W9-DHJ-593

MY LIFE
AS AN
EXPLORER

OTHER BOOKS BY SVEN HEDIN

MY LIFE
AS AN
EXPLORER

SVEN HEDIN

Illustrated by the Author

Translated by
ALFHILD HUEBSCH

With a New Prologue and Epilogue by
PETER HOPKIRK

KODANSHA INTERNATIONAL
New York • Tokyo • London

Kodansha America, Inc.
114 Fifth Avenue, New York, New York 10011, U.S.A.

Kodansha International Ltd.
17-14 Otowa 1-chome, Bunkyo-ku, Tokyo 112, Japan

Published in 1996 by Kodansha America, Inc.
by arrangement with W. W. Norton & Company, Inc.

First published in 1925 by Boni & Liveright, Inc.

This is a Kodansha Globe book.

© 1925 by Boni & Liveright, Inc. © 1953 by Alfhild Huebsch.
Prologue and epilogue copyright © 1996 by Peter Hopkirk.
All rights reserved.

Library of Congress Cataloging-in-Publication Data

Hedin, Sven Anders, 1865–1952.
    My life as an explorer : the great adventurer's classic memoir /
Sven Hedin ; with a new prologue and epilogue by Peter Hopkirk ;
illustrated by the author ; translated by Alfhild Huebsch.
        p. cm.—(Kodansha globe)
    Includes index.
    ISBN 1-56836-142-4 (pbk.)
        1. Hedin, Sven Anders, 1865–1952. 2. Explorers—Sweden—
Biography. 3. Asia—Description and travel. I. Title.
II. Series.
G306.H4A3 1996
910´.92—dc20   96-23143
[B]

Printed in the United States of America

96 97 98 99 00   Q/FF   10 9 8 7 6 5 4 3 2 1

TO
THE MEMORY
OF
MY BELOVED MOTHER

CONTENTS

CONTENTS

CONTENTS

ILLUSTRATIONS IN BLACK AND WHITE

ILLUSTRATIONS

xiii

PROLOGUE

Peter Hopkirk

During the early years of this century, in the remote and unexplored deserts of Chinese Central Asia, a great international race took place for the long-lost treasures of the ancient Silk Road. From the sand-buried cities and temples of a once flourishing Buddhist civilisation, archaeologists from seven nations removed, literally by the ton, huge wall paintings, sculptures, priceless manuscripts, and other works of art, and shipped them home. Today, to the anger of Chinese scholars, they are scattered throughout the museums and institutions of a dozen countries, including the United States.

The man who began this great treasure hunt was the Swedish explorer Sven Hedin, the author of this book. For in 1896 it was he who stumbled on the first of these thousand-year-old cities after hearing tales from local villagers of great riches, protected by demons, buried far out in the Taklamakan desert, into which entire caravans had disappeared without a trace over the centuries. When news of his discovery reached the West, other archaeologists and explorers—from Britain, Germany, France, and Japan, and later from America—mounted expeditions and joined in the search.

Hedin's discoveries in Central Asia and Tibet over the next forty years were to win him worldwide acclaim, including a British knighthood, honorary doctorates from both Oxford and Cambridge, and two of the Royal Geographical Society's coveted gold medals for his services to exploration. In Berlin a street and a square were named after him, and in other European countries he was festooned with honours, received by sovereigns and dictators, and lionised by the great.

His published works—some scholarly, others popular—ran to nearly fifty volumes, and were translated into thirty languages. His friends included the Tsar, the Kaiser, the King of Sweden, Field Marshal Hindenburg of Germany, and Lords Curzon and Kitchener of England, while other explorers and travellers were awed by his feats of endurance and his discoveries.

Yet, at first glance, he did not seem cut out to be one of the world's giants of exploration, being small in stature, bookish and bespectacled, and at times threatened by almost total blindness. But behind his mild, scholarly mien lay a man of iron will and determination, great strength and stamina, and an immense capacity for work. Furthermore, he was a gifted artist and writer, and was fluent in seven languages. Finally, he had been thoroughly schooled in the skills of the modern scientific geographer, having studied geology and zoology at the University of Stockholm, and physical geography under the great Baron von Richthofen, the man who first coined the phrase *The Silk Road,* in Berlin. In addition Hedin was a highly skilled mapmaker. "He seemed to possess every qualification of a scientific traveller," wrote Sir Francis Younghusband, who met him in Kashgar in 1890, when Hedin was still an unknown twenty-five-year-old.

And yet, when Hedin died in 1952, at the age of eighty-seven, he was an almost forgotten man. He died, moreover, reviled by many of those who had once honoured and admired him, though few to-day can probably recall what caused this abrupt reversal in his fortunes. The explanation is best left, I think, to its rightful place in the great explorer's career—that is, *after* the many adventures and misadventures that he unfolds in this remarkable narrative. For this reason I have included it in a brief epilogue summarising his various doings between 1908, when this book ends, and his death.

London
January 1996

MY LIFE
AS AN
EXPLORER

MY LIFE AS AN EXPLORER

CHAPTER I

How It All Began

HAPPY is the boy who discovers the bent of his life-work during childhood. That, indeed, was my good fortune. At the early age of twelve, my goal was fairly clear. My closest friends were Fenimore Cooper and Jules Verne, Livingstone and Stanley, Franklin, Payer, and Nordenskiöld, particularly the long line of heroes and martyrs of Arctic exploration. Nordenskiöld was then on his daring journey to Spitsbergen, Nova Zembla, and the mouth of the Yenisei River. I was just fifteen when he returned to my native city—Stockholm—having accomplished the Northeast Passage.

In June, 1878, Nordenskiöld had sailed from Sweden, in the "Vega," under the command of Captain Palander. He followed the northern shores of Europe and Asia, until he became stuck in the ice at the extreme eastern end of the Arctic coast of Siberia. The ice held him there for ten months. At home, a great anxiety was felt regarding the fate of the explorer and his scientific staff and crew. The first movement looking toward the rescue of the expedition came from the United States. James Gordon Bennett, famous for his command to Stanley, "Find Livingstone!" sent Captain De Long in July, 1879, in the American ship "Jeannette," to seek the North Pole, complete the Northeast Passage, and attempt to relieve the Swedish expedition.

Terrible misadventures awaited the Americans. The "Jeannette" was wrecked in the ice, and most of the party perished. The "Vega's" ice-bonds loosened, however; and, aided by her steam-power, she passed through Bering Strait into the Pacific. The Northeast Passage was accomplished with not a man lost. The first cable-message came from Yokohama, and I shall never forget the enthusiasm it aroused in Stockholm.

The voyage home, along the southern shores of Asia and Europe, was a journey of triumph beyond comparison. The "Vega" steamed into the harbour of Stockholm, on April 24, 1880. The entire city was illuminated. Buildings near the water-front were lit up by countless lamps and torches. On the Royal Palace, a star, Vega, shone forth in bright gas-flames; and amid this sea of lights, the famous ship came gliding into the harbour.

With my parents, sisters, and brother, I enjoyed a view of the city from the heights on the south side. I was a prey to the greatest excitement. All my life I shall remember that day. It decided my career. From the quays, streets, windows, and roofs, enthusiastic cheers roared like thunder. And I thought, "I, too, would like to return home that way."

Thereupon I delved into everything about Arctic expeditions. I read books, old and new, on the struggle for the Pole, and drew maps of every expedition. During our Northern winters, I rolled about in the snow, and slept by open windows, to harden myself. For as soon as I should be grown up and ready, and a benevolent Mæcenas should appear, throwing a bag of gold at my feet, with "Go and find the North Pole!" I was determined to equip my own ship with men, dogs, and sleds, and travel through night and ice-fields straight to the point where only south winds blow.

But it was written otherwise in the stars. One spring day, in 1885, shortly before I left school, the principal asked me if I would like to go to Baku, on the Caspian Sea, to serve for half a year as tutor to a boy in a lower class, whose father was chief engineer in the employ of the Nobel brothers. I lost no time in accepting. I might have to wait a long time for my Mæcenas, with his bag of gold. But here was a direct offer of a long journey, to the threshold of Asia, which was not to be slighted. Thus Fate led me toward Asiatic highways; and as the years ran their course, my youthful dreams about the North Pole gradually faded. And for the rest of my life I was to be held by the enchanting power that emanates from the largest continent in the world.

During the spring and summer of 1885, I was consumed with impatience for the moment of departure. Already, in imagination, I heard the roar of the waves of the Caspian Sea and the clangour of caravan-bells. Soon the glamour of the whole Orient was to unfold before me. I felt as if I possessed the key to the land of legend and adventure. A menagerie had just pitched its tents on a lot in Stockholm, and among the animals was a camel from Turkestan. I looked upon this camel as a fellow countryman from a distant land, and visited him again and again. Before long it would be my opportunity to convey greetings to his relatives in Asia.

My parents, sisters and brothers were afraid of letting me go on such a long journey. But I did not go alone. Not only my pupil, but his mother and a younger brother also went along. After a touching farewell from my family, we boarded a steamer, which took us across the Baltic and the Gulf of Finland. From Kronstadt we saw the gilded dome of St. Isaac's, gleaming like the sun; and a few hours later we landed at the Neva Quay in St. Petersburg.

We had no time to stay. After a few hours in the Czar's capital, we left on the fast train which passed through Moscow on its four-day

MOSCOW

journey through European Russia to the Caucasus. Endless plains rushed by rapidly. We shot through thin pine-woods and past fertile fields, where the ripening autumn grain swayed in the wind. South of Moscow we rattled along on shining rails across the undulating steppes of South Russia. My eyes devoured all of these prospects; for it was my first journey abroad. Small white churches lifted their green,

onion-shaped cupolas above pleasant villages.   Peasants in red blouses
and heavy boots worked in the fields, and transported hay and edible
roots in four-wheeled carts.   On the poor, undrained roads, which
harboured no dream of American automobiles then, *troikas* (three-
horse teams) dashed by like a streak, pulling *telegas* and *tarantasses,* to
the accompaniment of jingling bells.

Leaving Rostov, we crossed the mighty Don, not far from its outlet
into the Sea of Azov, an arm of the Black Sea.   The train rushed south
indefatigably.   At the stations there were Cossacks, soldiers, and gendarmes, and handsome, well-built specimens of Caucasian tribes, tall
men in brown coats and fur caps, with silver cartridges across breasts,
and pistols, *kinshals,* or daggers in their belts.

The train mounted slowly towards the northern base of the Caucasus Mountains, carrying us in between its foothills.   On the bank of

the Terek River lay the pretty little
town of Vladikavkaz, the "Ruler of the
Caucasus," just as Vladivostok is the
"Ruler of the East."   There my pupil's
father, the chief engineer, met us with
a carriage, in which we were to make
one hundred and twenty miles, in two
days, across the Caucasus, along the
Grusian army road.   This stretch was
divided into eleven stages, and horses
had to be changed at every station.
Seven horses were needed to haul the
heavy carriage up to the Godaur Station, 7,870 feet above sea-level.   The
down journey required only two or
three.   The slope was uneven.   Sometimes we drove up to the ridge of a steep
mountain, only to descend again, by four
or five zigzag curves, to the bed of the

THE   MILITARY   ROAD   ACROSS   THE
CAUCASUS

valley on the other side of the mountain;
after which a new height had to be scaled.

It was a magnificent journey.   Never before in my life had I
participated in anything comparable to it.   All around us rose the
giants of the Caucasus; and wonderful prospects, with snow-covered

peaks in the background, unfolded between steep mountain-walls. Highest of all, Kasbek bathed its dome, 16,530 feet high, in the sun.

The road itself was good. It was built, during the reign of Nicholas I, at so great a cost that upon opening it the Czar exclaimed: "I had expected to see a road of gold, but I find it all of grey stones." At the outer edge, a low stone parapet afforded protection against the abyss yawning below. On the slopes, where in winter huge avalanches come down across the road and fill the valley, we drove through snow-sheds, strongly built, with ten-foot walls.

KASBEK, 16,530 FEET HIGH, ONE OF THE HIGHEST PEAKS OF THE CAUCASUS

All the way, the horses maintained full speed. We moved at an insane rate. Seated next to the driver, I got dizzy every time the road turned abruptly; for it seemed to vanish into space, and I felt in danger of being hurled into the depths at any moment.

But nothing happened; and we drove into Tiflis, the principal city of Caucasus, safe and sound. What a swarming life! What colourful pictures! The houses rose amphitheatre-like on the steep, barren mountain-slopes, from the banks of the Kura. Streets and lanes were crowded with camels, mules, vehicles, and people of various races—Russians, Armenians, Tatars, Georgians, Circassians, Persians, gipsies, and Jews.

At Tiflis, we resumed the journey by rail. The summer was in full swing, and it was burning-hot. Taking a third-class compartment, because it was the airiest, we found ourselves in the company of Persian, Tatar, and Armenian merchants, with their children and wives, and other wonderful Orientals, picturesque in mien as well as in garb. In spite of the heat, they all wore big lambskin caps. I remember my feeling of wonder, when some pilgrims, returning from Mecca, spread their thin prayer-rugs on the floor of the compartment, while the train rolled on. The pilgrims all turned in the direction of the Holy City, and said their prayers, as the sun sank below the horizon.

Sometimes we were north of the River Kura, and sometimes south of it. Its fresh, green, cultivated banks frequently gleamed in the distance. Otherwise the country was desolate, mostly a steppe, where shepherds tended their herds; but in spots it was almost a desert. To the north, the mountain-range of the Caucasus appeared like an illuminated drop-scene, blue tones, with white streaks on the ridges. This was Asia! I could not look my fill at the fascinating picture. Already I felt that I would love this endless wilderness, and that during the years to come I would be drawn farther and farther toward the East.

At Ujiri, following my usual custom, I alighted to make some sketches in my book. I had not gone far, when heavy hands were laid on my shoulders, and I was seized by three gendarmes, with vise-like grips. Brusque and suspicious, they fired questions at me. An Armenian girl, who spoke French, became my interpreter; for I did not yet understand Russian. The gendarmes seized my sketch-book and laughed scornfully at my explanations. Evidently they scented a spy, who might be dangerous to the existence of the Czar's country. A dense crowd surrounded us. The gendarmes wanted to take me away, to lock me up, perhaps. The first signal for the train's departure sounded. The station-master made his way through the crowd to see what had happened. He took my arm and escorted me back to the train. The bell sounded the second time. I got up on a platform, the gendarmes at my heels. Creakingly the train started. Supple as an eel, I dashed through two or three coaches, and hid in a corner. By the time I returned to my companions, the gendarmes had jumped off the train.

We approached the Caspian Sea. There was a strong wind. Clouds of dust were swept along the ground. First the mountains disappeared and then the whole country was shrouded in an impenetrable haze. The wind increased. It became a gale, a hurricane. The engine worked desperately against the opposing head-wind. We puffed and panted heavily along the shore, seeing only indistinctly the white-capped waves, as they tossed and broke. The train stopped at last, at Baku, the "City of the Winds," which that evening surely deserved its name.

The Peninsula of Apsheron extends almost fifty miles eastward into the Caspian Sea. Baku is situated on the south coast of this peninsula, and east of it we found the "Black Town," where Nobel and other oil-kings have their huge refineries. From here the refined oil is piped through all of southern Caucasus to the Black Sea, while tank-steamers carry the precious fluid across the Caspian Sea to Astrakhan and Tsaritsyn on the Volga. The field which contains most of the oil-wells centres about Balakhany, a Tatar village thirteen versts [1] northeast

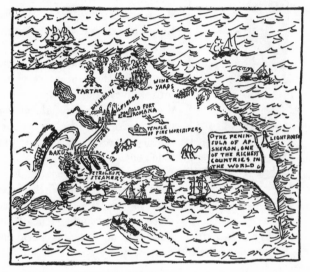

APSHERON

of Baku. It was long known that this region contained crude oil, but it was not until 1874 that the brothers, Ludwig and Robert Nobel, came and introduced the American drilling-method. During the following years, the industry prospered greatly; and in 1885, when I first visited Balakhany, there were three hundred and seventy drills, and as many wells, yielding oil by the hundreds of millions of puds annually. Sometimes it happened that the subterranean pressure caused the oil to gush like a spring. A single well would often eject half a million puds in twenty-four hours.

I spent seven months in the midst of this strange forest of derricks. I crammed history, geography, languages, and other useful subjects into my pupil; but I derived greater pleasure from accompanying Lud-

[1] A verst is two-thirds of a mile.

wig Nobel on his inspections of the oil-field.   Above everything else, I
loved to go through the villages on horseback, making sketches of the

OIL-WELL IN BALAKHAN

Tatars, their women, children, and
houses, or gallop into Baku on a frisky
horse, there to stroll round the "Black
Bazaar," where Tatars, Persians, and
Armenians, sitting in their dark little
shops, sold rugs from Kurdistan and
Kerman, hangings and brocades, slippers
and *papashs,* or big fur caps.   I watched
the goldsmiths hammering their ornaments and the armourers working iron
into knives and *kinshals.*   Everything
was enchanting and interesting to me,
the dervishes in their rags, as well as
the *begs,* or princes, in their long, dark-
blue coats.

A tempting objective for shorter
trips was the temple of the fire-worshippers.   Formerly, the sacred fire burned
there day and night, beneath the cupola
of the temple, fed by natural gas; but now it was permanently extinguished; and at night the old sanctuary lay on the steppe surrounded
by darkness and silence.

Late one winter evening, as we
sat around the lamp, ominous
cries of "Yango, yango!" (Fire,
fire!) were heard from the road-
way outside our windows.   Tatars were running from house
to house, rousing and warning
people, and shouting at the top
of their voices.   We hurried out.
The whole oil-field was lit up as
bright as day.   The heart of the
fire was only a few hundred

A BLAZING LAKE OF CRUDE OIL

yards away.   It was a blazing lake of crude oil, flaming between walls
of piled-up earth; and a derrick was ablaze too!   The wind whipped

the flames like torn, streaming flags, and heavy clouds of brown smoke welled up. Things were sputtering, boiling, and seething. The Tatars tried to choke the fire with earth, but in vain. The derricks were fairly close to one another. The wind carried sparks from derrick to derrick, destroying everything in the field that rose above its surface. The nearest drills looked like white phantoms in the glaring light. The Tatars were chopping them down as fast as they could. By superhuman effort, they thus succeeded in checking the fire; and after a few hours the lake was burnt out, and darkness again reigned over the land.

CHAPTER II

Across the Elburz Range to Teheran

DURING the winter evenings in Balakhany, I learned to speak the Tatar and Persian languages quite fluently. Baki Khanoff, a young Tatar of rank, was my teacher. Early in April, my term of service concluded, I decided to spend the three hundred rubles I had earned on a horseback-journey, southward through Persia, and thence down to the sea. Baki Khanoff was to go with me.

I took leave of my fellow countrymen, and late one evening boarded a Russian paddle-wheel steamer. A violent northern gale was sweeping over Baku, and the captain dared not leave port. By morning the gale had subsided. The paddles began their wrestling with the waves, and the steamer proceeded southward. After a thirty-hour sail, we landed at Enseli, on the southern shore of the Caspian Sea, and immediately went by launch across the big fresh-water lagoon, called Murdab, or the "Dead Water," to a lake village embedded in luxuriant green. From there we were to proceed on horseback to Resht, a trading-town.

I had changed all my funds into Persian *kran,* and at that time a *kran* was valued at a franc. The small silver coins were sewn in leather belts, which we wore around our waists. I had half the money, and Baki Khanoff the other. With this exception, we were dressed as lightly as possible. I carried no clothes, except the winter suit I wore, a short winter coat, and a blanket. I was armed with a revolver. Baki Khanoff had a gun strapped over his Tatar coat, and a *kinshal* in his belt.

The Royal Bengal tiger prowled in the dense jungles around Resht, and from the teeming marshes there rose fever-producing miasmata, which sometimes caused fearful epidemics. On one occasion, six thousand people perished in the little town; and the survivors, having no time to bury their dead, threw the bodies into the mosques. These mosques looked very picturesque, with their low minarets and red-slate roofs. The merchants' booths were covered with multi-coloured

24

draperies, as protection against the sun. Silk, rice, and cotton were the chief products of the country along this coast.

There was a Russian consul in Resht, a Mr. Vlassoff. I called on him, and was invited to dinner that same evening. Dressed in my simple travelling-suit and riding-boots, I entered a house decorated with Persian splendour, and regally illuminated; so that I felt very unhappy when my host appeared in formal evening clothes. I regretted that I had not stayed with Baki Khanoff in our humble caravansary. But I

A MOSQUE IN RESHT

had no evening suit; and I simply had to make the best of this Lucullian dinner for two.

The next morning, two rested horses stood pawing at the door of the caravansary, with two boys guarding them. A Tatar *kurchin,* or soft, double bag, tied behind the saddle, held all my luggage. We mounted, the boys following on foot, half running. The road led through a luxuriant forest. We met riders, and pedestrians, and big mule-caravans, with goods for transport over the sea to Russia, among them being dried fruits in leather-covered boxes. The forest resounded with the tinkle of mule-bells; and the first animal of each caravan wore a huge, bronze bell, which sounded dully.

We spent the night in Kodom, at an inn, where hundreds of swallows nested in the moss-covered roof, and flew in and out of the nests and through open windows.

Farther on, the ground sloped towards the mountains. We went along the valley-bed of the Sefeed-Rud, or the "White River," staying overnight in beautifully-situated villages, set among olive-groves, fruit trees, plane trees, and willows. We carried no provisions, but lived on what the country offered—poultry, eggs, milk, wheat-bread, and fruit, at an incredibly small cost. The road grew steeper. We were in the Elburz mountain-range and were ascending towards the heights. The forest thinned out and came to an end.

At Mendjil, we rode across an old, stone bridge, with eight arches. The day was grey and windy. All of the mountains were completely covered with a snow-blanket, which grew thicker, the higher we

ACROSS THE ELBURZ MOUNTAINS IN A SNOWSTORM

mounted. And now, too, snow began to fall. The whole country was enveloped in a blinding snowstorm. I was not dressed for that kind of weather. I was literally held fast to my saddle by snow, and felt the cold gradually penetrate bone and sinew. The blanket of snow obliterated the trail, the horses plunged into the drifts like dolphins, the driving snow beat on our faces, everything was white, and we thought we had lost our way, when something appeared dimly through the whirling snow. It was a caravan of horses and mules, moving in the same direction as we. Two men were riding in advance, probing the snow with long, thin lances, so as to avoid any treacherously-hidden crevices or menacing precipices. Chilled through and through, we finally reached the village of Masra; and there, in a dirty hovel, resembling a cave, we built a fire on the ground. Thus four Tatars, two Persians, and one Swede were seated, thawing out their stiff joints and drying their wet clothes in front of the fire.

The road wound up across the highest ridge of the Elburz Mountains. The snow soon disappeared on the southern slope, and the steppe slowly gave towards the city of Kazvin, concerning which the Prophet himself has said: "Honour Kazvin, for that city lies at the threshold of one of the doors of Paradise." Harun-ar-Rashid, the great Caliph, beautified Kazvin, and Shah Thamas I made it his own

IN THE REST-HOUSE OF MASRA

capital, as well as that of Persia (1548 A.D.), calling it Dar-es-Saltanet, or the "Seat of Royalty." Its glamour faded forty years later, when Shah Abbas the Great transferred his capital to Ispahan.

Legend has it that the Arabian poet, Lokman, who lived in Kazvin, when he felt death approaching, called his son to him, and said: "Treasures I have none to give you, but here are three bottles, filled with miracle-working medicine. If you pour a few drops from the first bottle over a dead man, his soul will return to the body. If you sprinkle him with the contents of the second bottle, he will sit up. If the contents of the third bottle are poured over him, he will be completely restored to life. But use this precious medicine sparingly." Arrived at old age, and knowing that his end was near, the son called his servant and directed that the remedy be applied to him as soon as he was dead. The servant carried his dead master to the bath-house, and poured the first and second bottles over him. Thereupon the son of Lokman arose, shouting at the top of his voice: "Pour, pour!" But the servant was so terrified at the dead body speaking that he dropped the third bottle on the stone floor, and ran away. There sat the poor son of Lokman, and had to return to the kingdom of the dead. But from the vault of the bath-house, still shown in Kazvin, the ghastly shouts of "Pour, pour!" are still to be heard.

Kazvin is situated on the plain south of the Elburz Mountains. A road, ninety miles long, divided into six stages, runs from Kazvin to Teheran, the capital of the country. Travelling is done by means of *tarantasses* and *troikas,* in the Russian fashion, the horses being changed five times.

The weather was now springlike and bright, and we enjoyed the swift drive. The horses went at full speed, and the wheels raised clouds of dust. Toward the north, the snow-covered ridges of the Elburz were visible. Toward the south the level plain extended to the sky-line; and here and there the fresh green of gardens, in various scattered villages, embellished the otherwise monotonously yellow-grey landscape.

Once we heard the rattling of another *tarantass* behind us, and the next moment it swept past at breakneck speed. The passengers, three Tatar merchants, shouted mockingly, "Happy journey!" as they rushed past our *tarantass.* Now *they* would be the first at the next station, and could appropriate the best horses. But presently my pride was stung. I promised the driver two *kran,* if he succeeded in overtaking the Tatars. So the horses were whipped up; and, near the next station, we passed the Tatars at a good clip. Now it was my turn to hurl a "Happy journey!" in their direction, which I did at the top of my voice.

I knew that a Swedish physician, ranking as a Persian nobleman, and bearing the honourable title of Khan, or prince, had been the dentist to the Shah of Persia since 1873; so, upon arriving at Teheran, I drove directly to his house. Happy at meeting a compatriot at last, he received me with open arms, and for a time I lived in his beautiful home, the decorations of which were an approach to Persian style. Day after day we tramped through this great city, about which I will speak more fully later on. Here I will relate only one incident, because of its future significance to me.

One day, Dr. Hybennet and I were walking between the yellow, clay walls and houses of Teheran's dusty streets. These streets, where sufficiently wide, had narrow, open ditches along their sides, and rows of plane trees, poplars, willows, or mulberry trees. All at once, we noticed a band of running *ferrashs,* or heralds, garbed in red, wearing silver casques, and carrying long, silver staffs in their hands. With these staffs they made a way through the crowd, for the King of Kings was out driving.   A troop of fifty horsemen followed these heralds, and then came the grey carriage of the Shah, drawn by six black stallions, in gorgeous silver caparisons, each left-hand horse bearing a rider.   The Shah wore a black cloak over his shoulders, and on his head a black cap, with a huge emerald and a jewelled clasp.   Another cavalcade followed the Shah's carriage, and in the rear of the procession came an emergency-carriage, always held in readiness, in case the other broke. Though the streets were not paved, there was no dust from the horses' hoofs; for before the Shah drove out, the roads to be traversed were sprinkled with water from leather bags, carried by mules.   In a minute or so, the magnificent cavalcade had disappeared in the distance between the trees.

That was the first time I ever saw Nasr-ed-Din, Shah of Persia.   He was regal in appearance, with dark eyes, aquiline nose, and a big, black moustache.   As we stood at the side of the road, and the carriage rolled past us, the Shah, pointing at me, called out to Hybennet: "In ki est?" (Who is that?)   Hybennet instantly replied: "A fellow countryman who is visiting me, your Majesty."   Years later, I was to have the opportunity of becoming better acquainted with this man, the last Shah on the ancient throne of Persia, who had the imperious temperament of a veritable Asiatic despot.

CHAPTER III

On Horseback Through Persia

SUMMER was approaching. It grew warmer every day, and I had no further reason to postpone my projected trip southward. But Baki Khanoff was taken down with fever, and so I had to go on alone. He went home to Baku, while I proceeded onward, without servants, on the twenty-seventh of April.

But one could not be quite alone, when travelling *chapari* (with hired horses) from one halting-place to another, through Persia. A groom went along, so that the two horses could be returned to the station from which they were borrowed. The horses cost a couple of *kran,* and a night's lodging in the *chaparkhaneh,* or station, about the same. Horse and groom were changed at every station. The traveller might ride day and night, if he felt equal to the strain. The stages ranged from twelve to eighteen miles. The double bag behind my saddle held all my belongings, but I still carried the silver coins, about six hundred *kran* (or francs) sewed up in the leather belt round my waist. The pockets of this belt were cut open as needed. Food was to be had cheaply everywhere.

Interminable stretches of a strange country lay before me, as I rode out of the south gate of Teheran with my first groom. The unrestrained, open-armed Asiatic reception made me happy. Horsemen, caravans, wandering dervishes, every living creature we saw, was my friend, and I felt boundlessly sorry for the tired little mules, sinking under their burdens of red watermelons and yellow sugar-melons, in plaited rush-baskets. The "Tower of Rages," the ancient city named in the apocryphal Book of Tobit, rose on the left. Beneath its golden cupola slumbered the holy Shah Abdul-Azim, in the burial-mosque where, ten years later, Shah Nasr-ed-Din was to fall by the hand of a fanatical mullah.

The country grew more desolate. Fewer gardens were to be seen, steppe appeared, and then all became desert-like. Now we trotted along, now we galloped. A band of pilgrims from Mecca met us. My companion dismounted in order to kiss the hem of their mantles.

In Koom, a holy shrine, visited by innumerable pilgrims, the holy Fatima sleeps her last sleep. A golden cupola glistens in the sunshine above her resting-place, two tall, slender minarets towering beside it.

Our road ran south through the important commercial city of Kashan, after which it ascended toward new mountains. I did not notice, at our departure, that the groom, a fifteen-year-old boy, had taken a fresh horse for himself, giving me an exhausted one. I changed horses with him out in the country, and he was no longer able to keep up with me. He nearly wept, and implored me not to ride away from him. But I was hard-hearted enough to say:

"You know the road and the country better than I. Surely you'll find your way alone to the station of Kuhrud. I'll wait for you there."

"Yes, but don't you see that

THE TOMB OF THE HOLY FATIMA IN KOOM

the night is approaching, and I shall be afraid to ride alone through the woods?"

"Oh, no! It isn't dangerous at all. You just ride along as fast as your horse can carry you."

I rode on southwards. The boy disappeared in the distance behind me. The sun went down. Twilight came, followed soon by darkness. It was all right, as long as I could see the road; but after that, I had to rely on my horse. Walking fast, he took me into the Kuhrud Mountains. I had no idea what the landscape looked like, but now and then I brushed past a tree-trunk, or felt leaves brushing my face. Maybe the horse was leading me astray. It would certainly have been wiser to have stuck to the boy, who knew the road. But now everything depended on the horse. He just walked and walked. The darkness was impenetrable. Only the stars twinkled over the valley, and time and again I saw the gleam of distant lightning.

After riding on in the dark for four hours, I noticed a streak of light glimmering through the trees. It was a nomad's tent. I tied my horse, and lifting the tent-flap, asked if anybody was at home. An old man answered me crossly that it was inconsiderate to disturb him and his family in the middle of the night. But when I assured him that I wanted nothing more than to know whether I was on the right road to Kuhrud, he came out and accompanied me part of the way through the forest, indicating the right direction, and disappearing again in the dark, without saying a word. I finally reached Kuhrud, where the boy whom I had so cruelly deserted stood laughing in the doorway. Arriving a few hours before me, he had wondered if I had been kidnapped. In the end, I had tea, eggs, salt, and bread, placed the saddlebag on the floor for a pillow, and was soon sound asleep.

The Anglo-Indian telegraph-line, which crosses Persia, reaches its highest point (seven thousand feet) at Kuhrud.

We approached a city, and life on the highway grew more diversified and colourful. The villages and the gardens were closer together, we passed little caravans of mules, horses, and donkeys, laden with fruit and grain, and finally entered a street. It was the famed Ispahan, the capital of Shah Abbas the Great.

The Zendeh-rud River rushed right through the city, and mighty bridges, more than three hundred years old, spanned its eddying, muddy waters. There was much for the stranger to see in Ispahan. He found there one of the largest plazas in the world, the Maidan-i-Shah, two thousand feet long and seven hundred feet wide. He could admire the glorious façade of the Mesjid-i-Shah, faced with beautiful faience. At Chehel Sutun, or the "Palace of Forty Pillars," he could count only twenty columns; but seeing their counterpart in the quiet pool extending before the façade, he readily understood how it got its name.

In Yulfa, the suburb inhabited by poor Armenians, I became aware of the aromatic scent of peaches, apricots, and grapes; and inside the masonry walls of the enormous bazaar, I heard a deafening noise, as the caravans made their way through the swarming crowds, and the merchants cried their wares and the coppersmiths hammered on their pans.

THE ROYAL MOSQUE OF ISPAHAN

It was truly a charming picture that unfolded itself before my gaze, when, from the heights south of the city, I turned in the saddle, and looked back on the innumerable houses, embedded in luxuriant gardens, and on the shining cupolas and minarets, rising above the fresh green.

Again I rode through wastes, where red spiders and grey and green lizards buried themselves, and where the nomads tended their grazing sheep. Through such a region I ascended to the ruins of Pasargadæ, and enjoyed a brief stay at a small, marble building, approached by

YESDIKAST, BUILT ON THE TOP OF AN ISOLATED ROCK

high stairs, which still defies the twenty-five centuries which have flown past its coping on the wings of time.

The Persians call this ancient monument Mader-i-Suleiman, or the "Mother of Solomon," believing that this grand lady's resting-place is in the sepulchral chamber, ten feet long and seven feet wide, at the top of the stairs. But the Europeans call it the Tomb of Cyrus, though it is very doubtful if the great king was really interred here in a gold-plated sarcophagus, with costly hangings from Babylon on the walls, and with the dead man's sword, shield and bow, his neck-chain, earrings, and royal attire.

I recalled the proud words of Cyrus: "My father's country is bounded on the south by lands so torrid as to be uninhabitable, and on the north by regions fettered with chains of ice. What lies between is subject to the satraps."

The mountainous district just traversed opened into the plain of Merdasht; and there I went on horseback to an ancient and even more remarkable monument, the ruins of Persepolis, capital of the Achæmenian overlords, the most beautiful relic of antiquity preserved in Persia. These ruins are situated in an almost complete waste. The yellow-clay soil is cracked from the heat. No life is to be seen. I sent the groom back to the station with the horse, and remained alone among the ruins all day long.

A flight of stairs, with double wings, and wide enough for ten horsemen abreast to ride up its low, marble steps, leads up to the gigantic platform, where still remain the foundation-walls of the palace of Darius I, and thirteen of the thirty-six columns which supported the roof-beams in the palace of Xerxes, two thousand four hundred years ago. One can picture it for oneself by reading the description of Ahasuerus' palace at Susa, in the Book of Esther (1:6): "There were white, green, and blue hangings, fastened with cords of fine linen and purple to silver rings and pillars of marble; the beds were of gold and silver upon a pavement of red, and blue, and white, and black marble."

All this splendour was destroyed, 331 B.C., when the victorious Alexander of Macedon, after a wild drinking-bout, set fire to the royal palaces and reduced Persepolis to ashes.

We proceeded toward the south. From a narrow pass, we had an unforgettable view over the city of Shiraz, lying on the plain below. They call this pass Tang-i-Allah Akbar, because Persians, approaching for the first time, and seeing Shiraz in the distance, exclaim in surprise, "Allah Akbar!" (God is great!).

Shiraz is famous for its wine, its women, its songs, and its luxuriant roses. There the wine ripens on the hillside, there the air is heavy with the scent of flowers, and there the cypresses rise above the graves of illustrious poets. The most notable tombs are the mausoleums over Persia's two greatest poets, Sadi (born 1176), author of "Gulistan," or the "Rose Garden," and Hafiz (born 1318), who wrote "The Divan" and his own epitaph: "O my beloved ones, approach my grave with wine and song, it may be that at the sound of your joyous voices and melodious music I shall awaken out of my slumber and arise from the dead." Tamerlane, admiring the poems of Hafiz, visited him in Shiraz, during one of his campaigns.

There are many orders of dervishes. The head of each order is called *pir*. They have different customs and rules. Some of them always cry "Allahum!" (O God!). Others, "Ya hu, ya hack!" (He is just, He is the truth!). Still others, who are stricter, flagellate their shoulders with iron chains. But almost all of them have one thing in common: their members carry a staff in one hand, and in the other, half of a cocoanut-shell, in which to receive alms.

In 1863, a Swedish doctor of medicine, named Fagergren, came to live in Shiraz, and spent thirty years in the City of Roses and Poets. He lies buried in the Christian churchyard there. One day a dervish pounded on his door. Fagergren opened it, and threw a copper coin to the beggar. The dervish exclaimed scornfully that he had not come to beg, but to convert the infidel to Islam. "First give me a proof of your miraculous powers," demanded Fagergren. "Yes," replied the dervish; "I can speak to you in any language you may name." "Well, then," said Fagergren, in his own tongue, "speak a little Swedish." The dervish lifted his voice, and in faultless Swedish recited some verses from Tegnér's "Frithiof's Saga." Our good doctor was amazed. He could hardly trust his ears. Then the dervish, thinking he had tormented the doctor long enough, removed his disguise, and revealed himself as Arminius Vambéry, professor of Oriental languages in the University of Budapest, who later became world-famous.

Quite without disguise I arrived at Shiraz, and lived for some days with M. Fargues, a very amiable Frenchman. In 1866, as a young official in his native country, he had received six months' leave, to make a little trip to Shiraz. But when I arrived there, in 1886, he had not yet left the city; and four years later I met him again, in Teheran, so completely had he fallen in love with Persia.

The roughest stretch of the entire journey from the Caspian Sea was that from Shiraz to the Persian Gulf. The roads over the Farsistan Mountains were steep and neck-breaking. We went up hill and down dale, among wild, crumbled, and sun-baked rocks, and crossed the three passes, Sin-i-sefeid (the White Saddle), Pir-i-san (the Old Woman), and Kotel-i-dukhter (the Girl's Pass). Once my horse lost his footing and rolled down a declivity, but I managed to free myself from the saddle in time, and remained on the path.

The heat was stifling. The mountains grew smaller, and gradually merged into flat coast-land, dry as a desert. On another night, I rode away from my groom, who was an aged man. There was little security in these regions, where highwaymen and bandits were wont to prowl. But everything went well. Dawn came. Before me appeared a shining streak, resembling a polished sword-blade. A few hours later I rode into Bushir, a port, having covered nine hundred miles in twenty-nine travelling-days, right through the Shah's vast realm.

CHAPTER IV

Through Mesopotamia to Bagdad

B USHIR was probably the most detestable city I visited in Asia! It must be a real punishment to have to live and work there. No vegetation, or at most a palm tree or two; two-story white houses; alleys reduced to the utmost narrowness for the sake of shade and coolness; an all-year-round sun-bath, especially intolerable in the summer; a temperature which I once found mounting to 110° Fahrenheit, but which can rise to 113° and more, in the shade; and, finally, the glittering sun over the warm, salt, lifeless water-deserts of the Persian Gulf.

I lived with kind European people. The beds, surrounded by mosquito-netting, were on the roof. But even before sunrise, I had to hurry below, to the shade, so as to avoid white water-blisters, which produce a smarting pain.

One day, an English steamer, the "Assyria," arrived, and anchored in the open harbour outside Bushir. I hurried on board. To conserve my rapidly shrinking funds, I booked my passage for the uncovered upper deck. The steamer carried freight and passengers between Bombay and Basra; and Orientals from India, Persia, and Arabia swarmed on board. The journey across the Persian Gulf was not long; and even before sighting land, while approaching the mouth of the big river, Shat-el-Arab, the engines slowed down, and the pilots navigated the ship carefully between the treacherous mud-banks in the water-covered area of the delta. This river is formed by the confluence of the Tigris and Euphrates, and carries with it such quantities of sand and clay, that the delta encroaches on the Persian Gulf a distance of one hundred and seventy-five feet a year.

We steamed up the river. On the low banks were palm-groves, huts and black tents, herds of cattle and sheep; and grey buffaloes, with receding horns, went grubbing in the mud. Outside Basra, the "Assyria" cast anchor, and about thirty boats, with water splashing at their bows, were rowed to her side. These *belem,* as they are called, carry passengers, as well as freight. Out on the river, where the water is deep, multi-coloured oars, with wide blades, are used; but in the shallows, the Arabian oarsmen jump onto the rail, and propel the boats with long, slender poles.

The European consulates, mercantile establishments, and warehouses are on the water-front. Having nothing to do there, I took a *belem,* no wider than a canoe, and had myself rowed along a winding creek, through a dense forest of luxuriant date-palms. It was humid, close, and warm, with never a breeze to afford relief. But there was an aromatic odour from the palms. A Persian poet avers that there are seventy different kinds of date-palms, and that they serve three hundred and sixty-three different purposes. And the palm is known as "Islam's blessed tree," its delicious fruit certainly being the principal nourishment of a great part of the population.

Arabic Basra, conquered by the Turks in 1668, is composed of two-story houses, with balconies, through the lattice windows of which the women observe the life of the narrow streets. There are cafés with open verandas, where Turks, Arabs, Persians, and other Orientals drink their coffee or tea, and smoke their narghilehs. The city is dirty and fever-infested. Its principal sanitary workers are the jackals and hyenas, which steal in at night from their dens in the desert, to clean up among the refuse and the carcasses decaying in the streets and lanes.

The paddle-wheel steamer "Mejidieh" left Basra, on the last of May, for Bagdad, and I had a cabin on its upper deck. The officers of the ship were Englishmen, the crew Turks. I was the only white passenger; all the others were Orientals. From the bridge one could enjoy the life of the forecastle-deck. Arabian merchants sat there playing tricktrack, while the Persians smoked their pipes and blew life into the glowing coals of the samovar. One could look right down into a harem, inside the temporarily-suspended blue hangings of which young women lounged on cushions and feather-beds, killing time by eating sweets, smoking, and drinking tea. A dervish was declaiming parables in a loud voice to listening boys, afterwards going among his audience with his cocoanut-shell for contributions of food.

The Tigris and Euphrates, the rivers of Paradise, meet at Corna; and the Arabs declare that in the beginning the Garden of Eden lay at the point of the peninsula between these two rivers. They even show you the Tree of Knowledge of Good and Evil. Others say that the Euphrates is male, the Tigris female, and that Corna is their wedding-place. Looking at the two rivers on the map, one cannot but notice their resemblance to a pair of ox-horns; and, as a matter of fact, the name Corna is strikingly like the Latin *cornu* and the English "corn."

The Euphrates, the largest river in western Asia, 1,665 miles long, has its source in the highlands of Armenia, not far from sacred Ararat. Together with the shorter Tigris, it encloses Mesopotamia, the "Land between the Rivers," the El-Yezireh, or the "Isle," of the Arabs. Here all the soil is redolent of bygone millenniums, when Assyria and Babylonia, then the great powers of their day, fought out their world-wars. There ancient Babylon flourished; there the presumptuous people evoked God's anger by building the Tower of Babel toward the sky; there, on the Tigris, we find the ruins of ancient Nineveh, the capital of Sennacherib, Asarhaddon, and Sardanapalus.

We left the mouth of the Euphrates and steamed slowly upstream on the winding Tigris. Armenia's and Taurus's melting snowfields sent freshets flowing through its bed. It would take us four days to reach Bagdad. At low water, and with the constantly shifting sandbanks lurking beneath the dirty, pea-soup-like water, the steamer frequently touched bottom; then the water ballast had to be emptied, and cargo and people discharged, in order to refloat the ship. When that happens, the journey takes as long as seven days. Going downstream, at high water, one can reach Basra, from Bagdad, in forty-two hours.

We anchored at the Tomb of Ezra, where palm trees were reflected in the river; and gay Jewish boys rowed out to fetch cargo and passengers. On the shore, half-savage nomads, of the Montefik and Abu Mohammed tribes, rode with their herds. They carried spears in their hands, and on their heads they wore horsehair wreaths, to hold the white veils, which fluttered over their shoulders and sides.

Sailboats (*kashti*) were skimming up the river, their white sails swelled by a light breeze. The mountains of Kurdistan were visible in the blue distance. A herd of buffaloes was swimming across the river, the herdsmen using spears to keep them in line. Black tents were pitched on the burnt steppe. The light from the camp-fires pierced the darkness of the night.

The sun was hardly risen, before the heat became suffocating. We were tortured by mosquitoes in the evening, and in the daytime the sky was literally clouded with grasshoppers. Entire swarms of grasshoppers flew over the river. They descended on the ship, creeping and crawling everywhere, on our clothes and hands, and in our faces; and we had to close the doors and windows of our cabins, to escape their company for the night. They struck the hot funnel, burned their wings, and fell in a steadily growing heap at its base.

At Kut-el-Amara, we took sacks of wool on board. Suddenly we stopped, and back-watered. We were aground on a sand-bank. The

THE TOMB OF EZRA ON THE TIGRIS

water ballast was emptied, and with the assistance of the stream, which here flowed at the rate of two and a half miles an hour, we worked ourselves loose. A little higher up, the river described a long curve, which the boat rounded in two hours and forty minutes, although a pedestrian might cross the base of the headland in half an hour. On this headland are the ruins of the city of Ctesiphon, where Parthians, Romans, Sassanids, and Arabs ruled successively. Here, too, rises the beautiful ruin of the castle Tak-Kesra, or "Khosru's Bow," so called after the Sassanian king, Khosru Nushirvan (531-578 A.D.).

The captain of the "Mejidieh" made no objection to my going ashore. I was rowed by four Arabs, two of whom accompanied me across the headland. Broken bits of faience rattled under our feet;

and at "Khosru's Bow" I stopped an hour to sketch. The desert had claimed the spot where once rose the walls of Ctesiphon, the capital. Then the king's garden unfolded in luxuriant splendour; but in the midst of the formal green there was a space where only weeds and thistles grew. A Roman legate asked for an explanation, and the king answered that the neglected ground belonged to a poor widow, who did not want to sell it, whereupon the Roman replied that this very piece was the most beautiful thing he had seen in the king's garden.

In 637, King Yezdegird III surrendered to the superior force of the rapidly advancing Arabs. To their negotiations, the King replied: "I have seen many nations, but never one as poor as yours; mice and snakes are your food, sheep and camel-skins your clothes. What makes it possible for you to conquer my country?" And the envoys answered him: "You are right. Hunger and nakedness were our lot, but God has given us a prophet whose religion is our strength."

We were nearing Bagdad! The desolate landscape was enveloped in a cloud of mist. I dreamt of the tales in the "Arabian Nights," and of all the wealth and splendour that gave the capital of the Abbasid caliphs such fame throughout the Orient. But the haze lifted. I saw only common, clay houses and palm trees. The dream vanished. A frail pontoon-bridge spanned the Tigris. The water for irrigation was drawn up the embankment by means of big wheels, propelled by horses. On the right bank appeared the Tomb of Zobeide, Harun-ar-Rashid's favourite wife. The "Mejidieh" cast anchor outside the custom-house. A swarm of shell-like boats (*guffas*), "with neither bow nor stern, and resembling a shield," according to Herodotus, surrounded the ship, and took us all ashore.

The powerful Caliph Abu Yafar Abdallah al-Mansur founded Bagdad, in 762 A.D., honouring his capital with the title of Dar-es-Salam, or "Dwelling of Peace." Under his grandson, Harun-ar-Rashid, "the Just," the city had its days of real glory. In 1258, Bagdad was plundered and burnt by the Mongolians, under Hulagu; yet, in 1327, Ibn Batuta was astounded at its greatness and splendour. But by 1401, the terrible Tamerlane was at its gates. He sacked and pillaged everything, except the mosques, and built a pyramid of ninety thousand human heads.

Little remained in Bagdad from the days of the caliphs—a caravansary, a city gate, Zobeide's Tomb, and the minaret Suk-el-Gazl, towering high and dignified above a sea of houses, in which the two hundred thousand people lived. The streets were narrow and picturesque, and I was swept into a throng of gaily-robed Arabs, Bedouins, Turks, Persians, Indians, Jews, and Armenians. In the bazaars, one's eyes could feed on glorious rugs, silk sashes, hangings, and brocades, largely importations from India.

The houses were two-storied, with balconies, and subterranean rooms that afforded refuge during the hot summer days. A *punka,* or fan, for comfort and ventilation, hung from the ceiling, and was kept in constant motion by a boy, with a rope. Tall palms rose over the flat roofs of the houses, and the summer wind sighed among their branches.

CHAPTER V

An Adventurous Ride Through Western Persia

IN Bagdad, I went to the house of Mr. Hilpern, an English merchant. He and his wife received me most hospitably, and I stayed with them three days. I strolled about the city and its environs, rowed in a *guffa* on the river, and fared royally at Mr. Hilpern's table.

He seemed to think that I was a reckless youth. I had come to Bagdad alone; and now, with no servant, I was going to ride back through the desert, through unsafe Kurdistan and western Persia, to Teheran. I could not bring myself to tell him that I carried in my belt no more than one hundred and fifty *kran,* or twenty-eight dollars. I was determined to hire myself out as a muleteer through waste regions, rather than reveal my poverty.

Mr. Hilpern accompanied me to the big caravansaries connected with the bazaar. In a courtyard, some men were packing bales of goods, to be loaded on pack-saddles. We inquired where they were going. "To Kermanshah," they answered.

"How many days does it take?"

"Eleven or twelve days."

"How large is your caravan?"

"We have fifty mules, with cargo. Our party consists of ten merchants, who will be mounted on horses, some pilgrims returning from Mecca, six pilgrims from Kerbela, and a Chaldean merchant."

"May I join your caravan?" I asked.

"Yes, if you will pay well."

"What does it cost to hire a horse for Kermanshah?"

"Fifty *kran.*"

Mr. Hilpern advised me to accept the offer. I was to be called for at his house on the evening of June 7. At the appointed time, two Arabs appeared. My Persian saddle was placed on the hired horse. I took leave of my kind host and hostess, mounted, and was conducted by the Arabs across Bagdad, to the caravansary on its outskirts.

It was Ramadan, the month in which the followers of the Prophet neither eat, drink, nor smoke while the sun is up. But after sunset, they make up for the deprivation. Then the men gather in the open-air cafés of the bazaars, and sup religiously. Our way led right through the throng. The smoke from their water-pipes floated like mist in the narrow passages, and the light from the oil-lamps struggled with the darkness.

It was not until two o'clock in the morning that our mules were loaded and the long caravan started off. Groves and gardens became rarer, and the silent, dark desert surrounded us. The bells tinkled, and the bronze mule-bells round the necks of the leaders sounded their dong-dong. Before dawn, lurking shadows appeared here and there at the sides of the road. They were jackals and hyenas, returning to their dens from their nocturnal raids.

At half-past four, the sun rose over the desert; and four hours later, we halted at the caravansary of Ben-i-Said. The mules were freed from their burdens, and the men lay down to sleep through the warmest hours of the day.

In the little city of Bakuba, on the Diyala River, a squad of soldiers, guarding the frontier, surrounded me, and declared that because my Swedish passport bore no visé I would not be permitted to cross the border between Turkey and Persia. When they tried by force to lay hold of my modest possessions, I defended them with the courage of a lion. A scuffle ensued, in which my Arabian fellow travellers sided with me. The fight ended with our going to the Governor, who regularized my papers for a fee of six *kran*.

During the next night's ride, I fought desperately against sleep; but for long spells I was asleep in the saddle. Once, when my horse shied, and gave a jerk at the sight of a dead

HYENAS FEASTING ON A DEAD CAMEL.

camel, I found myself on the ground before I realized what had happened. The animal galloped away in the darkness, but was caught by a couple of the Arabs; and by that time I was thoroughly awake.

On the evening of June 9, we were overtaken by an old Arab of our party, who rode a genuine, blooded Arabian horse. I had just decided to abandon the caravan, as I did not relish the thought of having to travel the entire distance of one hundred and eighty miles to Kermanshah at night, when the landscape was enveloped in darkness. I could not carry out that plan by myself; so I began a cautious conversation with the Chaldean merchant and the newly-arrived Arab. The former dissuaded me strongly, saying we would be attacked by Kurd robbers and killed. The latter was not afraid; but he demanded twenty-five *kran* a day for his splendid horse, though I had already paid in full for the journey. But, by riding with him, I would reach Kermanshah in four days, instead of in nine nights. What would happen afterwards, when my pockets were absolutely empty of money, remained to be seen. After all, death by starvation was not imminent. I might get a job as a mule-driver in a caravan, or beg my way like a dervish.

But another Arab was eavesdropping, and he betrayed our plan to his companions. They were firm in their refusal to let us depart. One infidel more or less did not matter, but a horse was not lightly to be lost. I pretended to yield, and we proceeded on our night-journey as usual. The moon was up. The hours passed slowly. Lulled by the monotonous tinkling of the bells, the tired merchants fell asleep on their horses. A few of them had been singing, to ward off sleep, but they soon stopped. No one seemed aware of the fact that the old Arab and I were riding side by side. Tempted by my shiny, silver coins, he was going to defy his companions. Slowly and imperceptibly we advanced to the head of the caravan. There we stayed till the moon went down and it got quite dark. Then we drew away little by little. The sound of the bells drowned the tramping of our horses. We increased our speed, while the tinkling of the bells grew fainter, and finally died away altogether. Then I pressed my heels into my horse's sides, and, with my companion, rode at a quick trot in the direction of Kermanshah.

After sunrise, we halted for a while at a village. The storks were coming home to their nests, with frogs in their bills. Then up and into the saddle again! A heavy rain was lashing us and the earth. The last palms were behind us. We were in the dangerous mountain-region, the

scene of many assaults and robberies. My revolver was ready, but we
met only peaceful riders, pedestrians, and caravans.

A group of pilgrims, mounted on mules, was on its way to Bagdad,
Damascus, and Mecca. The greatest desire of their lives would be
attained, when they viewed the Holy City from the top of Mt. Arafat.
And after saying their prayers at Kaaba, that sacred black stone, they
would acquire the honourable title of Hadji, or "Pilgrim to Mecca."

In a district regarded as particularly unsafe, we joined a caravan
going in our direction. For a time, also, a small troop of Persian
soldiers, in white-and-blue cloaks and silver-embroidered belts, kept us
company. They performed all kinds of equestrian feats, after which
they asked to be rewarded for having saved me from robbers, into
whose hands they declared I must have fallen, but for them. I had no
money to give them, and could save my honour only by asseverating that
I had never asked for their protection.

On June 13, we entered Kermanshah, riding through its noisy
bazaars, where we had to elbow our way among mules, dervishes, caravans, horsemen, buyers, and traders.

In the court of a caravansary, my old Arab dismounted, and I
followed his example. After paying him one hundred *kran* for the hired
horse, I still owned a few silver coins; but when the old man persistently
(and properly) demanded a tip for the happily-completed journey, he
got them too. I kept only one small coin, worth about fifteen cents,
with which to buy a couple of eggs, a piece of bread, and a few glasses
of tea, for supper. Then I took leave of the old man, threw my belongings over my shoulder, and walked into the town.

There was not a single European in Kermanshah, and I was without letters of introduction to Mohammedans. Not even in the desert
did I ever feel so lonely and abandoned as here. I sat down to think on
a dilapidated, clay wall, and watched the passing throng. The people
looked at me as though I were a wild animal, and they gathered about
me in a noisy group. Not one of them was as poor as I. What in the
world was I to do? Only a few hours remained until twilight, and
where was I to spend the night, safe from jackals? Crowds are always
cruel, and who cared about an infidel, a Christian dog?

"I suppose I shall have to sell my saddle and my blanket," thought I.

But all at once I remembered that in Bushir and Bagdad I had
heard of Aga Mohammed Hassan, a rich Arab merchant, whose cara-

vans went all over western Asia, between Herat and Jerusalem, Samarkand and Mecca. Furthermore, he was *wakil-et-dovlet-i-Inglis,* that is, "Agent of the British Empire," in western Persia. He was my man! If he should throw me out, I would have to go to a caravansary and get a job in a caravan.

I rose and asked a kind-looking man if he knew where Aga Mohammed Hassan lived. "Oh, yes," he replied. "Come along." We soon stopped before a door in a wall, and knocked on a plate with an iron knocker. The doorkeeper opened. I told him my errand, and he took me through a garden to a palatial house, ran up a flight of stairs, and soon returned to inform me that the wealthy merchant would receive me.

I was taken through stately rooms, decorated with Persian rugs, hangings, and fabrics from Kashmir, divans and bronzes, and finally

came to Aga Mohammed Hassan's study. He was seated on a floor-rug, surrounded by heaps of documents and letters. A couple of secretaries were writing from his dictation, while several visitors stood by the walls.

Aga Mohammed Hassan was an elderly man, with a grizzled beard. He had a kind and noble appearance. He wore eyeglasses, a white turban, and a white-silk cloak, interwoven with gold threads. He rose and invited me to come forward. I walked over the soft rugs in my dusty top-boots and my worn garments, the only ones I possessed. He extended his hand and asked me to sit down. He inquired about my journey and

THE WEALTHY ARABIAN MERCHANT, AGA MO-HAMMED HASSAN, RECEIVES ME WITH GREAT HOSPITALITY

my plans. To all my answers he nodded comprehendingly. The only stumbling-block for him was Sweden and its geographical location. I tried to orientate him by saying that Sweden was between England and

Russia. Pondering awhile, he asked if I was from the country where Temirbash was king, Temirbash, or the "Iron Head," being the name by which Charles XII is famous in the Orient to this day.

"Yes," I replied, "I am from the country where Temirbash was king."

Then Aga Mohammed Hassan's face was lit up, and he bent his head, as if paying tribute to a great memory. He said:

"You must stay here as my guest for six months. All I own is yours, you have but to command. You must now excuse me, for my duties tie me down to my work; but the *mirzas* who will be your servants will take you to a house in my garden, where I hope you will make yourself at home."

Thereupon I accompanied Khadik Effendi and Mirza Misak to a nearby house, in gorgeous Persian style, with elaborate rooms, lovely rugs, black-silk divans, and sparkling, crystal chandeliers. I heaved a sigh of relief, and was tempted to embrace the two men allotted to my service. Only half an hour before, I had stood in the dust of the street, a tatterdemalion, surrounded by other tatterdemalions; and now Aladdin's lamp was burning before my eyes with a clear light, and through the magic power of Fate I had been changed into a prince of the "Arabian Nights."

While we were chatting, some servants, silent as ghosts, entered the room, spread a thin cloth on the rug, and served a dinner to which I did full justice. There were small pieces of mutton, broiled on a spit, bowls filled to the brim with chicken, *pilaff* (rice), cheese, bread, sherbet (a drink made of date-juice and sugar) and, at the end, Turkish coffee and *kalian,* the Persian hookah or water-pipe.

When, at last, I wanted to go to bed, a divan was placed on one of the marble walls in the garden, at the edge of a marble basin, in the water of which goldfish played, and from the centre of which a jet, clear as crystal and fine as a hair, shot up, glistening in the moonlight like silver. The air was summer-like and fragrant with the scent of innumerable roses and lilacs. How different from the dirty caravansaries! It was like a fairy-tale or a dream.

The night was certainly delicious; yet I longed for the morning, to try out Aga Mohammed Hassan's horses. As early as I dared, I beckoned to a servant, and soon the horses were standing ready saddled outside my door. With Mirza Misak and a *gulam* (groom) I rode to Tak-i-Bostan, the Sassanian kings' grotto. There I saw figures, in high relief, carved from the solid mountain, representing mounted kings, from about 380 A.D., and Khosru II Parvez (590-628 A.D.), in armour, lance in hand, riding Shabdez, his spirited war-horse; also representations of royal hunting-expeditions, perfectly executed, with elephants to pursue boars, horses for antelopes, and boats for sea-fowl.

The days passed with excursions and banquets, but my pockets were as empty as ever. I had not a copper to give to a beggar; yet I tried to preserve the calm assurance of a gentleman, at least outwardly. But the situation could not be prolonged indefinitely; so, finally, I picked up courage, and confided to Khadik Effendi that my journey had lengthened beyond my calculations, and that I did not have a farthing left. He was surprised, but smiled compassionately. (Had he suspected something of the kind?) And then he spoke these words, which I shall never forget: "You may have as much money as you want from Aga Hassan."

My departure was fixed for June 16, after midnight. I was to accompany the courier, who travelled with a convoy of three armed horsemen as a protection against robbers. He looked at me doubtfully, and declared that I would probably be outdistanced, because, during the entire stretch between Kermanshah and Teheran, nearly three hundred miles, he was allowed only one day's or night's rest, in the city of Hamadan. At the other stations, he was permitted to tarry only long enough to change horses, and get his meal of eggs, bread, fruit, and tea. But I was twenty, and proud; and I decided that even at the risk of being shaken to pieces in the saddle, I would show Ali Akbar, the mail-guard, that I could stand it.

At midnight, I feasted for the last time with Aga Mohammed Hassan. We talked about Europe and Asia. He beamed with kindness and benevolence, but neither he nor I said a word about my financial ruin. I rose, thanked him, and took my leave. Smilingly he wished me a happy journey. It is many years now, since he went to his final rest, near the tomb of some saint; but I preserve his image in my memory with love and gratitude.

When, for the last time, I entered my "palace," Mirza Misak handed me a leather bag, full of silver *kran,* a loan which I later duly repaid.

Thereupon I vaulted into the saddle, and rode out into the night with Ali Akbar and the three armed men.

In truth, it proved to be a hard ride! During the first sixteen hours, we covered one hundred and two miles. On the following morning, the snow-covered peak of Alvand (10,700 feet) gleamed before us, and at its foot we spent our day of rest in Hamadan. I slept half the day; the other half I devoted to the Tomb of Esther and the ruins of Ecbatana.

Thus we went on from village to village, arriving at a station dead-tired, throwing ourselves down on the hearthstone to rest, while fresh horses were saddled and tea was brewed, then flying away again, over mountains and through passes, across gardens and valleys, over bridges

HUMAN CORPSES ON THEIR WAY TO KERBELA

and brooks. During the day, we were scorched by the sun; and at night we frightened off the hyenas, which were feasting on the remains of caravan-animals that had fallen by the wayside. We saw the sun rise, complete his course, and set; we saw the moon rise and set, floating like a silver shell, among the stars, in a blue-black sky. Once we met a funeral-caravan, identifiable beforehand by the stench arising from the dead bodies, which were wrapped in blankets, and were being borne by mules to Kerbela, to rest near the sepulchre of Imam Hussain. When, at last, we rode into Teheran, in the early morning of June 21, none of us had slept a wink during the preceding fifty-five hours. Each of us had worn out nine horses.

After a badly-needed rest, I rode across the Elburz Mountains to Barfrush, on the Caspian Sea, I proceeded by boat along the Turkoman shore to Krasnovodsk, thence to Baku, continuing by train, via Tiflis, to Batum, on the Black Sea, and thence by boat to Constantinople. In Adrianople, I was arrested, on account of my sketch-book. I arrived in Sofia on the 24th of August, and came near being shot by the guard, as I walked too close to the castle. Only three days had elapsed since the revolution which had cost Alexander of Battenberg his throne. At Stralsund, I boarded a Swedish steamer, and was soon received with rejoicing by my parents, brother, and sisters. Thus ended my first long journey on Asiatic soil.

CHAPTER VI

Constantinople

I NOW studied geography and geology at the Universities of Upsala and Berlin, and also at the Stockholm Högskola (literally "high school," but actually the equivalent of an American college). My teacher in Berlin was Baron Ferdinand von Richthofen, famous for his travels in China, and the greatest authority of his day on the geography of Asia.

I now also made my début as an author. In a volume illustrated by my own sketches, I told the story of my Persian journey. As I had never before written for publication, I hardly trusted my ears when a kind old publisher came to my home and offered me six hundred dollars for the right to publish my travel-experiences. I had only hoped to get the book published without having to pay for it myself and here was an amiable old gentleman, willing to buy my manuscript for a sum which, in my circumstances, seemed enormous. Fortunately, I grasped the importance of the situation, became a diplomat, quickly knitted my brows, and answered that the fee offered was not at all commensurate with the extreme dangers and hardships of the journey. But finally I yielded, and accepted the offer. As a matter of fact, I was ready to leap for joy.

Encouraged by this success, I translated and abridged the travels of the Russian general, N. M. Przhevalsky, in the interior of Asia, publishing them in one volume. As this was not an original work of mine, I got only two hundred dollars for it.

In the summer of 1889, Stockholm was the scene of a Congress of Orientalists, and our streets were filled with natives of Asia and Africa. Among the Asiatics were four distinguished Persians, charged by Shah Nasr-ed-Din to present a royal decoration to King Oscar II. It was like a breeze from home to speak to these sons of Persia, and I longed to revisit their country more than ever. Aladdin's lamp was lit anew, and it burned with as clear a flame as in the garden of Aga Mohammed Hassan.

I was spending a month in autumn with my mother and a sister on the seacoast south of Stockholm, on a farm belonging to Dalbyö, the estate of Nordenskiöld, the hero of the "Vega." One day, the mail brought a letter from my father which read: "You must be in town to-morrow at eleven o'clock, in order to pay your respects to the Prime Minister. The King is going to send an embassy to the Shah of Persia in the spring, and you are to go along. Hurrah!"

The cottage in which we were staying resounded with hurrahs. We sat for hours, discussing the event. There was hardly any sleep that night; for I had to get up at four o'clock. Transit between Dalbyö and Stockholm was wretched. I had to walk through forests, and row seven miles across the archipelago, to make the steamer-landing. But I ran through the forest and flew like a wild duck across the water, and arrived in Stockholm on time!

Sweden and Norway being still united under the same crown at that time, the King appointed F. W. Treschow, Chamberlain to the King, a Norwegian, to head the embassy. C. E. von Geijer was appointed secretary, Count Claes Lewenhaupt military attaché, and myself interpreter. We departed early in April, 1890, crossed the Continent, and arrived in Constantinople in Ramadan, the month of fasting.

Constantinople is one of the most beautiful cities in the world, situated as it is on the narrow Bosporus, the Sea of Marmora, and the Dardanelles, which latter connects two seas and separates two continents. As in Rome and Moscow, there are seven hills in the city. Its chief section is Stamboul, the specifically Turkish town, situated on a triangular tongue of land, protected on the land side by a wall with towers, and separated from Pera and Galata by a deep bay, the Golden Horn. Stamboul is a wavy sea of white and brightly-coloured houses, above which rise the mighty cupolas and tall, slender minarets of the mosques. During Ramadan evenings, the mosques are illuminated by hundreds of thousand of lights, arranged between the minarets so as to form the names of the Prophet and the holy Imams.

Biggest and most beautiful of all the temples of Stamboul is the Church of St. Sophia, the "Holy Wisdom," solemnly dedicated, in 548 A.D., by Justinian, the Byzantine emperor. The dome, with its galleries, is supported by one hundred columns, some of them of dark-green marble, others of dark-red porphyry.

In those days, the Christian cross surmounted the dome. But nine

THE GREEK BISHOP

centuries passed, and one warm summer night, on the 29th of May, 1453, Mohammed the Conqueror and his wild hordes, under the green flag of the Prophet, were standing outside the city gates. After a heroic defense, Constantine, the last emperor, having doffed his purple cloak, fell, unrecognized, among the piles of corpses. Observing the splendour of Constantine's palace, the victorious Sultan was seized with melancholy at the thought of the transitoriness of life and exclaimed, in the words of the Persian poet: "The spider has spun its web in the imperial palace, and the owl sings its twilight song from the tower of Afrasiab."

A hundred thousand terror-stricken Christians took refuge in the Church of St. Sophia, and barred the doors. But the Turks, maddened by blood-lust, battered down the doors, and rushed in. An awful slaughter began. At the high-altar stood a Greek bishop, in pontifical robes, reading the mass for the dead in a loud voice. Eventually he stood alone. Then he broke off in the middle of a sentence, took the communion-chalice, and mounted the stairs leading to the upper galleries. Like hungry wolves the Turks rushed after him. He directed his steps toward a wall, where a door opened. He entered, and the door closed again. In vain did the soldiers attack the wall with spears and axes. For more than four and a half centuries the Greeks have blindly believed that on the day when the Church of St. Sophia fell into the hands of the Christians again, the wall would open, and the bishop step out, with the chalice in his hand. At the high-altar he would continue the mass from the exact point at which he had been interrupted by the Turks. Nevertheless, during the last period of the World War, when Constantinople was held by the troops of the Allies, the bishop did not appear.

At the time of our visit, the crescent rested safely on the dome and the minarets, from the circular balconies of which the hours of prayer were proclaimed by the muezzin. Loud and clear in four directions, his voice rang out: "Allah is great! There is no other god but Allah! Mohammed is Allah's prophet! Come to prayer. Come to eternal bliss. Allah is great! La illaha il Allah!"

From the galleries of the great mosque, which was lit by innumerable oil-lamps, we saw thousands of the faithful, deep in prayer.

Mohammed the Conqueror laid the foundation of the seraglio, or palace, where twenty-five sultans have reigned until Abdul Mejid built the Dolma Bagche on the Bosporus, exactly four hundred years after the conquest. The seraglio occupies the highest point in the city. Its pinnacles are the first to be purpled by the morning light, and the last to pale when the evening glow fades. There is a grand view from its terraces, over the Sea of Marmora, the Golden Horn, and the Asiatic coast.

The seraglio consists of several groups of buildings and courts, separated by gates. The Orta Kapu, or "Middle Gate," at the Court of the Janizaries, consists of two pairs of doors, between which is a dark room, with vaults. A pasha coming there, in response to a summons from the Sultan, and hearing the first pair of doors slammed to behind him, without the opposite pair opening, understood that his hour had struck; for it was there that pashas who fell from grace were executed.

Inside the third gate, Bab-i-Seadet, the "Gate of Felicity," is the treasury, where, among other valuables, are the gold throne, pearls, rubies, and emeralds which Sultan Selim I seized from Shah Ismail of Persia. The Prophet's flag, cloak, staff, sabre, and bow are preserved in a secluded part of the palace, where no stranger is admitted. Only once a year did the Sultan betake himself to that sacred spot.

ABDUL HAMID II, THE LATE SULTAN OF THE TURKS

One day, we were invited to the Sultan's *iftar,* the evening meal in the month of Ramadan. It was served in the Yildiz Kiosk. The duties of host were performed by Osman Ghasi Pasha, famous for the bravery with which he defended Plevna, in 1877, when he held out against the superior force of the Russians for more than four months. The dining-room was small and dark-coloured, but flooded with light. Outside, the daylight was fading. And while waiting for the sunset-gun, all sat as silent as statues, leaning over plates of solid gold. At last the gun was fired, and the footmen served the dinner.

Afterwards, we were received by Abdul Hamid II. He was a small man, with fine, pale features, bluish-black beard, penetrating, dark eyes, and a Roman nose. He wore a red fez and a long, dark-blue uniform-coat. His left hand rested on the handle of his scimitar; and with a gracious nod he received the holograph letter which our King had charged us to deliver to him.

Nor did we neglect to visit the City of the Dead. There is an atmosphere of quiet and peace about the cemeteries outside Stamboul, and in Scutari. Tall, dark-green cypresses rise between the graves, and countless monuments mark the last resting-place of earth's weary pilgrims. A bowl-shaped hollow is often found on the horizontal monuments. Rain-water accumulates there, and small birds come to drink. On these visits, their song brings comfort to the dead who slumber beneath the stones.

CHAPTER VII

An Ambassador to the Shah of Persia

ON the 30th of April, we boarded the Russian ship "Rostov-Odessa," and steamed out through the Bosporus, with the European coast on our left, the Asiatic on our right, and on all sides a landscape fascinating in its peculiar beauty. Toward evening, the last lighthouses disappeared, and we glided out onto the Black Sea. I was familiar with the way we were about to take. We called at the towns on the coast of Asia Minor, landed at Batum, and went by rail, via Tiflis, to Baku. I saw the same scenes as on my former visit, the same caravans, riders, and shepherds, and the same picturesque carts, drawn by grey buffaloes.

This time, too, we visited the Nobel oil-fields at Balakhany. There were then (1890) four hundred and ten wells, one hundred and sixteen of which belonged to the Nobels. Of these, forty were being pumped, while twenty-five were being deepened. One of them gushed to the extent of 150,000 puds in twenty-four hours. The wells were generally 120 to 150 fathoms deep, and the largest pipe-line was twenty-four inches in diameter. Some 230,000 puds of crude oil were daily piped to the Black City, through two lines, yielding, after distillation, 60,000 puds of pure oil a day.

On the 11th of May, late in the evening, we boarded the steamship "Mikhajl," accompanied by some of Nobel's engineers. We were sitting aft, chatting, when we heard penetrating steam-whistles sounding on all sides. White flames rose from the Black City, dense brown clouds of smoke belching above them. The Swedish engineers hurried ashore, and were rushed to the seat of the fire in *isvostschiks*. In the light of the flames, the "Mikhajl" cast off, and we headed south for the Persian coast.

On disembarking at Enseli, trumpets blared, and a forty-gun salute was fired in our honour. On the shore stood two high dignitaries of the country, wearing uniforms resplendent with gold galloons and gewgaws,

with the cockades of the sun and the lion in their lambskin caps. One
of them was General Mohammed Aga, the *mahmandar,* or official host,
who bade us welcome on behalf of the Shah. He was to accompany us
to Teheran with a big suite, escort, and caravans.

We were towed in a boat to Resht by runners in loose garments, who
reminded me of forest trolls, or Robin Goodfellows, as they darted in
and out among bushes and beds of reeds. The Governor entertained
us at *dastarkhan,* a meal served on fifty platters. We left Resht on the
16th of May. Tents, rugs, beds, equipment, and provisions burdened
forty-four mules. The escort of soldiers, in their black uniforms, and
armed with rifles, sabres, and pistols, had their own caravans.

And now began a journey the like of which is to be found only in
ancient narratives. The Persians displayed the pomp and splendour
that were due to representatives of a great power. Spring was at its
height, the forest was heavy with fragrance, every brook rippled, and
all the song-birds greeted our brilliant procession. Each day's journey
was divided into two stages, one in the morning, the other in the evening. The warm hours of the day, when the temperature rose to more
than 86°, were spent in airy tents, pitched under olive and mulberry
trees. At every village through which we passed, we were welcomed by
the elders, white-bearded old men, wearing kaftans that reached to their
feet, and high, white turbans.

Our entry into Kazvin surpassed everything we had hitherto experienced. Far outside the city, the Mayor and a large escort met us,
and later the Governor, with a hundred horsemen. Our procession
swelled gradually into an enormous cavalcade, trotting along the road,
and sometimes disappearing in clouds of yellow-grey dust. Two heralds
rode ahead, one in black, the other in red, and both in white lambskin
caps and silver galloons. They were followed by horsemen, with blar-
ing trumpets, and, on either side, by running soldiers in blue uniforms.
They executed a *jigitovka* (equestrian manœuvres), in which one neck-
breaking feat followed another. Sometimes they stood on their saddles
while galloping at top speed, or threw themselves downwards, while in
full career, to snatch an object from the ground. Sometimes they threw
their rifles in the air, discharging them on the instant of their recovery,
or they would juggle thin, naked sabres, so that the blades flashed in
the sunshine. Thus our noisy procession went along through vineyards

and gardens, under the porcelain-tower of the gate of Kazvin, through bazaars, and across open squares.

Once we met a company quite different from ours. It was a Shiah funeral-procession. Two red banners and two black streamers came first, then huge trays filled with bread, rice, and sweets, with burning candles at the corners. Then followed a group of men, keening plaintively: "Hussain, Hassan." Behind them, the dead man's grey horse was led, with a gorgeous saddle and an embroidered cloth, the pommel bearing a green turban, the symbol of the owner's descent from the Prophet. The bier was high-arched, and covered with brown blankets. Any one of the spectators was allowed to relieve the carriers, and every-

ENTERING KAZVIN

body wanted to do so, for the dead man had been a high-priest of great distinction. The procession closed with an immense crowd of priests in white turbans.

Having received the honours due us in Kazvin, we proceeded by carriage to Teheran. Once we found ourselves in a shower of hail, and our vehicles became covered with slush. On another occasion, the road was blocked by a caravan of mules, laden with rugs. Hearing the carriages rattle behind them, the mules lost their heads and went off at a slow gallop. The ropes which bound their loads became loose, and one rug after another slid off. As their burdens grew lighter, the mules increased their speed. Gay and boisterous, they scampered away in front of the carriages. We laughed at this spectacle till we choked; but the poor caravan-conductors were far from laughing, as they went along picking their dusty rugs from off the road.

On the day that we entered Teheran, the Oriental splendour reached its climax. How different from my last entry! Then I had come as a poor student; now I came as one of the King's ambassadors. Whole regiments of cavalry were out in full uniform, and infantry lined the streets. Mounted bands played the Swedish national anthem, and we were received in a garden by the high dignitaries of the country. Here we arranged our cavalcade. Arabian horses, with saddle-cloths embroidered in gold and silver, and panther-skins under the saddles, were given to us. Even the horses took fire from the music, and went dancing gracefully through the city gate. The whole population seemed to be afoot to witness our entry. The procession ended in a garden, the like of which, for luxuriance and beauty, I had never seen before. In its centre stood the stately palace of Emaret Sepa Salar (the Marshal's Palace), where we were to reside.

One feast succeeded another for twelve days. We had cavaliers and officers waiting on us and following us everywhere like shadows. At meals, the Shah's brother-in-law, fine, old Yahiya Khan, presided; and in the evenings, a band played near the large, marble basin in front of the palace.

A few days after our arrival, we were summoned to an audience, escorted by chamberlains and state officials, in royal carriages, each drawn by four white horses with violet-dyed tails. Heralds, with silver staffs and *ferrashs,* dressed in red, ran ahead of us.

After some minutes' wait in an antechamber, a courtier announced that Ala Hasret (his Majesty) was ready to receive us. We were taken to a large room, decorated in fine Persian style, with rugs and hangings, along the walls of which a score of courtiers, ministers, and generals in old-fashioned, embroidered kaftans were lined up, as motionless as statues.

Shah Nasr-ed-Din was standing by the outer wall, between a single huge window, extending to the floor, and the famous peacock-throne. This strange piece of furniture, resembling a gigantic chair, with a back and an elongated seat, and with stairs leading up to it from the floor, is plated with thick gold, and set with precious stones in the form of an expanded peacock-tail. It was taken from the Great Mogul of Delhi, nearly two hundred years before, by Nadir Shah, during his Indian campaign.

Shah Nasr-ed-Din was in black. On his breast he wore forty-eight enormous diamonds, and on each epaulet three large emeralds. On his black cap was a diamond clasp, and at his side hung a sabre, the sheath of which was studded with gems. He observed us fixedly. He carried himself royally, and stood there like a real Asiatic despot, conscious of his superiority and power.

The head of our embassy delivered the decoration our King had sent to his Persian cousin. After it had been received by the interpreter and shown to the Shah, he conversed with each one of us for a while, asking several questions about Sweden and Norway. He told us that he had been in Europe three times, and that he intended to visit Sweden and America on his next journey.

There was an old-Persian glamour about the whole ceremony. But when I was received by Nasr-ed-Din's son, Shah Mussaffar-ed-Din, fifteen years later, it had faded considerably; and to-day it is gone altogether.

NASR-ED-DIN, LATE SHAH OR KING OF PERSIA.

In the days that followed, everything was done for our amusement and entertainment. A splendid feast was given in our honour at the royal palace, with all the state dignitaries present, and the Shah, invisible, watching us from a gallery.

We were shown the Shah's museum, the lock of which is sealed, and broken only for distinguished guests. Among its treasures we saw the diamond Daria-i-nur, or "Sea of Light," and a terrestrial globe, two feet in diameter, on which the oceans were represented by closely-set turquoises, the Arctic regions by diamonds clear as crystal, and Teheran by another jewel. We also saw glass cubes entirely filled with real pearls from the Bahrein Islands, turquoises from Nishapur, and rubies from Badakshan.

In the court in front of the Shah's stable, noble specimens of his nine hundred horses were displayed, each one ridden by a groom.

Most splendid of all were the manœuvres on a field outside the city. The troops, 14,000 strong, were drawn up in a square; and, in the train of the Shah, we rode by in review. Then the Shah established himself in a huge, red tent, and we did likewise in a rose-coloured one alongside of it, while the infantry marched past, saluting the monarch, and the cavalry spurred forward wildly. The most beautiful were the horsemen, clad in red cloaks, their heads bound with red fillets.

Finally, one day, we rode out to the ruins of Rages, the ancient city that flourished in the days of Salmanasar, and which is mentioned in the Book of Tobit. Alexander the Great rested there, when he was a day's march from the "Caspian Gates." More than a thousand years later, the city was beautified by the Caliph Al-Mansur. Within its walls Harun-ar-Rashid was born; and the Arabs sang of its glory, calling it the Gate of the Gates of the Earth. In the thirteenth century, Rages was totally destroyed by the Mongols, and now only a well-preserved tower rises above the ruins.

At Teheran, I found myself in a dilemma. Should I rest content with these mere feasts, that left no greater aftermath than do common fireworks? Ought I not rather to use this opportunity to get farther into Asia, to continue, in fact, to the heart of the continent? Such a journey might be a valuable preparation for bigger undertakings. My desire to make my way, step by step, to the still-unvisited parts of the desert region, and to the Tibetan highlands, was irresistible.

My travelling-companions of the embassy approved my plan. I telegraphed King Oscar for permission to continue eastward. The King not only assented, but also promised to pay the cost of my contemplated journey.

And so, when the other members of the embassy left Teheran, on the third of June, to return home by the route we had come, I remained with my friend Hybennet. I had funds sufficient to last me till I reached the Chinese border.

CHAPTER VIII

A Burial-Ground

ZOROASTRIANISM is one of the oldest religions in the world. It was founded by Zoroaster. Its sacred books are called the Zend-Avesta. It was practised by one of the mightiest peoples of the earth, flourished for a period of a thousand years, continued with diminishing vitality for another thousand years, and was finally crushed, in 640 A.D., when the Caliph Omar carried the banners of the Prophet against the Persians, whom he vanquished near Ecbatana. During the victorious progress of Islam, many of the Zoroastrians had already fled, in ships, from Hormus to Bombay. At present there are about 100,000 devotees left in India, and 8,000 in Persia. The sacred fire, therefore, is not yet extinguished.

In a previous chapter, we described a visit to a recently-abandoned fire-temple at Surakhani. In Yezd, Persia, there are a score of them. But in olden times it was different. There were several fire-altars in Persepolis, and Xenophon relates:

> "When Cyrus went out from his palace, horses were led before him to be sacrificed to the sun, also a white-garlanded carriage for the sun. Thereafter came a carriage with horses decorated in purple, and after this followed men carrying a fire on a big hearth. Then the horse was sacrificed to the sun, whereupon a sacrifice was offered to the earth according to customs set down by the Magi."

Magianism obtained in Persia and India before the age of Zoroaster. The celestial bodies and the two elements, fire and water, were deified. Sorcery and witchcraft flourished.

Zoroaster's teaching was dualistic. It recognized one god, Ahuramazda, the creator of all things light and good. Opposed to him was Ahriman, who represented the principle of darkness and evil, with evil-

minded demons in his train. The feud between Ahuramazda and Ahriman was never-ending; and it was the duty of the righteous to help
Ahuramazda to victory.

The oldest sacred fire was the one that burned at Rages. The sun
and the fire are symbols of God's omnipotence. Nothing on earth more
nearly approaches divine perfection than fire, because of the light, heat,
and purifying cleanliness which it distributes. Dead bodies pollute the
earth. The dead must therefore be buried on towers, separated from
their surroundings by high walls. The road leading to the tower is also
polluted by the passing of the corpse; but the way is purged, if a white
or yellow dog, with black spots around his eyes, is led in the wake of the
funeral-procession. The dog exorcises the demons. The flies that swarm
about the exposed corpses are goblins, female demons in the service of
Ahriman. Dead enemies do not pollute the earth, for they bear witness
to the victory of good over evil.

The fire-worshippers in Persia, known as Parsees, are despised and
detested by the worshippers of Islam. Hence they seclude themselves
in their own villages, that they may be able to devote themselves without interference to their religious observances. Many of them are
merchants and gardeners. After thousands of years, they still follow
the precepts of Zoroaster. A lamp burns in every house. Tobacco-
smoking is a sin against fire; and if a fire breaks out, one must not extinguish it, no mortal being allowed to fight the power of fire.

When a Parsee dies, he is robed in white, a white cloth is wrapped
round his head, oil-lamps are lit, and he is placed on an iron bier, with
a piece of bread at his feet. If a dog, on being admitted to the death-
room, eats the bread, the man is dead. Should the dog refuse to eat it,
the soul is regarded as still inhabiting the body, and the corpse is allowed to remain until decomposition sets in. The dead man is then
washed by the corpse-washer, who is considered to be impure, and in
whose house no one dares set foot.

Four porters, in white clothes that have been washed in running
water, carry the bier to the funeral-place, called the Tower of Silence.
It is not really a tower, but a wall, two hundred and twenty-three feet in
circumference, and almost twenty-three feet high. Inside this, the corpse
is laid in a shallow, open, rectangular cavity. Finally, the clothes of the
dead person are loosened and opened, the head-bandage is removed, the
funeral-guests walk backwards to the wall, and return home. During

the funeral, vultures perch on the ridge of the wall, and ravens circle over the place. When all is quiet, it becomes their turn to be active; and before long the skeleton lies bare, drying up in the burning sun.

The Parsees, or fire-worshippers, are said to be descended direct from the ancient followers of Zoroaster, and are thus the purest representatives of the Indo-European race.

Prior to my departure from Stockholm, a famous professor of medicine and anthropology asked me to try to obtain and bring home, in one way or another, the crania of some of these fire-worshippers. Accordingly, in the middle of June, when summer was at its height, and the thermometer registered 106° in the shade, I set out with Dr. Hybennet for the Tower of Silence, the funeral-place of the fire-worshippers, southeast of Teheran. We chose the early hours of the afternoon for our raid, because then everybody kept indoors, on account of the heat.

We took with us a *kurchin,* or soft saddlebag, in the two pockets of which we put straw, paper, and two watermelons, each the size of a man's head.

We drove, in a carriage, out through the gate of Shah Abdul Azim. The streets were as empty as dried-up river-beds. Camels, feeding on thistles, wandered about on the steppe outside the town, and here and there a cloud of dust passed over the baked earth like a ghost.

We took the road through the village of Hashemabad, in order to borrow a crock of water and a ladder from a peasant. Arriving at the Tower of Silence, we leaned the ladder against the wall; but it proved to be too short, by about three feet. However, I climbed to the top rung, managed to get a good hold on the coping, and swung myself up. Then I gave Dr. Hybennet a helping hand.

A rank, sickening smell of cadavers met us. Hybennet remained on the coping, to keep an eye on the driver, and to make sure that he was not spying on us, while I descended the cement stairs to the circular bowl of the funeral-place. There were sixty-one open, shallow graves. In about ten of them lay skeletons and corpses in various stages of putrefaction. Whitened and weather-beaten bones lay piled up alongside the wall.

After some deliberation, I selected the corpses of three adult men. The freshest corpse had been there only a few days; yet its soft parts, the muscles and entrails, had already been torn away and devoured by birds of prey. The eyes had been picked out, but the rest of the face remained, dried up, and as hard as parchment. I detached the dead man's skull and emptied it of its contents. I did the same with the second head. The third had been lying in the sun so long that its brains were dried up.

We had taken the saddlebag and the crock of water with us over the wall, pretending that we were going to have lunch there. I used the water to wash my hands. Then I emptied the bag, wrapped the skulls in paper, after first filling them with straw, and then put them in the bag in place of the watermelons. The bag thus retained its shape; and there was nothing to arouse the driver's suspicion, except the offensive smell, which may possibly have put strange ideas into his head. On our return to the carriage, we found the driver fast asleep, in the narrow shadow of the wall. As it was, he did not betray us. On the way back, we returned the crock and the ladder, and continued through the still-lifeless streets to Hybennet's home.

We buried the skulls in the ground, left them there for a month, and afterwards boiled them in milk, until they were as clear and white as ivory.

The need for all this secrecy is obvious. What would the superstitious Persians and Parsees have thought of us, had they learned that we infidels were driving about, stealing skulls from their funeral-places? Besides, Hybennet was physician-in-ordinary to the Shah, and, specifically, his dentist. People might have supposed that we intended to remove the teeth from the jaws of the skulls for subsequent use in the Shah's gracious mouth. There might have been disturbances and, riots, we might have been set upon, and finally delivered up to the people. But everything went off well.

Nevertheless, on arriving at the pier, in Baku, on my way home, next year, I nearly got into trouble with the customs officials. All my belongings were examined most carefully, and at last three round objects, wrapped in paper and felt, and resembling footballs, rolled out on the floor.

"What is this?" asked the customs inspector.

"Human heads," I answered, without blinking.

"I beg your pardon? Human heads?"

"Yes. Look, if you please!"

One of the balls was opened, and a skull grinned up at the inspectors. They stared at one another in perplexity. Finally, the surveyor said to the others: "Wrap the parcel up and put it all back!" And to me he said: "Take your traps and get out of here as fast as you can." He probably thought the skulls were evidence of a triple murder, and that it was the part of wisdom not to get mixed up in such an ugly affair.

Those Parsee skulls may be seen to this day in the Craniological Museum of Stockholm.

CHAPTER IX

To the Top of Demavend

EVERY year, Shah Nasr-ed-Din would make a summer trip to the Elburz Mountains, to escape the heat of Teheran and its environs. The departure this year was set for the fourth of July. As Dr. Hybennet's guest, I was invited by the Shah to join the party. We were to be gone for more than a month. One other European was, as a matter of course, attached to the party. This was Dr. Feuvrier, a Frenchman, who was first physician-in-ordinary to the Shah. Very few Europeans have, indeed, ever taken part in these royal excursions.

The spectacle was as unique as it was enchanting and impressive. On the day before setting out, we were visited by a chamberlain, who informed us of the route, and presented me with a handful of Persian gold coins from the Shah, a custom which implied the wish that the receiver might never lack money.

The journey took us northeast into the mountains, and to the basins of two rivers, the Jaje-rud and Lar, the former flowing south towards the desert, and the latter northward to the Caspian Sea. Our way included two high passes, the second being at an altitude of 9,500 feet.

We had reached the mountains, and were following the winding paths across cliffs and passes, and through valleys and pastures, when we suddenly found the road entirely blocked, both ways, by the two thousand beasts of burden—camels, mules, and horses—which bore the tents, provisions, and other equipment of the Shah, his ministers, and servants. Twelve hundred persons took part in the expedition, two hundred of whom were soldiers. When we encamped at night, a city of three hundred tents sprang up in the lonely valleys.

Everyone except the servants had a duplicate set of tents. No matter how quickly we rode, after breaking camp in the morning, we would find the tents ready pitched at the next stopping-place.

The Shah's tents were borne by camels, decorated with tall, red plumes. His boxes, covered with red cloth, edged with black, were carried by mules. His horses, too, wore red plumes; and the white horses had their tails dyed violet.

The arrangement of the tents was always uniform. Everybody knew the place occupied by his tents, and how the tent-streets ran. The Shah, in addition to his big, red living-tent, had one each for dining and smoking, and several other tents for the ladies of his harem. How many women he had brought along from his harem was not definitely known; but some said there were forty. This number included the maids of the harem ladies. Almost daily we rode past royal wives, thickly veiled, sitting astride their horses. Nevertheless, etiquette and tact made us avert our faces when these ladies were near. Eunuchs and dwarfs rode before and after them.

Surrounding the royal tents was a high screen of coarse, red cloth, on poles. This screen enclosed the inner royal courtyard. The outer court was enclosed by the tents that housed the main guard, the *ferrashs,* the supplies, the kitchen, etc. This was exactly the same tent-arrangement as the one which Xenophon tells us was used two thousand four hundred years before, in the camp of Cyrus.

Emin-i-Sultan, the Grand Vizier, was responsible for keeping order in the moving city. The kitchen-master and commissary-general was Mej-ed-dovleh, a relative of the Shah. Other functionaries of note were the master of the horse, the chief of the saddle-chamber, the chief of the body-guard, the head of the wardrobe, the chief of the Shah's bed-chamber (an old man, who always slept at the entrance of the Shah's sleeping-tent), the chief of the eunuchs, the chief of the *kalian* (the water-pipe rinser), the head chef, the butler, the chief barber, the chief of the *sakkas* (the men who constantly sprinkle water round the Shah's tent to lay the dust), and the chief of the *ferrashs.*

Hybennet and I had tents in the centre of the large camp-city. We had one for ourselves, one for the kitchen, and one for our servants. It is impossible to convey an idea of the commotion that prevailed in the evenings. The cries of the caravan-men and the gendarmerie, the jingle of bells, the neighing of horses, the braying of mules, and the roaring of camels were heard everywhere. At ten o'clock, a trumpet-signal indicated that only those who knew the day's password would be permitted within a certain distance of the Shah's tent. The watchman's warning cry was frequently heard when unauthorized nocturnal walkers were about. Gay camp-fires burned everywhere, lights shone from the tents, and anyone out calling on a friend was always preceded by a man carrying an oil-lamp in a paper lantern.

Justice was dispensed in the camp by especially trustworthy men. If the Shah's caravan-beasts trampled a villager's crop, the complainant received damages. But those who made false claims were bastinadoed.

The Shah would attend to the daily affairs of government with his ministers, and sometimes he would let his first interpreter, Etemad-e-Saltanet, read aloud from French newspapers. He often rode to the hunt with a large suite; and if the game was edible, he would distribute it among his suite, not forgetting us. When the expedition passed through a village, the people always came out to gaze at Shahinshah, the "King of Kings." At such times, he would distribute gold coins among them. When riding, he generally wore a brown coat and a black cap, and carried a black sunshade. The saddle and the saddle-cloth were embroidered in gold.

On the banks of the Lar River, our angling produced the most delicious trout. Large, nomadic communities camped in that vicinity, in black and coloured tents. Sometimes I looked in upon them, and made sketches. Once, when I wanted to draw a picture of a nice-looking nomad girl, her father absolutely refused to let her pose. Questioned regarding his fears, he answered: "If the Shah sees her picture, he will want her for his harem."

As the Shah himself was somewhat addicted to drawing, he was much interested in my sketches, and he sometimes had me bring them to him in his tent.

One interesting person who took part in this journey has not yet been mentioned. Asis-i-Sultan, which means "the king's affection," was a twelve-year-old, ugly, and consumptive whelp of a boy, the Shah's living talisman or mascot. Without him, the Shah could not travel or undertake any enterprise, or, indeed, live. His superstitious affection for this unlovable person was said to have had its origin in a prophecy which limited the Shah's years by the life of the boy. Thus the boy was looked after with the utmost solicitude. He had his own court, his dwarfs, jesters, negroes, *masseuses,* and servants to execute his slightest wish. And he was a marshal of the army. Because of his influence over the King, everyone was ready to stand on his head for him, though secretly they all wished him dead.

Nasr-ed-Din seemed always to need some living creature upon whom to bestow his affection. Prior to Asis-i-Sultan's accession to power, fifty cats were the Shah's favourites. These, too, had their own royal household; and whenever the Shah travelled, the cats were taken along in velvet-lined baskets. The name of the chief favourite was Babr Khan, or the tiger-cat. He had his breakfast daily at the Shah's table. When, as sometimes happened, the cats multiplied, they swarmed on the palace rugs, and then, God help the minister who should trip over them!

All in all, our summer days passed most pleasantly. I strolled about, drawing and writing; and as I was the only person in camp who knew English, I was sometimes asked to translate English despatches to Emin-i-Sultan. When we were in the valley of the Lar, not far from Demavend, I was seized with an irresistible desire to ascend the 18,700 feet of this, the highest mountain in Persia. It had been climbed frequently by European diplomats at Teheran.

Demavend was said to be a *solfatara,* a volcano no longer violently active, composed of trachyte, porphyry, and lava, with a crater of sulphur half a kilometre in circumference, capped by eternal snow. In ancient times, Persian poets celebrated it in song. Its original name was said to have been Divband, or "the Home of the Spirits"; and even in our day, jinn and divs—good and evil spirits—are believed to dwell on its summit.

When the Shah heard of my plan, he expressed great interest, and doubted whether I could reach the top without great preparations and a large escort. By his orders, the Grand Vizier wrote a letter to the elder of the village of Rahna, where the ascent was to begin, directing that everything be done to expedite my journey.

Jafar, one of the Shah's men, fetched me on the morning of July 9; and we rode, I on a horse, he on a mule, to Rahna, where we spent the night. The elder of the village declared, of course, that I had but to command and he would obey. I asked for the minimum of impedimenta, two reliable guides, and provisions for two days. Kerbelai Tagi and Ali were at once assigned to me. They told of having made thirty journeys to the top of Demavend, to procure sulphur.

The summit of Demavend was enveloped in clouds when we departed, at half-past four in the morning. The guides carried long, iron-tipped alpenstocks, together with our provisions and instruments.

We proceeded slowly, along steep gravel-slopes, between rocks, and across brooks. The whole day was thus consumed. At dusk the men stopped at a cave, where we were to pass the night. The top was still so far away, that I told them to continue. After dark, the terrain became so rough, that we had to proceed on foot among the rocks. When we reached the first snow, I ordered a halt for the night. We made a fire in the scrub. The smoke hung like a veil on the southern slope. We ate bread, eggs, and cheese, and then went to sleep under the open sky.

The night was cold and windy; but we kept the fire going, and hugged ourselves, like hedgehogs, as close to its warming flames as possible.

At four o'clock the next morning, I was waked by Ali, who stood at my side, shouting "Sahab berim!" (Sir, let us break up!). We drank a few mouthfuls of tea, ate some bread, and set out along a rocky ridge of porphyry and tuff. Demavend is shaped like a very regular volcano-cone. At an altitude of 11,000 feet, we came upon the ever-present snow, which lies like a cap on the skull of the mountain, and sends streaks down between the rocky ridges that extend along the slope. We made our way between two such snow-tongues.

The sun rose from a clear sky, spreading its gold over this glorious, wild landscape. In the southwest, at the stone bridge of Pul-i-Pulur, the valley-bed appeared white-spotted. This was, in fact, the three hundred tents of the Shah's camp, which had been moved thither the previous evening. But it soon became cloudy, and a hail-shower struck us like whip-lashes. We were forced to halt and crouch down between two rocks, the hail beating down on our backs.

Afterwards, we continued the steep ascent. My guides stepped as lightly as chamois, but to me the walking seemed terribly heavy. I was no mountain-climber, I had had no practice, and I had never before tried to ascend a high peak. Every ten steps I had to stop and catch my breath, after which I would again take a few steps. My temples throbbed, I had a violent headache, and I was tired to death.

The stony way ended, and we got into the snow. After a while, I threw myself headlong on its surface. Should I ever manage to get to the top? What was the good of it? Wouldn't it be better to turn back? No, never! For the life of me I could not appear before the Shah and admit that I had failed. After a minute I fell asleep. But

Ali pulled at me, calling again, "Sahab berim!" I rose and went on. The hours passed. At times the peak was infinitely distant, it seemed to me; at times it was shrouded in clouds or in whirling snow. Finally, Ali took off his girdle, and held one end firmly, while Kerbelai Tagi took the other, and I was jerked along at its centre. In this way they dragged me across the snow, which made things considerably easier.

Again it cleared, and the summit appeared to be nearer. We reached it at half-past four, after twelve hours' toil. It was no small matter to get the water to boil. The temperature sank to 29°, there was a strong wind, and it was biting-cold. I made a sketch, gathered a few specimens of sulphur, and admired the view through the rifts in the clouds, both toward the Caspian Sea and southward over the plains around Teheran.

TOP OF DEMAVEND. THE CRATER OF THE VOL-
CANO VISIBLE. ALTITUDE—18,700 FEET

After a rest of three-quarters of an hour, I gave the order to start. My two guides took me to a point at the beginning of a crevasse, covered with snow, which tapered

DOWN THE SNOW-COVERED SLOPE OF DEMAVEND

far down along the mountainside. Here they squatted down on the thin crust of snow, pressed their iron-tipped staffs into the surface, and slid downhill at a breathless speed. I followed their example. We had to use our heels as brakes, and the snow sputtered before them like spray at the bow of a steamer. For about seven thousand feet we went sizzling along in this way. Finally the snow grew so thin, that we preferred making our way through the rocks on foot. Just as the sun was setting, the clouds lifted. We reached the cave at nightfall. Jafar and some shepherds were waiting there with my horse, and in a few minutes I was sleeping like a rock.

A few days later, I was sent for by the Shah. He was seated in his large, red tent, surrounded by several of his court. Some of them doubted that I had really reached the top. But when the Shah saw my sketches, he turned to them and said: "Refte, refte, bala bood" (He has walked, he has been up there). The courtiers bowed down to the rug, and all their doubts vanished like the clouds around Demavend. We remained in the refreshing mountains for some time, and then returned to the capital with the Shah and his court.

My last recollection of Teheran is a bloody one. *Kurban bairam,* or the sacrificial offering, was being celebrated in the town. A camel, with silver bridle, tall plume, and costly, embroidered cloths, was led to an open place, where thousands of people were assembled. A band played, horsemen on frisky mounts rode about, and *ferrashs* with long switches tried to keep the crowd in check.

The sacrificial camel was made to lie down in the midst of the crowd. A bunch of grass was held before him, and he ate, the while his trappings were removed. Ten butchers, in aprons, and with rolled-up sleeves, appeared. One of them, a big, heavy-built man, stuck his knife into the camel's breast with a powerful movement. The beast gave a jerk and fell on its side, its head sinking to the ground. At the same moment, another butcher appeared, and with two cuts severed the head from the body. The camel was then skinned and cut up, and as many of the crowd as could get to it fell like hungry wolves upon the gory cadaver. As soon as one succeeded in tearing off a small piece of meat for himself, he withdrew, to make place for another. Within a few minutes there was nothing but a red spot to show where the camel had lain. But the proper sacrifice had been made to the high powers which forge the destiny of man.

CHAPTER X

Through Khorasan, the Land of the Sun

ON September 9, 1890, I started off on the long caravan-road, marked by twenty-four stations, which connects Teheran with Meshhed, the capital of Khorasan, the Land of the Sun, and the chief shrine of pilgrims of Persia proper.

As long ago as the time of Xerxes and Darius, a postal system was operated along this road; and in the days of Tamerlane, whose couriers traversed the road with messages, the stations were about the same as now.

The soil reeks with memories of the past. There Alexander the Great overtook the fleeing Darius III, Codomanus; there Harun-ar-Rashid and his hordes sallied forth; there the wild Mongolian tribes pillaged and murdered; there the waste reverberated with Nadir Shah's clatter of arms; and there hundreds of thousands of tired pilgrims have bent their steps toward the grave of Imam Riza, at Meshhed.

Two days before starting, I bade farewell to the aged Shah Nasr-ed-Din. He was walking alone on a path in the garden of Sultanetabad, leaning on a gold-headed cane. He wished me a happy journey, and continued his lonely walk. His great-great-grandson is now on the throne of Persia. He himself reigned for forty-eight years. But in the twenty-nine years following his death, the throne has been occupied by four generations!

I was setting out on a journey of 3,600 miles, to be made on horse-back, by sleigh, carriage, and train. I travelled as cheaply as possible, and the expenses totalled only $1,011.

I had three horses: one for riding, one to bear my luggage, and one for the stable-boy who accompanied me. As on the journey to the Persian Gulf, stable-boy and horses were changed at every station.

We rode out of Teheran through the Khorasan gate, which has four small towers, in yellow, blue, and white faience. In return for a coin, the keeper of the gate called out to us a kind "Siaret mubarek," or "A happy pilgrimage!"

On the right, the cupola over the grave of Shah Abdul Azim shone like a golden ball; and, at the foot of its knoll, the Tower of Silence appeared. On the left, Demavend, enthroned in light clouds, was about to be shrouded in its white, winter garb. The black tents of the nomads lay scattered on the steppe. At dusk, we reached the village of Kubed Gumbed, where we spent the evening among dogs and cats.

The mounted mail-carrier was expected momentarily; and as he

THE MONGOLS PLUNDERING AND BURNING KHORASAN

would have the first choice of fresh horses, we continued on our way at midnight. We changed from a trot to a gallop, and again to a walk, so as not to tire the horses. The air was mild, Orion reigned, and the moon was up. In the distance, dull caravan-bells sounded; and soon the camels glanced by like shadows.

We rode most of the following day. Sometimes we stopped at a *kavekhaneh,* or coffee-house, on the roadside; sometimes with a resting caravan, or at a nomad-tent, where copper-brown children played with dogs and lambs. Once I fell asleep, but was waked by a sonorous "La illaha il Allah!" as the sun disappeared. At five o'clock in the afternoon, the heat was still up at 93°.

In the village of Deh-i-Namak, we were overtaken by the first mail-rider. He was a decent sort of chap, and suggested that we join him. So we rode out in the night, five horses strong. The road was marked by many parallel tracks, worn through thousands of years by camels' pads, horses' hoofs, and human feet.

Thus we proceeded from village to village, via Semnan, to Gusheh. Once we met twenty-four dervishes, in white-and-green turbans. They were returning from Meshhed to their home in Shuster. Another time, we met some white-bearded pilgrims, whose weakness obliged them to travel on their camels in litters (*palekeh*).

In Gusheh there were but two houses: the caravansary and the station. From the station-roof, toward the south and southeast, Kevir, the "Salt Desert," could be seen, resembling a frozen sea. I devoted a day to riding to its shore, and out on its dazzling-white surface. After a ride of thirty-one miles, I reached a spot where the salt surface was nine centimetres thick. Toward the south, the white surface extended to the horizon. Sixteen years later, I crossed this terrible desert by two different routes.

Once again on the caravan-road, we soon beheld, from a hill, the city of Damghan, with its gardens, a place which was devastated by the Mongolians, and where one may now find a beautiful mosque, with high minarets, and an older mosque, much dilapidated, but having picturesque archways and cloisters.

Here I decided to make a side-trip to Asterabad, a city sixty miles further north. In order to get there, I had to cross the Elburz Mountains and the forests on its slopes. I hired a *charvadar*, or caravan-driver, and two horses, and set out.

The second day's journey took me to a poor little village, Chardeh, surrounded by naked hills. My *charvadar* did not take me to the village itself, which was known for its poisonous vermin, but to a garden a few hundred yards away. This garden was surrounded by a five-foot-high clay wall, without doors; so we had to climb it to get in. The *charvadar* spread my rug on the ground under an apple-tree, arranged my blanket, ulster, and pillow into a bed, placed the two leather boxes at the side, and went off with the two horses to the village, to buy eggs, poultry, apples, and bread. After a while, he returned with two other men, and we prepared our supper. What was left over was placed on the boxes next to my bed, whereupon the three men went back to the village.

As long as there was daylight, I sat on the bed, writing. Not a living creature was to be seen. Now and then I heard a dog bark far away. When darkness fell, I lay down and went to sleep.

Sometime during the night, a rattling sound from the boxes woke me, and I sat up and listened. All was still, and I fell asleep again. But before long I awoke once more, and again heard the scratching on the leather. I started up, and, by the light of the stars, distinguished faintly half a dozen jackals, who, taking alarm, slunk into the shadow of the wall. I was wide awake now, and on a sharp lookout. I saw them slink by like shadows, and heard their pattering steps behind me. Their number was increased by new arrivals from the waste and the steppe.

I knew that jackals, as a rule, were harmless animals; but I was alone, and one never could tell. To pass the time, I thought of going on with the supper. But the boxes had been swept clean: the jackals had taken everything except the apples. As they grew bolder and approached the bed, I took an apple and hurled it with all my force straight into the pack. A whining, plaintive sound indicated that one of the nocturnal robbers had been hit. They returned, however, and their boldness increased. Seizing a riding-whip, I tried to frighten them by beating heavily on the leather boxes. The hours passed slowly. I might certainly have lain down again; but one does not sleep peacefully with a lot of jackals pattering round and stepping on one's face.

Dawn came at last, and the roosters of Chardeh began to crow. The jackals leaped the wall and did not return; and so I was able to rest till the *charvadar* waked me. At our next camping-place I was regaled with several jackal-anecdotes. Not long before, a man was on his way from one village to another, on muleback. He was pursued by ten jackals, and had great difficulty in keeping them off. Tales were also told of people who had been killed by hungry jackals.

We rode on through juniper-woods and slept at open fires. We passed through dense forests of oak, plane, and olive trees. The road followed steep precipices. The valleys to the north were filled with white mist. We passed through districts inhabited by the once powerful Yomud Turkomans, and eventually reached Asterabad, entering by the gate named after the province of Masenderan.

I remained, here as the guest of the Russian consul for a few days. On the Shah's birthday, we were invited to the Governor's. I shall never forget that festival. It was celebrated at night, with spectacular fireworks. Horsemen, on paper horses, entered the lists in a tournament, carrying wooden lances dipped in tar. A noisy band, composed of copper cymbals, flutes, kettledrums, and drums, furnished the music. Boys, disguised as women, danced; and, notwithstanding the prohibition of the Koran, considerable quantities of wine were drunk.

We proceeded onward, through luxuriant woods and along dangerous precipices, following a road further east, and rejoined the main caravan-route at the cities of Bostan and Sharud. In Bostan, we found several old buildings, covered with sea-green faience, a mosque named after Sultan Bayasid, and two minarets, known as the Trembling Towers.

Then we went on eastwards, over slightly undulating wastes and steppes, hemmed in on the left by the mountain-ranges which form the boundary of the country of the Turkomans to the north. As recently as fifty years ago, the name "Turkoman" aroused the greatest terror among the inhabitants of this region. The Turkomans organized marauding-expeditions into Persian territory, and returned with rich spoils, comprising goods, cattle, and slaves. The slave-trade flourished. When Muravieff was Russian Ambassador at Khiva, in 1820, there were thirty thousand slaves there, Persians and Russians. Christians who rejected Islam were buried alive, or were nailed by the ear to a wall, where they were left to starve. Skobeleff freed twenty-five thousand slaves, when he took Geok-Tepe, in 1881.

Roadside towers, forty and fifty feet high, locally known as *burj,* appeared in ever-increasing numbers. These towers were once occupied by Persian lookouts, who watched the north and the east, warning the inhabitants of adjacent villages to flee and hide in time. This district was called Ja-i-kuf, or the Tract of Terror, because of the predatory exploits of the Goklan Turkomans.

The Miandasht caravansary, situated in the midst of the desert, is doubtless one of the largest in all Islam. It is a halting-place for caravans from east and west; and pilgrims rest here for a day or two. Women, crying children, dervishes, soldiers, and merchants crowd together in a mass of vibrant colour. Some of them are to be heard disputing about advantageous positions, others fetch water from the wells in the court, and still others are to be seen buying fruit from vendors in little booths. One caravan was getting ready to depart, while the camels of another were being relieved of their burdens. I saw a fine lady enter the caravansary, seated in a *takhterevan* (a sort of sedan-chair, but borne by two mules) and accompanied by pedestrians and riders.

A PERSIAN CAMEL'S HEAD

Eastward of this place, the country took on the appearance of a desert. We rode past a dying camel, which had been abandoned by its owner; and we met four dervishes, carrying their shoes on their shoulders, so as not to wear them out. A flock of ravens preceded us for a long time, like an advance guard. In the upper room of the shelter where I spent the night, dancing clouds of dust came whirling in.

We reached Sabzevar next, the City of Vegetables, with fifteen thousand inhabitants, two big and several small mosques, and a bazaar under a raftered roof, amply stocked with miscellaneous goods. An *ark,* or fort, is also to be seen; but it is only a relic, now that the pillaging-expeditions of the Turkomans have ceased. And then there are the opium-dens, which, for very shame, are kept hidden

A MONEY-CHANGER IN THE BAZAAR OF SABZEVAR

underground. Accompanied by an Armenian, I entered one of them. Two men were smoking, stretched out on rugs spread on the earthen floor. The opium-pipe consists of a long tube and a clay ball with a small hole. An opium-pill as big as a large pea is deposited in the hole, the pipe is held over a flame, and the smoker inhales the poisonous smoke. Pill after pill is inserted, and gradually the smoker passes into a world of bright dreams. Four smokers, already insensible, lay in the darkness along the walls. I took a few puffs, and can compare the smoke only to that of burnt horn.

OPIUM-SMOKERS IN SABZEVAR

On the way to Nishapur, we passed a trading-caravan of two hundred and thirty-seven camels; also a company of pilgrims, the women, of whom there were ten, travelling in *kajeveh* (bearing-baskets). The men slept on their mules. A priest was conducting this group of pilgrims to the grave of Imam Riza, relating sacred legends on the way.

The next city we passed through was Nishapur, which is famous throughout the Orient for its turquoises, the finest in the world. The mountains of Binalud, north of the city, contain silver, gold, copper, pewter, lead, and malachite.

Nishapur has been destroyed and rebuilt several times during the past centuries, Alexander the Great being numbered among the destroyers.

A few days more, and we reached Tepe-i-salam, the Hill of Greeting, where, for ages, innumerable pilgrims have knelt in prayer, upon seeing Meshhed, the Place of Martyrdom; for, from this hill, the Holy City can be seen. Every pilgrim lays a stone on one of the many thousand cairns and pyramids that tower on the height, as simple ceremonial-tributes of their piety.

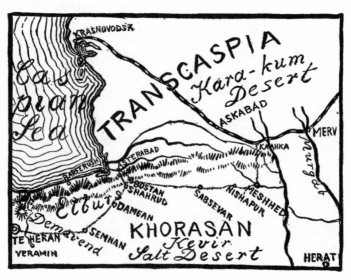

ROUTE FROM TEHERAN TO KAAHKA

CHAPTER XI

Meshhed, the City of Martyrs

THREE famous men are buried in Meshhed. In 809, the Caliph Harun-ar-Rashid, of Arabian Nights fame, died on his way to this city, whither he was going to suppress a revolt.

Nine years later, the eighth *Imam,* Imam Riza, was buried in Meshhed. The Persian Mohammedans, called Shiahs, regard Ali and eleven of his successors as *Imams.* Ali and his sons, Hussein and Hassan, were the first ones; Imam Riza was the eighth; and El-Mahdi, the Mystic, was the twelfth, the one who expected to re-establish the Kingdom of God on earth, at the Day of Judgment.

The third grave is that of Nadir Shah. He was a Tatar robber, who ravaged Khorasan, became mighty and powerful, offered Shah Thamas II his support, reconquered for him all the provinces taken by the Turks, expanded the borders of Persia in all directions, dethroned the Shah and had him assassinated, drowned Delhi in blood (1738), blinded his son, built pyramids of human heads on the mosque-roofs, and stamped on his coins, "O coin, announce to all the earth the reign of Nadir, the king who conquers the world." In the spring of 1747, he lay with his army outside Meshhed. Indignant at his Persian soldiers and officers, he ordered them to be stabbed at a given signal. The plan proved abortive. The Turkish, Uzbeg, Turkoman, and Tatar soldiers were discovered sharpening their knives and swords. Thus there was no recourse but to murder Nadir. Sale Bek, a colonel of the guards, stole into his tent at night, and cut his head off. The body was buried in a mausoleum; but Aga Mohammed Khan, founder of the present royal house (the Kajars), on attaining power, in 1794, opened the grave of the conqueror, and let the body be devoured by dogs. It is said that the remains of Nadir Shah now rest beneath a hillock, in a court shaded by four mulberry trees.

The holy place almost forms a little town by itself, in the heart of Meshhed. But the most beautiful objects in the city are the eighty-foot-high gilded cupola over the grave itself, the faience-covered façades and minarets, and the courts, with their alcoves for three thousand pilgrims, their basins, and their pigeons. A mosque, with a blue cupola and two minarets, was built by the favourite wife of Tamerlane. Treasures of incalculable value are kept in these sacred edifices. At the time of my visit, it was said that a hundred thousand pilgrims flocked to Meshhed every year, and that ten thousand dead bodies were taken to be buried near the *Imam*, so that he might lead them by the hand to Paradise on Resurrection-Day. The jackals prowl about the cemetery, and at night they even come into the town and enter its gardens. Three-fifths of the estimated population of eighty thousand was said to consist of priests, dervishes, and pilgrims. Near the grave, food was given to the poor, sight was restored to the blind, and the paralyzed recovered the use of their limbs.

All streets leading to the sacred area are shut off with chains. Within its bounds all malefactors are safe, and many confessed murderers and bandits take advantage of this asylum.

From *Nagara-khaneh*, or the Drum Tower, a curious orchestra plays every morning, to greet the sun at his rising, and every evening, to bid farewell when he sinks in the west, far beyond Khorasan.

CHAPTER XII

Bokhara and Samarkand

IT was the middle of October, and autumn was approaching, when I left Meshhed with a *charvadar* and three horses, and went through the narrow corridors, defiles, and passes of the Hesar-mestjid Mountains, and past the strong, natural fortress of Kelat-i-Nadir, on my way northward to the Transcaspian Railway, which I reached at the station of Kaahka.

At Askabad, the capital of Transcaspia, I made the acquaintance of the military governor, General Kuropatkin. He had fought at Plevna, during the Russo-Turkish War, and had taken part in the conquest of Transcaspia. In the war against Japan, he was commander-in-chief of the Russian armies. I met him several times later, at Samarkand, Tashkent, and St. Petersburg; and I remember his name with gratitude, for he was one of the men who made travelling easier for me.

I made excursions around Askabad. I observed that the Turkomans had already partly progressed from nomad life to agriculture, near villages which had been settled by them. I visited the beautiful mosque at Anau, famous for the yellow Chinese dragons interwoven in the design of its faience-covered façade. Here I got my first sight of Kara-kum, the Black Sands desert, which lies between the Caspian Sea and Amu-daria, and between Khorasan and the Aral Sea, and where roamed the wild ass, the boar, the tiger, and the jackal. Parts of Turkestan had already been conquered: Khiva and the entire eastern shore of the Caspian Sea were under the Czar's sceptre. The country lying between —the desert of Kara-kum, in whose oases the herds of the Tekke-Turkomans grazed—still remained to be conquered.

In the beginning, the Russians met with reverses, losing seventeen thousand of their eighteen thousand camels in one campaign. The arrogance of the Turkomans increased. A blow had to be dealt them which they would never forget. So Skobeleff inaugurated a campaign which became one of the most cruel in the history of Asiatic warfare, and which resulted in keeping the Turkomans crushed up to the days of Lenin.

With seven thousand men, and seventy guns, Skobeleff marched into the desert, in December, 1880, while General Annenkoff, with surprising rapidity, laid among the shifting sand-dunes the string of rails which served as a supply-line for the operating corps. The Turkomans called Annenkoff the "Samovar Pasha," and the locomotives the "carts of the Devil." A great number of the Akhal-Tekke-Turkomans, forty-five thousand people, of whom ten thousand were armed horsemen, embattled themselves, w i t h women and children. in the fort of Geok-tepe (the Green Hill), surrounded by high, clay walls. Makdum Kuli Khan was their leader. They had rifles, side-arms, and a cannon, from which they shot stone balls.

A TURKOMAN

In January, 1881, the Russians moved their entrenchments forward, close to the fort, and were planting a mine that was to make a breach in the wall. The Turkomans, hearing the underground boring, believed that a hole would open in the wall, through which the Russians would crawl one by one. They therefore kept themselves in readiness, with drawn sabres, till the fatal day, when a ton of powder exploded, and did great execution.

The Russian army rushed into the breach in three columns, two of which were commanded by Kuropatkin and Skobeleff. Skobeleff rode a white horse, wore a white uniform, and was perfumed and frizzed like a bridegroom, while the regimental band played a march. Twenty thousand Turkomans were killed. Five thousand women and children, together with the Persian slaves, were spared. The Russians lost four

officers and fifty-five men. For many years thereafter, the Turkomans
would weep whenever they heard the sound of Russian military music;
for there was not a Turkoman in the country who had not lost a relative
at Geok-tepe.

It took only a few years for the Russians to conquer the country as
far as a day's journey from Herat. The danger to India, together with
the rapid advance of the Russians into Central Asia, gave rise to the
justifiable fears of the English.

In 1888, the railway to Samarkand, 870 miles long, was opened;
and about the end of October, I travelled by that line to the oasis of
Merv, which, in the Avesta, is called Moru and by Darius Hystaspes,
one of whose satraps was established there, Marga.

Merv is situated on the boundary between Turan and Iran. It
passed from one ruler to another during thousands of years. In the
fifth century A.D., a Nestorian archbishop lived in Merv. In 651,
Yezdegird III, the last Sassanian king, came fleeing with four thousand
men, and bearing the sacred fire from Rages. The Tatars stormed
the town. Alone, and on foot, the King fled, seeking refuge with a
miller, who agreed to hide him, provided the King paid the miller's
debts. Yezdegird handed him his sword and its precious scabbard.
During the night, the miller, tempted by the King's brilliant attire,
murdered him. But the Tatars were driven away, and the miller was
torn to pieces.

Jakut, the learned Arab, studied in the library of Merv, and wrote
in praise of the fresh water, juicy melons, and soft cotton of the oasis.
In 1221, the district was devastated by Tulai, son of Jenghiz Khan;
and in 1380, the oasis was taken by Tamerlane. The Merv Turkomans
were dreaded. At Khiva and Bokhara, it was said of them: "If you
meet a viper and a Mervi, kill the Mervi first and then the viper!"

When I was in Merv, a market was held in the oasis every Sunday.
Products of native industry, particularly the beautiful rugs, of ox-blood
colour, with rows of white figures, were on sale, in canvas booths and
in the open. A charming sight was presented by the throngs and the
commotion—men in high, fur caps, Bactrian camels, the famous Turkoman horses, with clumsy heads and slender necks, horsemen, caravans,
and carts. And no less charming were the ruins and cupolas of old
Merv (Baïram Ali).

From Merv, the railway winds between the shifting dunes. Saxauls, tamarisks, and other desert plants are grown on top of these dunes, to counteract their tendency to bury the rails with their shifting sands. Over a wooden bridge, two versts long, the train crosses the great Amu-daria, which measures 1,450 miles from its source, in Pamir, to its mouth in the Aral Sea.

The next important centre of West Asiatic culture and history which we encountered, was Bokhara-i-Sherif, the Noble Bokhara, one of the jewels among the cities of the earth—an Asiatic Rome.

Greek, Arabian, and Mongolian armies have passed like devastating avalanches over this region. It is the Sogdiana of the Greeks, and the

MOLLAHS—OLD WISE PRIESTS.

Transoxiana of the Romans. In the eleventh century, Bokhara was the centre of Islam, as regards classical learning. A proverb tells us: "In all other parts of the world, light descends upon the earth from above; but in Bokhara it comes from below, and rises." And Hafiz's impression of it, and of Samarkand, its sister city, is reflected in his verses, of which one runs thus:

Agger on turchi shirafi bedast dared dill i ma ra
Be halu hinduiesh bakshem Samarkand ve Bokhara ra.

The beauty in Shiraf who holds my heart in her hand—
For the birth-mark on her cheek I would give Samarkand
and Bokhara.

There were one hundred and five *madrasahs,* or religious training-schools, and three hundred and sixty-five mosques, which enabled the faithful to perform their devotions in a different mosque each day in the year.

This city, too, was sacked by Jenghiz Khan and taken by Tamerlane. In 1842, Colonel Stoddart and Captain Connolly visited Bokhara. The cruel Nasr-ullah was then Emir. He arrested the two Englishmen, tortured them, threw them into the famous vermin-pit, and beheaded them. Vambéry, disguised as a dervish, managed to get to the city in 1863, and described its remarkable features.

The population is composed of several diverse elements. The most important are the Tajiks, of Iranian stock, to which the educated classes and the priests belong; the Uzbegs and Jaggatai Turks, of the Mongolian race; and the Sarts, a mixed race, to which the populace and the permanent population in general belong. Many other Oriental peoples are represented, among them being Persians, Afghans, Kirghiz, Turks, Tatars, Caucasians, and Jews.

In the archways of the bazaars, where twilight always reigns, the bustling life of the Orient has a motley of its own. There one may admire the marvels of the Bokharan textile art;

AN OLD TAJIK OF BOKHARA

and in the antique-shops one runs across Greek and Sassanian silver and gold coins, and other rarities. Cotton, sheep-wool, lambskins, and raw silk are exported in great quantities; and in the caravansary courts, connected with the bazaars, bales are piled mountain-high. There are nice restaurants and coffee-houses; and from a distance one detects the odour of pastry made with onions and spices, and of coffee and tea. A small tart costs one *pool* (64 pool = 20 copeck = 1 tenge; 20 tenge = 1 tillah = 4 roubles).

I never tired of walking in the beautiful, narrow streets, between funny, two-story houses, with camel-caravans jostling their way among carts, horsemen, and pedestrians. I stopped frequently to sketch a mosque or a tempting street-scene. A noisy crowd would gather round me, and Saïd Murad, one of the servants of the Russian legation, would

A STORY-TELLER IN BOKHARA

keep bold urchins at a distance, by using his braided knout. Once I went for a stroll without him, and then the lads took their revenge, bombarding me systematically, which rendered drawing out of the question. They rushed at me from all sides, their missiles being rotten apples, lumps of earth, and all sorts of refuse. After vainly trying to defend myself, I hastily retreated to the Legation and fetched Saïd Murad.

In 1219, Jenghiz Khan entered the door of Mestjid-i-Kalan, the Great Mosque, and ordered a general massacre. Not quite two hundred years later, Tamerlane restored the temple.

Not more than thirty-five years ago, criminals were still hurled from the top of a minaret, one hundred and sixty-five feet high, the judge having previously announced their crime from the same place, in a resounding voice. A couple of storks now had their nest there, and nobody was allowed on the top, because the nearby harem courts were visible therefrom.

Opposite the Great Mosque is Mir-Arab, a *madrasah* more famous than all others in Central Asia. It has circular towers, two cupolas of brilliant, green faience, and a house with four portals and one hundred and fourteen rooms for two hundred *mollahs,* or priests.

Yet the pearl among the cities of Central Asia is Samarkand, where I took up my abode on the first of November. When Alexander the Great conquered these countries, the capital of Sogdiana was called Maracanda. Even at the present day, the Macedonian name survives in the form of Iskander Bek. Though Samarkand was defended against Jenghiz Khan by a hundred and ten thousand men capable of bearing arms, it had to surrender and was completely razed.

The name of a third conqueror is associated with Samarkand even more closely than those just mentioned. Tamerlane was born in 1335, in a Tatar tribe. A refugee from Khiva, he met saga-like adventures in the desert of Kara-kum. He was wounded in Sistan and became lame. Therefore he was named Timur Lenk or Timur Lane, a name later corrupted into Tamerlane. In 1369, he was safely seated on his throne in Samarkand. Afterwards, the great conquests began. Persia was taken. At Shiraz he met Hafiz, as mentioned before. Between campaigns, Tamerlane erected incomparably magnificent edifices in Samarkand, which made this city unique in its kind. Even at this day, the shining, green cupolas rise from the verdure of the gardens; and minarets and cupolas, of the deep, pure-blue colour of a turquoise, stand out against the lighter blue of the sky.

In 1398, Tamerlane marched across the Hindu kush, defeated King Mahmud of Hindustan, and pillaged Delhi, carrying incalculable loot home to Samarkand on stolen elephants. Bagdad, Aleppo, and Damascus were taken; and, in 1402, he defeated Sultan Bajazet at Angora. According to a legend, of small reliability, the lame conqueror put his one-eyed prisoner, the Sultan, in an iron cage, in order to exhibit him later in the cities of Asia. As Tamerlane returned to Samarkand by the way I have described, from Teheran to Meshhed, he was followed closely by Ruy Gonzales de Clavijo, ambassador of King Henry III of Castile and Leon, who wrote a capital account of his journey.

In January, 1405, Tamerlane set out from Samarkand on his last campaign. He wanted to defeat Yong Loh, the greatest emperor of the Ming dynasty.   But he died in Otrar, on the other side of the Sir-daria (Jaxartes), sixty-nine years of age.   His body was taken back to Samarkand, where one of the most beautiful mausoleums in the world was built, according to his own design.   Embalmed in musk and rose-water, and wrapped in linen, the body was laid in an ivory coffin.   In the burial-vault, beneath the cupola, the place was marked by a solid piece of jade, six feet long, one and one-half feet thick, and one and one-half feet wide, this being the largest piece of jade known.   On one of

THE TOMB OF TAMERLANE

the walls, the following words appear, written in relief, in Arabic, in alabaster: "Were I still alive, mankind would tremble."

At the beginning of the Mohammedan era, one of the descendants of the Prophet, Kasim Ibn Abbas, came to Samarkand to preach Islam. Being seized and beheaded by the ungrateful people, he put his head under his arm and disappeared in a subterranean cave.   It was on the top of this cave that Tamerlane later built his splendid summer-palace, the graceful lines of whose seven blue-green cupolas still rise above the yellow ground.   The conqueror held his drinking-bouts there, and the biggest drinker was declared *bahadur,* or knight.   There is an opening through which one may look into a subterranean cave for this man walking around with his own head under his arm.   He is called "Shah-i-sindeh," or the Living King, a name which the palace itself still bears. When the Russians advanced, step by step, into Asia, it was prophesied that when they reached Samarkand, Shah-i-sindeh would emerge from his cave, and, with his head held high, would liberate Tamerlane's city. But he failed to appear, when Kauffmann conquered Samarkand; and he thus lost much of his prestige among the Mohammedans.

Mirza Ullug Bek, Tillah Karch, and Madrasah-i-Shirdar are three religious colleges, built, after the era of Tamerlane, around Rigistan, the most beautiful open place in the world. The colleges are resplendent with the most glorious designs in faience, and their cupolas and minarets have been splendidly pictured, in oils, by the Russian painter Verestchagin.

Outside the city, I visited the mosque in which Bibi-Khanum, Tamerlane's favourite wife, daughter of the Emperor of China, is buried. It dates from the year 1385, and is magnificent even in its dilapidated state.

In the company of a Frenchman, I also took a nocturnal walk to Pai-Kabak, the not-too-savoury quarter of the women dancers. We were ushered into perfumed rooms, carpeted with rugs, and with divans along the walls. Beautiful women played the *sitara* (zither) and *chetara* (guitar), manipulating the strings with dainty little fingers. Others, with like skill and grace, played the tambourine. In order to keep the drumhead tight, they would now and again hold the instrument over a *mangal,* or glowing brazier.

As the music rose in the night, the dancers appeared, in light, floating garments, with movements full of grace. Some of them were Persians or Afghans, others had Tatar blood in their veins. And to the rhythmic sounds of music from the stringed instruments, they danced in undulating measure, like fairies in a dream—messengers from Bihasht and the joys of Paradise.

CHAPTER XIII

Into the Heart of Asia

THE bells jingled on the arch of the *duga* as I drove away from Samarkand, while the blue cupolas disappeared in the distance, and the rising sun gave life and colour to the hills of Afrasiab.

I drove in a *troika* through a wealth of gardens, shimmering in the yellow-and-red autumn. I crossed the Zerafshan—the Gold Roller—the river which irrigates Samarkand and the nearby oases. I drove through the narrow, rocky pass called "Tamerlane's Gateway," and through "Golodnaya," or the Hunger Steppe, which is a corner of the desert of Kizil-kum, or the Red Sand, between the Oxus and Jaxartes, the giant rivers of Russian Turkestan.

We were taken across the last-mentioned river (whose Turkish name is Sir-daria) on a huge ferry, which carried ten camels and twelve carts with their horses, besides us. After further changes of horses, we reached Tashkent, the capital of Russian Central Asia.

Once upon a time, Jagatai Khan, son of Jenghiz Khan, reigned here; and in 1865, General Cherniaieff brought the city under Russian rule. The city then numbered one hundred and twenty thousand inhabitants. Cherniaieff captured it with only two thousand men. On the evening of the surrender, Cherniaieff, accompanied by two Cossacks, rode through the streets, went to bathe in a Sart *hammam,* and dined in the bazaar. This boldness made a great impression on the inhabitants.

Baron von Wrewski, the Governor General, resided in Tashkent at the time of my arrival; and his house became my home during the period of my stay. He provided me with maps, a passport, and letters of introduction, and overwhelmed me with kindness and hospitality. He had been one of the Russian ambassadors at the coronation of my King, in Stockholm, in 1873.

We continued our journey in fresh vehicles, crossing the Sir-daria again to Khojent, going on into the fertile valley of Ferghana, to Khokand, where we visited the palace of Khodier Khan (the last Khan) and the hovels of the singing-dervishes, and thence to Margelan, a city that can coolly point out Gur-i-Iskander-Bek—the grave of Alexander the Great—to strangers.

In bright moonlight, we went tinkling along to Osh. Colonel Deubner was at that time head of the district. I had decided to go as far as Kashgar, the most westerly city of China, on the further side of the mountain-ranges that link the Tian-shan with Pamir. Their highest pass is crossed by the caravan-road running between Osh, in Russian Turkestan, and Kashgar, in Chinese Turkestan, and is named Terek-davan, or the Poplar Pass. Its altitude is 13,000 feet.

Colonel Deubner told me that the last caravans had already left, that the snowstorm season was due, and that only those hardy Kirghiz who knew the road ever ventured over the pass. This was not sufficient to deter me; so the Colonel did everything in his power to expedite my journey. I bought provisions, a fur coat, and felt rugs; hired four horses, for each of which I had to pay sixty copecks a day; and employed three servants, Kerim Jan, the *jigit* or postilion, Ata Baï, the groom, and Ashur, the cook.

Heavily clothed, and in *valenki*, or soft, felt boots, we set forth on the first of December. The snow was falling thickly; and between the mountains, the landscape, white as chalk, revealed the *kibitkas*, or big, arched blanket-tents of the Kirghiz, looking like black dots. Our longest day's march was that to Sufi-kurgan, a record one of forty-two miles. Here, as at all our other camps, we lodged in the tents of the Kirghiz, and ate, rested, and slept around their cheerful fires. At Sufi-kurgan, there was an *aul*, a village of fifty tents. Khoat Bi, the old chief, received us amiably; and at his camp-fire, Ashur made a soup, called *besh barmak* (the five fingers), because it is thick enough to be eaten with the hand. It consisted of mutton, cabbage, carrots, potatoes, rice, onions, pepper, and salt, all boiled in water.

On December 5, we departed towards Terek-davan, in fairly cold weather (6°). My men wore leather trousers, roomy enough to cover their entire clothing, including their fur coats. They extended, in fact, as high as the armpits.

The road crossed ice-bound brooks over small, frail, wooden bridges. Birch trees and junipers grew on the slopes of the valley through which we passed. We came to a passage, hardly twenty feet wide, between sheer mountain-walls, which was known as Darvase (The Gate). The steep road made zigzags through the snow. The day was almost gone when we reached the top of the pass, a sharply-defined ridge. The bones of human beings and of horses, mute symbols of fatal snowstorms, lay hidden under the snow.

To the east and south, a magnificent landscape unfolded, a labyrinth of wild mountain-ranges. The brooks which flowed eastward, during the warm season, ended at Lop-nor; those flowing westward emptied into the Aral Sea.

Descending, we frightened a herd of *kiyiks* (wild goats), who, with sure, elegant movements, disappeared over a declivity. On we went,

A KIRGHIZ AT IRKESHTAM, ON THE BORDER BETWEEN RUSSIAN AND CHINESE TERRITORY

from tent to tent, down through the valleys, by way of the Russian border fort of Irkeshtam, and the Kizil-zu River, to the woodland region of Nagara-Chaldi, where a hundred Yoash Kirghiz lived in twenty tents. Their chief invited us to a dinner of sour milk, greasy mutton, bouillon, and tea.

In the Chinese frontier fort of Ulugchat, a garrison of eighty Kirghiz and twenty-five Chinese soldiers was commanded by one Khoang Darin. In the evening, he called on me, accompanied by three *beks* and twelve men, with a gift of a fat-tail sheep.

Day by day, the country unfolded itself. Toward the east, our eyes surveyed endless stretches, extending far into the desert. On the fourteenth of December, we rode through the first villages surrounding the oasis of Kashgar, and so to the Russian consulate, situated outside the city wall. A tall, elderly, bearded man, with gold-rimmed eyeglasses, a conical, green cap, and a long Sart *khalat,* or cloak, came out and received us graciously in the court. He was Nicolai Feodorovitch Petrovsky, Privy Councilor and Imperial Russian Consul General for East Turkestan. I stayed at his house for ten days. He proved to be my friend in later journeys, also, when I again made Kashgar my headquarters.

Kashgar has passed from one conqueror to another, representing many different peoples, of Aryan or Mongolian descent; and this soil, too, recalls memories of the days of Jenghiz Khan and Tamerlane. The Chinese ruled the country at various times. From 1865 to 1877, Yakub Bek, a conqueror from Russian Turkestan, ruled despotically all the country between Tibet and the Tian-Shan. Since his death, the Chinese have again held the reins of power.

Kashgar is a peculiar city in that it is more distant from the ocean than any other city in the world. Dao Tai was the Chinese governor of Kashgar; but the most powerful man in the place was Petrovsky, who was dubbed "the new Jagatai Khan" by the native Sart population. The consulate boasted a military force of forty-five Cossacks and two officers.

I remember, too, with gratitude and sympathy, four other men who lived there, though death has separated me from two of them, and the World War from the other two. These last two were Captain (later Colonel Sir Francis) Younghusband and Mr. Macartney (later Sir George Macartney). Younghusband had quite recently completed his first long journey through Asia, across the pass of Mustagh, and was now living in the garden of Chinne-

HINDU MERCHANT IN KASHGAR

bagh, outside the city wall. He had no house, but a huge *kibitka* instead, with wooden floors, covered with carpets, and on the walls of which hung costly shawls and rugs from Kashmir. Macartney was his Chinese interpreter. Gurkhas, Afghans, and other Indian natives were in his suite. I spent many a memorable evening with these two amiable Englishmen.

One day, as we were chatting in the consul's study, a bearded spectacled priest, in the long, brown garb of a monk, entered and greeted me with a few Swedish words. Father Hendricks was a Hollander. In 1885, he had arrived in Kashgar, from Tomsk, by way of Kulja, accompanied by a Pole, Adam Ignatieff. He had not received a single letter since his arrival, and mystery seemed to surround his past. Nobody knew anything about that past, and he himself was silent. But regarding Ignatieff—a tall man, clean-shaven, with close-cut hair as white as chalk, robed in white, and with a crucifix and chain around his neck—it was known that he had assisted in hanging a Russian priest during the last Polish revolution, a deed that warranted deportation to Siberia. He lived in a poor hovel near the consulate, and took all his meals at the consul's house.

At an Indian caravansary, Father Hendricks occupied an equally bare room, with earthen floor and paper windows, a chair, a table, a bed, and a few wine-barrels—for he was an expert wine-maker. The room, one wall of which was adorned by a crucifix, also served as a church. He never failed to celebrate mass. His congregation consisted of Adam Ignatieff. Father Hendricks preached to Ignatieff for a few years, and then they had a falling-out. Adam Ignatieff was barred from the church, and the congregation ceased to exist. But the priest continued to say mass to the bare walls and the filled wine-barrels, while poor Adam had to stand outside, with his ear glued to the keyhole.

Some Chinese soldiers were stationed at the city gates, but most of the garrison was at Yangi Shahr, a walled city, seven miles away. At the Sart Kashgar, the open market-places, with their booths, where unveiled women were among those selling, were most picturesque. Here and there, too, a mosque broke the monotony of the yellow-grey, clay houses. Yakub Bek rests in the court outside the funeral-mosque of Hazret Apak, under mulberry and plane trees. The Chinese are said to have burnt his corpse when they recaptured the city.

There are many other saints' graves around Kashgar. Indeed, there are so many of them, that the people themselves see the ludicrousness of it. The following anecdote was current at the time:

A sheik used to teach the Koran to his disciples at a saint's grave outside Kashgar. One day, one of the pupils came to the sheik and said: "Father, give me money and food, so that I may go out into the world and try my luck." The sheik answered: "I have nothing else to give you but a donkey. Take it, and may Allah bless your journey." With his donkey, the youth wandered for days and nights, and finally crossed the great desert. There the donkey pined away and died. Bewailing his loss and his loneliness, the youth dug a grave in the sand, buried the donkey, and sat down on the grave to weep. Then some rich merchants passed by with their caravan. Seeing the youth, they asked: "Why do you weep?" He answered: "I have lost my only friend, my faithful travelling-companion." The merchants were so touched by this fidelity, that they decided to have a magnificent mausoleum erected on the hill. Huge caravans carried bricks and faience to the place, and a sacred edifice, with a shining cupola and minarets reaching to the clouds, rose in the desert. The tale of the new saint's grave travelled fast, and pilgrims from far and near thronged there to perform their devotions. After many years, the old sheik from Kashgar also went there. Astonished at finding his former pupil a sheik at so prominent a saint's grave, he asked: "Tell me, in confidence, who is the saint that rests under this cupola?" The pupil whispered: "It is only the donkey you gave me.—Now you tell me who was the saint that reposed where you used to teach me?" To which the old sheik replied: "It was the father of your donkey."

CHAPTER XIV

With the Emir of Bokhara

ON Christmas Eve, I started on a jolly journey, a wild and whizzing expedition, on horseback, by sleigh, and by carriage, through all of western Asia. Three Cossacks from the consulate, who had finished their term of service, were returning to Narinsk, in Semiryetchensk, the Country of Seven Rivers, on the Russian side, and I was going with them.

We travelled northward with our little caravan of pack-horses. The way took us through narrow valleys, in a biting cold (−4°). We crossed rivers that were only partly frozen. There the Cossacks proved invaluable. They rode out on the ice near the shore till it broke, and the horses plunged like dolphins among the ice-cakes. I often feared the animals would rip their bellies open on the sharp edges of the ice. The water reached to the middle of our saddles, and we had to balance ourselves cross-legged in order to keep our felt boots dry.

THE PONIES HAD TO JUMP INTO THE ICY WATER
AS WE CROSSED THE HALF-FROZEN RIVERS

Higher up, the watercourses were frozen solid. The horses slid along, and danced like maniacs, on the crystal-like surface of the ice. We crossed the Chinese border, rode through the pass of Turugart (12,740 feet), across the frozen and snow-covered lake of Chatyr-kul, and over the pass of Tash-rabat (12,900 feet). We were in a labyrinth of valleys, in an entanglement of grand, wild mountains, belonging to the Tian-shan range, or the "Celestial Mountains," as the Chinese call them.

From the last-mentioned pass, the path descended in countless, sharp turns, between sharp-edged, rocky points and spurs, at that season partly covered with snow or ice. Here a pack-horse slipped, rolled down the precipice, broke his neck, and died where he fell.

It snowed frequently; and on New Year's Day, 1891, the flakes fell like a closely-woven, white veil. At Narinsk, the caravan dispersed, and I drove alone, for one thousand miles, to Samarkand. The sledge-road was splendid. We usually drove with two horses; but, where the snow was deep and loose, three horses were used. The driver sat on the right side of his seat, his legs dangling outside, and urged his horses on with an encouraging,—"Well, little dove, that's it, my boy, try again, pull away, little father." The bells tinkled merrily, the snow fell and fell, wrapping its veil around us, and the drifts at the sides of the road grew several feet deep. We went along at breakneck speed. The sled pitched like a boat on the uneven road, but it was not easily upset, being provided with two horizontal safety-runners that acted as buffers when the sled was on the verge of tipping over. Only once, at night, we capsized completely in a snow-covered ditch, but we soon righted the sled on a more even slope, and on we went, jolting and tossing, through the dark.

On arriving at the most westerly narrow end of the big lake of Issik-kul—the Warm Lake, as it is called, because its tepid sources and depth prevent freezing—I decided to make a pilgrimage to the grave of Przhevalsky, the great Russian traveller, located near the town which now bears his name. The distance was one hundred and twenty-six miles. A black, wooden cross, with a figure of Christ and a laurel-wreath, rose on the hillock. It was barely two years since Przhevalsky had passed away in this waste land, at the threshold of a new journey of discovery into the heart of Asia.

We journeyed westward, along the northern base of the Alexander Range, to the little town of Aulie Ata. At the ford across the Asa River, travellers and fragile baggage were taken through water three and one-half feet deep, in an *araba,* a cart on two high wheels, while the horses pulled the empty sled across, floating like a boat.

It snowed incessantly. The temperature sank to −9°, and thus the snow remained loose. The three-horse team jumped through drifts several feet high, the snow flying round the sled like foam. But as I approached Chimkent and Tashkent, the drifts grew smaller; and west of the capital, where the ground was bare, the sled was abandoned, and I continued the journey in a *tarantass*.

At Chinas, I reached the shore of the Sir-daria. The ferries could not be operated in the drift-ice. A small, frail boat had to be used instead; and I and a young lieutenant from Courland were poled across the river by three sturdy men, with iron-shod poles, amid drifting, crackling ice-floes.

After we had crossed, we each took a three-horse *tarantass* and went on. Half-way to the station of Mirsa-rabat, the rear axletree of my vehicle broke. One wheel got loose, the body of the carriage scraped the ground, the horses became frightened, and ran wildly towards the steppe. The carriage jumped, bumped, and was knocked about among the hillocks. I had to hold on for dear life. The horses, exhausted, stopped at last. The driver and I salvaged our scattered belongings and loaded everything onto one of the horses. Then riding bareback on the other two, and abandoning the wrecked *tarantass,* we proceeded to Mirsa-rabat, where the young lieutenant was awaiting our arrival.

Our next misadventure occurred at the Jisak River, whither we had proceeded late in the evening. The sky was clouded, there was a strong wind, and it was nasty-cold. Shortly before midnight, we reached the bank of the river. The water was high, and the drift-ice abundant. Not a living creature was to be seen, when our two *tarantasses* halted at the ford.

The lieutenant from Courland entered the ice-strewn water first. His carriage had not proceeded more than a few lengths, before it was stuck in the broken ice. The cakes piled up on the carriage, and the horses could not budge it. After several vain attempts, the horses were unharnessed. The Courlander took his belongings, and, together with his driver, rode safely back to shore. The carriage had to be abandoned. It probably remained there till the following spring, unless it was crushed to pieces when the ice broke up.

The drivers knew of another fordable place, where the river branched into two arms. Two of the Courlander's horses were accordingly harnessed to my *troika,* and his things stowed with mine. He himself sat on the driver's seat, his back to the horses, steadying himself by the fore edge of the hood.

When everything was ready, we set out to cross the first branch.

The ice bore us splendidly, while the heavy vehicle rumbled across. Powdered ice flew about the horses' hoofs. One of them slipped, but recovered himself in time. All went well until we got to the other branch, where the bank sloped steeply down toward the water, and turned sharply towards the right.

Uttering wild shouts, and swishing his whip, the driver urged the horses on. Foaming and rearing, their every muscle twitching, they plunged spiritedly downhill, until they were half in the water. We reached the turning. The two right-hand wheels were still on the ice-slope, when those on the left slipped down into the river. It all

A TERRIBLE ACCIDENT AT NIGHT IN THE RIVER JISAK

happened in an instant. Seeing what was coming, I pressed myself against the right side of the hood. The horses were going full speed when they made the turn. The carriage upset in three feet of water, and with such force that the hood was smashed to pieces. The two leading horses fell and got so badly entangled in their harness that they nearly drowned. At just the right moment, the driver jumped into the river to their assistance. The water reached to his middle. The Courlander was hurled from his seat, and had a bloody encounter with a block of ice. Only the corners of my boxes stuck out of the water;

and my blanket, my fur coat, and my rug were nearly carried away by the current. Many of our things were ruined; and everything was soaked, including ourselves. Little by little, we fished out our belongings. They were sent across the river on horseback, and we followed, jumping from floe to floe. The next station was not far away. We dried our things there, and I salvaged what I could. But the poor Courlander barely escaped death. When I took him to a hospital, in Samarkand, he had a very high fever.

I had received an invitation to visit Emir Saïd Abdul Ahad, of Bokhara, who at that season of the year lived in his castle at Shahr-i-sabs, not quite fifty miles from Samarkand. Not the least of Shahr-i-sabs' titles to fame is the fact that Tamerlane the Great was born within its walls, in 1335. I was now to pay my respects to his successor, a shadow of a shadow—in reality a vassal of the Czar—a king who, attending the coronation of Alexander III, at Moscow, and being asked what aroused his greatest interest, answered, "The iced lemonade."

A DERVISH IN TURKESTAN

I was received at the frontier by a troop of horsemen, and rode from village to village, accompanied by them and by a gradually increasing escort. When we halted for the night, we found nice, warm rooms, strewn with rugs, and everywhere a *dastarkhan,* or "treat," consisting of mounds of pastry, raisins, almonds, fruit, and sweets, besides the regular meat. Shadibek Karaol Begi Shigaul, a court official, with a group of gentlemen dressed in red or blue velvet *khalats,* riding splendid horses that were covered with gold-embroidered saddle-cloths, met me, and extended a welcome from the Emir. At all points, the people flocked to watch our imposing cavalcade.

In the city of Kitab, where the magistrate honoured me with a banquet, I was questioned about my country, and about the relations between Sweden and Russia. This fact explains why, later on, the Emir was so well informed about Sweden.

Clavijo's account of his reception on the way to Tamerlane's court at Samarkand, shows that the ceremonial has not altered much in the course of nearly five hundred years.   In the memoirs of Sultan Babur, the first Grand Mogul of Hindustan, we read that Shahr-i-sabs and Kitab were formerly surrounded by a common wall, which in spring was covered by verdure so luxuriant, that it gave rise to the name of Verdant City.

A stately palace was placed at my disposal.   The *dastarkhan* was served on thirty-one huge platters.   My bed was covered with red silk, and large, wonderful Bokhara rugs were spread on the floor.   If only I had been allowed to take a couple of them home!

The next morning, at nine o'clock, the reception took place.   Dressed in my best, I rode through the door of Ak Seraï, once Tamerlane's palace.   Officers in blue uniforms accompanied me, fifty men presented arms, and a band of thirty musicians played.   The procession was led by two heralds, in *khalats,* gold-embroidered, carrying gold staffs in their hands.

We rode through three castle courtyards before we were met by the court officials at the new castle.   I was ushered into a big reception-room, in the centre of which stood two armchairs.   One of them was occupied by the Emir.   He rose, and bade me welcome, in Persian.   He was a tall, handsome, black-bearded man, with pure Aryan features.   He wore a white-satin turban, a blue-velvet *khalat,* epaulets, a belt, and a scimitar; and his dress sparkled with diamonds.

For twenty minutes we talked about my journey, about Sweden, Russia, and Bokhara.   Afterwards, the governor of the city gave a stupendous banquet of forty courses.   On this occasion, he handed me a gold souvenir from the Emir, together with an address that be-

SAID ABDUL AHAD, EMIR OF BOKHARA

gan with these wonderful words:

"At this time Aga Sven Hedin of Istokolm has arrived in Turkestan in order to see the land.   Owing to the bonds of friendship which unite us with H.M. the Emperor of Russia [!] he has been allowed to enter the domains of blessed Bokhara and has had the honour to appear before our eyes to make our acquaintance. . . ."

I had nothing to give the Emir and his gentlemen in return, my travelling-funds permitting no extravagances.   All that I could do was to try, by seemly behaviour, to uphold the good name which Sweden evidently enjoyed with this last kind, but impotent occupant of Timur's throne.

I next spent a week with Lessar, the Russian Minister at Bokhara, one of the most learned and noble men who ever represented the Czar at an Asiatic court.

I finally returned, through the desert of Kara-kum, across the Caspian Sea, through Caucasia, Novorossiysk, Moscow, St. Petersburg, and Finland, to my old home in Stockholm.

PERSIA

CHAPTER XV

Two Thousand Miles in a Carriage—A Winter Ride on the "Roof of the World"

WHEN I reached home, in the spring of 1891, I felt like the conquerer of an immense territory; for I had traversed Caucasia, Mesopotamia, Persia, Russian Turkestan, and Bokhara, and had penetrated into Chinese Turkestan. I therefore felt confident that I could strike a fresh blow, and conquer all Asia, from west to east. My years of apprenticeship in Asiatic exploration were indeed behind me; yet before me lay great and serious geographical problems. I was burning with desire once more to take the road of wild adventure. Step by step I had worked my way deeper and deeper towards the heart of the largest continent of the world. Now I was content with nothing less than to tread paths where no European had ever set foot.

Eventually it proved to be a journey which lasted three years, six months, and twenty-five days, and covered a distance greater than that from Pole to Pole. About 10,500 kilometres—equivalent to one-fourth the circumference of the earth, or two and a half times the distance between New York and San Francisco—was mapped out. The charts, in five hundred and fifty-two sheets, measured three hundred and sixty-four feet. Of this mapped portion, nearly one-third, or 3,250 kilometres, represented land hitherto absolutely unknown. The expense of the trip was less than ten thousand dollars.

I did not wish to start until I had been thoroughly drilled in Asiatic geography by Baron von Richthofen; and so it was October 16, 1893, before I bade a long farewell to my family, cast off from my moorings, and started eastward to St. Petersburg.

On the way from the Czar's capital to Orenburg, a distance of 2,250 kilometres, we whizzed through Moscow and the Tamboff forests, and across the Volga on a bridge 4,867 feet long. Orenburg is the capital of the "Orenburg Cossacks," and the governor is their *ataman,* or chief.

The presence of Bashkirs, Kirghiz, and Tatars showed that this was the threshold of Asia.

My first objective was Tashkent. I was already familiar with the southern route from the Caspian Sea. This time I wanted to try the northern route, through the Kirghiz Steppe, 2,080 kilometres long, and divided into ninety-six stages. The entire journey—a distance as great as that from Los Angeles to Omaha—was made by *tarantass;* and, in order to avoid transferring baggage ninety-six times, the traveller usually bought his own carriage and spare parts, besides carrying lubricants and provisions. The *staresta,* or station-master, was always a Russian. The *yamshchiks,* or drivers, were Tatars or Kirghiz, who earned a yearly salary of sixty-five roubles, besides one and a half puds of bread and half a sheep a month. The station houses had rooms furnished with tables, chairs, and couches, where travellers could rest overnight. In one corner there was an icon, and on the table a Bible, the gift of Przhevalsky.

Annenkoff's railroad to Samarkand, which was soon extended to Tashkent, dealt a hard blow to the wagon-road through the Kirghiz Steppe. The road was, however, still kept up, for strategic reasons, until finally it was supplanted by a railway.

As it was, I bought a *tarantass* at Orenburg for seventy-five roubles, and sold it afterwards at Margelan for fifty. My baggage weighed three hundred kilograms. The boxes were sewed up in rush mats, and were fastened behind the car, as well as to the driver's seat. Among them were two heavy ammunition-boxes. Had not my guardian angel protected me, I must certainly have been blown up; for the violent jouncing reduced the cartridges to powder, and it was a miracle that the priming did not make the whole thing go off.

When I left Orenburg, on the fourteenth of November, it was 21°, and the first blizzard of the winter was raging. I sat on a small bundle of hay, covered with a rug, wrapped in furs, blankets, and *bashlik,* while the swirling snow blew under the raised hood in suffocating clouds. During the night, I was overtaken by the post-courier, a grey-bearded old man, who for twenty years had travelled to and fro, thirty-five times a year, between Orenburg and Orsk, a distance equal to that between the earth and the moon, plus six thousand miles. Powdered with snow, and with hoar-frost in his beard, he sat down at the samovar and drank eleven glasses of scalding-hot tea during the short rest.

Orsk is a small town on the Asiatic shore of the Ural River. "Good-bye, Europe!" thought I, as the *tarantass* left the last street behind, and started on its journey through the immense Kirghiz Steppe, lying between the Caspian Sea, the Aral Sea, the Ural River, and the Irtysh. Wolves, foxes, antelopes, and hares abounded, Kirghiz nomads wandered there with their herds, pitching their *kibitkas,* or black, hive-shaped tents, and their reed tents along the frequent rivulets which empty into the salt-lakes. A well-to-do Kirghiz often owns three thousand sheep and five hundred horses. In 1845, the Russians conquered this part of the Steppe, and built some forts, which are still occupied by small garrisons.

The wheels creaked on the frozen snow. The horses trotted and galloped, and the *troika* burnt up the road. The constant jolting nearly bumped me to pieces. We continued hour after hour, yet the *tarantass* remained the centre of a never-changing circle of plain land. Now and then the driver stopped for a spell to let the perspiring horses catch their breath. Occasionally he pointed his whip in the direction we were going and said: "After a while we'll meet a *tarantass* from the south."

With my field-glasses I scanned the horizon, and discovered nothing more than a tiny speck. But the driver could even make out the colour of the approaching horses. Their outdoor life on the steppe has sharpened the senses of the Kirghiz incredibly. In the middle of the night, when it is pitch-dark and cloudy, they find their way. Nothing baffles their sense of locality but the blizzards. Of course, the telegraph-poles mark the road, to a certain extent; but in heavy blizzards one can lose one's way between two poles, leaving no choice but to wait for the dawn. During such nights it behooves one to beware of the wolves.

At Tamdy, where I rested a few hours, and where the *staresta* fed the oven with dried steppe-plants, wolves came and stole three geese.

On the twenty-first of November, the temperature fell to $-4°$, that being the coldest night I experienced on my way to Tashkent. The next station, Constantinovskaya, was of the humbler kind, consisting of only two *kibitkas*. Here the road ran along the Aral Sea, a salt-lake rich in fish, about the size of Victoria Nyanza, being smaller than Lake Superior, yet larger than Lake Huron. For seventy-two miles, our way ran through sand-dunes. Three Bactrian camels were accordingly hitched to the *tarantass*. The driver rode the centre camel. It was funny to see them run through the passes, their humps swaying from side to side.

Soon we approached a warmer zone.   It was raining, and the camels' cushion-feet flopped against the wet sand.   Thus we arrived at Kazalinsk, a small town on the Sir-daria (Jaxartes), where Ural Cossacks fish for sturgeon and do a good business in caviar.   The road follows the bank of the great river.   Countless tigers, boars, and pheasants inhabit the dense, almost impenetrable bush.   A hunter gave me a proof of his skill by supplying me with pheasants enough to last me to Tashkent.

We were still one hundred and eight miles from the city of Turkestan, when our front axle broke.   After it had been temporarily mended, we drove cautiously and slowly to this ancient city, where a beautiful memorial mosque, with cupolas and minarets, had been erected, by Tamerlane, over Hazret Sultan Khoja, the patron saint of the Kirghiz.

We rolled farther and farther on this endless journey through the Steppe.   Once the *tarantass* got so hopelessly stuck in the mud, that the three horses could not budge it an inch.   It was a pitch-dark night. The horses kicked, reared, and broke their harness.   Finally the driver had to ride one of them back to the station, to fetch help.   Hours passed, and the night-wind howled.   I waited and waited, wondering if the wolves would take advantage of this opportunity.   At last the driver returned, with one man and two horses; and after a while we were able to go on.

We crossed the Aris River on a ferry.   The terrain undulated slightly, and we were drawn by an ordinary *piatorka*, or five-horse team, a man riding the leader.   As the heavy carriage rolled downhill at a dizzy speed, and the horses ran in full career, I was in deadly fear lest the rider's horse fall and he himself be crushed under the wheels. But nothing untoward happened.   At Chimkent we came to the first of the places that I had learned to know on my previous journey; and on the fourth of December, with bells jingling, we rolled into Tashkent.

Thus, in nineteen days, I had traversed eleven and a half degrees of latitude, passed thirty thousand telegraph-poles, employed one hundred and eleven drivers, used three hundred and seventeen horses and twenty-one camels, and passed from a Siberian winter to a temperature that, in the daytime, rose to 54°.

At Tashkent, where I again made myself at home in the house of the Governor General, Baron von Wrewski, and at Margelan, where I stayed with General Pavalo-Shweikowsky, Governor of Ferghana, I completed the purchase of my heavier impedimenta—tents, blankets, fur coats, felt boots, saddles, provisions, kitchen-utensils, fresh ammunition, and maps of Russian Asia—as well as presents for the natives, such as cloth, dresses, revolvers, tools, knives, daggers, silver cups, watches, magnifying-glasses, and other curious objects. For all this heavy luggage, I bought leather-covered, wooden, Sart chests (*yakhtan*), which could be adjusted to the pack-saddles of the horses.

I had decided to go to Kashgar by way of Pamir, one of the most notable mountain-regions in the whole of Central Asia. Pamir is like a knot of enormous, clustered masses of snow-covered mountains, from which radiate the highest and mightiest ranges of the earth: to the northeast, the Tian-shan, to the southeast, the Kuen-lun, the Mustagh Range, or Kara-korum, and the Himalayas, and to the southwest, the Hindu Kush. It is thus properly named *Taghdumbash,* or "The Roof of the World."

Russian Turkestan, Bokhara, Afghanistan, British Kashmir, and Chinese Turkestan are the countries whose political interests meet in Pamir. At the time of which I write, this region gave cause for considerable political tension between Russia and Great Britain. The British and the Afghans had strongholds in the western and southern parts of the country. The Chinese likewise maintained themselves in the east. In 1891, the Russians asserted their claim to the northern parts by means of a military display; and, two years later, they built the fort of Pamirsky Post, on the Murgab, one of the sources of the Amu-daria. The slightest imprudence capable of interpretation as a challenge, would have precipitated war.

The road from Margelan to Pamirsky Post was two hundred and ninety-four miles long. The distance was not great, yet the winter road was to be dreaded because of the cold and the snow. The mercury still froze at night. Everybody warned me that I would never emerge alive from the deep snows of the Alai Valley. Only the *jigits,* the Kirghiz couriers who bore the mail between Margelan and the fort, could manage it; and even they often met with terrible misadventures and suffering.

Nevertheless, I persisted. To try conclusions with the winter snow on "The Roof of the World" was just what tempted me. General

Pavalo-Shweikowsky sent a mounted messenger to the Kirghiz tent-villages along the road, ordering them to receive me and to assist me in every way; and Captain Saitseff, commander of the fort, also was notified of my coming.

I had no elaborate or heavy encumbrances. Only three men were to go with me: Rehim Baï, my body-servant, and two caravan-men, one of whom, Islam Baï, became my faithful servant through many difficult years. I hired a riding-horse and seven pack-horses, at one rouble a day per horse, thus relieving myself of responsibility for the care and feeding of the beasts. The caravan-men brought three more horses, laden with grain and hay, at their own expense.

On the twenty-third of February, 1894, we started. Our way took us through the valley of the Isfaïran River, which cuts through the northern slopes of the Alai Mountains.

ONE OF OUR HORSES FELL DOWN TO THE BOTTOM OF THE VALLEY AND WAS KILLED IMMEDIATELY

The higher we rose, the worse the path became. We left the last settlement behind, and the last frail, wooden bridges. The valley narrowed down to nothing more than a corridor, and the path climbed the steep mountain-slopes, now on the right, now on the left. Ice marked the sites of springs along the path. At one of these places, a pack-horse slipped, turned a double somersault, broke his spine against a projecting point of slate, and died on the river-bank.

A crowd of natives accompanied us from the last village—and they certainly were needed! What remained of the road was terrible. The path ran like a cornice along precipices. Sometimes it was buried under snow, sometimes covered with ice. Picks and axes were constantly in use, and the most slippery spots had to be sanded. Twilight crept silently over the district, and night set in. We still had a three hours' tramp to our camping-place. We climbed, crawled, and slid on the brink of abysses, the bottoms of which we could not see in the dark. Each horse was led by one man, while another man held onto its tail, ready to help, in case the animal slipped. Wild shouts reverberated in the valley. Our progress was constantly interrupted. A horse would slip on the edge, and would have to be held until help arrived, so as to free him of his load. It was the season of avalanches. Every minute we were in danger of being buried by loosened masses of snow. Skeletons of horses were lying around. Not infrequently, whole caravans, men and all, were buried by such avalanches.

At last we reached a place where the valley expanded, and it was with a sense of indescribable relief that we saw flaming camp-fires in the distance. After twelve hours' hard march, we brought up wearily at Langar, where the Kirghiz had pitched a nice *yurt,* or blanket-tent, for my benefit.

From here, I sent eight Kirghiz, with shovels, picks, and axes, to the Tengis-Bai Pass, in the Alai mountain-range, to dig a path for our horses; and the next day, we rode to Rabat, a small shelter, at an altitude of 9,550 feet, where I and several of my men became thoroughly acquainted with the headache, heart-palpitation, ear-buzzing, and nausea which constitute mountain-sickness. I could not bear the sight of the evening meal, and I slept badly. Later on, in Tibet, I got used to rarefied air, and did not feel the slightest distress, even at 16,000 feet.

Early the next morning, we started off along the trail which the Kirghiz had dug. The Alai mountain-ridge towered before and above us. We emerged into a steeply ascending trough, that was as white as chalk. On the six-foot-deep snow the Kirghiz had trodden a narrow path that was as ticklish as planks on a marsh; for a misstep meant sinking into the snow. After zigzagging hundreds of times, we reached the pass (12,500 feet) and had a splendid view over a vast region of snow-covered ridges. Southward, the Alai Valley stretched between the Alai and the Transalai mountain-ranges, running east and west.

A glen led down to the Alai Valley. We followed it, crossing and recrossing a small brook, on bridges and arches of snow. The horses frequently broke through, and it took our united efforts to haul them out and reload them. A huge avalanche had come down the day before, filling the glen and obliterating the road. The Kirghiz congratulated us on having escaped it. We were now walking on top of it, with perhaps twenty or thirty yards of snow under our feet.

At Daraut-kurgan, where we entered the Alai Valley, there was an *aul,* or tent-village, of twenty *yurts.* We could see a blizzard raging over Tengis-bai, and again the Kirghiz congratulated us. One day earlier, and we would have been buried underneath the avalanche; and one day later, we would have been snowed up and frozen to death in the blizzard.

The blizzard had reached Daraut-kurgan the night before the first of March. It nearly wrecked the *yurts,* which had to be stayed with ropes and stones. When I awoke, I found a small snow-wall across my pillow. The *yurts* were embedded in snow a yard deep.

Having rested for a day, we continued our journey with Kirghiz pilots, who sounded the snow with long staffs. Far ahead, on the boundless expanse of white, I saw, with satisfaction, a small, black spot, the *yurt* where we were to spend the night. A fire was burning there, the smoke swirling out through the opening in the smoke-board. That evening, a Kirghiz entertained us by playing on a stringed instrument. During the night, the blizzard raged again.

Our way continued eastward along the Alai Valley, down which the Kizil-zu River (the "Red Water"), one of the sources of the Amu-daria, flows eastwards. Here we had to set four camels to treading down a path for our horses. Sometimes they sank completely into the snow, and had to be taken to less-deep places.

We approached the *yurt* of our next night's camp to within one hundred and fifty paces. But that short distance was traversed with difficulty. Between us and the tents was a ravine, filled with nine feet of snow. The first pack-horse disappeared completely, but was freed from his boxes and hauled up by means of ropes. It was useless to try to shovel the snow away. The Kirghiz hit upon the expedient of removing pieces of blanket from the *yurt,* and spreading them out on the snow. The horses were then led, one by one, over the blankets, step by step. It seemed an eternity before we got them all across.

Complete walls of snow surrounded the blanket-tent. During the night the temperature was −5°. The next morning, the highest point of the Transalai, Kauffmann Peak (23,000 feet), stood forth in all its splendour.

From Jiptik, our camp, I sent a Kirghiz to fetch help. His horse plunged in the snow up to the rider's knees. It looked too funny for anything. He soon had to give up the attempt. We were literally snowed in, and we had no choice but to wait.

At last, some Kirghiz arrived with camels and horses, and they helped us along for a while. They told us that deeper snows were not uncommon, and that yaks were employed to butt their way through, thus making a tunnel, through which horses and men followed.

They also told of forty sheep, belonging to one of their friends, which had been bitten to death by a wolf during the last blizzard. Another man had recently lost a hundred and eighty sheep. The wolf is the Kirghiz's worst enemy. A single wolf, stealing up on a herd of sheep, at night, during a blizzard, will bite them all to death. His thirst for blood is unquenchable. But God help him if the Kirghiz capture him alive! They tie a heavy pole to his neck and a piece of wood between his jaws, and wind ropes about them. Then they let the wolf loose, torture him with whips and scourges, blind him with glowing coals, and stuff his mouth with dry snuff. On one such occasion, I had a chance to shorten the wolf's agonies.

Many a wild sheep (called *Ovis Poli,* after Marco Polo) has been torn to pieces by the wolves, who hunt systematically, establishing outposts and pursuing the sheep to a steep declivity. The sheep, on seeing their panting, red-eyed persecutors behind them, prefer a leap over the precipice, breaking the fall, so the Kirghiz say, by landing on the pads at the base of their powerful and beautifully-shaped horns. But even so, the sheep are doomed; for other wolves are waiting for them at the foot of the precipice.

One of my Kirghiz, with a companion, travelled through the Alai Valley the previous winter, and was attacked by twelve wolves. But fortunately the men were armed. They shot two of the wolves, which were at once devoured by the rest.

Not long before, a Kirghiz had gone from one tent to another, but did not return. A search revealed his skull, and other parts of his skeleton, together with his fur coat, in the snow, where bloody traces of a hopeless and desperate struggle could be seen. I could not rid myself of the image of that solitary man; and I lay awake at night, thinking of his plight when he found himself surrounded by the wolves. He must have tried to reach the tent-village, but the wolves undoubtedly attacked him on all sides. He probably drew his dagger and stabbed right and left, which only increased the fury and bloodthirstiness of his assailants. Finally his strength must have failed him, he staggered from exhaustion, all grew dark, and he entered the endless night, as the fangs of the nearest wolf sank into his throat.

We crossed the Kizil-zu at a point where a huge strip of ice outlined the shore, while in the middle the water flowed fast and deep. The horses had to jump from the slippery ice into the angry waters, and then gather themselves for a leap to the rim of ice on the other side.

Not far from here, we camped in deep snow, of which enough had been cleared away to make room for a tent. The night was sparklingly clear and still, and beautiful with its shining stars and snow. The temperature was −30°. I felt sorry for the horses. They had to stand outside and freeze.

Riding eastward, as we were, I found that the right side of my body was kept quite warm by the sun, while the left side, being in the shade, got frost-bitten. The skin of my face became chapped, and flaked off, but eventually it hardened and became tough as parchment.

Bordoba is a small mud-hut where post-couriers put up. I went there in advance, with a Kirghiz. We ploughed through a three-foot snow, and did not arrive until late at night. We could see the tracks of seven wolves near by.

From this place, the ground rises to the pass of Kizil-art (14,000 feet), in the Transalai. At the top stands a cairn and some poles with fluttering streamers. The Kirghiz kneel there and thank Allah for granting them a safe journey across this holy but dreaded pass. Later, in Tibet, I frequently encountered the same custom—the same cairns, the same poles and streamers, and the same veneration of the mountain-spirits.

On the south side of the pass there was much less snow. The lowest temperature we experienced during the entire expedition was −37°. This was at the mud-hut of Kok-sai.

The next day, we crossed a small, threshold-like ridge, from the crest of which one's eye embraced the entire prospect of Kara-kul, the "Black Lake." The sun was setting, and the shadows of the western mountains moved quickly over the desolate, cold spaces.

On March 11, I walked out on the immense ice-surface of Kara-kul, with four men, five horses, and provisions for two days. The rest of the party were to meet us on the southeastern shore. The area of this lake is one hundred and thirty square miles. It is thirteen miles long, and nine and a half miles wide. I thought of measuring its depth. We made soundings through holes in the eastern end, and spent the night on a small, rocky island. The ice made strange sounds, as if drums and bass-viols were being moved, or the doors of closed automobiles were being slammed. My men believed that giant fishes were beating their heads against the ice-roof.

After the large western basin of the lake had been sounded, and had shown a maximum depth of seven hundred and fifty-six feet, my Kirghiz and I followed the trail of the others, who had gone ahead. Twilight had already merged into darkness. We came upon bare ground, and lost the trail; and we failed to pick it up, when we reached snow-covered ground again. We rode for four hours, shouting all the while; but there was no answer. Finally we halted where dry steppe-plants were growing, and we made a fire, not only to warm ourselves, but also to serve as a signal to our men. We sat and chatted until one o'clock, with never a piece of bread or a drop of tea, frightening one another with tales of wolves. Then we wrapped ourselves up in our furs and went to sleep before the fire.

Next morning we found the caravan. We went on into the valley of Mus-kol, which leads to the pass of Ak-baital (15,300 feet). There were "ice volcanos" in the valley, formed from the water that welled up and froze, layer upon layer, the strata forming cones. The largest of these was twenty-six feet high, and six hundred and fifty feet around the base.

The snow swirled and blew like a white bridal veil on the pass. We had to abandon one of our horses here. Kul Mametieff, the interpreter of Pamirsky Post, met us on the other side. He was a gay and agreeable Kirghiz, and had been educated in Russia. When we had ridden some distance, he pointed southward over the wide valley of Murgab, and said: "Do you see that flag over there? It is waving over Pamirsky Post, the highest of all Russian forts!"

CHAPTER XVI

With the Kirghiz

THE fort was built of blocks of earth and sand-bags. Guns were mounted on barbettes at the four corners. As we advanced towards its northern front, the entire garrison of one hundred and sixty soldiers and Cossacks, drawn up on the parapet, began to cheer. At the main entrance, we were met by the commander, Captain Saitseff, who had been Skobeleff's adjutant, and by the six officers of his staff.

My arrival made a welcome break in their monotonous life. They had not seen a white man the whole winter long; and as my presence was like a godsend from the outside world, I was overwhelmed with hospitality and good-will, and was held a voluntary prisoner for twenty days.

It was a splendid rest! We talked, I sketched and took photographs, and we made excursions on horseback to the Kirghiz chiefs of that region. On Sundays, games were organized, and the garrison danced to the music of a concertina. On Tuesdays we swept the northern horizon with field-glasses, hoping to pick out the longed-for mail-courier, bearing letters and newspapers.

Before I was aware of it, the pleasant period of rest came to an end. On April 7, I said farewell, mounted my horse again, and rode northeast with my small company to Lake Rang-kul, where I stayed overnight in a *yulameika*, or flueless, conical tent. The lake, though only six feet deep, was covered with three feet of ice. Where the springs fed it, there was no ice. This lake was frequented by swarms of wild geese and wild ducks.

Continuing eastward, we crossed the Sarik-kol Mountains through the Chugatai Pass, on the further side of which we camped in the first Kirghiz tent-village located on Chinese soil. Three *beks,* or chiefs, from Bulun-kul, a nearby Chinese fort, met us; and after counting us and looking us over carefully, they returned to the fort. A rumour was afloat that a Russian army was on its way to conquer Chinese Pamir. It was even believed that we were concealing soldiers and weapons in our boxes. But, seeing that I was a lone European, with a few natives, they were reassured.

Not far from Bulun-kul, the commander himself, Chao Darin, called with an escort of ten men. He made no objection to my plan of proceeding to the western base of Mustagh-ata, but stipulated that I should leave one man and half of my luggage with him as security. The only road to Kashgar open to me was the one leading through the valley of the Gez-daria, which began at Bulun-kul.

The Chinese were rather suspicious, and they kept guards and spies at our tents all night. But they did not bother us much. On April 14, I left with four men and four pack-horses, going southwards through the wide valley of Sarik-kol, past the beautiful little mountain-lake of Kara-kul, and arrived at the tent-village of Togdasin Bek, a hospitable Kirghiz chief. The Kirghiz, on learning that a European was encamped in the neighbourhood, brought their sick to my *yurt,* and I doctored them, as best I could, with quinine and other harmless, bitter things, which proved to be wonderfully efficacious!

Mustagh-ata Mountain, the "Father of the Ice-Mountains," towered above us, its summit 25,500 feet high, and crowned with a shimmering field of eternal snow. Like a beacon, visible from the interior of the deserts to the east, it rears its dome on the meridional mountains, known as the Kashgar Range, which border the Pamir highlands toward the basin of eastern Turkestan.

The Kirghiz have many legends concerning Mustagh-ata. It is believed to be a gigantic *masar,* or saint's tomb, in which Moses, as well as Ali, rests. Some hundreds of years ago, a wise old man climbed the mountain. He found a lake on its summit, and a river, on the shore of which a white camel grazed. Venerable men, garbed in white, were sauntering in a garden of plum-trees. The sage partook of the fruit, whereupon one of the old men approached and congratulated him on not having spurned the fruit; for otherwise he would have had to remain there forever, like the rest. Then a rider on a white horse lifted him into the saddle, and rushed with him down the precipice.

On the top of the "Father of the Ice-Mountains" there is also believed to be a city, called Janaidar, inhabitants of which are absolutely happy, and know neither cold, nor suffering, nor death.

Wherever I went, and wherever I was a guest at the *auls* of the Kirghiz, I heard new tales of this sacred mountain. So it was only natural that I at length developed an irresistible desire to get better ac-

quainted with it, and to storm its steep slopes—not necessarily mounting to the summit, but going part of the way, at least.

I accordingly left my horses and a couple of men in the valley, engaged six hardy Kirghiz, hired nine splendid yaks, and moved my camp two thousand feet higher, to a region free from snow, with rocky beds and gravel-piles and murmuring glacier-brooks. We spent the first night out of doors, by a fire of dry steppe-plants.

TWICE I TRIED TO ASCEND THE MUSTAGH-ATA, OR
"THE FATHER OF THE ICE-MOUNTAINS"

But my first attempt to approach this giant mountain ended sadly. Aided by yaks, we climbed laboriously through the snow, up to the edge of the steep mountain-wall which borders the deep furrow of the huge Yam-bulak glacier on the north. From this point, we had a magnificent view of the Sarik-kol Valley to the west, and of the mighty glacier, which was fed by the *névé* basin under the top, and glided down, white and shimmering-blue, through its deep furrow, right below our feet, and emerged from its rocky abode proud as a king.

But we were given little time for contemplation. The wind rose, and on the higher slopes a raging blizzard had begun. Clouds of snow whirled above us, it grew dark, and we had to return hastily to camp.

During our absence, Togdasin Bek had come up to our camp with a big blanket-tent. He came at a most opportune moment! Before long, the blizzard enveloped the whole mountain. Everything was lost to view, and it was an agreeable thought to know that we were adequately protected against the wind.

Realizing that it might be long before the weather would permit of a fresh ascent, I sent several Kirghiz down to the valley to fetch provisions.

But now ill-fate crossed all my plans. I became afflicted with a violent rheumatic inflammation of the eyes, which compelled me to seek warmer regions without delay. The expedition was broken up; and, blindfolded, I proceeded, with my little caravan, past Kara-kul and Bulun-kul, and farther along the wild, narrow valley of the Gez-daria, notorious as the resort of robbers and escaped thieves.

Time and again we had to cross the river, which hurled itself between mighty boulders, foaming and roaring. The men waded through the water, in order to support the horses, which might have drowned but for this assistance. We found bridges only at a few places. One of them had a gigantic block of stone for a pier, and afforded an interesting view, as our horses crossed its sagging planks.

The temperature rose quickly. We descended into summer air, the thermometer recording 66°. My eyes were nearly well again when we finally rode into Kashgar, on the first of May.

I will relate only a few memories of my stay in Kashgar, which was largely spent with my old friend Petrovsky, the consul-general, and with the hospitable Mr. Macartney and the witty Father Hendricks.

My first duty was to visit Chan Dao Tai, governor of the city and the province, a splendid man, whom I knew from my first visit. He received me kindly and benevolently, granting every wish of mine as to passports and permission to go about freely.

He came the next day to return my visit; and it was really a sight for the gods, his many-coloured procession marching into the court of the consulate. First came a herald, on horseback, who thumped a sonorous gong at every fifth step. Then followed a group of men on foot, carrying switches and daggers, with which to keep a path clear for His Excellency. He himself rode in a small, covered carriage, drawn by a fine mule. On each side walked attendants, carrying sunshades and yellow standards, inscribed in black, on high poles. The procession ended with a troop of gaily-uniformed riders, on white horses.

One day, Adam Ignatieff, the Consul, and I were invited to a state dinner at Chan Dao Tai's. Our Russian procession was plainer than that of the Chinese. The *aksakal*, or elder (literally "white-beard"), of the western Turkestan merchants rode at its head, and a horseman carried the flag of the Russian Empire in front of our carriage. The two officers of the escort and twelve Cossacks in white uniforms followed

us. Thus we went through the entire city and its bazaars, across
Rigistan, the market-place, and through the "Flea Bazaar," where one
could purchase old clothes and have the vermin thrown in.

When we reached the office and residence of the governor, two guns
were fired. In the inner court, our host and his suite met us. A large,
round table stood in the centre of the dining-room. Our host shook the
chairs, to indicate to us that they could bear our weight. He waved his
hand over table and chairs, to indicate that everything was dusted and
fine. He touched his forehead with the ivory chop-sticks, and then restored them to their place.

We sat down and worked our way, by degrees, through forty-six
courses. At intervals, hot liquors were served. Adam Ignatieff evoked
admiration by his appetite and
by his contempt of death, he having emptied seventeen cups of
spirits without becoming intoxicated. The following motto was
posted on the wall: "Drink and
tell piquant tales." We did
both. But I am afraid we frequently violated the laws of the
best Chinese etiquette. Our
hosts would probably have
turned pale, had not their colour, since childhood, been as yel-
low as sun-dried peaches. A Sart orchestra played throughout the meal.
As soon as the last course was finished, we departed.

AN ORCHESTRA IN KASHGAR

Summer was now in full swing and the heat rose to 95°. I could
not forget the "Father of the Ice-Mountains," the permanent snow-
fields, and the shimmering-blue glaciers. With a small, light caravan,
led by Islam Baï, I left Kashgar, in June, and went on horseback to
Yangi-hissar, a small town, whose *amban* warned me about swollen
rivers in the narrow valleys, and, to facilitate my journey, gave me some
Kirghiz under the chieftancy of Nias Bek, as companions.

Thus we penetrated the mountains, and were welcomed at the Kip-
chak Kirghiz villages. These consisted sometimes of *yurts,* and at other
times of clay and stone huts. Time and again the dazzling-white dome
of Mustagh-ata rose above the rest of the earth. The valleys were

wild and picturesque, the rivers foaming and deep. But we got on without mishap. Here and there, the villages lay in spreading valleys, where the grass was luxuriant, and where wild roses, hawthorns, and birches grew. In the village of Pas-rabat, pouring rain overtook us; and after this, the rivers were swollen in earnest, the water becoming brownish-grey, and roaring dully and heavily in the valleys.

The hardest part of the road led through the glen of Tengi-tar, the Narrow Corridor, hemmed in between steep mountain-walls only a few yards apart. The river fills the whole valley-bed, and the traveller to Pamir is actually compelled to ride in the river itself. The water surged among tumbling rocks. A deafening echo filled the narrow gorge. The horses, uncertain of their footing, felt their way carefully between the large, round blocks. Now and then they leapt onto a block and set their muscles for a jump to the next one, always with the luggage-boxes balancing on their backs. At the most difficult places, two men would alight on conveniently-placed blocks, and guide and support the horse on either side.

It was a great relief when the narrow, blue strip of sky that had hitherto been visible between the tops of the grey, granite walls, extended itself

DIFFICULT PASSAGE BETWEEN PERPENDICULAR
ROCKS

over more open and rounded mountains. After leaving the pass of Kòk-moinak (15,540 feet), we found ourselves again on the "Roof of the World," where the *beks,* in the large, open valley of Tagarma, received us courteously.

The most beautiful prospects of alp and alpine life unfolded before us in the clear, pure air. Mustagh-ata shot its tongue-like glaciers through its deep and narrow clefts; and from them, crystal-clear brooks rippled down the slopes, crossing green pastures, where large herds of yak and sheep grazed, and on which about eighty *yurts* had been pitched.

We continued northward to the plains at Su-bashi, where we were met by our friend, Togdasin Bek, who placed one of his best *yurts* at our disposal. For nearly three months thereafter, I stayed with the Kirghiz. I lived as they did, rode their horses and yaks, ate their food —mutton and sour milk—and became their friend. Later on, they often said: "Now you have become a real Kirghiz."

On the eleventh of July, Togdasin Bek prepared a *baiga,* or tournament, on the plains at Su-bashi in my honour. Dressed in their gold-trimmed, gaily-coloured, sumptuous cloaks, or *khalats,* all the *beks* of the region assembled at our tents; and, accompanied by a resplendent retinue of forty-two mounted men, I rode to the scene of the wild riot which was about to take place. Crowds awaited us there, among them old Khoat, a hundred and eleven years of age, and his five sons, all white-bearded old men.

The whole plain was full of riders, eager for the signal that was to start the sports. The signal was given. A rider dashed up to us at full gallop. He circled before us, directing his horse with his knees, for in his left hand he held a live goat, and in his right hand a sharp-edged sabre. With a well-directed blow he cut off the goat's head, and the body dangled at his side, writhing and bloody.

Then he completed the circuit of the arena; and, with eighty horsemen at his heels, he approached us again in wild career. The ground trembled under the clattering hoofs. They came nearer and nearer, now and again disappearing in clouds of dust, until they were quite close to us, and in another minute must have crushed us like a devastating avalanche. But, when only a few paces away, with sand and earth already sprinkling us, they wheeled about; and, casting the goat's carcass at my feet, the leader disappeared into the plain, shrouded in dust.

In a few seconds, however, they were back; and then the fight for the goat's carcass began. We retreated hastily. The object was to reach the carcass from the saddle and ride away with it. It was a most fantastic fracas. All of the eighty riders crowded together. Some horses reared, others fell. Riders were thrown, and had to find their way out of the mêlée to avoid being crushed to death. From the edge of the circle, other Kirghiz pressed forward, worming their horses in among the others, who were already as tight-packed as could be. One might have taken them for Huns, pillaging.

At length, a strong Kirghiz secured the goat and circled with it wildly over the plain, the others pursuing him like a pack of hungry wolves. And in this way the spectacle was repeated over and over again.

Togdasin Bek became so excited over it, that he flung himself headlong into the game. But during its progress, he turned a somersault with his horse, and got some Chinese ideographs printed in red on his forehead, whereupon he desisted from the sport.

Afterwards, we were treated to an elaborate *dastarkhan* of mutton, rice, sour milk, and tea; and I distributed prizes, in the form of silver coins, to all the winners. Among the victors were Yehim Baï and Mollah Islam, two lusty Kirghiz, whom I took into my service.

As twilight advanced, the hordes of riders went home to their tents, and the darkness of a new night fell upon the plains at the foot of Mustagh-ata.

CHAPTER XVII

My Struggle with the "Father of the Ice-Mountains"

THE task I had set myself was to map out the region around Mustagh-ata, the "Father of the Ice-Mountains." Accompanied by my servants and some Kirghiz friends, I went to the shore of Kara-kul, the "Little Black Lake." A fine blanket *yurt* was placed at my disposal, and our neighbours provided us with sour milk, fresh milk, *kumiss* (fermented mare's milk), and sheep. The daylight hours were devoted to field-work. In the evenings, the Kirghiz would come to visit us, and I drew out of them all that they knew about their country. Whenever there was a strong wind, or pouring rain, I stayed indoors, and made notes, or drew portraits of the Kirghiz.

One day, the watch-dog which we had brought along from Ferghana

TWO KIRGHIZ BOYS

disappeared. Later on, during one of our excursions near Kara-kul, a yellowish-white, emaciated Kirghiz dog came to us. Islam Baï and the others tried to chase him off by throwing stones at him, but he always returned. So I let him stay. With liberal rations of meat and bones, he soon picked up, and became a general favourite. We called him Yoldash, or the "travelling-companion." He kept faithful watch at my tent. He was my best friend for ten months, and I did not take a step without him. He left us under tragic circumstances. But that is another story, which will be told later on.

The Kirghiz pasture their sheep, yaks, and horses around Mustagh-ata. Each family has its fixed summer and winter pastures. Although they are Mohammedans, the women do not appear veiled, but expose their faces freely, and wear high, white, turban-like head-coverings. Their lives are bound up with the well-being of their herds. At sunset, the sheep are taken to the folds. Half-wild dogs protect them against the wolves. The women have to do the heavier work connected with the sheep, ewes, and lambs, and they also provide the fodder. The men are mostly in the saddle, visiting one another, riding to the fair at Kashgar, and supervising the care of the horses and yaks. Children play around the tents. They are often sweet and pretty. We observed one of them, an eight-year-old youngster, walking perfectly naked, except for his father's boots and lambskin cap.

Through fog and mist, we advanced towards the northern slopes of Mustagh-ata, where the glacier-tongues pointed downwards, like so many fingers, to the Sarik-kol Valley. We had only yaks for riding- and pack-animals. It takes a certain amount of patience to ride a yak. Although the beast has an iron ring fixed in the cartilage of its nose, together with a guide-rope, yet the yak, obstinate and grunting, goes as it pleases.

Having examined the northern glaciers, we moved our camp to the western side of the mountain, and made excursions, on foot, along those enormous ice-streams which go by the name of Yam-bulak and Kamper-kishlak. Brooks of melted ice rippled over the bluish-green ice, clear as crystal. Here and there deep clefts yawned in the glacier, and in some places large rocks formed beautiful glacier-tables.

At sunrise, on August 6, I began the ascent of a steep cliff on the northern side of the Yam-bulak glacier, with five Kirghiz and seven yaks. The weather was glorious. At eight o'clock we were already higher than the top of Mont Blanc; and at 16,000 feet, we met the snow-line. The snow rapidly increased in depth, and its surface became frozen. We advanced slowly. The yaks were stopping continually, to recover their wind. Two of them were quite done up, and had to be abandoned, to shift for themselves.

Again we came to the edge of a cliff, with the Yam-bulak glacier, at 12,000 feet, directly below us. About a thousand feet higher, Mollah Islam and two other Kirghiz dropped down on the snow, fell asleep, and were left thus. I went on, with two Kirghiz and two yaks. The yaks were plainly discontented at this seemingly useless and stupid climb through never-ending snow.

At 20,160 feet, we had to pause for a long rest. The yaks stood with their tongues hanging out, and their breathing sounded like the sawing of wood. I and the Kirghiz were suffering from headache, as we sat eating snow. I now realized that if we were to ascend another one or two thousand feet, it would be necessary to bring provisions and tents, and prepare to spend the night at this 20,000-foot altitude. Determined on repeating the attempt, I returned to camp.

After further tramps among the glaciers, we finally, on August 11, made our second attempt to ascend the mountain, this time along the steep slope which rises immediately south of the Chal-tumak glacier. Carrying a small blanket-tent, food, and fuel, the yaks and Kirghiz struggled until we were up 17,000 feet, where we took a long rest.

All at once, a deafening roar, which filled the deep ravine with its echo for a long time, came from the perpendicular cliff that bounded the northern side of the glacier-corridor. The higher reaches of the mountain, it seems, are covered with a hood of ice, which projects over the top of the rocky wall, and, breaking of its own weight, hurtles down to the surface of the glacier. Huge blocks of this ice-armour presently descended, and, striking the protruding rocks, were converted to powder, as white and churning as foaming water.

Further up, we saw four wild goats, nervous and frightened, fleeing across the snow-crust. Shortly before that, we had seen two big, light-grey wolves, who were evidently chasing the goats into the permanent snow, but who, for want of strength, had not pursued them further.

The snow, lying two feet deep on the ice-armour, made our ascent even harder than before. Mollah Islam led the way with a yak that bore two big bundles of a steppe-growth, hard as wood, which the Kirghiz call *teresken*. Suddenly, the yak vanished, as though a trap-door had opened under him. We hurried to the spot, and found the yak suspended by his right hind leg, his horns, and the bundles of *teresken*. He had stepped through a treacherous snow-bridge that spanned a cleft about a yard wide, and beneath him there yawned a black abyss. Fortunately, the frightened animal did not move, otherwise he would have been lost. The Kirghiz got a rope around his belly, and the other yaks, uniting their strength, pulled the wretched beast up.

Slowly and cautiously we made a second attempt. Another yak was nearly engulfed, and one of the Kirghiz escaped a like fate only by hanging onto the edge. We came to a crevasse, three or four yards wide, and seven yards deep, between steep walls of azure-blue ice. This we negotiated carefully. The crack extended as far as the eye could see, in both directions. It put an absolute stop to all further advance. Our altitude was 19,100 feet.

On my return to the camp, I decided to try the ascent once more, this time by way of the slope north of the Yam-bulak glacier, which we had climbed twice before.

We spent one day getting to the 20,160-foot level, at the edge of the abyss, which we had previously attained. We had to make up our

SAVING A YAK THAT HAD FALLEN INTO A DEEP CREVICE

minds whether or not to go on; but as the ten yaks we had brought along were dead-tired, we decided to spend the night there, and continue the climb the following morning.

The yaks were tied to the few slate-rocks sticking out of the snow; and a small *yurt* was pitched on the precipice, and well stayed with ropes to several rocks. The fire inside made the eyes smart, and the air was suffocating for lack of a vent. The melting snow made a pool around the fire; but after that went out, in the evening, the water froze into a cake of ice. I let two sick Kirghiz go down to where the air was less rarefied. We all showed symptoms of mountain-sickness—singing in the ears, deafness, a quick pulse, a temperature below normal, and insomnia.

The sun went down, and its purple light died on the western slopes of Mustagh-ata. When the full moon had risen over the crest of the rocky wall south of the glacier, I went out into the dark to admire one of the most magnificent spectacles I have ever witnessed in Asia.

The permanent snow-fields on the highest dome of the mountain, the firm basin that feeds the glacier, and the highest regions of the glacier were bathed in the silver light of the moon; but where the ice-stream lay, pitch-dark, in its deep cleft, fathomless shadow prevailed. Thin, white clouds floated across the hilly snow-fields, like so many mountain-spirits engaged in dancing. Perhaps they were the souls of departed Kirghiz, with their guardian angels, passing on, from the wear and tear of the earth, to the joys of Paradise; or the fortunate beings in the enchanted city of Janaidar, who, in the light of the full moon, were dancing around about the "Father of the Ice-Mountains."

We were almost as high as the top of Chimborazo or Mt. McKinley, and higher than Kilimanjaro, Mont Blanc, and all the mountain-peaks of at least four continents. Only the highest peaks of Asia and the Andes rose higher than our present elevation. The top of Mt. Everest, the highest mountain in the world, extended 8,880 feet higher. Yet I believe that as regards wild and fantastic beauty, the picture that unfolded itself about me surpassed anything else that could be presented to man on this earth. I felt as if I were standing on the edge of the immeasurable space where mysterious worlds revolve forever and ever. Only a step separated me from the stars. I could touch the moon with my hand; and under my feet I felt the globe of the earth, a slave to the unyielding laws of gravitation, continuing to revolve, in its orbit, through the night of universal space.

Sharply-defined shadows of the tent and the yaks fell across the snow. The beasts, tied to the rocks, stood silent, but for an occasional creaking sound, as they rubbed the teeth of the lower jaw against the cartilage of the upper; and sometimes the snow crunched beneath their hoofs, as they changed their position. Their breathing was inaudible, yet visible in the shape of white clouds of vapour issuing from their nostrils.

The Kirghiz's camp-fire, between two large rocks, had gone out; and now and then the hardy, weather-beaten mountaineers grumbled, as they lay huddled up, face down, their foreheads touching the snow.

I tried in vain to go to sleep in the small tent. The cold was not severe (only 10°), but my fur coat felt as heavy as lead. Suffering from a shortness of breath, I rose time and again to get air.

Before dawn, we heard a roar, which gradually increased in volume; and by morning, a storm enveloped our camp with impenetrable clouds of whirling snow. We waited hour after hour. No one wanted to eat, and everyone had a headache. I hoped that the gale would subside, so that we might proceed to the summit. It only increased in violence, however, and toward noon I realized the hopelessness of our situation. Wishing to try the mettle of the Kirghiz, I ordered them to load the yaks and continue our climb through the storm. Every one of them obeyed. But when I said that we would have to return to our camp below, they were glad and grateful.

With two men I began the descent. I rode a big black yak, strong as an elephant. I left him to his own devices, for it was useless to try to guide him. I could not see my hand before my face, on account of the whirling, whipping snow. The yak waded, plunged, jumped, and slid downward through the snow, diving like a dolphin in the drifts. I had to press my knees hard, or I would have been thrown from the saddle by the yak's sudden and spasmodic jerks. At times, I lay back to back with the yak, only to feel, a moment later, the tips of his horns in my stomach. But finally we left the snow-clouds behind, and reached the camp, which was on a level with

A HURRIED RETREAT IN A SNOW-STORM DOWN THE
SLOPES OF MUSTAGH-ATA

the top of Mt. Whitney, in the Sierra Nevada.

Thus ended our struggle with the "Father of the Ice-Mountains." I had had my fill of this mountain, and decided to pay a short visit to

Pamirsky Post. But the Russian frontier would have to be crossed without arousing the suspicions of the Chinese; for they might take alarm, and refuse to let me return to their district. All my baggage was put away in a Kirghiz *yurt,* in a remote region; and, with two companions, I departed in the middle of the night, threading inaccessible, secret paths towards the Russian frontier. Distant Kirghiz tent-villages were visible in the moonlight, but their dogs kept quiet, and in a whirl of snow we safely crossed the Mus-kurau Pass into Russian territory.

It was a long and trying ride. Yoldash, our dog, got sore hind paws, and we had to make socks for him. He felt very much embarrassed in these garments. He tried to walk in a squatting posture, with his hind legs in the air. Finding that he was falling behind, he elected to run on three legs, keeping the right and the left stocking alternately raised in the air.

With Captain Saitseff and two other officers, I traversed a great part of Pamir, eventually pitching my tent on the shores of Yeshil-kul, a lovely alpine lake. And from there I returned quietly and unnoticed to Chinese territory. During my absence, the Chinese had missed me and had instituted a search. The Kirghiz who concealed my baggage would have got himself into trouble, if he had been found out. To free himself of suspicion, he had moved my boxes up to a stone-pile, hiding them between two rocks. And so, on September 30, when my *yurt* had again been pitched on the eastern shore of the Kara-kul, no one dreamt that I had spent twelve days on Russian territory.

One task still remained to be done at the charming little lake, before I returned to Kashgar, my headquarters. I wanted to take soundings of the lake. But there was not the slightest sign of a boat. None of the Kirghiz had seen a boat, or knew what such a thing looked like. So I made a small model, of wood and paper, and the work of construction began at the "shipyard," under the direction of Islam Baï.

A horse's hide and a lamb's skin were sewed together and stretched over a framework of tent-ribs. Oars and a mast were made from other ribs, and a spade served for rudder. It was a wonderful boat, dented and jagged like a discarded sardine-tin! Inflated goatskins were fastened to port and starboard, and also at the stern, to steady the craft. This strange turnout resembled some prehistoric animal, sitting on its eggs. One of the Kirghiz said he never thought that a boat would look like that, and Togdasin Bek remarked: "You will surely drown, if you go out on the water in this thing. Better wait till the lake freezes."

But the boat carried me all right, and the Kirghiz Turdu soon learned how to row. On the occasion of its launching, the nomads assembled on the shore, with their wives and families, and watched the proceeding in silence. They probably thought that I had gone crazy, and were only waiting to see me disappear in the clear, crystal depths.

Soundings were made in several directions, and one day we were

OUR "BOAT" ON THE LITTLE KARA-KUL, EASTERN PAMIR

destined to cover the longest route of all, that from south to north. We rowed and sailed out from the south shore, but had not gone far, when a south wind of hurricane force sprang up. We furled our sail. The waves mounted higher and higher, the foam hissed on their crests, and the boat jumped about like a refractory yak.

I sat steering with the spade. Suddenly the stern went down, and a wave surged over me, filling half the boat. One of the inflated goat-skins had got loose, and was floating away over the waves like a wild duck. Every new wave gave us a new cold shower. Turdu bailed for dear life, and I tried to thwart the assaulting waves with the spade. The boat sank deeper and deeper, and there was a whistling and peeping sound from the starboard goatskins, as the air was squeezed out of them. We listed dangerously. Unplumbed depths yawned beneath us. Would we keep afloat till we reached land? Or would Togdasin Bek prove that he had been right? The Kirghiz, both mounted and on foot, assembled on the nearest shore to see us drown; but we finally made shallow water, and landed, soaked through and through.

On another occasion—it was at twilight and we were but a few hundred feet from the north shore—a violent north wind sprang up and sent us out over the lake. Night came on; but fortunately there was a moon. The wind died down after a while. Islam Baï had lighted a fire on shore, which served us as a beacon. The greatest depth sounded was only seventy-nine feet.

Time and again, I was forced by blizzards and hail-showers to stay indoors. At such times, the Kirghiz would visit me; and I was never bored. They told me of their adventures and experiences; and sometimes they told me their troubles also. A young Kirghiz who had fallen in love with the beautiful Nevra Khan, but who was not able to pay the requisite *kalim,* or dowry, to her father, came to my tent and tried to borrow the needed sum. But my purse was too slender for such an undertaking.

A rumour had already spread all over Pamir that a European had arrived, had leaped up Mustagh-ata like a chamois, and had flown across the lake like a wild goose. This legend, appropriately elaborated and improved upon, probably survives to this day.

I had found life among the Kirghiz congenial; and when I left, there was emotion in their voices as they bade me farewell. Had I not lived with them, and become their friend? Their life was care-free, but not joyous. They fought a bitter fight against a cold and parsimonious Nature. And when they completed their span of life, they would be carried to their tombs in the valley where a holy man slumbered beneath a simple, white cupola.

I returned to Kashgar by a new route, and there summed up my findings and worked over my notes.

On November 6, we were seated around the bubbling samovar on the dining-room table, at Consul Petrovsky's. Breathless and dusty, a Cossack courier entered, and delivered a telegram to the Consul. It contained only the brief statement that Alexander III had died. Everyone rose, and the Russians crossed themselves, evidently deeply moved.

Christmas came around again. I spent it with Mr. Macartney, Father Hendricks, and my compatriot, Höglund, a missionary, who, shortly before, had arrived at Kashgar, with his family. Father Hendricks left at midnight, in order to celebrate Christmas mass in his little room, with the wine-barrels and the crucifix. I pitied him, as he made his way through the dark, sleeping town, alone, ever and unchangingly alone.

BOKHARA AND RUSSIAN TURKISTAN

CHAPTER XVIII

I Approach the Desert

ON February 17, 1895, I left Kashgar, and began a journey which proved to be one of the most difficult I ever undertook in Asia.

We had two *arabas,* or carts with two high wheels, drawn by four horses, one of them between the shafts, and the other three in front, harnessed with ropes. Each team was driven by an *arabakesh,* or driver. The carts had arched roofs made of rush-mats. I drove in the first one, with part of the luggage, and Islam Baï, with the heavy boxes, in the other. We had two dogs, Yoldash, from Pamir, and Hamra, from Kashgar. They were tied to Islam Baï's cart.

Squeaking heavily, and stirring up big clouds of yellow dust, our *arabas* rolled out through Kum-darvaseh, the "Sand Gate" of Kashgar. In Yangi-shahr, the Chinese quarter, we had a little adventure. A Chinese soldier stopped us, and declared that Hamra was his dog. When he found that we would not release the dog, he lay down on the ground, right in front of a wheel, shrieking and behaving like a madman. A big crowd gathered around us. Finally I made this declaration: "We will let the dog loose. If he goes with you, he is yours. If he goes with us, he is ours."

The wheels had made only a few revolutions, when Hamra came dashing like an arrow in our direction; and I could hear how the crowd behind laughed mockingly at the soldier.

Our way went eastward, close to the Kashgar-daria. Here and there we drove across frozen marshes. The wheels of my cart broke through the ice once up to the axle, and the team-leaders fell. This happened at night. So we made a big fire, unloaded the baggage, hitched the horses to the rear of the cart, and pulled it out; after which we tried another place.

In the villages, where we spent our nights, the drivers slept in the carts, so as to protect the baggage against thieves.

Passing through poplar-forests and tamarisk-steppes, we reached the small town of Maral-bashi.

We had been regaled, at every stopping-place, with tales of the Desert of Takla-makan, our present objective. One legend told of an ancient town, Takla-makan, that had been buried under the sand in the middle of the desert. Among the ruins of its towers, walls, and houses, gold ingots and lumps of silver lay exposed. But if a caravan went there, and loaded its camels with gold, the drivers would become bewitched, and would walk round and round in a circle, till they collapsed. They would think they were going in a straight line, but actually they would be moving in a circle all the time. Only by throwing away the gold could they break the enchantment and be saved.

It was said that a man went alone to the old city, and loaded himself down with as much gold as he could carry. Countless wild-cats attacked him. He threw the gold away, and lo, the cats vanished, leaving not a single trace.

An old man told me that when a traveller is lost in the desert, he hears voices calling his name. He becomes bewitched, follows the voices, and is lured deeper and deeper into the desert, only to expire from thirst.

This is exactly the same story that Marco Polo told, six hundred and fifty years ago, when he travelled along the edge of the desert of Lop, situated further east. In the famous account of his travels, he says:

"There is a marvellous thing related of this Desert, which is, that when travellers are on the move by night, and one of them chances to lag behind or to fall asleep or the like, when he tries to gain his company again he will hear spirits talking, and will suppose them to be his comrades. Sometimes the spirits will call him by name; and thus shall a traveller ofttimes be led astray so that he never finds his party. And in this way many have perished. Even in the daytime one hears those spirits talking, and sometimes you shall hear the sound of a variety of musical instruments, and still more commonly the sound of drums."

As we were on our way to the large Desert of Takla-makan, the temptation to penetrate to its interior increased day by day, and I could not resist its mysterious lure. In every village where we halted, I pumped the natives for everything they knew of the desert. A child could not have listened more attentively to a fairy-tale than I did to the stories of these simple, superstitious peasants. The ridges of the yellow sand-dunes, resembling sea-waves, were already visible here and there through the forest. At whatever price, I was determined to break through them.

We left the Kashgar-daria and turned southwest, along the bank of Yarkand-daria, the main river. Our road led alternately through fields of dense reed, where there were boars in large numbers, and through forests. And on March 19, we pitched camp in the village of Merket, near the right river-bank. This became our headquarters for a time.

While I went off on short excursions in the district, Islam Baï made all the purchases needed for our approaching journey. The most difficult thing was to find suitable camels. Impatiently, I awaited the return of my caravan-leader. One week passed, then another, and still another. Spring made its appearance at the edge of the desert. The warmer it got, the more dangerous a desert-journey became.

I had nothing to complain of otherwise. I lived in the pleasant home of Togda Khoja Bek, the chief of the village. He was clothed with judicial authority, and I witnessed the daily administration of justice in his court. One day, an adulteress was brought before him. She was found guilty, and was sentenced to have her face painted black, and to ride backwards through the ba-zaar, on a jackass, with her hands tied behind her back.

CRIMINALS FORCED TO TELL THE TRUTH

On another occasion, he interrogated a woman who had been terribly beaten. She accused her husband of having attacked her with a razor. When the man denied this, his hands were tied behind his back, a rope was fastened around his wrists, and he was thus hoisted up into a tree. He thereupon confessed, and received a flogging. Later on, he declared that his wife had beaten him, too; but he was convicted of lying, and so he got another flogging.

It was evident that the religion of the Prophet was held in veneration; for those persons who, in the fasting-month of Ramadan, had partaken of food while the sun was up, were painted black, and led by a rope, like wild animals, through the bazaar, to be jeered and scoffed at by the crowd.

I suffered from a sore throat for a couple of days, and Togda Khoja came and asked me to let him cure me, with the assistance of the village exorcist (*peri-bakshi*). "With pleasure!" I answered. I thought it might be amusing to see how they went about the chasing-off of the evil spirits that possessed my body. Three tall, bearded men entered my room, seated themselves on the floor, and, with fingers, fists, and palms, began beating the drums they held before them, the calfskins on which were stretched so tight that they resembled sheets of metal. They beat the drums with amazing strength, and in unison, so that it sounded like one drum; and all the while they grew more excited from the deafening roar, and the rhythm and constant crescendo. They rose, danced, threw the three drums in the air simultaneously, and caught them again, all together, with a united snap of their fingers on the drumhead. They kept this up for an hour. When the exorcism was over, I really felt much better; but all the following day I was half deaf.

Islam Baï returned on April 8. He had bought four iron tanks and six goatskins, to carry the water; sesame-oil to nourish the camels in the desert; various provisions, such as flour, honey, dried vegetables, macaroni, etc.; spades and kitchen-utensils; and many other things indispensable for a caravan. Most important of all, he had bought eight splendid camels, at thirty-five dollars apiece. They were all males. All but one were Bactrian, or two-humped camels. We named them, in Jaggatai Turki, the language of the country, as follows: "The White," "Boghra" (the Stallion), "One-Hump," "Old Man," "Big Blackie," "Little Blackie," "Big Fawnie," and "Little Fawnie."

The big bronze bells which three of the camels bore round their necks, clanged as they were led into Togda Khoja's court, where Yoldash, never having seen camels before, barked himself hoarse with rage at their intrusion.

Besides Islam Baï, I hired three new men, to go with me to the interior of the desert. They were Mohammed Shah, an old, white-bearded camel-driver, whose wife and children lived in Yarkand; Kasim, black-bearded, powerful, and dutiful, accustomed to handling camels;

and lastly a man who lived in Merket, also named Kasim, but whom we called Yolchi, or "the guide," because he asserted that he was well acquainted with the desert, and could find his way everywhere. At the last moment, our provisions were augmented by two bags of freshly-baked bread, three sheep, ten hens, and a rooster to enliven the quiet of our camps in the eternal sand. The iron tanks and the goatskins were filled with 455 litres of water, designed to last us for twenty-five days.

The portion of the large sand-desert that I was about to traverse was triangle-shaped. It was bounded on the west by Yarkand-daria, on the east by Khotan-daria (a tributary of the Yarkand), and on the south by the Kuen-lun Mountains. Our route ran, roughly, from west to east; and as Khotan-daria flows from south to north, we would sooner or later strike this river, provided we did not die of thirst. Ten years before, in 1885, Carey and Dalgleish, two Englishmen, and Przhevalsky, the Russian, had travelled through the valley of Khotan-daria. The location of the river was therefore known. On its western shore, they had observed a quite small mountain-range, called Masar-tagh, or the "Mountain of the Saint's Tomb." Another small mountain, situated in the angle between Kashgar-daria and Yarkand-daria, and which I had visited on my way to Merket, was also known as Masar-tagh, from which I surmised that the two mountains formed the extreme wings of one and the same range, extending through the entire desert, and running from northwest to southeast. If this was so, we ought to find earth free of sand at its foot, and, perhaps, traces of a civilization of bygone millenniums. The distance from Merket to Khotan-daria was 175 miles; but it was made much longer for us by the innumerable bends our route made between the sand-dunes. I hoped to cross the desert in less than a month, and move towards the cool heights of northern Tibet during the warm summer months. We therefore took fur coats, blankets, and winter clothes. Our arsenal consisted of three rifles, six revolvers, and two heavy ammunition-boxes. I had three cameras, together with a thousand glass and celluloid plates, the usual astronomical and meteorological instruments, and finally, some scientific books and a Bible.

On April 10, in the morning, our eight stately camels and their leaders marched out of Merket. The camels were heavily laden, and the bronze bells tolled solemnly, as if for a funeral. The villagers had assembled on the roofs and in the streets. They all looked grave.

We heard an old man say, "They will never come back." Another added, "Their camels are too heavily laden." Two Hindu money-changers threw some copper coins over my head, and shouted, "Happy journey!" About one hundred mounted men accompanied us a short distance.

The camels proceeded in two divisions, the first one led by Kasim, the second by Mohammed Shah. I rode Boghra, the first camel in the second division, and from my elevated place I had a splendid view of the flat land.

The camels were fat and rested, and consequently in high spirits, as they started out on their march. First, two of the younger ones, then another pair broke loose, and began a lumbering gallop around the steppe, so that their burdens fell to the ground. One of the ammunition-boxes dangled at a camel's flank. After the refractory ones had been rounded up, each camel was led separately by a man from Merket.

We pitched our first camp in a ravine, in the midst of dunes and steppe. All the animals were set loose. A fire was made and supper was prepared. It consisted of mutton and rice-pudding. I ate the same food as the men. My tent was furnished with a rug, a camp-bed, and two boxes, containing instruments and such things as were in constant use. The men from Merket had gone home.

The next day, we came upon such high dunes, that two of the camels slipped and had to be reloaded. But they soon accustomed themselves to the soft, undulating, sandy ground, and stepped steadily and safely. It seemed wise to avoid the deep sand a few days longer, so we moved along the edge toward the northeast. At every camp, we dug a well, and found water at a depth of from three to five feet. It was salty, but not too salty for the camels. We therefore emptied most of the contents of the iron tanks. We intended to refill them before heading definitely into the desert. On the fourteenth of April, we missed the dogs for quite a while; and when they returned, they were wet up to their bellies. We found the sweet-water pool where they had drunk, and camped that night at its edge.

Poplars grew here and there, and vast reed-fields extended between waste stretches of desert-sand. We generally covered fifteen or sixteen miles a day. Sounds like whistling or soughing were heard in the dense

reeds, as the camels pushed their way through the undergrowth. On
April 17, we glimpsed occasional hills in the northeast. They were the
northern Masar-tagh. We had not known that they extended so far
toward the desert; for no one had ever been there before.

The following day, we came quite unexpectedly upon a sweet-water
lake, the shore of which we followed eastwards. We went through a
truly primeval forest, so dense that we were frequently forced to retreat
and make a detour. At times we were unable to proceed without using
our axes. I dismounted, so as not to be swept from Boghra's back by
the overhanging branches.

On the nineteenth, we camped under some leafy poplars, on the
shore of yet another lake, and stayed there more than a day. A few
days later, when we were in the sterile desert, we looked back, in
imagination, on this encampment as on an earthly paradise. The
mountain shimmered in violet tints, the lake was ultramarine, the poplars
a vernal green, and the reeds and sand yellow. One of our sheep had
already been slaughtered; and now the second one was sacrificed. The
third one we were going to conserve.

On the twenty-first of April, our track lay between two isolated
mountains and along the western shore of a long lake. We went around
the southern end of this lake, and camped on its eastern shore. No
more mountains were discernible in the southeast. Our camp lay at the
southern point of a ridge which was like the outermost cape on a seacoast. On April 22, which was devoted to rest, I walked up on this
mountain. To the east, south, and southwest, nothing was to be seen
but sterile, yellow sand-dunes. The desert-sea yawned before us.

Up to this evening, we had a whole lake of water right outside our
tents. The men, the camels, and the other animals could drink their fill.
Reeds grew abundantly on the banks; so the camels and the surviving
sheep could graze without stint. Perhaps the animals, too, dreamt of
this camp, during the nights that followed, as a blessed and happy spot.
Yolchi, the guide, who was in disfavour with the other men, and kept
to himself most of the time, only crawling up to the fire, to revive its
embers, when the others had gone to sleep, now declared that it was
but a four days' journey eastwards to Khotan-daria, and that we would
be able to strike water even before reaching the river. But I told the
men to take water for ten days, as the distance might be greater than

the guide said.   If the tanks were half filled, we would be able to water the camels twice in the interior of the desert.   The tanks were put in wooden frames, and protected from direct exposure to the sun by bundles of reeds.   To the sound of the splashing water, as the men poured it into the tanks, I fell asleep, on the shore of this last lake.

CHAPTER XIX

The Sand-Sea

EARLY in the morning of April 23, the camels were reloaded, and we started off towards the southeast. I wanted to satisfy myself that our last mountain did not extend into the desert.

In two hours, we had passed the wisps of reeds, and the sterile, sandy dunes grew higher. Another hour, and they were sixty feet high; and presently they rose to eighty and ninety feet. Plains of level, dry, hard clay disclosed themselves here and there between the dunes. From this solid ground, the camels looked quite small, as they trod the ridge of the nearest dune. We zigzagged and turned in all directions, to avoid the difficult crests of the dunes and remain as nearly as possible on one level.

After a while, we saw the last tamarisks, and passed the last spots of level, clay soil. There was nothing now but fine yellow sand. As far as the eye could reach, only high dunes, quite bare of vegetation, were visible. Strange, that I was not terrified at this sight, and that it did not make me halt! It should have occurred to me that the season was too far advanced, and that the risk was too great! If ill-luck prevailed, I might lose everything. But I did not hesitate for a moment. I had determined to conquer the desert. No matter how many weary steps I might have to take to Khotan-daria, I would not retrace a single step of my trail. I was swept away by the irresistible *desiderium incogniti,* which breaks down all obstacles, and refuses to recognize the impossible.

Yet here I already observed how my men were labouring with their spades, to make the difficult places easier for the camels.

After sixteen miles, marching, we camped, at dusk, on a small spot of even clay-ground, entirely surrounded by high sand-dunes. Here grew the last two tamarisks, which the camels stripped of their bark in a few bites. Later on, we had to tie the camels, in order to prevent them from fleeing back to the lake, at night. We dug for water; but as the sandy clay proved to be dry as tinder, we gave up the attempt.

Hamra was missing. We went up on the dunes and whistled, but the dog never came back. Plainly, he had been wiser than we, and had returned over the caravan-trail. Yoldash, however, had to pay for his fidelity with his life.

After midnight, a strong westerly wind rose over the desert; and, when we started to load the camels at dawn, sand-plumes were fluttering from every dune-crest, and a yellow-red haze floated above the horizon. Later on, we were to become acquainted with the eastern gales, which carried clouds of fine dust, and turned day into night.

We kept to the southeast; but after we had made sure that Masartagh did not stretch out in that direction, I decided to change our course to due east. This direction promised the shortest distance to Khotandaria. Islam Baï led the procession, compass in hand. Seeing him climb high, pyramid-like dunes, we gathered that he was looking for a practicable path for the camels. One camel fell, at the top of a dune, in so awkward a posture, that he could not get up on all-fours again, until we had rolled him down sixty feet to more solid sand. At noon, we made a halt, and everyone got a drink, even Yoldash and the last sheep. The temperature of the water was more than 86°.

The camels had eaten the reeds which served to upholster the tanks. At the evening camp, not a trace of vegetable or animal life was to be seen, not a wind-driven leaf, not a moth. We gave the camels each a few mouthfuls of vegetable-oil, mornings and evenings.

On April 25, we were waked by a northeast wind and flying dust. Colours faded, and distances and dimensions became distorted. A nearby dune took on the appearance of a remote, high mountain.

When the tanks came to be reloaded on their three bearers, the sound of the splashing water was such that I examined the supply. To my surprise, I discovered that it was sufficient for only two days. I questioned the men, and reminded them of my order to bring water for ten days. Yolchi, the guide, answered that we were within two days of Khotan-daria. I dared not scold them, for I myself should have watched how much water was taken from the lake. We had travelled only two days, and it would have been wise to retrace our steps. The caravan would have been saved, and no life would have been lost. But I could not bring myself to go back, and I reposed undue confidence in the guide. In the presence of all, I charged Islam Baï with responsibility for the water-supply. The water-rations were reduced for the men, and the camels had to go without a single drop.

From that moment, I, as well as my men, went on foot. Entire ranges, plateaus, and stretches of sand extended in all directions.

The "Old Man" became tired, and he had to be led along minus his burden. During one of the halts, he got a mouthful of water, and an armful of hay, taken from his own pack-saddle. The dunes were still sixty feet high. A heavy and ominous mood prevailed throughout the caravan. Conversations had ceased. There were no sounds but the soughing of the wind, the tired breathing of the camels, and the funeral tolling of the bronze bells.

"A raven!" Islam exclaimed. The black bird of death circled over the caravan a few times, alighted several times on a dune-ridge, and disappeared in the haze. We were encouraged by the thought that he must have come from woods and waters in the east.

Presently "Big Blackie" also tired, and so we were obliged to pitch camp. All the hay in the "Old Man's" pack-saddle was distributed among the camels. I ate only tea, bread, and some tinned food; the men, tea, bread, and *talkan* (roasted barley-flour). There was no more fuel; so we sacrificed a wooden box, in order to make the tea. Two gnats were the only sign of life. But perhaps they had come with the caravan.

On April 26, I departed alone, at dawn. I held the compass in my hand, and counted my steps. Every hundred represented a gain, every thousand increased my hope for salvation. The day grew warm. The silence was deeper than in a graveyard. Only the headstones were wanting. The sand-ridges now mounted to a height of one hundred and fifty feet. The exhausted camels had to get over them all. Our situation was desperate. At noon, the sun was like a glowing oven. I myself was dead-tired. I had to rest for a while. But no! First another thousand steps, and then rest!

Worn out by tramping in the soft sand, and overcome with fatigue, I threw myself on my back on a dune-crest, and pulled my white cap over my face. Rest was sweet. I dozed off, and dreamt that I was camping on the shore of a lake. I heard the wind murmur in the trees, and the waves sing, as they broke against the shore. But suddenly I was awakened to the horrid reality by the cruel tinkling of the bronze bells. I sat up. There came the funeral-procession! There was a dying look in the camels' eyes. Their gaze was indolent and resigned. They breathed heavily and measuredly, and their breath gave forth a nasty stench.

There were only six of them now, and they were led by Islam and Kasim. The "Old Man" and "Big Blackie" had been left behind. Mohammed Shah and the guide stayed with them.

We camped on a small spot of hard clay-ground, not larger than the deck of a brig. I gave up pitching my tent. We slept under the open sky, all of us. The nights were still cold. We were always in higher spirits when settling down for the night, than in the daytime; for then came rest, the distribution of water, and the evening coolness after the heat of the day.

The two played-out camels were led to the camp that evening. At six o'clock, I said to the men: "Let us dig for water." Everyone was inspirited by this. Kasim took a spade, and straightway began to dig. Only Yolchi, the guide, made fun of the others, saying that water might be struck here at thirty fathoms. They asked him where the river was which he had said we would reach in four days. He was put to shame further, when, at a depth of three feet, the sandy ground became moist.

The tension grew indescribably. We worked, all five of us, as though for our lives. The wall of sand thrown up around the well grew in height. The sand had to be hauled up in a bucket. At a depth of four and a half feet, the temperature of the sand was 55°, as compared to 84° in the air. The water in the tanks was warmed by the sun to 85°. We placed an iron jug, filled with water, in the cold sand, and drank recklessly; for soon we were going to be able to fill the tanks again to the brim.

The further down we went, the moister the sand grew. We could now squeeze it into balls that did not crumble. As each digger wearied, he was replaced by a fresh one. The upper part of our bodies was bare, and we perspired freely. Now and then we lay down on the cool, moist sand to cool our fevered blood. The camels, Yoldash, and the sheep waited impatiently around the well. They knew that their thirst would eventually be quenched.

It was pitch-dark; so we placed a couple of candle-ends in small niches in the sides of the well.

How far down might the water be? If we had to dig all night, and all the next day, we were determined to find water! We worked

with the determination of despair. I sat watching Kasim, who, illuminated from above by the candles, looked fantastic at the bottom of the
well, ten feet down. I was waiting to see the reflection thrown back
by the first drops of water!

Suddenly Kasim stopped abruptly in his work. The spade slid from
his hands. With a half-choked cry he collapsed at the bottom of the
well. Fearing that he had had a stroke, I shouted down to him: "What
has happened?"

"The sand is dry," he answered; and it sounded like a voice from
the grave, like the death-knell of our unfortunate caravan.

The sand was as dry as tinder. We had exhausted our strength in
vain. We had used up nearly our whole meagre supply of water, and
had worked up a violent perspiration, all for nothing. Without a word,
the men threw themselves on the ground, hoping to forget the sorrows
of the day in sleep. I talked with Islam for a while, and did not conceal
the danger of our situation. Yet Khotan-daria could not be far away.
We had to see the undertaking through. We had water for one day
more. It would have to do for three days. That meant two cups a
day per man, one bowl for Yoldash, and one for the sheep. The camels
had not been watered for three days. They would not get another
drop. Our entire supply was less than a tenth of what a camel would
need to drink its fill.

As I rolled myself in a blanket, and lay down on my rug, the camels
were still lying at the well, waiting in vain for water, patient and
resigned, as always.

Having discarded such superfluous belongings as tent-rugs, tent-
cot, stove, etc., we set out early on the twenty-seventh of April. I went
on foot, in advance. The dunes were now only thirty feet high. My
hopes rose. But again the dunes mounted to double and treble size,
and again our situation seemed hopeless.

The sky was covered with thin clouds, and the glowing heat of the
sun was slightly moderated thereby. After four hours' walking, I
waited for the caravan to catch up. The camels were still game. We
saw two wild geese fly towards the northwest. They roused our hopes.
And yet, what were one or two hundred miles to a wild goose?

Worn out by fatigue and abstention from water, I mounted Boghra.
I felt the camel's legs tremble weakly; so I jumped down again, and
walked on with tottering steps.

Yoldash always kept close to the tank in which our little supply of water still swished about. During one of our innumerable halts, the faithful dog came up to me, wagged his tail, whined, and looked at me fixedly, as if asking if all hope was gone. I pointed toward the east, shouting, "Water, water!" The dog ran a few steps in the direction indicated, but came right back, disappointed.

The height of the dunes was now one hundred and eighty feet. From the highest crest, I searched the horizon with a field-glass.

SOME OF OUR CAMELS GOING DOWN A SAND DUNE AT SUNSET

Nothing was to be seen but high, shifting dunes. A sea of yellow sand, without the slightest trace of a shore. Countless dune-waves rose all the way to the eastern horizon, where the sand disappeared in the haze of distance. We had to get over them all, and over those beyond the horizon! Impossible! We had not the strength! Both men and animals grew weaker with every day that passed.

The "Old Man" and "Big Blackie" were not able to follow us to that evening's camp. Mohammed Shah and the guide, who had been leading them, came to the camp alone. The former told us that the "Old Man" had lain down, his legs and head stretched out on the sand, while "Big Blackie" had stood erect, with trembling legs, unable to take another step. When his six comrades disappeared among the dunes, he had sent a long, wondering glance after them. And then the men had abandoned the two dying camels. A couple of empty water-tanks were abandoned at the same time.

I thought of those two camels, with horror, as I lay awake at night. First, they had merely enjoyed the rest. Then the night had come, with its coolness. They would be expecting the men to return to fetch them. The blood flowing in their veins grew thicker and thicker. The "Old Man" probably died first. Then "Big Blackie" was alone. Finally, he too died, in the majestic stillness of the desert; and in due time the shifting sand-hillocks would bury the remains of the two martyrs.

Steel-blue, rain-filled clouds appeared in the west before sunset. Our hopes revived again. The clouds expanded and approached. We

HOLDING UP THE TENT TO GET A FEW DROPS OF RAIN WATER

kept the last two empty tanks, placed all the bowls and jugs on the sand, and spread the tent-covering on the surface of the dune. It grew dark! We took the tent-covering by the corners, and stood ready to collect Life, the rescue which was to come from the sky. But when close upon us, the clouds thinned out gradually. One man after another let go the cloth, and walked away sadly. The clouds vanished without trace, as though the aqueous vapour had been annihilated in the warm desert-air. Not a drop reached us.

In the evening, I listened to the conversation of the men. Islam said: "The camels will collapse first, one by one; then it will be our turn." Yolchi, the guide, thought that we had come in for *telesmat*, or witchcraft.

"We only imagine that we are walking straight ahead; but in reality we are walking in a circle all the time. We exhaust ourselves uselessly. We might just as well lie down to die anywhere."

"Haven't you noticed the regular course of the sun?" I asked. "Do you think that one walks in a circle, when one has the sun at one's right every day at noon?"

"We only think so; it is *telesmat*," he insisted. "Or the sun itself has gone mad."

Thirsty, after the two miserable cups of water which was our dole for the whole day, we again went to rest.

CHAPTER XX

The Caravan Meets with Disaster

EARLY in the morning of April 28, a sandstorm, the like of which we had never seen, broke over our camp. The wind heaped piles of sand on us, on our belongings, and on our camels; and, when we rose, at dawn, to meet another terrible day, we found we were nearly buried in sand. Everything had sand in it. My boots and my cap, my leather instrument-bag, and other articles had disappeared; and we had to dig the things out again with our hands.

There was little actual daybreak to speak of. Even at noon the darkness was more pronounced than at dusk. It was like marching at night. The air was filled with opaque clouds of drift-sand. Only the nearest camel was dimly visible, like a shadow in this otherwise impervious mist. The bronze bells were inaudible, even when quite near. Shouts could not be heard. Only the deafening roar of the storm filled our ears.

With such weather, it was wise for all of us to stick together. To fall behind the caravan, or to let it get out of sight, was to lose it forever. The traces of camels and men were obliterated almost instantly.

The gale grew into a hurricane. The velocity of the wind was fifty-five miles an hour. During the most violent blasts we nearly choked. Sometimes the camels refused to walk, but lay down and stretched their necks along the sand. Then we also threw ourselves down, pressing our faces against their flanks.

One of the younger camels began to stagger during that day's march. He was being led in the rear of the caravan by Yolchi. As I walked along, I kept my hand on one of our boxes, so as not to lose my way. Yolchi came up and shouted in my ear that the camel had fallen on a steep sand-ridge, and could not be induced to get up. At once I ordered a halt, and sent Mohammed Shah and Kasim to save the camel. They returned in a few minutes and reported that the trail had disappeared, and that they had been unable to find the camel in the thick clouds of whirling sand. As it was a question of life and death for all of us, we had to leave him, as well as his load, consisting of two boxes of provisions, ammunition, and furs. He was doomed to die of thirst in this suffocating, murderous desert.

In the evening, when we camped, we got rid of the other boxes, which contained provisions, furs, blankets, rugs, pillows, books, cooking-apparatus, kerosene, pots and pans, a set of agate-ware and china, etc. Everything that could be dispensed with was packed in boxes, which we

WORKING OUR WAY THROUGH THE SANDSTORM

stowed between two dunes. Into the crest of the higher dune we drove a pole, to the top of which we tied a newspaper, to serve as a beacon. We kept only enough food for a few days. All the liquid tinned food was distributed among the men. They ate it, first satisfying themselves, however, that it contained no pork. They greedily drank up the oil in the sardine-tins. Another pack-saddle was emptied of its hay stuffing; but the camels ate the hay without relish, their throats were so parched. In the evening, I drank my last cup of tea. Only two small iron jars of water were now left.

The gale subsided during the night. At sunrise, on the twenty-ninth

of April, Islam reported that one of the water-jugs had been stolen
during the night.   Everyone suspected Yolchi, especially as he did not
show up until the next morning.

We started off with the remaining five camels.   Again we made observations from the high dunes.   There was only a sea of yellow sand in
all directions.   Not a sign of organic life even the size of a pin-head.
Yet, to our surprise, we found the grey, porous .trunk of a poplar,
withered for centuries, perhaps for thousands of years.   How many
dunes had passed over this tree, dead ever since its roots had ceased
to reach the moisture of the subsoil.

As a result of the storm, the air was filled with flying particles of
sand, which tended to moderate the sun's heat somewhat.   Yet the
camels walked slowly, with tired, deliberate steps.   The last two bronze
bells tinkled in slow, solemn measure.   We moved on for twelve and
a half hours, with countless stops and interruptions.   From our night's
camp, nothing could be seen to indicate that the desert sea had a shore.

The next morning, the thirtieth of April, the camels got all the
butter that was left.   There still remained a few cups of water in the
last iron jar.   While the camels were being laden, we came upon Yolchi,
with the jug to his mouth.   Foaming with rage, Islam and Kasim fell
upon him, beat his face, threw him to the ground, kicked him, and
would have killed him on the spot, had I not intervened.

Hardly one cup of water remained.   I told the men that at noon I
would dip the corner of a handkerchief in it and moisten my lips and
theirs, and that the last drops would suffice for a small mouthful for
each.   At noon I moistened their lips, but in the evening the jug was
empty.   I do not know who the guilty one was, and it was no use holding a trial.   The desert was endless, and we were all headed toward
certain death.

When we had gone along for a while, the dunes became lower,
averaging about twenty-five feet.   A wagtail was hopping on a dune-
comb.   Islam Baï was so buoyed up by this, that he begged permission
to hurry eastward with the empty iron jugs, and to return after he had
filled them at the nearest water.   But I would not allow it.   He was
more necessary to us now than ever.

Yolchi was missing again; and the others were furious.   They
thought he had deliberately understated the distance, after he had
stolen the water from us that night, in the hope that we would die of

thirst, and that afterwards he could steal our Chinese silver and find refuge in the woods along the Khotan-daria. But I think their suspicions were groundless.

That night, I wrote what I supposed were to be my last lines in my diary: "Halted on a high dune, where the camels dropped. We examined the east through the field-glasses; mountains of sand in all directions, not a straw, no life. All, men as well as camels, are extremely weak. God help us!"

May Day, a springtime feast of joy and light, at home in Sweden, was for us the heaviest day on our *via dolorosa* through the desert.

The night had been quiet, clear, and cold (36°); but the sun was hardly above the horizon, when it grew warm. The men squeezed the last drops of the rancid oil out of a goat's skin, and gave them to the camels. The day before, I had not had a single drop of water, and the day before that, only two cups. I was suffering from thirst; and when, by chance, I found the bottle in which we kept the Chinese spirits for the Primus stove, I could not resist the temptation of drinking some of it. It was a foolish thing to do; but nevertheless I drank half the bottle. Yoldash heard the gurgling sound, and came toward me, wagging his tail. I let him have a sniff. He snorted, and went away sadly. I threw the bottle away, and the rest of the liquid flowed out into the sand.

That treacherous drink finished me. I tried to rise, but my legs would not support me. The caravan broke camp, but I remained behind. Islam Baï led, compass in hand, going due east. The sun was already burning-hot. My men probably thought I would die where I lay. They went on slowly, like snails. The sound of the bells grew fainter, and finally died away altogether. On every dune-crest the caravan reappeared like a dark spot, smaller and smaller; in every hollow between the dunes, it remained concealed for a while. Finally I saw it no more. But the deep trail, with its dark shadows from the sun, which was still low, reminded me of the danger of my situation. I had not strength enough to follow the others. They had left me. The horrible desert extended in all directions. The sun was burning and blinding, and there was not a breath of air.

Then a terrible thought struck me. What if this was the quiet before a storm? At any moment, then, I might see the black streak, across the horizon in the east, which heralded the approach of a sandstorm. The trail of the caravan would then be obliterated in a few moments, and I would never find my men and camels again, those wrecks of the ships of the desert!

I exerted all my will-power, got up, reeled, fell, crawled for a while along the trail, got up again, dragged myself along, and crawled. One hour passed, and then another. From the ridge of a dune, I saw the caravan. It was standing still. The bells had ceased tinkling. By superhuman efforts, I managed to reach it.

Islam stood on a ridge, scanning the eastern horizon, and shading his eyes with his hand. Again he asked permission to hurry eastward with the jugs. But seeing my condition, he quickly abandoned the idea.

Mohammed Shah was lying on his face, sobbingly invoking Allah. Kasim sat in the shadow of a camel, his face covered with his hands.

ALL, MEN AND CAMELS, WERE DYING FROM THIRST

He told me that Mohammed Shah had been raving about water all the way. Yolchi lay on the sand, as if he were dead.

Islam suggested that we continue, and look for a spot of hard clay ground, where we might dig for water. All the camels were lying down. I climbed on the white one. Like the others, he refused to get up. Our plight was desperate. Here we were to die. Mohammed Shah lay babbling, toying with the sand, and raving about water. I realized that we had reached the last act of our desert-drama. But I was not yet ready to give in altogether.

The sun was now glowing like an oven. "When the sun has gone down," I said to Islam, "we will break camp and march all night. Up with the tent!" The camels were freed from their burdens, and lay in the blazing sun all day. Islam and Kasim pitched the tent. I crawled in, undressed completely, and lay down on a blanket, my head pillowed on a sack. Islam, Kasim, Yoldash, and the sheep went into the shade, while Mohammed Shah and Yolchi stayed where they had fallen. The hens were the only ones to keep up their spirits.

This death-camp was the unhappiest I lived through in all my wanderings in Asia.

It was only half-past nine in the morning, and we had hardly traversed three miles. I was absolutely done up, and not able to move a finger. I thought I was dying. I imagined myself already lying in a mortuary chapel. The church-bells had stopped tolling for the funeral. My whole life flew past me like a dream. There were not many hours left me on the threshold of eternity. But most of all, I was tormented by the thought of the anxiety and uncertainty which I would cause my parents and brother and sisters. When I should be reported missing, Consul Petrovsky would make investigations. He would learn that I had left Merket on the tenth of April. All traces after that, however, would then have been swept away; for several storms would have passed over the desert since then. They would wait and wait at home. One year would pass after another. But no news would come, and finally they would cease hoping.

About noon, the slack flaps of the tent began to bulge, and a faint southerly breeze moved over the desert. It blew stronger, and after a couple of hours it was so fresh that I rolled myself up in my blanket.

And now a miracle happened! My debility vanished and my strength returned! If ever I longed for the sunset, it was now. I did not want to die: I *would* not die in this miserable, sandy desert! I could run, walk, crawl on my hands and feet. My men might not survive, but I had to find water!

The sun lay like a red-hot cannon-ball on a dune in the west. I was in the best of condition. I dressed, and ordered Islam and Kasim to prepare for departure. The sunset-glow spread its purple light over the dunes. Mohammed Shah and Yolchi were in the same position as in the morning. The former had already begun his death-struggle; and he never regained consciousness. But the latter woke to life in the cool of the evening. With his hands clenched, he crawled up to me, and cried pitifully: "Water! Give us water, sir! Only a drop of water!" Then he crawled away.

"Is there no liquid here, whatever?" I said.

"Why, the rooster!" So they cut off the rooster's head and drank his blood. But that was only a drop in the bucket. Their eyes fell on the sheep, which had followed us as faithfully as a dog, without complaining. Everyone hesitated. It would be murder to kill the sheep to prolong our lives for only one day. But Islam led it away, turned its head toward Mecca, and slashed its carotids. The blood, reddish-brown and ill-smelling, flowed slowly and thickly. It coagulated immediately into a cake, which the men gulped down. I tried it, too; but it was nauseous, and the mucous membrance of my throat was so dry, that it stuck there, and I had to get rid of it quickly.

Mad with thirst, Islam and Yolchi collected camel's urine in a receptacle, mixed it with sugar and vinegar, held their noses, and drank. Kasim and I declined to join in this drinking-bout. The two who had drunk this poison were totally incapacitated. They were overcome with violent cramps and vomiting, and lay writhing and groaning on the sand.

Islam recovered slightly. Before darkness fell, we went over our baggage. I laid everything that was irreplaceable in one pile: note-books, itineraries, maps, instruments, pencils and paper, arms and ammunition, the Chinese silver (about $1,300), lanterns, candles, a pail, a shovel, provisions for three days, some tobacco, and a few other things. A pocket-Bible was the only book included. Among the things abandoned were the cameras and about a thousand plates, of which about one hundred had already been exposed, the medicine-chest, saddles, clothes, presents intended for the natives, and much besides. I removed a suit of clean clothing from the pile of discarded things, and changed everything, from head to foot; for if I was to die and be buried by the sandstorms in the eternal desert, I would at least be robed in a clean, new shroud.

The things we had decided to take along were packed in soft saddle-bags, and these were fastened to the camels. All the pack-saddles were discarded, as they would only have added unnecessary weight.

Yolchi had crawled into the tent to lie down on my blanket. He looked repulsive, soiled as he was with blood from the lungs of the sheep. I tried to brace him up, and advised him to follow our track during the night. He did not answer. Mohammed Shah was already delirious. In his delirium, he muttered the name of Allah. I tried to make his head comfortable, passed my hand over his burning forehead, begged him to crawl along our trail as far as he could, and told him that we would return to rescue him as soon as we found water.

The two men eventually died in the death-camp, or near it. They were never heard of; and when, after a year had elapsed, they were still missing, I gave a sum of money to their respective widows and children.

All five camels were induced to get up, and they were tied to one another in single file. Islam led, and Kasim brought up the rear. We did not take the two dying men along, because the camels were too weak to carry them; and, indeed, in their deplorable condition, they could not have kept their seats between the humps. We also cherished the hope that we would find water, in which case we were going to fill the two goatskins that we still carried, and hurry back to save the unfortunate ones.

The hens, having satisfied their keen hunger with the dead sheep's blood, had gone to rest. A silence more profound than that of the grave prevailed around the tent. As twilight was about to merge into darkness, the bronze bells sounded for the last time. We headed eastward as usual, avoiding the highest ridges. After a few minutes' walk, I turned about, and gave a farewell-glance at the death-camp. The tent stood out distinctly in the vanishing daylight that still lingered in the west. It was a relief to get away from this ghastly place. It was soon swallowed up by the night.

When it was pitch-dark, I lit the candle in the lantern, and walked ahead, looking for the easiest way. One of the camels collapsed during the march, and lay down immediately, prepared for death, neck and legs stretched out. His bag was placed on "White," the strongest of the four survivors. The dying camel's bronze bell remained with him. Its tinkling was now a thing of the past.

Our progress was desperately slow. Every step was an effort for the camels. Now one, then the other stopped, and had to rest for a while. Islam suffered from fresh attacks of vomiting, and lay writhing on the sand like a worm. In the faint light from the lantern, I lengthened my stride, and went on ahead. I walked thus for two hours. The sound of the bells died away behind me. There was no sound discernible, save the swishing of the sand under my heels.

At eleven o'clock, I struggled up onto a flat, sandy ridge, to listen and to reconnoitre. The Khotan-daria *couldn't* be far away. I scanned the east, hoping to detect the fire of a shepherd's camp; but everything was pitch-dark. Only the stars shone. No sound interrupted the silence. I placed the lantern in a position to serve as a beacon for Islam and Kasim, laid myself on my back, and pondered and listened. My composure, however, remained unshaken.

Far away, the clanging of the last bell again became audible. There were intervals of quiet, but the sound came nearer. After I had waited for what seemed like eternity, the four camels stood forth like phantoms. They came up to me on the ridge and lay down right away. They probably mistook the lantern for a camp-fire. Islam staggered along, threw himself on the sand, and whispered labouredly that he could go no farther. He would die where he was. He made no answer when I tried to encourage him to hold out.

On seeing that the game was up, I decided to forfeit everything except my life. I even sacrificed diaries and records of observations, and took along only what I always carried in my pockets, namely, a compass, a watch, two chronometers, a box of matches, handkerchief, pocket-knife, pencil, a piece of folded paper, and, by the merest chance, ten cigarettes.

Kasim, who still bore up, was happy when I told him to come with me. Hurriedly he took the shovel and pail, but forgot his cap. Later on, he used my handkerchief to protect himself against sunstroke. I bade farewell to Islam, and told him to sacrifice *everything,* but try to save himself by following our track. He looked as if he were going to die, and made no answer.

After a last look at the patient camels, I hurried away from this painful scene, where a man was fighting death, and where the veterans of our erstwhile proud caravan would end their desert-journey for good. I caressed Yoldash, and left it to him to decide whether he would stay or go with us. He stayed, and I never saw the faithful dog again. It was midnight. We had been shipwrecked in the middle of the sea, and were now leaving the sinking ship.

The lantern was still burning beside Islam, but its light soon died out behind us.

CHAPTER XXI

The Last Days

THUS we walked on through the night and the sand. After two hours of it, we were so exhausted, from fatigue and from lack of sleep, that we flung ourselves headlong on the sand, and dozed off. I was wearing thin, white, cotton clothes, and was soon awakened by the cold night-air. Then we walked again, till the limit of our endurance was reached. We slept once more on a dune. My stiff-topped boots, reaching to my knees, made progress difficult. I was on the point of throwing them away several times; but fortunately I did not do so.

After another halt, we walked on for five hours more, that is, from four to nine in the morning. This was on the second of May. Then one hour's rest again, and one and a half hour's slow march. The sun was blazing. All became black before our eyes, as we sank down on the sand. Kasim dug out, from a northerly slope, sand which was still cold from the night. I stripped and laid myself down in it, while Kasim shovelled sand over me up to my neck. He did the same for himself. Our heads were quite close to each other, and we shaded ourselves from the sun by hanging our clothes on the spade, which we had stuck in the ground.

All day long we lay like this, speaking not a word, and not getting a wink of sleep. The turquoise-blue sky arched over us, and the yellow sea of the desert extended around us, stretching to the horizon.

When the ball of the sun again rested on the ridge of a dune in the west, we got up, shook off the sand, dressed, and dragged ourselves slowly, and with innumerable interruptions, towards the east, until one o'clock in the morning.

The sand-bath, although cooling and pleasant during the heat of the day, was also weakening. Our strength was ebbing. We could not cover as much ground as the night before. Thirst did not torment us, as it had done during the first days; for the mouth-cavity had become as dry as the outside skin, and the craving was dulled.   An increasing feebleness set in, instead.   The functioning of all the glands was reduced. Our blood got thicker, and flowed through the capillaries with increasing sluggishness.   Sooner or later this process of drying-up would reach its climax in death.

From one o'clock until half-past four in the morning, on May 3,

we lay inanimate; and not even the cold night-air could rouse us to go on. But at dawn we dragged ourselves f o r w a r d again. We would take a couple of steps intermittently. We managed to get down the sandy slopes fairly well; but climbing the waves of sand was heavy work.

At sunrise, Kasim caught me by the shoulder, stared, and pointed east, without saying a word.

"What is it?" I whispered.

KASIM AND I CREEPING AND STRUGGLING FOR LIFE

"A tamarisk," he gasped.

A sign of vegetation at last! God be praised! Our hopes, which had been close to extinction, flamed up once more. We walked, dragged ourselves, and staggered for three hours, before we reached that first bush—an olive-branch intimating that the sea of the desert had a shore. We thanked God for this blessed gift, as we chewed the bitter, green needles of the tamarisk. Like a water-lily, the bush stood on its wave of sand, basking in the sun. But how far below was the water that nourished its roots?

About ten o'clock, we found another tamarisk; and we saw several more in the east. But our strength was gone. We undressed, buried ourselves in the sand, and hung our clothes on the branches of the tamarisk, to make shade.

We lay in silence for nine hours. The hot desert-air dried our faces into parchment. At seven o'clock, we dressed, and continued onward. We went more slowly than ever. After three hours' walk in the dark, Kasim stopped short, and whispered: "Poplars!"

Between two dunes there appeared three poplars, standing close together. We sank down at their base, exhausted with fatigue. Their roots, too, must derive nourishment from below. We took hold of the spade, intending to dig a well; but the spade slipped from our hands. We had no strength left. We lay down and scratched the ground with our nails, but gave up the attempt as useless.

Instead, we tore off the fresh leaves, and rubbed them into our skin. Then we collected dry, fallen twigs, and made a fire on the nearest crest, as a signal to Islam, should he prove to be still alive, which I very much doubted. The fire might also, perhaps, attract the attention of a shepherd in the woods along the Khotan-daria. But even if a shepherd should see this fire in an area of deathly silence, he was more likely to become frightened and believe it was the desert-spirit who haunted the place and practised witchcraft. For fully two hours we kept the fire going, regarding it as a companion, a friend, and a chance of rescue. Nowadays, those who are shipwrecked at sea have other means of sending out their S.O.S., in moments of extreme danger. We had only this fire; and our eyes were glued to its flames.

The night was coming to an end; and the sun, our worst enemy, would soon rise again above the dunes on the eastern horizon, to torment us anew. At four on the morning of the fourth of May, we started off, stumbling along for five hours. Then our strength gave out. Our hope was again on the decline. In the east there were no more poplars, no more tamarisks, to stimulate our dying vitality with their verdure. Only mounds of sand, as far as the eye could reach.

We collapsed on the slope of a dune. Kasim's ability to dig out cold sand for me was gone. I had to help myself as best I could.

For fully ten hours we lay silent in the sand. It was strange that we were still alive. Would we have strength enough to drag ourselves through one more night—our last one?

I rose at twilight and urged Kasim to come. Hardly audible was his gasp: "I can't go on."

And so I left the last remnant of the caravan behind, and continued on alone. I dragged myself along, and fell. I crawled up slopes, and staggered down the other side. I lay quiet for long periods, listening. Not a sound! The stars shone like electric torches. I wondered whether I was still on earth, or whether this was the valley of the shadow of death. I lit my last cigarette. Kasim had always received the butts;

but now I was alone, and so I smoked this one to the end. It afforded me a little relief and distraction.

Six hours had passed since the beginning of my solitary journey, when, totally overcome with feebleness, I sank down by a new tamarisk, and went off into the doze which I feared, for death might come while I was asleep. As a matter of fact, I hardly slept at all. All the time, in the grave-like silence, I heard the beating of my heart and the ticking of the chronometers. And after a couple of hours, I heard the swish of steps in the sand, and saw a phantom stagger and struggle to my side.

"Is that you, Kasim?" I whispered.

"Yes, sir."

"Come! We have not far to go!"

Heartened by our reunion, we struggled on. We slid down the dunes; we struggled upwards. We would lie, motionless, where we fell, in our battle against the insidious desire for sleep. We slackened our pace, and grew more and more indolent. We were like sleep-walkers; but still we fought for our lives.

Suddenly Kasim grabbed my arm and pointed downwards at the sand. There were distinct tracks of human beings!

In a twinkling we were wide awake. It was plain that the river *must* be near! It was possible that some shepherds had noticed our fire and had come to investigate. Or maybe a sheep, astray in the desert, had been searched for by these men who had so recently passed over the sand.

Kasim bent down, examined the prints, and gasped:

"It is our own trail!"

In our listless, somnolent state, we had described a circle without knowing it. That was enough for a while; we could not endure any more. We collapsed on the trail and fell asleep. It was half-past two at night.

When the new day dawned, on the fifth of May, we rose heavily, and with difficulty. Kasim looked terrible. His tongue was white and swollen, his lips blue, his cheeks were hollow, and his eyes had a dying, glassy lustre. He was tortured by a kind of death-hiccup, which shook his whole frame. When the body is so completely dried up that the joints almost creak, every movement is an effort.

It grew lighter. The sun rose. From the top of a dune, where nothing obstructed the view towards the east, we noticed that the horizon, which for two weeks had revealed a row of yellow saw-teeth, now disclosed an absolutely even, dark-green line. We stopped short, as though petrified, and exclaimed simultaneously: "The forest!" And I added: "The Khotan-daria! Water!"

Again we collected what little strength we had left, and struggled along eastwards. The dunes grew lower, we passed a depression in the ground, at the bottom of which we tried to dig; but we were still too weak. We went on. The dark-green line grew, the dunes diminished, stopped altogether, and were replaced by level, soft ground. We were but a few hundred yards from the forest. At half-past five we reached the first poplars, and, wearied, sank down in their shade. We enjoyed the fragrance of the forest. We saw flowers growing between the trees, and heard the birds sing and the flies and gadflies hum.

A DARK LINE OF FOREST FAR AWAY IN-
SPIRED US WITH NEW HOPE

At seven o'clock we continued. The forest grew thinner. We came upon a path, showing traces of men, sheep, and horses, and we thought it might lead to the river. After following it for two hours, we collapsed in the shade of a poplar-grove.

We were too weak to move. Kasim lay on his back. He looked as if he were going to die. The river *must* be quite near. But we were as if nailed down. A tropical heat surrounded us. Would the day never come to an end? Every hour that passed brought us closer to certain death. We would have to drag ourselves on to the river, before it got too late! But the sun did not go down. We breathed heavily, and with effort. The will-to-live was about to desert us.

At seven P.M., I was able to get up. I hung the iron spade-blade in the crotch of a tree, and used the wooden handle for a cane. The blade would serve to mark the way, in case we returned with some shepherds to rescue the three dying men and recover the lost baggage. But it was four whole days since we had deserted the men. They were sure to be dead already. And it would take us several days more to reach them. Their situation was clearly hopeless.

Again I urged Kasim to accompany me to the river to drink. He signalled with his hand that he could not rise; and he whispered that he would soon die under the poplars.

Alone I pulled myself along through the forest. Thickets of thorny bushes, and dry, fallen branches, obstructed my way. I tore my thin

clothes and scratched my hands; but gradually I worked my way through. I rested frequently, crawled part of the way on all-fours, and noticed with anxiety how the darkness grew denser in the woods. Finally the new night came—the last one. I could not have survived another day.

The forest ended abruptly, as though burnt by a fire. I found myself on the edge of a six-foot-high terrace, which descended almost perpendicularly to an absolutely level plain, de-

I CREPT, DYING, THROUGH THE FOREST IN SEARCH OF WATER

void of vegetation. The ground was packed hard. A withered, leafless twig was sticking out of it. I saw that it was a piece of drift-wood, and that I was in the river-bed of the Khotan-daria. And it was dry, as dry as the sandy desert behind me!

Was I to die of thirst in the very bed of the river, after having fought my way so successfully to its bank? No! I was not going to lie down and die without first crossing the Khotan-daria and assuring myself that the whole bed was dry, and that all hope was irretrievably gone.

I knew that the course of the river was almost due north. The shortest distance to the right-hand shore would therefore be straight eastward. Although the moon was up, and I watched the compass, I was all the time, and unconsciously, being drawn toward the south-east. There was no use fighting this force. I walked as though led by an invisible hand. Finally I resisted no more, but walked towards the southeast, where the moon was. I frequently sank down and rested. I was then overcome by a terrible desire for sleep. My head sank to the ground, and I had to use all my will-power not to go to sleep. Had I gone to sleep, exhausted as I was, I am sure I should never have waked again.

Like the beds of all desert-rivers in Central Asia, that of Khotan-daria is very wide, flat, and shallow. A light haze floated over the desolate landscape. I had gone about one mile, when the outlines of the forest on the eastern shore appeared below the moon. Dense thickets of bushes and reeds grew on the terraced shore. A fallen poplar stretched its dark trunk down towards the river-bed. It looked like the body of a crocodile. The bed still remained as dry as before. It was not far to the shore where I must lie down and die. My life hung on a hair.

Suddenly I started, and stopped short. A water-bird, a wild duck or goose, rose on whirring wings, and I heard a splash. The next moment, I stood on the edge of a pool, seventy feet long and fifteen feet wide! The water looked as black as ink in the moonlight. The over-turned poplar-trunk was reflected in its depths.

In the silent night I thanked God for my miraculous deliverance. Had I continued eastwards I should have been lost. In fact, if I had touched shore only a hundred yards north or south of the pool, I would have believed the entire river-bed to be dry. I knew that the freshets from melting snow-fields and glaciers in northern Tibet flowed down through the Khotan-daria bed only in the beginning of June, to dry up in the late summer and autumn, leaving the bed dry during the winter and spring. I had also heard that in certain places, separated some-times by a day's journey or more, the river forms eddies, which scoop the bed into greater depths, and that the water may remain the year round in these hollows near the terraced shore. And now I had come upon one of these extremely rare bodies of water!

I sat down calmly on the bank, and felt my pulse. It was so weak that it was hardly noticeable—only forty-nine beats. Then I drank, and drank again. I drank without restraint. The water was cold, clear as crystal, and as sweet as the best spring-water. And then I drank again. My dried-up body absorbed the moisture like a sponge. All my joints softened, all my movements became easier. My skin, hard as parchment before, now became softened. My forehead grew moist. The pulse increased in strength; and after a few minutes it was fifty-six. The blood flowed more freely in my veins. I had a feeling of well-being and comfort. I drank again, and sat caressing the water in this blessed pool. Later on, I christened this pool Khoda-verdi-kol, or "The Pool of God's Gift."

The reeds grew thick on the shore, and the bushes formed tangled thickets. The silver crescent of the moon hung in the crown of a poplar. There was a rustle in the thicket. Brittle, dry reeds were displaced as

THE POOL WHICH SAVED MY LIFE

by a body propelling itself. Was it a tiger, stealing to the pool to drink? With the smile of a conqueror I waited to see his eyes shine in the dark. "Come on, you!" I thought. "Just try to take my life, which but five minutes ago was granted me a second time!" But the swishing sound among the reeds died away; and whether it was a tiger or some other forest inhabitant that had come to the pool to quench his thirst, he evidently thought it best to retire, on discovering the intrusion made by this lone man, gone astray.

CHAPTER XXII

Robinson Crusoe

I HAD quenched my thirst; and, strangely enough, I suffered no
harm from my injudicious drinking.

My thoughts now flew to Kasim, who lay, faint from thirst,
on the edge of the wood on the western shore. Of the stately
caravan of three weeks ago, I, a European, was the only one that had
held out till the moment of rescue. If I did not waste my minutes, perhaps Kasim, too, might be saved. But in what was I to carry the water?
Why, in my water-proof boots! There was, in fact, no other receptacle.
I filled them to the top, suspended them at either end of the spade-
handle, and carefully recrossed the river-bed. Though the moon was
low, my old track was plainly visible. I reached the forest. The moon
went down, and dense darkness descended among the trees. I lost my
trail, and went astray among thorny bushes and thickets, which would
not give under my stockinged feet.

From time to time, I called "Kasim!" at the top of my voice. But
the sound died away among the tree-trunks; and I got no answer but
the "clevitt" of a frightened night-owl.

If I lost my way, perhaps I would never again find the trail, and then
Kasim would be lost. I stopped at an impenetrable thicket of dry
branches and brush, set fire to the whole thing, and enjoyed seeing the
flames lick and scorch the nearest poplars. Kasim could not be far
away; he was certain both to hear and to see the fire. But he did not
come. I had no choice but to await the dawn.

At the foot of a poplar, out of reach of the fire, I lay down and slept
for some hours. The fire protected me against any prowling wild
beasts.

When dawn came, the night-fire was still glowing, and a black
column of smoke was rising above the forest. It was easy now to find
my trail, and the place where Kasim lay. He was still in the same position as the night before. Upon seeing me, he whispered: "I am
dying!"

"Will you have some water?" I asked, letting him hear the splashing sound. He sat up, dazed and staring. I handed him one of the
boots. He lifted it to his lips and emptied it to the last drop. After
a short pause he emptied the other one, too.

"Come along now to the pool," said I.

"I can't," Kasim answered.

"Follow my track, then, as soon as you can. I shall go to the pool,
first, then southward along the river-bed. Good-bye!"

I MADE A LARGE FIRE TO ATTRACT THE ATTENTION OF KASIM

I could do no more for Kasim at the moment; and I thought he was
now out of danger.

It was five o'clock in the morning of May 6. I drank again at the
pool, bathed, and rested awhile. Then I walked south, following the
woody terrace of the eastern, or right bank. I had walked for three
hours, when it grew dark, and a *kara-buran,* or black storm, swept over
the waste.

"These are the first shovels of earth over my dead men on the sand
in there," thought I.

The outlines of the forest vanished, and the whole country was shrouded in a haze. After three hours' walk, I again suffered from thirst, and it occurred to me that days might elapse before I reached another watering-place. It was clearly unwise to have left the first pool, Khoda-verdi-kol.

I said to myself: "I'll go back to the pool and find Kasim."

After a half-hour's walk towards the north, I came right upon a very small pool, with bad water. I stopped there and drank. I suffered from hunger now, not having eaten in a week. I ate grass, reed-shoots, and leaves, and I even tried the tadpoles in the pool; but they tasted bitter and disgusting. It was now two o'clock in the afternoon.

"I'll leave Kasim," thought I, "and stay here till the storm passes."

Thereupon I went into the wood, sought and found a dense thicket, which sheltered me from the strong wind, arranged my boots and cap into a pillow, and slept soundly, and well, for the first time since the thirtieth of April.

I awoke at eight o'clock. It was dark. The storm roared and rushed above me, the dry branches groaning and creaking. I gathered fuel for the "camp," and made a fire. Then I drank again at the little pool, ate grass and leaves, and sat watching the play of the flames. If I had only had the company of our faithful Yoldash! I whistled, but the storm drowned every sound, and Yoldash never returned.

When I awoke at dawn, on May 7, the storm was over, but the air was still full of fine dust. I was alarmed at the thought that the nearest shepherds might be several days distant, and that I could not survive long without food. It must be a hundred and fifty miles to Khotan. With my reduced strength, I would need at least six days to cover that distance.

I started as early as half-past four, and made towards the south, walking right in the middle of the river-bed. To be on the safe side, I half filled my boots with water, and carried them suspended from the spade-handle, like a yoke, on my shoulders. After a while, I approached the left bank, where I saw an abandoned sheep-pen and a well. At noon, the heat was unbearable. I walked into the forest and lunched on grass, leaves, and reed-shoots. Twilight took me by surprise. I made a fire, and spent the night there.

On the eighth of May, I set out before the sun was up, and walked nearly the whole day. Before nightfall I made a startling discovery on the shore of a little island. In the hard-packed sand of the river-bed, there appeared quite fresh prints of two barefoot men, driving four mules northwards! Why had I not met them? Very likely they had passed me during the night, while I was asleep. Now they were far ahead, and it would be useless to turn back and try to overtake them.

I thought I heard an unusual sound from a jutting tongue of land, so I stopped short and listened. But the forest was dead-silent; so, concluding that it must have been some bird's call, I went on.

But no! After a minute, I heard a human voice and a mooing cow! It was no illusion. There were shepherds!

I emptied the water out of my boots, put them on, wet as they were, and hurried into the forest, breaking through thickets and jumping over fallen trees. Presently I heard the bleating of sheep. A herd was grazing in a glen. The shepherd stood as if petrified, when I burst forth from the jungle.

At my greeting, "Salam aleikum!" (Peace be with you), he turned on his heels and disappeared among the trees.

He soon returned with an older shepherd. They stopped at a safe distance. I then told them in a few words what had happened.

"I am a European," I said. "I entered the desert from the Yarkand-daria. My men and camels died of thirst, and I have lost everything. For ten days I have had nothing to eat. Give me a piece of bread and a bowl of milk, and let me rest near you; for I am tired to death. In time I shall be able to pay you for your help."

They looked at me with suspicion, evidently thinking that I was lying. But after some hesitation, they asked me to come along; and I accompanied them to their hut. It stood in the shade, at the foot of a poplar, and consisted of only four slender poles, supporting a roof of twigs and brush. A worn felt rug lay on the ground, and I dropped down on it. The younger shepherd brought out a wooden vessel, and offered me a piece of maize-bread. I thanked him, broke a piece off, and at once felt as if I were stuffed. Then he gave me a wooden bowl, filled with the most delicious sheep's-milk.

Without a word, the shepherds rose and disappeared. But their two big half-wild dogs stayed and barked incessantly.

At nightfall they returned with a third shepherd. They had just taken the sheep to the pen near by. Now they made a big fire in front of the hut; and when it had burned itself out, all four of us went to sleep.

The shepherds were named Yusup Baï, Togda Baï, and Pasi Ahun. They tended a hundred and seventy sheep and goats, and seventy cows, which belonged to a merchant in Khotan.

At daybreak, on May 9, I found a bowl of milk and a piece of bread beside me; but the shepherds were gone. I ate my breakfast with Lucullian appetite, and then went to inspect my immediate surroundings. The hut lay on a sandy height, from which one could view the dry bed of the Khotan-daria, near the bank of which the shepherds had their well.

Their clothes were worn and ragged. Their feet were covered with plain pieces of sheepskin, laced together; and in their waist-belts they carried their supply of tea. Their household-utensils, consisting of two crude wooden vessels, lay on the roof of the hut, together with the corn-supply and a primitive guitar with three strings. They had also axes for cutting their way through the forest, and a fire-steel, for which there was little use, as they had only to blow the glowing coals, underneath the ashes, into life again.

A very strange thing happened that afternoon. The shepherds were in the woods with the sheep. I sat looking out over the river-bed, and saw a caravan of a hundred mules, laden with bags, going from south to north, from Khotan to Aksu. Should I hurry down to the leader? No. That would have been of no use, as I did not have even a copper in my pocket! I would certainly have to stay with my shepherds as a hanger-on, get thoroughly rested at their place for a couple of days, and then walk to Khotan. I lay down to sleep under the brushwood roof.

Awakened suddenly by voices and the clattering of horses, I sat up, and saw three merchants, in white turbans, ride up to the hut, dismount, and approach me, bowing humbly. Two of my shepherd friends had shown them the way, and were now holding their horses.

Seating themselves on the sand, they told of having ridden in the river-bed the day before, on their way from Aksu to Khotan, brushing past the wooded terrace on the left shore, when they saw a man, apparently dead, lying at the foot of the terrace. A white camel was grazing among the trees.

Like the Good Samaritan, they had stopped to ask what ailed him.

He had whispered, "Su, su" (Water, water). They sent their servant with a jug to the nearest pool, probably the same one that had saved my life. Afterwards they gave the man bread and nuts.

I realized at once that it was Islam Baï. He had told them the story of our journey, and had asked them to look for me, although he really believed I was dead. Yusup, the chief of the merchants, offered me one of his horses, and asked me to accompany them to Khotan, to seek rest and quiet.

But I did not want that at all! Their news instantly changed my situation, which had been so gloomy a moment before. Perhaps we might be able to go back to the death-camp and find out if the men we left there were still alive. Maybe we could save the baggage, and equip a new caravan. Perhaps my money could be found. The future seemed bright once more.

The three merchants said good-bye, and continued their journey, after lending me eighteen small silver coins, worth two dollars, and giving me a bag of white bread.

The shepherds were abashed when they realized that I had told them the truth.

On the tenth of May, I slept all day. I felt like a convalescent after a long illness. At sunset I heard a camel roar, and went out. There was one of the shepherds leading the white camel, with Islam and Kasim staggering behind them!

Islam threw himself at my feet, weeping. He had thought we would never meet again.

When we were seated around the fire, supplied with milk and bread, Islam related his adventures. After a few hours of rest, during the night of May 1, he and the last four camels had recovered sufficiently to follow our track in the sand. On May 3, at night, he had seen our fire, and had been greatly encouraged thereby. On reaching the three poplars, he bruised one of the trunks, and sucked the sap. As two of the camels were dying, he unburdened them at the poplars. On May 5, Yoldash, our dog, died of thirst. Two days later, the two dying camels collapsed. One of them had been carrying all of our hypsometrical instruments and many other things of importance. One of the last two camels broke loose, and went to graze in the wood; while Islam continued, with "White," to the river, which he reached on the morning of May 8. Finding the river-bed dry, he despaired, and lay down to die.

Yusup and the other two merchants rode by a few hours later, and gave him water. Later on, they discovered Kasim, too; and now they were here.

In the white camel's pack we found my diaries and maps, the Chinese silver, two rifles, and a small supply of tobacco. Thus, at a single stroke, I became quite rich again. But all the instruments for measuring heights, and many other indispensable articles, were lost.

We bought a sheep from Pasi Ahun, and that evening, beside the fire, we lived high. My pulse was now up to sixty, and it rose slowly to normal during the next few days.

The following day, the shepherds moved their camp to a better pasture. Here Islam and Kasim built a nice bower for me between two poplars. My bed consisted of the torn felt mat, and my pillow of the bag in which I kept the Chinese silver. The white camel grazed in the forest. He was the only one left of our fine string. Three times a day we got milk and bread from the shepherds. We had nothing to complain of; but my thoughts sometimes ran to Robinson Crusoe.

AHMED MERGEN, THE HUNTER

On the twelfth of May, we saw a caravan from Aksu, going south, in the river-bed. Its owners, four merchants, accompanied it. Islam brought them to the bower; and our situation was again improved by the trading which then took place. We bought three horses, for 750 tenge (1 tenge = 10 cents); also three pack-saddles, one riding-saddle, bits, a bag of maize, a bag of wheat-flour, tea, jugs, bowls, and a pair of boots for Islam, who had lost his in the desert. We were once more free to move, and could go wherever we wished.

Two young deer-hunters visited us. They hunted the deer for the sake of their horns, which the Chinese use for medicinal purposes. They presented me with a fresh-slain deer. The next day, Ahmed Mergen, their father, also came to our camp; and it was arranged that Islam, Kasim, and the three hunters should try to find the camel that bore the instruments, recover the things that had been left at the poplars, and, if possible, make their way to the death-camp.

They departed with the white camel and the three horses; and again I was alone with the shepherds.

The period that followed was trying to my patience. I recorded my recent adventures in the recovered diaries; and the rest of the time I lay in the bower and read. Only one book had been rescued from the caravan-wreck; but it was a book that one can begin all over again, when one has read it to the end, namely, the Bible. The shepherds, who were now my friends, were solicitous for my welfare. The heat was tropical. But I was well shaded; and the wind coursed kindly through the poplars. One day, some passing merchants sold me a big bag of raisins. Another time, my dreams were disturbed by a large yellow scorpion, crawling over my felt mat. My dreams were of Tibet. As soon as Islam and the others returned with the lost instruments, we would go there, by way of Khotan. My strength returned. It was a delightful period of rest and solitude in the forest.

The rescuing-expedition returned on the twenty-first of May. The goods that Islam had left at the three poplars were found. The corpses of the dead camels were emitting an unendurable stench. But "One-Hump," the camel that had carried the boiling-point thermometer, the three aneroids, a Swedish army-revolver, etc., was gone forever.

It was out of the question to go to Tibet without instruments for measuring altitudes. A new outfit would have to be procured from Europe; and so I had to return to Kashgar. We took leave of the shepherds, after compensating them royally for their services. Thereupon we rode to Aksu, which is two hundred and seventy miles from Kashgar. We arrived there on June 21, and thence I sent a mounted messenger to the nearest telegraph-station on the Russian border. The new outfit could not get to Kashgar in less than three or four months. How was I to use this long time of waiting? For another expedition to the Pamirs, of course. Consul Petrovsky and Mr. Macartney lent me the necessary instruments.

One day, I was invited to dine with Dao Tai. As I entered his *yamen*, he pointed to a revolver on the table, and inquired: "Do you recognize that?"

It was my Swedish army-revolver, which had been packed with the hypsometrical instruments!

Amazed, I asked him:

"Where does that come from?"

"It was found on a peasant, in the village of Tavek-kel, on the Khotan-daria, below Khotan."

"But where are the other things that were borne by the same camel?"

"They have not been found. But a careful search is being made all along the Khotan-daria. You need not worry."

Thieves and traitors were evidently involved in this. What satisfaction could these simple people derive from scientific instruments, which meant nothing to them, but everything to me! I would have given ten camels to get them back.

The revolver and its discovery are another story; but that must be left for a later chapter.

Fate was now taking me back to the Pamirs.

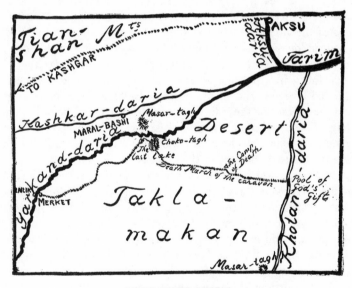

MARCH OF THE CARAVAN

CHAPTER XXIII

Second Expedition to the Pamirs

MY faithful servant, Kasim, having been appointed watchman at the Russian Consulate, I took Islam Baï, two other men, and six horses, and left Kashgar on July 10, 1895.

The following day, we arrived at Upal, a large village, situated in a deep ravine worn out of the soft soil. In the afternoon, a heavy rain came down, the like of which I have never again seen. An hour before sunset, we heard a furious roar, hollow and mighty, which gradually came nearer. In a few minutes, the river-bed was turned into a raging torrent, which soon overflowed the banks, flooding large sections of the village. Great volumes of water hurled themselves past, with tremendous violence, forming a boiling, seething mud-flood, which carried everything before it. The ground trembled under the weight. The whirling spray lay like a mist on the brown waves. The bridge was carried away, as though its posts and planks were made of straw; and, on the surface of the water, uprooted trees, carts, household-goods, and haycocks tossed about in a wild dance. The awe-struck villagers ran about, shrieking, as the water washed away their frail clay houses. Mothers, with their babies on their backs, were fleeing through water that rose to their waists; while others attempted to save their furniture from huts and hovels already invaded by the water. Willow and poplar alleys were bent down; and at one exposed point, fifteen houses were washed away. From a melon-field which was menaced, the melons, nearly ripe, were hurriedly carried to safety. And as for myself, it was only by a hair's-breadth that this caravan, too, was not destroyed. Fortunately, our quarters were sufficiently far from the bank. At twilight, the water receded quickly; and the following morning, the river-bed was again empty.

We were now about to climb the mountain-range again, and we chose the pass of Ullug-art, which is 16,900 feet high, and closed by snow for ten months of the year.

We rested at the *aul,* or tent-village, of Ullug-art, in whirling snow;

and the Kirghiz thought we would have a difficult journey. But their chief undertook, with the assistance of ten men, to carry all our baggage across the most difficult ridge of the pass, for a remuneration equivalent to eight dollars.

We departed, early, through the narrow valley; and, by making hundreds of zigzag bends, we ascended the extremely steep slope. Enormous, steep mountains rose on both sides; and tongues of glaciers were in evidence here and there. The snow was about a foot deep. The loads were fastened to the backs of the Kirghiz; and slowly and heavily we began the climb to the entrance to the pass. At the very saddle of the pass, stood a pile of stones, with staves and rags. The Kirghiz prostrated themselves before it.

If the ascent was difficult, the descent was quite neck-breaking. The snow-covered path was like a cork-screw; and, in places, it dropped perpendicularly between the jutting rocks. We hewed ridges in the ice-surface; and little by

A KIRGHIZ MOTHER WITH HER CHILD

little, hauled the boxes down with ropes. Each horse was assisted by two men; but one of those that I had bought at the shepherds' camp on the Khotan-daria, lost his footing, tumbled down the steeps, and was killed. We ourselves slid down on all-fours.

We proceeded southward through familiar territory, and up the Hunserab River, to the Hindu-kush, where I crossed four high passes, from which—with my eyes, at least—I could command Kanjut. I had asked the British authorities for permission to go there, but was told: "This road is closed to travellers."

We continued to the pass of Vakjir, where the water flows in three different directions: through the Panj River, to the Amu-daria and the Aral Sea; through the Taghdumbash-daria, to the Yarkand-daria and Lake Lop-nor; and through the rivers beginning on the southern side of the pass, to the Indus and the Indian Ocean.

At Chakmakden-kul, I learned that the Anglo-Russian Boundary

Commission was in the region of Mehman-yoli, a day's journey toward the northeast. The commissioners were determining the boundary between the Russian dominions in the north and those of the English in the south, from Victoria Lake to the Chinese Pamirs.

I decided to visit the Commission's camp. So I sent a Kirghiz, with letters to the English general, Gerard, and to the Russian general, Pavalo-Shweikowsky; and, after a day, I received cordial invitations from both of them.

On August 19, I rode there with my small caravan, intending to pitch my tent on neutral ground between the two camps. As a guest of the two generals, I had to observe strict neutrality. But I thought I ought to visit Pavalo-Shweikowsky first, having been his guest in Margelan. To reach his large Kirghiz *yurt,* however, I had to pass between the English officers' tents. My old friend, Mr. Macartney, came running out of one of them, bringing a dinner-invitation from General Gerard for that evening. So there I stood, between two fires, wondering how my neutrality was to be maintained. I took refuge in my acquaintance with the Russian general, and asked to be permitted to visit Gerard the next day. During my stay at the camp, I visited the Russians and the English on alternate days.

It was certainly the most picturesque camp ever pitched among the desolate ranges of the Pamirs. From the snow-covered crests, wild sheep looked down on the motley, humdrum life of the valley, quite unconcerned about political boundaries. The English had sixty Indian army-officers' tents; while the Russians had a dozen large Kirghiz felt *yurts,* certain conspicuous ones being covered with white blankets and gaily-coloured ribbons. The place teemed with Cossacks, Gurkhas, Afridis, Hindus, and Kanjutis; and, at mealtime, bands of music played English and Russian compositions.

There were many distinguished personages among the English. First there was the chief, General Gerard, the most daring tiger-hunter in India, who, with his own hand, had shot two hundred and sixteen tigers, thus breaking all records. Then there was the splendid Colonel, Sir Thomas Holdich, one of the greatest authorities of our day on the geography of Asia; and, finally, Captain McSwiney, whose friendship I shall never forget. I met him again, years later, shortly before his death, when he was Brigadier-General at Umballa, India. Among the Russians, not the least conspicuous was the topographer, Bendersky, who was one of the embassy which visited Shir Ali Khan, Emir of Afghanistan, at Kabul. Abdurrahman Khan, the then Emir, also had a representative on the Boundary Commission. He was Gulam Moheddin Khan, a silent, dignified, fine old Afghan.

As for me, after my wandering through the desert, it was like a resurrection to take part in all the festivities and parties at Mehmanyoli. And there was certainly no danger of dying of thirst at the hospitable officers' mess. When we assembled at the large casino of the Russians, Cossacks with lighted petrol-torches stood guard in front of the *yurts;* and when we were guests of the English, the lonely mountains echoed the strains of the band which played during our meals.

For the entertainment of the men, there were field-sports in front of the camp. There was a tug-of-war between eight Cossacks and eight Afridis, and the Cossacks won. The Cossacks were victorious, too, in a horse-race, beating the Indians by two minutes. But in lime-cutting, and tilting at the ring, the Indians had their revenge. One event, which made everybody, Europeans and Asiatics alike, choke with laughter, was a foot-race between different nationalities, the competitors running in sacks tied round their waists, and having to hop over a tape during their course. A race between camels and yaks was just as ludicrous. But the last event was the most exciting of all. Two bands of Kirghiz horsemen, twenty in each, took positions, face to face, at two hundred and fifty yards' distance. At a signal, they dashed off at full gallop, met half-way,

DOST MOHAMED KHAN, AN AFGHAN OFFICER BELONGING TO THE BRITISH GUARDS

and tumbled about in the greatest confusion. Many of them went headlong to the ground; others got bruises, and were dragged along on the ground; and only a few emerged from the encounter without injury.

Meanwhile, an agreement was reached as to the boundary-line. The pyramids were accordingly erected, and the Commission's work was done.   On the last evening, when the English gave a splendid farewell-banquet, the Indian soldiers performed their national sword-dances around a huge fire.   Then the guests scattered to the four winds; the region sank back into its accustomed quiet; and, after all had departed, the valley was swept by a blizzard.

I returned to Kashgar with my caravan.   We had to traverse four high ranges, but the greatest adventure was the crossing of the Yarkand-daria at the village of Tong.   The river was magnificent, in its narrow, pinched valley.   The enormous volume of water rolled down heavily and mightily between steep mountains.   Hassan Bek, the chief of the village, prepared to ferry us across.   Six naked Tajiks, of Iranian origin, with inflated goatskins tied to their chests, conveyed our baggage, in four separate trips, on a raft composed of a stretcher attached to a dozen inflated goatskins.   A horse was yoked to the raft, while a swimmer threw his arm around the horse's neck, and guided him across the river.   But during the trip, the current carried the raft a good mile down the river, and the problem was to get the raft to the opposite bank before it was ground to pieces in the eddies where the main rapids began.

I was seated on a box in the centre of the raft.   The strange contrivance was swept madly down the torrent; but to me it seemed as if the cliffs on the opposite bank were racing upstream.   The raft oscillated and careened; I became dazed and dizzy by the wild dance; the dull and menacing roar of the rapids increased in strength; and the raft was sucked, unresisting, toward the foaming witches' cauldron, where, the next moment, we might have been ground into atoms against the cliffs. But our swimmers were well-practised, and sure in their calculations. At the point of almost inescapable danger, they forced the raft into the counter-current, at the foot of a projecting cliff, and we reached the opposite bank safe and sound.

CHAPTER XXIV

I Discover 2000-Year-Old Cities in the Desert

FEVER kept me in Kashgar a long while. Meanwhile, the new equipment arrived from Europe; and on December 14, 1895, a small caravan was again ready to start. It included Islam, three other men, and nine horses. The distance to Khotan was three hundred and six miles. We knew that road from experience; and its difficulties were not going to hinder us this time. It ran by way of Yarkand, the largest city of East Turkestan, with a hundred and fifty thousand inhabitants, seventy-five per cent of whom were afflicted with a strange tumour, called *boghak,* affecting the throat, and often growing to the size of the head.

East of Kargalik, where I spent Christmas Eve, the country became more barren; yet the ancient caravan-road was always marked with *potai,* or flattened pyramids of clay. Some of our nights were spent in large caravansaries, where the drinking-water was obtained from deep wells. One of them was a hundred and twenty-six feet deep.

Kum-rabat-padshahim, or "My King's Serai in the Sand," was a point on the road where thousands of sacred pigeons filled the air with their cooing, and with the sound of wing-beats, when they flew. Every traveller must bring the pigeons an offering of maize; and we carried a whole bagful just for that purpose. Standing there, feeding the beautiful blue-grey birds, I became enveloped in a cloud of pigeons, which boldly settled down on my shoulders, cap, and arms. High poles, hung with rags, represented offerings, and served as scarecrows against birds of prey. But the pious folk on the spot assured me, that if a falcon were to capture a pigeon, the falcon itself would be sure to die.

On January 5, we arrived at Khotan, in ancient times called Kustana, in Sanskrit, known to the Chinese for thousands of years, and revealed to Europe by Marco Polo. Fa Hien (400 A.D.), the famous Chinese monk, describes Khotan as a magnificent city, where the cult of Buddha flourished.

A legend, dating from 632 A.D., tells of an ancient town, buried in the desert-sand. It was said that in the village of Pima, west of Khotan, there had then been an image of Buddha, in sandalwood, twenty feet high, which glowed with light. Before that, it had belonged to the town of Ho-lao-lo-kia, farther north. Once a sage came to Ho-lao-lo-kia, to worship at this image of Buddha. The inhabitants treated him harshly, seized him, and buried him up to his neck. A pious man brought food to him secretly, and eventually rescued him. Before hastening away, the sage said to his saviour: "Within seven days, Ho-lao-lo-kia shall be buried by sand from heaven, and thou alone shalt be saved." The pious man warned the people in the town; but they all laughed him to scorn. Then he took refuge in a cave. On the seventh day, there came a rain of sand, which buried the town, and suffocated every person in it. The pious man crept out of the cave and went to Pima. Hardly had he arrived, when the sacred image of Buddha came flying through the air, having chosen Pima as its sanctuary in place of the buried Ho-lao-lo-kia.

A Chinese traveller of the same period—the T'ang dynasty—writes of the desert regions north of Khotan: "There is neither water nor vegetation, but a hot wind often rises, which takes away the breath of man, horse, and beast, and not seldom is the cause of sickness. You hear almost always shrill whistlings, or loud shouts; and when you try to discover whence they come, you are terrified at finding nothing. It very often happens that men get lost, for that place is the abode of evil spirits. After four hundred li, you come to the ancient kingdom of Tu-ho-lo. It is a long time since that country was changed into a desert. All its towns lie in ruins and are overgrown with wild plants."

No wonder, then, that in spite of my unfortunate journey into the desert the preceding spring, I was again drawn irresistibly toward the mysterious country under the eternal sand! The inhabitants of the oasis of Khotan, which extends round the town of the same name, told me of buried towns; and two men offered to guide me to one of those cities for a liberal remuneration.

In Khotan, as also in the ancient village of Borasan, I bought antique relics from the natives: small objects in terra-cotta, representing two-humped camels; monkeys playing the guitar; griffins, on the Indian "Garuda" motif; lion-heads which had adorned jars of the Græco-Buddhistic or Indo-Hellenic school, and which betrayed the Greek influence after Alexander; beautifully-executed jars and bowls in terra-cotta; images of Buddha; and other things. My collection numbered 523 articles, not counting some ancient manuscripts and a mass of coins. I also purchased some Christian gold coins, a cross, and a medal with a representation of "St. Andrea Avelin" worshipping before a crucifix, and, on the reverse, St. Irene crowned with a nimbus. Marco Polo speaks of Nestorian and Jacobite sects, which, in 1275, had their own churches in Khotan.

Liu Darin, the city governor, was an elderly, amiable, and benevolent Chinese. He assisted me in all my enterprises and purchases, and did not object to my visiting an old river-bed, where nephrite was to be found. There the Chinese obtained the beautiful jade, which they esteem so highly. It appears in kidney-shaped pieces among the boulders. It is mostly green. Yellow jade, or white, with brown spots, is the most precious.

On January 14, I was again ready to leave. This time I travelled lighter than ever before, taking only four men, three camels, and two donkeys. The journey was to be only a quite short one, namely, to the sand-covered city of which I had heard. I therefore took only enough provisions for a few weeks, and left my heavy baggage, most of my money, my Chinese passport, the tent, etc., with a merchant in Khotan. I wanted to sleep under the open sky, the same as my men, though the temperature might sink to −6°.

Actually, four and a half months were to pass, before we returned to Khotan; and part of this expedition became a veritable Crusoe ro-mance. When I took leave of Liu Darin, he wanted to give me two camels, because he thought my caravan was much too small. But I refused his kind offer.

My four men were Islam Baï, Kerim Jan, and the two hunters—Ahmed Mergen and his son Kasim Ahun—who had taken part in the expedition of Islam Baï the year before, after our disaster in the desert. We also took along the two men who had promised to show us the ancient town.

We followed the Yurun-kash, the eastern head-stream of the Khotan-daria, to the village of Tavek-kel, where my Swedish army-revolver had been found. Our search for the rest of the outfit was fruitless. In fact, it was not conducted at all vigorously; for I had replaced everything that had been lost, except the cameras.

On January 19, we left the river, and again wormed our way into the deadly, sandy desert. But this time it was winter. Our water-supply, in four goatskins, froze into chunks of ice. At our camps, we found water by digging from five to seven feet; and if we had walked eastward, we would have been near the Keriya-daria, which runs north, parallel to the Khotan-daria.

The dunes in this part of the desert were not as high as those in the region where our caravan had been lost the year before. Their ridges were thirty-five to forty feet high.

On the fourth day, we camped in a hollow, where a dead, dried-up forest provided us with excellent fuel. The next day we went to the ruins of the ancient city, which our guides called Takla-makan, or Dandan-uilik, the "Ivory Houses." Most of the houses were buried in the sand. But here and there, posts and wooden walls stuck out of the dunes; and on one of the walls, which was possibly three feet high, we discovered several figures, artistically executed in plaster. They repre-sented Buddha and Buddhistic deities, some standing, some seated on lotus-leaves, all robed in ample draperies, their heads encircled by flaming aureoles. All these finds, and many other relics, were wrapped up carefully, and packed in my boxes; and the fullest possible notes on the ancient city, its location, sand-covered canals, dead-poplar avenues, and dried-up apricot-orchards were entered in my diary. I was not equipped to make a thorough excavation; and, besides, I was not an archæologist. The scientific research I willingly left to the specialists. In a few years, they too would be sinking their spades into the loose sand. For me it was sufficient to have made the important discovery, and to have won, in the heart of the desert, a new field for archæology. And now, at last, I felt rewarded and encouraged, after the preceding year's vain search for traces of a dead civilization. The ancient Chi-nese geographers, as well as the present-day natives living on the edge of the desert, were now vindicated. My rejoicing over this first find, which was to be followed by similar discoveries in later years, is evident from notes made at the time.

"No explorer," I wrote, "had an inkling, hitherto, of the existence of this ancient city. Here I stand, like the prince in the enchanted wood, having wakened to new life the city which has slumbered for a thousand years."

During several successive sandstorms, I measured the rate at which

sand-dunes move; and, guided by that, and by the course of the prevailing winds, I calculated that it had taken about two thousand years
for the sand-desert to extend from the region of the ancient city to its
present southern border. Discoveries made at a later date warrant the
conclusion that the age of the ancient city was about two thousand years.

On receiving their well-earned pay, the two guides returned over our
trail. The following morning, we continued on our way through the
eternal sand.

The air was laden with the finest dust. In the dense haze, we had
not even an idea of where the sun was in the sky. The dunes grew in
height. We climbed the crest of a sand-wave one hundred and twenty
feet high, wondering whether we were headed toward another such
murderous labyrinth as that of the year before. Because of the haze,
we could discern nothing in the east. It was as though a curtain had
been drawn in front of us, and as if we were walking towards an unknown abyss. Yet we went on, and nothing untoward happened. The
dunes became lower and lower, gradually merging into level, soft, sandy
ground. One evening, we camped in the forest, on the banks of the
Keriya-daria. The river was a hundred and five feet wide here, and
covered with thick ice. The camels got liberal rations of grass, and
drank their fill, after the desert-journey. No human beings were in
sight. There was only a deserted shepherd's hut. We built a big log-
fire, and kept it burning through the night. The winter cold did us no
harm. Sleeping in the open brought nothing but satisfaction.

No European had ever followed the course of this river to its end
in the desert-sand, and nobody knew where the last drops of water disappeared after their hopeless struggle with the dunes. I decided, therefore, to follow the river northwards to its very end. It served us as
a guide, and thus we were independent of men. Not a shepherd was
to be seen; and we had killed our last sheep. But there were lots of
hares, roe-deer, and red deer, so we had no fear of hunger. On the
banks, we would occasionally disturb whole families of boars, which
fled noisily into the dense growths of reed. Sometimes we also surprised a fox, who would dart subtly and speedily into the forest-glen.

Ahmed Mergen, the elder deer-hunter, once made an excursion into
the woods, and returned with a shepherd. The shepherd told us he
had thought we were robbers and that his last hour had come. We

camped beside his reed hut.   All the information which he and his wife
could give me, was duly set down in my diary.

"What is your name?" I asked.

"Hassan and Hussein," he replied.

"How's that?   Have you two names?"

"Yes.   But Hassan is really the name of my twin brother, who lives
in Keriya."

On our way northward, through the river-forests, we met shepherds
constantly.   In order to get information about the various forest regions, and their names, we always took one or two shepherds with us.
In this way we got farther north, day by day.   The frozen river extended much farther into the desert than we thought.   I measured its
width, across the ice, and found it to exceed three hundred feet.   Further down, where the Keriya-daria became wider, it frequently appeared
majestic, between its wooded banks.   Every morning brought new
excitement.   How far would we be able to go before the river merged
into the surrounding sand, which, in some places, extended to the very
brink?   Finally, I hatched the hazardous plan of crossing the desert as
far as to the Tarim River, which must be its northern frontier, if the
river flowed far enough.

Near Tonkuz-basste (the Hanging Wild Boar), a shepherd told me
that by striking out into the sand to the northwest, we would soon find
the ruins of an ancient town, named Kara-dung (the Black Hill).

February 2 and 3 were devoted to it.   Here, too, we found houses
buried in the sand, the largest of them measuring 280 by 250 feet, and
many traces of other structures made by human hands, dating from the
period when Buddha's teachings prevailed in the far interior of Asia.
The site of this town, too, was carefully determined, so that archæolo-
gists would be sure to find it later on.

Thereupon we continued our journey, through forests and fields of
reed.   The river showed a tendency to divide into a number of branches,
and to form inland deltas.   On February 5, we encountered four shepherds, in charge of eight hundred sheep and six cows.   Two days later,
Mohammed Baï, an old denizen of the forest, told us that the point
where the river died out in the sand was only another day and a half's
journey distant.   He lived in such seclusion, that he did not know
whether Yakub Bek (died 1878) or the Emperor of China ruled over
East Turkestan.   He also told me that no tiger had been seen in the

last three years. The last one had clawed one of Mohammed Baï's cows, after which it went northward, but only to return.   Finally it struck out across the desert toward the east.

"How far does the desert reach to the north, from the point where the river ends?" I asked. And Mohammed Baï replied:

"To the end of the world.   And it takes three months to get there."

CHAPTER XXV

The Wild Camels' Paradise

ON February 8, we camped at a point where the river was hardly fifty feet wide; and at our next camping-place, the ice-crust had narrowed to fifteen feet. The forest was still luxuriant, and the reed-fields so impenetrable, that we had either to make detours or use the axes to blaze a path. Parts of boar-trails formed veritable tunnels through tangled growths of reeds.

I shall never forget the thrill with which I saw the thin crust of ice end, like the point of an arrow, at the base of a dune!

But for one more day we walked through real jungle, and the river-bed was plainly visible. In its deepest hollows, we dug for water, and with success. On all sides rose the yellow crests of dunes.

As far back as February 1, we had heard the shepherds tell of the wild camel, whose habitat was in the sand below the delta of the river. With rising excitement I longed to see this wonderful animal, whose existence in this part of the large desert no European had hitherto suspected. Przhevalsky, who brought the skin of a wild camel home to St. Petersburg, in 1877, assures us that the royal animal is to be found only far to the east of where we then were, in the Lop-nor Desert. In that region, General Pievtsoff, his officers, and Mr. Littledale had succeeded in shooting a few specimens, which they likewise took home. According to the shepherds, the wild camel travels in small herds. They avoid the forests and undergrowth, and roam in the open. They never drink water in the winter, but only in the summer, when high water reaches further north. They are frequently the victims of deer-hunters. The truth of these statements was confirmed by several things, as, for example, the fact that several shepherds wore shoes made of wild-camel skin, taken from the feet;—horny nails, pads, and all.

One of the shepherds told us that God had sent a spirit to the earth in the form of a dervish, and had bidden him go to Hazret Ibrahim (the Patriarch Abraham) to ask him for a flock of domestic animals.

Abraham complied with the dervish's request so generously, that he impoverished himself.   Then God ordered the dervish to return all the animals to Abraham.   But Abraham refused to take back what he had once given.   Then God's anger was aroused, and He commanded the animals to wander about homeless on the earth.   Any man, who so wished, might kill them.   The sheep became wild sheep, the goats wild goats, the yaks wild yaks, the horses wild horses, and the camels also ran wild.

Old Mohammed Baï, whose gun was impotent at a range greater than one hundred and fifty feet, had shot three wild camels that year. He told us that they were in the greatest terror of smoke from camp-fires, and that no sooner did they scent burning wood than they fled into the desert.

I am not a hunter myself; and I never was.   This is not because of the first commandment of Buddha, not to destroy life.   But I have always been unable to bring myself to extinguish a flame that I could not light again.   Least of all could I kill such a noble animal as the wild camel.   He was master in his desert land, whereas I was a mere intruder.   On the other hand, I have always taken hunters along with me, deeming it necessary, not only for the sake of provisions, but also for the sake of scientific collections.   Islam Baï handled the Berdan rifle skilfully; and Ahmed Mergen and his son Kasim were professional huntsmen.   None of my four servants had ever seen a wild camel; and it had long been a dream of mine to see the stately animal move majestically over the sand.

With ever-growing tension, we marched north, on February 11, between dunes of increasing height, seeing the river-bed becoming less and less distinct.   Only now and again we sighted a solitary poplar, but more often dead, withered tree-trunks, brittle as glass.   It was a hundred and fifty miles of sand-desert, as the crow flies, to the Tarim River, a distance greater than that covered by the caravan which was destroyed between April 23 and May 5, the year before.   And now we could take no more water than four goatskins would hold!   It was a bold venture. But the winter cold was to our advantage.   Would we succeed?   Or was there a new disaster awaiting us?   Is it any wonder that we watched the dunes grow, and the vegetation vanish, with breathless tension?

On February 9, we saw the first signs of wild camels—a tuft of light reddish-brown hair stuck on a tamarisk bush.   But on the next day, we came across many fresh tracks, crossing the sand in various directions. On the eleventh, we kept a sharp lookout. Kasim, the hunter, went ahead, shouldering his primitive flint-lock.

Suddenly he stopped, as though struck by lightning. He motioned for us to stop, crouched down, and crept among the bushes like a panther. I hurried forward. A shot rang out. It was a small herd. The animals started, gazing in our direction. Then they turned right around, and fled. But their leader, a twelve-year-old male, took only a few steps, and fell.

We camped on the spot. The fallen desert-king was a beautiful specimen. He measured ten feet, ten inches, in length, and seven feet in girth. The rest of the day we devoted to skinning him, and covering the inside of the skin with heated sand, to make the burden lighter.

THE FIRST WILD CAMELS WE CAME ACROSS

We dug a well, in a depression; but even at the depth of ten and a half feet it yielded no water. We therefore resolved to stay where we were for one day longer, and not advance so far into the desert as to jeopardize our return.

The well was made deeper; and at a little more than thirteen and a half feet, water began to trickle. It was gradually transferred to a bucket, and hauled up. The camels and donkeys were allowed to drink their fill. Then the four goatskins were filled.

The following day, we proceeded into the unknown desert. One of the donkeys carried the skin of the wild camel. The river-bed was still visible; but toward evening, it disappeared under the moving dunes, which were now twenty-five feet high.

On our left, we saw a herd of six camels—one old male, two young ones, and three females. The old male was shot by Islam Baï. The fat in his humps, as also some pieces of flesh, were removed, and the hair was cut off, to be made into twine and rope. Before I could prevent it, Islam had shot a she-camel, in a second herd of five animals. She sank into the posture in which camels usually rest. We hurried to her, and I made a few sketches, while she was still alive. She did not look at us, but seemed to be in despair at having to part forever with her otherwise inviolate desert land. Before she died, she opened her mouth, and bit into the sand. I now forbade any more shooting.

I was surprised to find the wild camels so little on their guard. When the wind was against us, we were able to get within two hundred feet of them. They would gaze in our direction; and, if they lay ruminating, they would rise. The last-mentioned herd ran about fifty steps, repeated this twice, stopped, and looked attentively at us, and seemed so preoccupied by their curiosity, that its members forgot to flee. The hunters had therefore no difficulty in getting within range.

Our three tame camels got quite frantic when they saw their wild relatives. It was their rutting-season. They roared dully, lashed their backs with their tails, and ground their teeth, the foam dropping in white flakes from their mouths. When they saw the dying she-camel, they were quite beside themselves, and had to be tethered. They rolled their eyes, and bellowed horribly with passion. At night, they were always tethered, else they would have run away to their free kindred in the desert.

During the next days, we sighted several herds, as well as single camels; and finally we became so used to the beasts, that they ceased to arouse any particular attention. But I, for my part, never tired of following their movements with my field-glasses. I enjoyed a commanding view from my tall riding-camel; and I saw them move along with ease across the sand, now ambling, now at a gallop. Their humps were smaller and firmer than those of the tame ones, whose humps are pressed down by pack-saddles and burdens.

Every step took us deeper into the great, unknown desert, and further away from the last delta-arms of the Keriya-daria. As late as February 14, we could still see traces of the old river-bed. Luck was with us. Every evening, we succeeded in obtaining water at a depth of five or six feet. The next day, the dunes rose to more than one hundred feet, and there was much dead forest. One day more, and we were surprised to find an oasis, of seventy vigorous poplars, in a hollow. We saw the track of a panther; and dry camel-droppings were plentiful. The cold was bitter, but we did not lack fuel. We always encamped not far from dead tree-trunks. I lay on my stomach, on the sand, writing up my diary, by the light of the camp-fire; while my men prepared the evening meal, looked after the animals, dug a well, or collected fuel. I was monarch of all I surveyed! Never before had a white man set foot on this part of the earth's surface. I was the first one. Every step was a new conquest for human knowledge.

On February 17, the goatskins were empty; but we found water at six feet. It trickled so slowly, that we secured only enough for the men and to fill one skin. The next day, the dunes rose to a hundred and thirty feet, and only high, barren sand was visible to the north. The men now became depressed. We used up the water in the last goatskin, and in the evening all our digging was in vain. The hay from a pack-saddle was given to the camels to eat. The trail of a fox, which went north, inspired us with the hope that the Tarim forests might not be far away.

When we broke camp, on February 19, without a drop of water, we resolved that if we found no water in the evening, we would return to the place of our last supply.

Thus we walked on. Camel-tracks were again numerous. The dunes grew lower; and, in the hollows between them, we often found wind-driven leaves from forest-trees. We halted at a field of reeds, for the sake of the camels. We found water at five feet, but it was so salty, that even the thirsty camels refused to drink it.

In spite of this, we decided to continue northward. We had not gone far, when the dunes dwindled to an insignificant height. From the crest of one of the last of them, we saw the dark line of the forests of the Tarim in the distance. In what was once an arm of the river, we came upon a frozen pool, where we should have camped. But we thought the river was so near, we might as well walk on. And on we went, through patches of reeds and forests. One hour after another passed. Evening surrounded us with its twilight; and at nightfall we were literally stuck fast in an impenetrable thicket. Here we spent a second night without water.

At daybreak, we broke through the thicket, and again found a frozen pool, where we camped, and where man and beast drank without stint. The following day we crossed the ice-lid of the Tarim, five hundred and twenty feet wide. I released Ahmed Mergen and his son Kasim, and they returned to Khotan. In addition to their remuneration in money, I gave them the donkeys. They took with them, to Khotan, the wild-camel hide.

By the time we reached the small town of Shah-yar, forty-one days had passed. We had crossed the huge desert, had mapped all the hitherto unknown lower part of a river, discovered two ancient cities, and the hardly-accessible paradise of the wild camel.

Not wishing to return to Khotan, my headquarters, along roads that I knew already, I decided to take the long, roundabout route, across the Lop-nor, in the east, and then ride back to Khotan along the southern road, once traversed by Marco Polo. It was a route of some twelve hundred miles. Our provisions were used up; but we could live on the same food as the natives. I had not brought any maps of the eastern regions; but I was prepared to make new ones myself. I had left my Chinese passport in Khotan, but we might possibly manage without it. My diaries and sketch-books were full, so I bought Chinese paper in Shah-yar. My supply of tobacco had gone up in smoke, so I would have to content myself with a Chinese water-pipe and the sour, native tobacco.

Temir Bek, the chieftain of Shah-yar, asked to see my Chinese passport. As it was impossible for me to show it, he declared that the road to the east was closed to us. But we outwitted him, and escaped surreptitiously into the thickets of the Tarim, leaving no trace.

CHAPTER XXVI

Retreating Twelve Hundred Miles

AS space in this book is limited, I must make the long journey to Khotan at breakneck speed; and I am the more willing to do so, because of the opportunity a later chapter will afford me of returning to the most interesting part of it, the Lop Desert and the moving lake of Lop-nor.

For two weeks we travelled through the forests along the banks of the Tarim, always with shepherds to guide us. I derived special pleasure from the wild geese, which had begun to flit at that season. They were seen daily, in flocks of from thirty to fifty, flying east. As long as the sun was up, they rose high above the earth; but after dark, they flew low. At night we could hear their gabbling conversation, on the invisible roads of the air. It was evident that they were all flying along exactly the same route.

On March 10, we were in the little town of Korla, and were received hospitably by Kul Mohammed, of Margelan, the *aksakal,* or "white-beard," of the merchants from West Turkestan. He rode with me to the town of Kara-shahr—a profitable excursion, from the scientific point of view—where I risked calling on Hven Darin, the Chinese governor. I entered his *yamen,* and told him frankly that I had no passport.

"A passport!" exclaimed this courteous gentleman, with a pleasant smile. "You do not need any passport. You are our friend and guest. You are your own passport."

And he added to his kindness by providing me with a document that facilitated our way everywhere in his own province.

When I returned to Korla, Islam Baï told me, with a lump in his throat, that he had had an unpleasant experience during my absence. One day, he was sitting quite peacefully in the bazaar, talking to a West Turkestan merchant, when a Chinese chieftain, with four soldiers, rode by. They carried a pole with an emblem of the power of the

Emperor. Everybody had to rise, as a mark of respect to this symbol. But Islam, being a Russian subject, sat still. Thereupon the Chinese soldiers halted, seized him, bared his neck, and flogged him till the blood flowed.

The insulted man foamed with rage against his tormentors, and demanded revenge and satisfaction. I wrote to Li Daloi, the commander, asking where it was written that Chinese soldiers could beat

THE CITY GATE OF KARA-SHAHR

Russian subjects, and making an imperative demand that the culprit be punished. Li Daloi came to me instantly, begged pardon, and regretted that the guilty persons could not be identified. I then demanded that the entire *lansa* (troop) should be paraded, and Islam took it upon himself to point out the guilty man.

"There he is," cried Islam, as the perpetrator of the outrage passed. Now it was this poor sinner's turn to get a thrashing. And so, justice having been appeased, Islam declared himself satisfied; and Li Daloi marched off with his *lansa*.

We bought a little flame-coloured puppy at Korla, an Asiatic savage, who inherited Yoldash's name, and soon became everyone's favourite. When I left Korla, at the end of March, accompanied by Islam, Kerim Jan, two natives who knew the road well, and our three camels and four horses, following the left bank of the Konche-daria, the largest tributary of the lower Tarim, going southeast, Yoldash was still too young to go with us on his own legs. Ensconced in a basket, on top of one of the camels, he became terribly seasick from the constant swaying to and fro. In time, he grew, developed, and became my best friend.

He went with me through Tibet and China, to Peking, through Mongolia and Siberia, to St. Petersburg, and would have made his entry into Stockholm, too, had I not heard that it was impossible for me to bring him in, because of rabies in Russia. I therefore boarded him with Professor Backlund, a fellow countryman of mine, who was Director of the Pulkova Observatory, and intended to fetch him when the quarantine had been removed. But Yoldash was an Asiatic savage, and remained one, being used to defend our caravan against all sorts of more or less imaginary enemies; and he was totally devoid of the polish of civilization necessary for a respectable house in Pulkova. To start with, he bit to death every cat he could get hold of, within a radius of half a mile; and later on, he became too expensive a luxury, because of his taste for tearing the trousers of visitors to the observatory. And when, finally, he bit an old woman in the leg, Backlund considered it the part of wisdom to board him with a peasant, at an appreciable distance from Pulkova. Thus I lost track of my faithful travelling-companion, and I am still in the dark as to the end of this hero's tale.—But at this point of my story, he was in the bloom of youth, on his first voyage, and lay whining in his rocking basket on a camel's back, on the bank of the Konche-daria.

Our goal was the inland delta of the Tarim, and the Lop-nor. Marco Polo was the first European to write about the Lop Desert, and the large city of the same name. The famous Venetian merchant did not know the lake of Lop-nor. But the Chinese had known of its existence, and its geographical location, for several hundred years; and they had indicated the lake on maps at various periods. The first European to penetrate to its shores was the great Russian general, Przhevalsky, during his journey of 1876-77. He found the lake a full degree farther to the south than the Lop-nor of the Chinese maps. This caused Baron von Richthofen, the famous explorer of China, to advance the theory that, because of changes in the Tarim delta in subsequent years, the lake had moved one degree to the south.

Four expeditions (those of Carey and Dalgleish, of Bonvalot and Prince Henry of Orleans, of Littledale, and of Pievtsoff and his officers) visited the Lop-nor after Przhevalsky; and all of them faithfully followed the track of the Russian general. None of them seem to have considered the importance of ascertaining whether there were any other waterways farther east. I wanted now to make this investigation. It was the first step toward a solution of the Lop-nor problem, which later aroused so much debate.

Already, on my way to the delta, I heard of an eastern waterway, fed mainly by the Konche-daria, forming a whole string of lakes east of the route my predecessors had once followed, and situated on the same degree of latitude as the Lop-nor of the Chinese. I followed the eastern shore of all these lakes. They were nearly overgrown with reeds. In 1893, Kozloff, a Russian captain, discovered a river-arm, long since dried up, which had once been the bed of the Konche-daria, and which seemed to continue eastward from a point above my chain of lakes. The natives called it "The Sand River" or "The Dry River." During a later expedition, I was to have the opportunity of mapping out its entire course, and of discovering its importance.

Thus we travelled south along the lakes. Sand-dunes, forests, some old and dead, others fresh and living, and vast fields of reed made progress difficult. At Tikkenlik, a little village, we had great trouble in taking the camels across the Konche-daria. The water was still too cold for them to swim across. So we tied a few of the natives' long, narrow canoes together, covered them with boards and reeds, and took first one camel across, and then the two others. The poor animals were frightened, they resisted desperately, and had to be tethered on board the strange ferry-boat.

It had now grown warm. By day, the temperature was 91.6°; and in the evenings, and at night, we were much tormented by gnats. I smeared tobacco-oil on my face and hands; and on one occasion we set fire to a whole field of dense, dry reeds, to keep the bloodthirsty insects away. It sounded like rifle-shots, when the reed-stalks burst from the heat; and all night we lay under that constant crackling. The flames swept across the quiet region, and it grew as light as day.

From Kum-chekkeh, a fishing-place, Islam went on along the main road, to a spot we had agreed upon, where the arms of the delta met. I myself hired a canoe, twenty feet long, and one and a half foot broad, hollowed out of a poplar-trunk, and went with two oarsmen along the long watercourse, over lakes and river-branches, to the rendezvous. It was a delightful voyage! I sat amidships, as in an easy-chair, with compass, watch, and map on my lap, and mapped out our route. Yoldash, who lay at my feet, found this mode of travelling more pleasant than rocking on the camel's back. The oarsmen stood erect, dipping their thin, broad-bladed paddles almost perpendicularly into the water. The canoe glided so swiftly through the water, that there were eddies about its stern. The banks glided past. There was a swishing and creaking sound, as we broke through the dense growth of reeds. One of my oarsmen, old Kurban, had hunted in this region for fifty years, and remembered the time when the country was dry, and when, twenty years before, he had killed a wild camel and sold its skin to the first European who had ever appeared in this country, namely, Przhevalsky.

One day, a first-rate *kara-buran,* or black storm, swept the country, and the majestic old poplars meekly bowed their heads before the wind. We could not think of going out in the canoe. We lay quietly waiting, in reed huts, the inhabitants of which received us hospitably and treated us to fresh-caught fish, wild duck, goose-eggs, and reed-shoots. All the time, we lived on native food, which, supplemented by salt, bread, and tea, was quite excellent.

KUNCHEKKAN BEK, OR "THE CHIEF OF THE RISING SUN," A FORMER FRIEND OF PRZHEVALSKY, WHO BECAME MY FRIEND

A few days later we arrived at Abdal, a small village, composed of the most primitive reed huts, on the bank of the Tarim, just above the point where the river emptied into the Lopnor. The chieftain of the place, eighty-year-old Kunchekkan Bek (the Chief of the Rising Sun), had been a friend of Przhevalsky, and received us with the greatest hospitality. He told us of wonderful events in his own life, about rivers, lakes, deserts, and beasts, and he invited me to a long canoe-excursion eastward across this strange combination of reed-marsh and fresh-water lake.

The Tarim branched off into several arms below Abdal. We followed one of them; and before long, we saw in front of us a growth of reeds, which seemed to form an effective bar to our journey. But our oarsmen knew how to manage. They steered the canoe to the opening of a corridor in the reed-palisade. This corridor was so narrow, that we could not see the water below us, nor the sky above. These labyrinths of narrow canals among the reeds were permanently navigable, because the reeds were uprooted and new growths checked. Here the small nets of plant-fibre were set in long rows; and here the delicious fish were caught, which constitute the staple food of the Lop men.

The tallest reeds I measured were twenty-five feet, from the root to the pasque-flower. At the level of the water, one could hardly encircle them with one's thumb and middle finger. Here and there, the reeds

NARROW, DARK CORRIDORS IN THE REED-THICKETS

were battered and broken by heavy storms, and were so densely matted that we could walk on them. The wild geese used to lay their eggs in such places; and a couple of times one of my guides, as supple as a cat, jumped over to such a roof of broken, entangled reeds, as we passed by, and returned with his arms full of fine goose-eggs.

Toward evening, we glided out of the close, narrow passages, and reached wide, open water, where innumerable flocks of wild geese, wild ducks, swans, and other water-fowl swam about. We camped, on the northern bank, in the open, and went on, the next day, to the end of the lake. In the evening, we returned, in brilliant moonlight. It was a nocturnal journey in a Venetian atmosphere, in the heart of Asia.

There remained the six-hundred-and-twenty-mile stretch from Abdal to Khotan; and I wanted to cover that distance as quickly as possible. This could only be done with horses; and so, in the little town of Charkhlik, with an aching heart, I sold the three veteran camels which had so signally helped us in our important discoveries in the geographical and archæological fields. I was particularly sorry to part with the splendid camel which had for so long carried me through desert and forest, and which, every morning, had given me a poke with its nose,

OUR PASSAGE BLOCKED BY   REEDS

to wake me and to remind me of the two cakes of maize-bread that were its due. But now the moment of parting had come. The merchant who bought them came to fetch them himself. I hated him; and there were tears in my eyes, when I saw the camels disappear from the empty court. Patiently and calmly, and with majestic mien, they went away to new toil and new adventures.

We soon had something else to think about. Li Darin, the civil governor, sent a messenger to my house, asking to see my passport. I answered that I had left it behind, in Khotan. Li Darin thereupon informed me that the road to the west, leading to Khotan, was closed to me, but that I might return the same way I had come! And if I tried to take the shorter way, via Cherchen and Keriya, against his orders, he would have me arrested!

There I stood, facing a journey through forests and deserts, in the suffocating summer heat, and by roads that I had already charted! In the evening, Shi Darin, the commandant, came to my quarters to call on me. He was an amiable and sensible man; and he informed himself thoroughly of my travels.

"Was that you," he asked, "who last year lost your caravan, and yourself almost perished from thirst, in the Takla-makan Desert?"

I confirmed his surmise; and he was pleased beyond all bounds, and asked me for a detailed account of my adventures. He listened, as a child listens to a wonderful story. In the end, I complained of Li Darin's severity; but Shi Darin begged me not to worry.

The next day I paid him a return-visit.

"What about my arrest?" I inquired.

Shi Darin laughed loudly, and said:

"Li Darin is crazy. I am the commandant; and without me he cannot get a soldier to arrest you. You just take the shortest way to Khotan. I will take care of the rest."

I thanked him for his kindness, bought four new horses, bade farewell once more to our faithful camels, and rode through the woods of the Cherchen-daria, to Kopa—a place where gold-dust is extracted from the river-bed—and finally, via Keriya, to Khotan, where we—three dusty horsemen—made our entrance on May 27.

CHAPTER XXVII

A Detective-Story from the Heart of Asia

MY first task, after returning to Khotan, was to call on Liu Darin, the governor. And then the whole sequel to our disastrous desert-journey began to unfold itself like a thrilling detective-story. Some of the men whom we had regarded as rescuing angels the year before, were now revealed as rascals and thieves.

It seems that Yusur, one of the three merchants who gave Islam Baï water, and thus saved his life, visited Said Akhram Baï, the *aksakal*, or "white-beard," of the West Turkestan merchants, in Khotan, and gave him a revolver, in order to secure his silence and good-will. But Said Akhram, having been forewarned by Consul Petrovsky, subjected Yusur to a sharp examination. Thereupon Yusur confessed that Togda Bek, chief of Tavek-kel, had presented him with the revolver. Said Akhram immediately handed the weapon over to Liu Darin, who, in turn, sent it to Dao Tai, in Kashgar. It was the same Swedish army-revolver that Dao Tai had returned to me.

On feeling the ground give way under him, Yusur fled to Urumchi. Said Akhram sent a cunning spy to the village of Tavek-kel, where he obtained a position with Togdasin Bek as keeper of his sheep. One day, the spy-shepherd went to Togdasin Bek's house, to ask for his wages. He was prevented from entering. But he had already seen how Togda Bek and three other men were sitting crouched around some dusty old boxes, the contents of which were scattered about the earthen floor. These three men were Ahmed Mergen and his sons, Kasim Ahun and Togda Shah, the hunters who had accompanied Islam on the expedition of recovery after the destruction of our caravan in the desert. Two of them had been with me on my journey to the ancient cities and the region of the wild camels. I had no idea, at the time, that two of my four men were thieves, and had robbed me.

Meanwhile, the spy had seen enough. He walked slowly back in the direction of his herd of sheep; but, once out of sight, he caught the first horse he saw, and galloped as fast as he could to Khotan. As he was missed before long, Togda Bek began to suspect that something was wrong, and sent men on horseback to pursue him. But it was too late; he was too far ahead.

Arrived in Khotan, the spy told his story to Said Akhram, who reported it to Liu Darin. The latter sent two Chinese officials and some soldiers to Tavek-kel.

Togda Bek now realized that he was in for it, and would have to act diplomatically. Thinking it was better to sacrifice his illicit possessions than his standing and his job, he packed the stolen articles in the boxes, and took them to Khotan. On the way, he met Liu Darin's men, and concocted the story that the objects sought for had been found and taken to his house only a few days before, and that he was now on his way to hand them over to the Chinese authorities. The entire party then went to Khotan, where Togda Bek and the other thieves put up at a caravansary. But there, too, Said Akhram had spies, who overheard Togda Bek instructing the three hunters what to answer in case they were questioned.

Having thus informed himself sufficiently, Said Akhram held an inquiry, and got the three hunters to confess that in the course of the winter they had followed up the trail of a fox in the sand, which led them into the desert, far west, to a place where there was a dune, white with flour. Attracted by the smell of our discarded eatables, the foxes had probably gone out to the death-camp repeatedly.

As the fox-trail did not continue further west, the hunters had drawn the correct conclusion that this must be the place where we had abandoned the tent and the boxes. After some digging, they found the tent, which had probably been overturned by the wind before it was buried by the sandstorms of the summer. Thereafter, it was a simple matter to dig out the boxes which we had left in the tent. They knew nothing of our two men, who had most likely died outside the tent. They loaded the boxes on their donkeys, and themselves carried what remained of their water-supply in goatskins.

In some way or other, Togda Bek, in Tavek-kel, got wind of the find, and persuaded the hunters, who were otherwise honest men, to take the boxes to his house. They had been hidden there for some time. Ahmed Mergen and Kasim Ahun then entered my employ, and took part in my journey to the ancient cities. Thus they knew a good deal, while on this journey; but they were quiet about it. But when they returned to Khotan with the wild camel's skin, Liu Darin, who had learned all in the meantime, arrested them, gave them a thrashing, and threw them into jail.

On my return to Khotan, Liu Darin gave back to me all that was left. There was nothing of great value to me, for I had meanwhile got a new outfit from Europe. And what was I to do with the large camera, and its stand, after all the glass plates, both the exposed and the non-exposed ones, had had their films removed and been used for window-panes in Tavek-kel!

Liu Darin wanted to resort to the rack and grill, in order to squeeze the whole truth out of the guilty ones, a measure which I, of course, prevented. When, at a final examination, Togda Bek and the hunters threw the blame on one another, Liu Darin delivered the Solomon-like judgment that each of them should pay back to me the value of the missing articles, which, at a low valuation, I estimated at five hundred dollars. But I declared that I did not want their silver, and that the damage done could not be repaired by money. As a warning to others, Liu Darin insisted that they should not come off quite without penalty; and so I claimed a sum equivalent to three caravan-horses, or about one hundred dollars. Togda Bek doubtless had to stand that loss; for the hunters had nothing. And I really felt sorry for them.

It would not surprise me if some of my readers were to raise the question:

"What was the good of your exposing your own life, as well as those of your men and camels, and your whole outfit, to the tremendous risks of those long journeys across sandy deserts devoid of water?"

To this I should like to reply that though the best existing maps of the interior of Asia indicated sandy deserts in the section of eastern Turkestan in question, no European had ever traversed them; and thus an investigation into the nature of this part of the earth's crust remained an unfinished task for geographical research. Nor was it beyond question that traces of ancient civilization might be discovered in the regions which had been completely buried in the drift-sand. We have also seen, in a previous chapter, that those hopes of mine were finally crowned with success through my discovery of two ancient cities.

I have also mentioned my hope that these ruined cities would some-

time be made the subject of expert archæological excavation and examination. In this, too, I was not disappointed, although my hopes were
not realized until twelve years afterward. It was my friend, Sir Aurel
Stein, the famous English archæologist, an Hungarian by birth, who,
supported by the Indian Government, took upon himself this difficult
but grateful task. And my old cities could hardly have fallen into better
hands than his. For his achievements there, as well as in other parts
of Asia, the Retzius Gold Medal of the Swedish Geographical Society
was later awarded to him, on my recommendation.

Once, at the beginning of February, 1908, he boldly ventured to
follow the same route along the Keriya-daria, and through the desert,
which I have described in two of the foregoing chapters. He was
guided by my maps. But he made the journey in the opposite direction,
that is, from north to south. He describes it thus (*Ruins of Desert
Cathay*, II, 379):

"Had I known in Kuchar that guides were not to be secured from
Shahyar, I might, perhaps, have hesitated before attempting to strike
right across the desert to the Keriya River; for without such guides
I could not for a moment hide from myself the serious difficulty of the
task, and its inherent risks. Hedin, coming from the south, had left
the end of the Keriya River with the certainty of striking the broad
goal of the Tarim right across his route at some point or other, if
only he kept long enough to an approximately northern course. For
us, coming from the north, the case was essentially different. Our hope
of reaching water within reasonable time depended solely on our ability
to steer correctly across some hundred and fifty miles of high dunes
towards a particular point—the termination of the Keriya River, which
flowed, not right across our route, but practically in the same direction;
it involved also the assumption that the river still actually sent its
water to where Hedin had seen it.

"Now I knew well by experience the difficulty of steering a correct
course by the compass alone in a real sea of sand devoid of all directing
features. Nor could I overlook the fact that, however justified my
reliance in Hedin's careful mapping was, differences in longitude deduced
from mere route-traverses were bound to be considerable on such ground,
and in our case all depended on the assumed longitude being right.
If we failed to strike the river-end in the confused delta of dry beds
which the river has formed since early periods in its death-struggles

with the sands, our position was certain to be dangerous. There would be nothing to indicate whether the actual bed, in which we might hope to find at least subsoil-water by digging wells, lay to the east or west. If we continued our course to the south, there would be great risk of our water-supply getting completely exhausted, and of animals—if not of men, too—succumbing through thirst long before the line of wells and oases at the foot of the Kuen-lun could be reached."

Thus his own life, as well as those of his men and his caravan-animals, depended on my map. Had this been unreliable, and he been led to steer to the right or the left of the point where I had found the river-end in the sand-desert, he would have been lost beyond rescue. I had, therefore, a great responsibility; and even to this day I am happy in the confidence he reposed in my map. One cannot stake more on a single card than one's own and other people's lives. He had one advantage over me, in that he knew from my account that the dunes *could* be traversed with camels and donkeys. I was in the dark about that, when I ventured into the desert from the point where the river ended. Stein's journey was accomplished without mishap; and he writes, when every danger was past:

"I . . . saw to my delight a broad valley-like belt of dead forest and living tamarisks stretching away below to south-southwest. The high sands we had just crossed, and this continuous stretch of dead jungle, agreed well with the description Hedin had recorded of the ground where, on his march from the south, he had finally lost touch with the dry river-bed marking the former extension of the river. I felt, indeed, almost assured of having hit the very point which his map shows as Camp XXIV. It seemed like a triumphant vindication of the accuracy of Hedin in mapping, and of our own steering."

A few months later, Stein travelled north, down the dry bed of the Khotan-daria; and it is of great interest to hear what he says, thirteen years after my desert-journey, about the pool that saved my life, and from which I carried water in my boots to Kasim. I quote from his book (II, 420):

"On April 20, I started from Mazar-tagh down the dry bed of the Khotan River, for Aksu. During the eight rapid marches which carried us north to the river's junction with the Tarim, we suffered a good deal from the increasing heat of the desert, and a succession of sand-storms. Such conditions made me realize with full intensity the experiences of

Hedin on his first disastrous crossing of the Takla-makan, in May of
1896 [really 1895]. Kasim, who had met him afterwards during his
enforced rest at the shepherd-camp of Böksam, was able to show me
the pool of fresh water, some twenty miles lower down on the right
bank, which had proved the great traveller's saving when he struggled
through from the 'sea of sand,' exhausted by thirst. The constancy of
these pools, found at considerable intervals along that side of the river-
bed where the current sets, and the delicious freshness of their water,
furnish proof that there must be a steady flow of subsoil-water, making
its way down the bed of the river, often over a mile wide, even at the
driest season."

The same geographical problem which had tempted me to undertake
the disastrous journey in the Takla-makan Desert, also prompted Stein,
eighteen years later, to take the same route. Like myself, he thought
that the Masar-tagh was a mountain-range extending all through the
desert, from the northwest to the southeast. But he chose a more suitable season than I did; for he began his journey on October 29 (1913),
whereas I had made the start on April 23. He had the winter, with
its cold, before him. He chose the same starting-point as I did, namely,
the southern end of the long lake I had discovered. When, after sixteen
miles, I found that the range did not continue through the desert, I
changed my course to one straight east, and crossed the entire desert.
When Stein, after twenty-five miles, found the enterprise a too risky
one, he abandoned it, and returned to the lake. He was wiser than I—
vestigia terrent. He says about this (*Geographical Journal,* August,
1916):

"From a lake near it [the hill], which inundations from the Yarkand
River feed, but which we found brackish at its end, Hedin had started,
in May, 1896 [really April, 1895], on that bold journey through the
sandy wastes eastward which ended with the destruction of his caravan
and his own narrow escape. Steering a southeasterly course, we forced
our way for three trying marches into the sea of dunes. Closely packed
and steep from the start, they grew steadily higher, and invariably
rose in a line running diagonally across our intended direction. By the
second day, all trace of vegetation, dead or living, was left behind,
and an endless succession of mighty ridges, with not a patch of level
sand between them, faced us. The ridges to be climbed soon reached
two hundred to three hundred feet in height, and progress became pain-

fully slow with the heavily laden camels. . . . It was by far the most forbidding ground I had ever encountered in the Takla-makan. By the evening of the third day, the hired camels . . . had either broken down completely, or showed serious signs of exhaustion. Next morning, I ascended the highest dune near our camp, and carefully scanning the horizon, saw nothing but the same expanse of formidable sand-ridges, like huge waves of an angry ocean suddenly arrested in movement. There was a strange allurement in this vista, suggesting Nature in the contortions of death. But hard as it seemed to resist the siren voices of the desert which called me onwards, I felt forced to turn northward. . . . It was as well that I took that hard decision in time; for, by the third day after, there sprung up a violent *buran* (storm). . . ."

He still had eighty-five miles to go, from his turning-point, to the little mountain of Masar-tagh, on the western shore of the Khotan-daria. It was no doubt fortunate for him and his companions that he turned in time. In a similar situation, I should never have made such a decision. I should have continued through the desert. It might have been the death of me and my men. I might have lost everything, as in 1895. But the adventure, the conquest of an unknown country, the struggle against the impossible, all have a fascination which draws me with irresistible force.

CHAPTER XXVIII

My First Entry Into Tibet

OH, sweet summer in Khotan! Oh, delicious rest, after endless rides in desert and woods!

With tender sadness do I remember the month I spent in the old city. From morning to night, my days were filled with work. I completed maps and notes, wrote letters, read, and made preparations for a journey to northern Tibet. I lived quite by myself, in a spacious wooden pavilion, containing only one large room, with windows, opening on all sides, that were closed at night with wooden lattices. The building was erected on a brick terrace, and stood in the middle of a large garden, surrounded by a high wall. There was only one door in the wall; and there was a keeper's lodge, where Islam Baï and my other servants lived, and which housed the kitchen. The distance between the pavilion and the kitchen was too great for me to shout for the servants. We therefore installed a very simple bell-system between the two houses.

Fifteen new horses stood in the garden, eating grain out of their cribs. Liu Darin was magnificent in his generosity. Every day he sent me provisions for the horses, as well as for the men. I had asked him to recommend to me a young Chinese, whom I could take along to Peking, and who could give me lessons in Chinese, during the journey. One day, my new travelling-companion appeared. His name was Fong Shi. He was a pleasant, willing man, and was extremely happy to be able to go to Peking. We began the lessons at once, and I made daily notes in Fong Shi's strange mother-tongue.

It was hot; but in our garden we did not mind 100.4°. There was enough shade for us, and the water rippled in rivulets among the trees. At times, violent storms passed over the district. Then the wind whistled and sang in the tree-tops, and one could hear the branches creak and rub against one another, or snap off.

One dark night, a storm swept Khotan. I lay awake, listening comfortably to the roaring wind outside. Yoldash, who had grown, and had developed into a good watch-dog, rushed up suddenly, and began to bark wildly at one of the farther windows. The wooden gratings were down. The dog quivered, and foamed with rage. I crept to the wire attached to the bell. It was cut. I slipped out onto the terrace, and saw a couple of dark shadows, hard pressed by the dog, disappear among the bushes. I woke Islam up. We fired a few shots at random. The next morning, we found, inside the wall, a ladder, which the thieves had left behind them in their hurried flight. After that, we always kept a night-watchman in the garden. Once every minute, the watchman was to sound three strokes on his drum. From that time on, no more thieves disturbed our rest.

When everything was ready for our departure, I took leave of fine old Liu Darin, and presented him with a gold watch and chain as a memento. A rousing farewell-feast was held around a big fire in the garden, where all who had assisted us, and also my own men, were treated to mutton, rice-pudding, and tea, while they regaled their eyes with the dancing, and their ears with string-music. On the following morning, our caravan-beasts were laden, and we went off to Keriya and Niya, where we bought six fresh camels, and then to Kopa, a small, insignificant village of a few stone huts, at the foot of the mountains, where gold was to be found.

A "TAGHLIK" OR MOUNTAIN INHABITANT OF DALAI-KURGAN

On July 30, we entered in among the mountains, which are the outworks of the highest and most gigantic natural fort on earth, the high plateau of Tibet. A valley led us up to the Dalai-kurgan district, where we were already at a height of 11,000 feet. This part of the country was still inhabited by Taghliks, or mountaineers of East Turkestan ex-traction. Here there were but eighteen families, with their tents and their six thousand sheep. But after leaving Dalai-kurgan, we came to unpopulated country, and were to travel east for two months without meeting a human being.

What was worse, we left the last good pasture-land at one day's remove from Dalai-kurgan. Then the grass grew worse and worse, and finally ended entirely. We departed from Dalai-kurgan with twenty-one horses, twenty-nine donkeys, and six camels. Of these, only three horses, three camels, and one donkey got through northern Tibet with their lives. We also had twelve sheep, two goats, and three dogs— my faithful Yoldash, or the "Travelling-Companion," Yolbars, or the "Tiger," and Buru, the "Wolf." A sheep-dog, limping on three legs, as a result of a fight with wolves, joined our caravan of its own accord.

I had only eight steady retainers: Islam Baï, Fong Shi, Parpi Baï, Islam Ahun, Hamdan Baï, Ahmed Ahun, Roslak, and Kurban Ahun. We took with us also seventeen Taghliks from Dalai-kurgan, and their *aksakal,* or chief, who was to accompany us for two weeks, and help us over the most difficult passes.

Parpi Baï was a man of fifty, with nice features, full black beard, and lively dark-brown eyes, dressed in a sheepskin coat and a fur-edged cap. He had been a servant of Dalgleish, when the latter was assassi-nated at the Kara-korum Pass, and of Dutreuil de Rhins, who was murdered in eastern Tibet, and of Prince Henry of Orleans, who died in the French East Indies. At the camp-fires, there seemed to be no end to the tales of his own wonderful adventures, experienced on his long journeys in Asia.

We noticed, from the very beginning, that the Taghliks were un-trustworthy. One night, two of them ran away, and later on two more. They had got their wages in advance. Their *aksakal* had to answer for the liberties taken by his men. Among the labyrinth of valleys and mountains which we had to cross, to reach the Tibetan plateau, the men were sorely needed.

The caravan proceeded in five divisions. The camels, with their leaders, went first; then the horses; then the donkeys, in two groups; and, last, the sheep and the goats, with their shepherds. Accompanied by Fong Shi and a Taghlik acquainted with the district, I always brought up the rear; for I was busy drawing a map of our route, and making sketches of the glorious mountains that rose on all sides, and also collecting plants and rock-specimens. Islam Baï picked out the camping-places, which were always chosen with due regard to water, grazing, and fuel. By the time I reached camp the tents would already be pitched, the animals would be grazing on what sparse grass there might be, the fires would be burning, and Yoldash, who generally deserted me upon seeing the camp in the distance, would be standing in the opening of my tent, wagging his tail, and bidding me welcome as though he were the master of the house.

The valley turned southeast, and narrowed. It took us to the first high pass over which the Taghliks were to guide us. The caravan traversed it without loss. Its height was 15,680 feet; and from its fairly sharp ridge, we had a magnificent view over a world of snow-covered mountains. South of it, the terrain opened out again. Here we startled the first wild ass, who disappeared among the mountains, pursued by the dogs. The three-legged dog found he could not keep up with the caravan. He stood alone and abandoned on a projecting rock, and howled as the caravan went on its way.

Bulak-bashi (the Head of the Spring) was the last place for which the Taghliks had a name. Going east from there, we were to wander long through nameless regions, where no European had ever set foot. The mountains to the south, between the snow-covered ridges and summits of which glacier-tongues led down, were known to the Taghliks merely as Arka-tagh, or "the Farther Mountains."

Winter comes early in these high regions. One morning we were awakened by a snow-storm. My tent was upset by the wind, and had to be guyed with ropes and boxes. The temperature fell to 20°, in spite of the fact that we were well along in August. The whole country was white, and it was not always easy to find the trail of the caravan. Mountain-sickness also claimed its victims. Most of the men complained of headache and palpitations. But nobody was in so sad a plight as Fong Shi, whose condition grew worse, day by day. He had a high fever, and could hardly keep in the saddle. To take him farther along would have been to risk his life; so I had to send him back to East Turkestan. I let him keep his horse, gave him money and food, and a Taghlik as escort. He was deeply grieved at his ruined hopes of getting to Peking. He really presented a disconsolate sight on the morning when we parted at the embers of one of our camp-fires.

My faithful servant, Islam Baï, was ill too. He coughed blood, and asked to be left behind, with two Taghliks. But after a few days' rest, in a valley where we found tolerable grazing, he improved. The animals had not had any green fodder for four days.   But they always got maize.   The donkeys carried the maize for the horses and camels. They themselves were less particular, and even put up with the droppings of wild asses and yaks.   We had maize to last us for a month, and provisions for the men for two months and a half.   Every evening, at sunset, the camels would return from grazing, and come waddling up to the camp, where their maize-rations were poured out on a piece of tent-cloth.

It was with a group of invalids that I made my entrance into northern

THE CARAVAN ATTACKED BY A STORM OF HAIL AND RAIN

Tibet.   We were at an altitude of 16,300 feet, and the temperature at night sank to 13°.   A western storm, with hail and snow, swept the tableland every day.   No matter how clear the sky, the west would darken, and lead-coloured clouds filled the spaces between the snowy peaks.   A roaring sound became audible, and approached at a terrific speed.   It grew as dark, at midday, as after nightfall.   The thunder rumbled and a dull echo reverberated among the mountain-walls.   And then came the hail-shower, like a veritable artillery-fire from an enemy's battery. The beatings of the innumerable little ice-balls, as they whipped our poor bodies, could be felt right through the thickest sheepskin coat. It was impossible to see anything. We sheltered our heads underneath our coverings. Night surrounded us, and the caravan stopped. The poor horses got frightened, and winced at their undeserved hail-whipping. But these storms, as regular as they were violent, passed quickly. They were generally followed by a snowfall; but about an hour later, the sky would clear, and the sun would sink behind the mountains in all its glory.

We were now to cross the Arka-tagh, and our guides accordingly led us up through a steep valley. I followed the horses, which that day were in the lead. After many difficult hours, we reached the pass, at a height of 17,200 feet. At the moment of surmounting the saddle of the pass, the usual hail-storm arrived. We could not go on; for we were unable to see our way. So we decided to camp, temporarily. The tents were pitched and guyed, and the animals tethered. Water, grazing, and fuel were lacking; but the hailstones that collected in the crevices gave us water; and a wooden box was broken up for firewood. It was a horrible camping-place. The thunder pealed all around us. The ground trembled under the shock. The camels and donkeys had disappeared. In the evening, the sky cleared, and the moon rose, shining like silver.

The next day, we discovered that our Taghliks had led us astray, and that the pass on which we were camping led over a smaller ridge, not over the Arka-tagh itself. We had to descend again, to look for the right pass, and to find the divisions of the caravan that had gone astray.

We accomplished the latter task; but, as everyone was exhausted, we no sooner found some tolerable pasturage on a brookside, than we encamped.

It was now arranged that three Taghliks should return home, but that the others should go with us till we got in touch with other human beings. The latter asked for half their wages in advance, in order to send the money home to their families by their three returning comrades.

Silence fell on the camp at an early hour that evening. Our Taghliks used to arrange the maize-bags and the provision-boxes in a small, circular barricade, in the centre of which they built their fire, and afterwards found shelter from the constant wind.

On the morning of August 19, the alarm was sounded. Every one of the Taghliks had disappeared, probably as early as midnight! Tired out as we were, we had all slept soundly, and nobody had noticed anything. The Taghliks stole two horses, ten donkeys, and a supply of bread, flour, and maize. And to bewilder us, they left the camp in groups, proceeding in different directions, as was evident from their tracks. Afterwards, by prearrangement, they met at a rendezvous, and continued west together.

Parpi Baï was entrusted with the task of pursuing the fugitives with two men and our three best horses. A day and a half later, he returned with the sorry-looking gang, and made the following report:

After the Taghliks had covered a distance equal to that which we would traverse in three days, they felt themselves safe; so they stopped and made a fire. Five of them were sitting around it, and the others were already asleep. When Parpi Baï rode up, they leapt to their feet and fled in different directions. He fired a shot in the air and shouted: "Come back, or I'll shoot you down!" Thereupon they returned, flung themselves on the ground, and cried for mercy. Parpi Baï took their money, and bound their hands behind their backs. Early the next morning, they started for our camp; and at ten o'clock at night they arrived, half dead, poor fellows, from exhaustion.

It was indeed a picturesque court-scene which was presented before my tent in the mixed light from the camp-fire and the moon. They were sentenced to be kept tethered, and under watch, at night, and to compensate Parpi Baï and the two other men for their trouble; upon which they went to sleep behind their barricade of bags and boxes, and, being completely exhausted, they slept heavily, while the moon shone brightly on a ground covered with a thin layer of snow.

A few days later, having made a thorough reconnaissance, we crossed the principal crest of the Arka-tagh, by a pass 18,200 feet high; and on the other side we descended into a vast valley, stretching as far east as the eye could see. We followed this valley for almost a month. On our left, rose the Arka-tagh, with mighty summits, perpetual snowfields, and blue glaciers; and on the right, or south of our route, the mountain-range, the extreme eastern end of which is called Koko-shili (the Green Hills) by the Mongolians.

No human beings ever find their way to these regions. Neither nomads nor their herds can live there. The altitude is too great. Even in the lowest part of the mountains we were at a higher level than the top of Mont Blanc, and most of the time we were at an altitude of 16,200 feet.

Already at our first camp, the mountain-spirits greeted us with a thunderous sound. Fantastic, wild, purple-black clouds rose at sunset, filled the valley, and floated eastward like a lava-stream. It grew dark all around us. The gale threatened to carry off the whole camp; and we all had to hold onto the tent to keep it in place. The hail lashed the whole region like a scourge. But within five minutes the heavy squall was past, and the cloud-formations moved on to the east like great fleets of warships. Impervious fog followed in their wake, to be succeeded, in turn, by night, with its unsolvable mysteries.

CHAPTER XXIX

Wild Asses, Wild Yaks, and Mongolians

WE were now on the crest of the huge Tibetan plateau, the largest and highest mountain-accumulation on earth. Our period of hardships began when the rarefied air and absence of pasture-land broke the caravan's power of resistance, and when, almost daily, our track was marked by the beasts of burden which we left lying on the road.

Now, too, we were in the Eldorado of the wild animals. In a country where we looked in vain for grass, wild asses and antelopes found their way to the scarce pastures, and wild yaks got their subsistence from the lichens and mosses growing among the gravel and on the cliffs, all the way up to the edge of the glaciers. We saw them daily, singly and in herds; and the desolate and sterile landscape was enlivened by these masters of the highland.

Some of the four-legged members of the expedition, i.e., the dogs, were at least as interested as the men in the wild animals. Once an inquisitive wild ass kept running ahead of the caravan for two hours. Time after time, it stopped, sniffed, snorted, and ran ahead again. When Yolbars, the "Tiger," chased him, he turned round to attack the dog. We all laughed to see the dog run away, with his tail between his legs.

Another time, my favourite tent-companion, Yoldash, shot like an arrow after a wild ass, who fled and disappeared over the nearest hills, tempting the dog to follow. But the brave pursuer did not return. We camped, and the evening passed, and also most of the night. But at three o'clock in the morning, I was awakened by Yoldash wriggling in underneath the tent-cloth. Whining with joy, he came up to me and licked my face. He had evidently lost our trail, had wandered in search of us for fourteen hours, and had probably found our camp by mere chance.

One day, Islam Baï sent a bullet after a lone wild ass, and shattered one of its legs. The animal went only a short distance, and then fell, landing picturesquely in my sketch-book. He measured seven and a half feet, from his upper lip to the root of his tail. His colour was a beautiful dark reddish-brown, his belly and legs white, the nose grey. The hoofs were as large as those of a horse, the ears fairly long, the nostrils large and broad, the tail like that of a mule, the lungs well developed. We kept the skin, and the flesh was a welcome addition to our food-supply.

The beautiful, elegant antelopes were not molested by Islam Baï; but a few yaks fell before his bullets. One was a cow, measuring eight feet in length, whose tongue, kidneys, and marrow provided a welcome

A WILD YAK CHARGING OUR DOGS

variety to my meals. The men appropriated the flesh to themselves. Another, a bull, was not brought down so easily. Islam came triumphantly to camp and told us he had shot a stately bull yak at some distance from our tents. Seven bullets were required to make the beast take final leave of his familiar grazing-grounds. As he lay near the road over which we were to go the next day, it was decided that Islam should show me the spot, so that I might draw a picture of the animal.

So Islam took the lead next morning. Imagine my surprise, on finding the place empty, and the "killed" bull yak gone. At first, I wondered if the whole thing was the usual hunter's yarn. But no! The trail showed quite clearly that the yak, after recovering from the string of shots, had got up and wandered to a spring. There he was walking, on the edge of the pool, and grubbing in the ground. When he sighted us, he raised his head, and presented a magnificent picture of compact strength and glowing rage. When the eighth bullet, with a dull sound, lodged in his body, he lowered his horns and rushed at us. We wheeled our horses, and fled at top speed. But the yak pursued us, and gained upon us. The distance between us grew shorter. He was quite near, when all of a sudden he stopped short, tossed up the sand with his horns, lashed the air with his tail, and rolled his red, bloodshot eyes wildly. Then we stopped, too, and the hunter sent another bullet into him, which made him whirl round several times, while earth and sand flew all about him. Yoldash, who was with us, aroused the bull's anger; but he saved himself in time. The eleventh ball penetrated the region of the heart, and the wild old yak fell heavily on the ground where he had spent his life in undisturbed freedom.

This bull was about twenty years old, and a fine specimen, being ten and a half feet long. The outside measurement of the horn was two and a half feet; and the thick, black, woolly fringes on the sides, which form soft, warm cushions for him to lie on, were a little over two feet long.

From this it appears that the yak is not easily brought down. He does not collapse, unless shot behind the shoulder. He merely grunts, and shakes his head at a ball sent into his massive, low forehead. But if he is struck in a more vital spot, he becomes dangerous, and will charge the hunter. He is built for the high, rarefied air, and does not get short of breath. The chances are, therefore, that he will overtake the hunter and his horse, who are both accustomed to breathing denser air.

On our way east, we discovered a whole line of lakes, most of them more or less salt. Instead of giving them European names, I designated them by Roman numerals. Lake Number XIV was at an altitude of 16,750 feet. A week later we went along the shore of a large lake for seventeen miles.

The country continued to be monotonous. But every day new views over snowy peaks and glaciers opened out on both sides. No trace of any human being was ever to be seen. But yes! Once, when we crossed the route of Bonvalot and the Prince of Orleans, we found a felt rag, which had probably belonged to one of their beasts of burden. The dry droppings of the wild yak were collected in bags during our march. They burned with a bluish-red flame and gave intense heat. The worst thing was that pasturage became more and more scarce. One horse or donkey after another collapsed; and we considered ourselves lucky on those days when we had no losses to record. The camels were the hardiest. But their pads became sore from rubbing against the sand; and so we made socks for them. When hunting was poor, the dogs had to content themselves with the flesh of dead caravan-animals. The tension grew day by day; and in the end we doubted whether we would stumble on any nomad-tents before the last caravan-beasts succumbed. In that event we would have to discard our luggage, and make our way on foot, until we found men.

As a matter of fact, our hunting had been unsuccessful for some time; and we had already killed our last sheep. When the first camel collapsed, the men cut out the best of its flesh for food. One morning, my faithful riding-horse, which had carried me for sixteen months, was found dead between the tents.

On September 21, we camped on the western shore of a lake, which barred our way diagonally. We could not make out its southeastern extremity, and we might have imagined ourselves standing on the shore of a bay. We followed the lake to the northeast, and lost two days by this roundabout journey. One day, we were caught here by a storm, surpassing in magnitude and violence all previous ones. The sky darkened rapidly. The blue lake turned dark-grey, and its surface rose in white, foaming, roaring waves. The mountains disappeared behind impenetrable clouds. The hail-storm lashed the rocks, while the waves interrupted our progress, and forced us to encamp hastily at the entrance to a valley.

We now had five camels, nine horses, and three donkeys left. The animals got grain for the last time. There was still sufficient flour for a month, therefore the last horses got a small roll of bread each day.

On September 27, we left the wide valley with the many lakes, and went northeast over a pass. On the farther side, we surprised a herd of yak, numbering about a hundred. Islam sent a bullet into the group. The frightened animals separated into two groups, one of which, about forty-seven animals, headed straight toward me and the Taghlik who accompanied me. A huge bull ran in front. When about a hundred

paces away, they saw us, and swerved aside. Islam fired a second shot.
The bull charged; and he was on the point of tossing horse and rider
in the air, when, at the last moment, Islam turned in his saddle and
gave the beast a fatal shot in its breast. We encamped near the fallen
animal. Its carcase yielded food for several days.

We could not be very far now from human beings! On the summit
of the next pass, there was a stone cairn, evidently erected by Mongolian yak-hunters. We still saw herds numbering two hundred wild
asses. Another couple of our horses died. How long would the caravan
survive? Our food-supply was nearly exhausted; and tents, beds, boxes,
and specimens weighed as much as before, and possibly more.

On the last day of September, we reached an opening of the valley,

AN "OBO" OF 49 STONE SLABS WITH THE SACRED INSCRIPTION TO THE
SPIRITS OF THE MOUNTAINS

and came upon a very beautiful *obo*, or religious monument, dedicated
to the mountain-deities. It consisted of forty-nine slabs of dark-green
slate, some of them four and a half feet long, placed edgewise one
against the other, like a stable with three cribs. They were covered
with Tibetan ideographs. I had never before seen an *obo*. Very likely
one of the pilgrim-roads of the Tsaidam Mongols, leading to Lhasa,
crossed here. Did the writing on these slate slabs perhaps contain some
important historic information? But I did not have to study the inscrip-

tions long, before discovering that the same signs recurred invariably, and in the same order, on all the slabs. It was of course the usual formula of prayer, "Om mani padme hum!" (Oh, the jewel is in the lotus!).

The next day, going down a valley, between granite mountains, we found another *obo,* as well as some fireplaces and abandoned tent-grounds. A herd of yak grazed on a slope. Islam took a shot at the animals at long range; but they never budged. Instead of that, an old woman came running forward, shouting at the top of her voice. We learned from her that the yaks were tame. This we could see for ourselves, when we got closer; for the tame yak is smaller than the wild one. A brooklet rippled down the valley; and on its shore we pitched our tents, quite close to the one belonging to the old "lady of the mountains."

It was quite interesting to meet a human being again, after fifty-five days of solitude. But none of us understood Mongolian, the language of that human creature. Parpi Baï knew only the single word, *bane* (there is), and I knew five, *ula* (mountain), *nor* (lake), *gol* and *muren* (river), and *gobi* (desert). But it was difficult to make the old woman understand by means of this vocabulary that our first and foremost wish was to buy a fat, juicy sheep. I tried to bleat like one, and showed her two Chinese silver coins; whereupon the fate of one of her sheep was sealed. The meat soon found its way into our frying-pan.

The old woman was dressed in a sheep's skin, a belt, and boots, and had a kerchief wrapped round her forehead. She wore her hair in two plaits. Her eight-year-old son was similarly dressed, but had three braids. Their black felt carpet-tent was supported by two upright poles, and was kept taut with ropes. Its interior revealed a picturesque disorder of saucepans, wooden bowls, ladles, hunting-utensils, furs, skins, sheep-bladders filled with yak-fat, and big pieces of meat cut from the carcase of a wild yak. Two small Buddha-images and some sacred vessels were standing on a wooden box toward the back. This, according to my Mohammedan men, was the house-altar, or the family's *budkhaneh* (shrine of Buddha).

The head of the family came home in the evening. His name was Dorche, and he was a professional yak-hunter. He was not a little amazed at having acquired neighbours right in the wilderness, who came from God only knows where. He stood as if paralyzed, staring at us, uncertain whether we were real, or whether he was labouring under an hallucination.

The old woman and the boy probably told him that we were not bandits, but fairly decent men, who paid honestly for what they got, besides presenting them with tobacco and sugar.

Thereupon Dorche gradually melted; and he was quite amiable, when later we took him to my tent. He became our friend and our confidant, and afterwards served as our guide for several days, and took us to his tribesmen, the Tajinoor Mongols of Tsaidam. Already on the first day, he sold us three small horses and two sheep.

In the beginning, we had great difficulty understanding each other. When we did not grasp what Dorche said, he shouted as though we were stone-deaf. I began immediately taking lessons in Mongolian from him. I first wrote down the numerals. Then I pointed to the forehead, the eyes, the nose, the mouth, the ears, hands and feet, tent, saddle, horse, etc., to get the names of these objects. It was more difficult to learn the verbs. We first disposed of the simpler ones, such as to eat, drink, lie, walk, sit, ride, smoke, etc.; but when I wanted to know the Mongolian word for "beat," and accordingly thumped Dorche on the back, he started up quite scared, thinking that I was angry. The lessons continued on the days following; and after a few days' rest, during a ride down the valley of the Naïji-muren, I kept Dorche constantly by my side, asking him the names of valleys and mountains. I wanted to learn Mongolian; and, besides, necessity forced me to it. It is sometimes an advantage not to have an interpreter; for then one must perforce acquaint oneself with the language. After a few weeks, I spoke the simple vernacular of the nomads without difficulty.

On October 6, I left before the caravan was ready, Dorche and Yoldash, the dog, being my sole companions. We rode, mile after mile, down the widening valley; and finally the level horizon of the lowlands of Tsaidam appeared in the north. The whole day passed. We were crossing a belt of desert land, when twilight set in; and then we entered a path, which wound its way across a tamarisk-steppe.

Dorche stopped, and pointing in the direction from which we had come, he declared that our caravan would never find its way to my camp without a guide. He would therefore have to go back and lead it. But first he indicated with his hand in which direction I was to proceed; and when I intimated that I understood what he meant, he laughed, nodded, and jumped up and down in the saddle, out of sheer delight. Then he disappeared in the darkness, and I rode on.

The night became pitch-dark. The newly-purchased horse evidently knew his way, for he just walked on and on. The way seemed endless. Eventually, the light of some fires appeared in the distance. Slowly the light increased. Dogs could be heard barking to the north; and, after a while, a lot of furious dogs attacked us. They would probably have torn Yoldash to pieces, if I had not jumped off of my horse and got the poor creature up on the saddle. Thus, after a ride of nearly thirty miles, we made our entrance—the horse, Yoldash, and I—into

"GAO" BOXES, WHICH THE MONGOLS HANG ROUND THEIR NECKS

the tent-village of Yike-tsohan-gol. I tied my horse, and stepped into a tent, where half a dozen Mongols sat round the fire, drinking tea, and kneading *tsamba,* or roasted maize-flour, in their wooden bowls.

I greeted them with "Amur san bane?" (How is your health?).

They stared at me, speechless. I drank a good mouthful out of a pan of mare's milk, and lit my pipe with imperturbable coolness. The Mongols were exceedingly amazed. They apparently did not know what to make of me. I tried to impress them by uttering some of the words Dorche had taught me. But they only stared; and I could not get a sound out of them.

Thus we sat, staring at one another, and at the fire, for fully two hours, when the tramping of horses and voices announced that the caravan had at last arrived. Two horses and one donkey, veterans from East Turkestan, had died; and only three camels, three horses, and one donkey remained of the original fifty-six animals.

After Dorche explained things to the Yike-tsohan-gol Mongols, we soon became friends. We stayed with them five days, organizing a new caravan.

The Mongols who dwelt near by, hearing that we wanted to buy horses, came and offered their animals for sale. We bought twenty of them. Parpi Baï, being a saddle-maker, made pack-saddles for them. Sonum, the chief of the district, came to visit me, wearing a red mantle, and bringing us milk, sour milk, and *kumiss* (fermented mare's milk), in wooden vessels. I returned his visit in his tent, outside the entrance of which a spear was stuck in the ground. The interior was adorned with a fine domestic altar. Agriculture was not carried on at all in this district; but the people kept herds—sheep, camels, horses, and horned cattle—and some of them were very well off.

They wore small cases of brass, copper, or silver round their necks. These contained images of Buddha, in clay or wood, and slips of paper bearing the sacred prayer. The cases were called *gao*. I bought a whole collection of them. They were beautifully decorated. The silver ones, in particular, were embellished with turquoises and coral. But the Mongols did not dare to reveal to one another that they were selling the holy relics to an infidel; and so they would steal to my tent at night, where, under cover of darkness, they delivered the images of the unfathomable Buddha into my hands.

CHAPTER XXX

In the Land of the Tangut Robbers

WHEN we left our new friends, on October 12, and proceeded eastward across steppes, deserts, and knotty, salty ground, we had an entirely new and splendid caravan of well-conditioned horses. On the left rolled the boundless, level plains of Tsaidam; and on the right were the Tibetan mountains. We spent the nights in Mongol tent-villages, eating the same food as the Mongols. After a few days, Dorche was paid off. He was superseded by Lobsang, a fine, big Mongol. We were still a month's journey from Si-ning, and twelve hundred and fifty miles from Peking. Winter, with its cold, was approaching; but we had reached lower regions, and were usually at an altitude of from 9,000 to 10,000 feet.

Then we swerved toward the north, and reached the Tossun-nor, a salt-lake of a beautiful dark-blue colour. That region was almost uninhabited. But on the shores of the river of Holuin-gol, we saw fires at night. There was a wonderful, mysterious air about that country! Here and there a picturesque *obo* rose, with ghostly, fluttering prayer-pennants. Where fresh-water sources existed near the shores of the Tossun-nor, white swans could be seen swimming about on the blue water. The temperature had fallen to −14.8°, the air was still, and the full moon silvered the desolate country, its beams tracing a vibrant path on the lake.

As we rode along the southern shore of Kurlyk-nor, a fresh-water lake, Lobsang sat silent and serious in his saddle, incessantly mumbling the sacred formula, "Om mani padme hum." I inquired after the cause of his gloom, and he answered that he had learned from the last Mongols we met that Tangut robbers had been to Kurlyk a few days before, and had stolen horses from the nomads. He advised us, in consequence, to have all our firearms in readiness. Our three rifles and five revolvers were accordingly distributed among the men. At night, our horses were tethered close to the camp. Night-sentries were stationed about the tents, and the three dogs were depended upon to warn us of danger.

On the last day of October, we camped on the shores of Khara-nor, where bear-tracks were numerous, and where we had to keep more careful watch than ever on the horses. Though the bear contents himself with wild berries, in the late autumn he will attack any grazing horse that he encounters.

The next day, we rode east, through a broad valley, surrounded by low mountains. The track of a bear that had loped along, in the direction we were taking, was visible on the path in the centre of the valley. Islam Baï and Lobsang rode out in pursuit. At the end of an hour, they came galloping back at full speed, looking as if they had seen the Devil himself. On coming up to us, they shouted, with what breath remained: "Tangut robbers!"

Close behind them, and stirring up a cloud of dust, appeared a band of about a dozen mounted Tanguts, all with rifles on their shoulders or in their hands. They raced straight towards us. We halted, and arranged our position of defense in a trice. We happened to be on a mound, six or seven feet high, on the top of which Islam, Parpi, Lobsang, and I stationed ourselves, with rifles and revolvers ready for action. The other men, with the caravan, took position behind us, where they were protected by the mound. The men thought their last moment had come, and their knees trembled. We had thrown off our furs, so as to be freer to receive the shock. The outcome was doubtful. We were only three rifles against twelve. I lit my pipe, in the hope of imbuing my men with a calmness that I hardly felt myself.

When the robbers saw that they had to deal with a whole caravan, they stopped short, at a hundred and fifty paces, and held a council of war. They crowded together, talking and gesticulating, their rifles gleaming in the sunshine. After a moment, they turned back. We mounted our horses again, and resumed our journey. The Tanguts kept on our right, at a distance of two rifle-shots. They separated into two platoons, one riding up a side-valley, the other skirting the foot of the mountain on the right side of the valley. They kept together, and seemed to have their minds set on anticipating our arrival at the narrow passage into which the main valley tapered. We perceived the danger ahead of us, and hurried on as fast as our horses could go. Lobsang was nearly scared to death.

"They will shoot us down from the top of the rocks," he said. "We had better turn and take another way."

But I urged my men on, for all they were worth. The Tanguts showed themselves again at the rocks near the narrow entrance. Our situation was most exciting. The Tanguts might hide among the rocks far above us, and pick us off, one by one, without exposing themselves. They had chosen a veritable Thermopylæ, which we, with our three rifles, had small chance of forcing.

Puffing vigorously at my pipe, I rode into the narrow, rocky passage. "Here goes," thought I. "I will be struck down by a bullet, while my brave Mohammedans will flee for dear life."

But nothing happened. We passed safe and sound through the defile, and were relieved to see the valley on the other side open out into a large plain. The Tanguts had disappeared, leaving no trace. We continued our march, until we found a frozen fresh-water pool, surrounded by grass, in the middle of the plain. There I ordered a halt, and we pitched camp for the night.

The horses were instantly turned loose in the grass, and were kept out, under watch, until it grew dark. Then they were tethered between the tents. Islam and Parpi took the night-watch. No extra measures were needed to keep the men awake; for everyone expected the Tanguts to return in greater numbers. Przhevalsky was once attacked by three hundred Tanguts; and if their kinsmen east of Khara-nor had been a little bolder, they would have made a great haul.

No sooner was it pitch-dark than we heard the wildest howling—long-drawn, plaintive whines, like the hungry wails of hyenas, jackals, and wolves at night. It came from all around our camp, and quite close by. Lobsang assured us it was the Tangut war-cry, designed to frighten us, and to find out how attentive and brave our watch-dogs were. The bandits crawled through the grass, on their elbows and knees, and they could get quite close without being seen in the darkness. Every moment we expected to hear the first shots of an attack, which we could only have returned blindly. We did our best to drown the noise they were making. Twice a minute, Parpi Baï would call out "Khabardar!" (Are the sentries awake?). And, in the absence of drums, two of the men banged a couple of rattling saucepans as hard as they could.

Hour after hour passed, and no shots were exchanged. The Tanguts evidently still felt unsure, and therefore postponed their attack. I grew drowsy, and lay down, hearing the indefatigable Parpi Baï's "Khabardar" till I fell asleep.

Thus the night passed without further adventure; and when the sun rose, the Tanguts had mounted their horses and were out of range. We loaded our animals, and started east. No sooner had we left our camping-place, than the Tanguts rode up to it and dismounted. We saw them scratch and search where the tents had stood and the fire had burned. Empty match-boxes, ends of candles, and pieces of newspaper doubtless informed them that the caravan was under European direction. At any rate, they did not pursue us, and we saw nothing more of them.

Now that we felt ourselves again secure, I let my men, after so hard a night's work, sleep the whole day. Never before, or after, did I hear people snore as they did.

TANGUT BANDITS CREEPING AROUND OUR CAMP AT NIGHT

Thereafter, we often passed Tangut nomad-tents, and bought sheep and milk. The Tanguts are a Tibetan tribe, but they are considered to be more savage and ferocious than the Tibetans. They rob weak caravans and steal horses whenever they can. Once I took Lobsang and entered a tent unarmed. A couple of women sat there, nursing their babies. I made a note of all their house-furnishings, and asked them the names of the various objects. The women laughed, believing I was crazy. Lobsang was of the opinion that we would get into trouble if the husbands happened to return at that moment. On one occasion, we came upon twenty-five tents; but, bargain as we would, none of the Tanguts was willing to accompany us as guide.

The valley grew more lively as we approached the monastery of Dulan-kit, where a *Hutuktu Gigen,* or "Living Buddha," resided. On the night of our encampment at the small Tsagan-nor (the White Lake), we again heard ghastly howls near by, which led us to believe that the Tanguts were collecting for a decisive attack. But I was tired, and fell asleep. In the morning, I was told that this time the howling had been that of wolves, who had approached as far as the tents, and had had an encounter with our dogs.

The next day, we met a caravan of about fifty Tanguts. They had been to Tenkar, a small town, to buy flour and other supplies for the winter. They camped near us, and prowled around our tents during the night, hoping to be able to steal something.

Next came a desolate region, where we saw neither man nor beast. But at night, the miserable howling of the wolves was heard, and the dogs barked themselves hoarse.

After crossing the half-frozen Yak River (Bukhain-gol), we beheld a magnificent view in the east, the enormous Koko-nor (the Blue Lake), the colours of which shifted from one glorious malachite-green shade to another. The lake was large, but not so large that "periodic ebb and flood" was noticeable on its shores, as good Abbé Huc (1846) tells us in his travel-records. Its altitude is 10,000 feet. Tanguts tented along its shores in winter; but in summer they moved to fresh pasturage in the highlands. From our road along the northern shore, we had a fine view of the mountains south of the lake-basin. There was a small, rocky island in the lake, inhabited by some poor hermits. They lived on voluntary offerings from pilgrims and nomads, who, when the winter was at its coldest, would walk across the ice to the island. This was quite a risky walk, because a heavy storm might arise and break the ice up, when the walkers were midway. But their errand was one that was acceptable to the gods, and they willingly took the risk.

Large herds of antelope grazed on the shores of this lake; and once we surprised six wolves lying in wait for them in a ravine. We often saw tents and herds of sheep. On one occasion, we met a caravan of sixty yaks, laden with maize, which the merchants were going to sell to

the Koko-nor Tanguts. Another time, a whole valley seemed to be
filled with men and animals. It was a travelling train of Dsun-sasak
Mongols, who had been in Tenkar, laying in their winter supplies. It
comprised one thousand horses, three hundred camels, three hundred
horsemen, with a hundred and fifty rifles, besides women and children.
A rumbling noise from the tramping of the horses' hoofs filled the valley
as they went past.

When the Tanguts asked Lobsang what was in our boxes, he, without winking an eye, replied that the large ones contained two soldiers,
and the small ones only one. I had a small, light stove, of sheet iron,
with a stovepipe, for heating my tent. Lobsang said it was a gun.
The Tanguts expressed their astonishment that a gun should be heated,
whereupon Lobsang explained that this was the common practice when
the weapon was ready for action. He told them that balls were
showered over the enemy through the tin pipe, and that no earthly
power could resist such a hail of bullets.

Beyond the Khara-kottel Pass, we came to regions which had an
outlet to the sea by the Hwang-ho (the Yellow River). I had spent
fully three years, up to that time, in territory from which no drop of
water reached the ocean. But I was still nine hundred miles from
Peking. I was longing to reach the capital of China; and yet it seemed
unattainable to me.

The farther east we got, the livelier the country became. We met
camel-caravans, horsemen, pedestrians, carts, droves of cattle, and
sheep-herds. We rode through villages surrounded by poplars, birches,
willows, and larches; passed bridges, temples and *chortens* (sacred
monuments) ; and at last entered the city gate of Tenkar.

I had heard that there was a Christian mission in this city, and so I
betook myself to the Chinese house where the missionaries lived. The
head of the mission, Mr. Rijnhart, a Dutchman, had gone to Peking;
but Dr. Susie C. Rijnhart, his wife, a learned, amiable, and talented
American, received me most hospitably, and secured lodgings for my
men and myself. This brave and capable lady was soon to meet with
the most terrible misfortune that can befall a woman. In 1898, accompanied by her husband and her little son, she tried to penetrate to
Lhasa. At Nakchu, they were forced to turn back. The child died;
and the Tibetans stole their horses, not far from the place where the
Frenchman, Dutreuil de Rhins, was murdered, in 1894. Bereft of every-

thing, Mr. and Mrs. Rijnhart rested on the bank of the Tsachu River, on the opposite bank of which some Tibetan tents were visible. Mr. Rijnhart attempted to swim across the river. His wife saw him disappear behind a rock; and as he had espied other tents, nearer by, she thought he would soon return. But he did not come. She waited all day. Days and nights passed, but he was never heard from again. Nobody knows whether he was drowned or killed. After sorrows and sufferings almost too great to be borne, Mrs. Rijnhart finally managed to reach China, and then went home to America.

From the hospitable house of the Rijnharts, I went to the famous monastery of Kum-bum, a whole city of temple-buildings, resplendent under gilded roofs. There I paid my respects to the prior, a "Living Buddha," who gave his blessing to my friend Lobsang. I viewed the colossal figure of Tsong Kapa, the reformer, and also saw the wonderful tree, of which Abbé Huc relates that every spring the sacred formula, "Om mani padme hum," is lettered automatically on its leaves. But Lobsang whispered in my ear that the lamas themselves printed the holy syllables on the leaves at night.

On November 23, we got a late start, and night was quite far advanced before we stopped, in the darkness outside the city gate of Si-ning. A watchman was pacing the wall, and beating a drum. Having pounded in vain on the gate with our riding-whips, we hailed the watchman, and promised him a liberal tip if he would open for us. After much arguing, he sent a messenger to the governor's *yamen* for orders. We waited an hour and a half before the reply came. It was to the effect that the gate would be opened at daybreak!

We had no choice but to spend the night in a nearby village. The next day, we went to see Ridley, Hunter, and Hall, of the China Inland Mission, who, during the days I spent with the family of the first-mentioned, overwhelmed me with indescribable kindness and hospitality.

My manner of living, as well as my mode of travelling, underwent a change here. I dismissed *all* my attendants except Islam Baï. I paid them twice the amount due them, and made them a present of all but two of the horses. As they were Chinese subjects, it was easy to get them a pass to their mother-country through the Dao Tai of Si-ning.

And there I was, with seven hundred and seventy *taels* left, and still three months distant from Peking!

CHAPTER XXXI

On to Peking

THE remaining months of my long journey resembled very much a race back to civilization; and so I will now quickly relate our adventures.

Islam Baï was, as I have said, my sole retainer now. He was responsible for the baggage. We drove with carts and mules to Ping-fan, and with large Turkestan carts and horses on to Liang-chow-fu. Upon crossing the Shi-ming-ho, the wheels of our first cart cut like knives through the none-too-strong ice, but eventually the vehicle got over safely. The other cart got hopelessly stuck in the ice-sludge. All of the baggage in it had to be carried ashore; and a Chinese—I still shiver when I think of him—stripped and walked out into the deep river, to remove the lumps of ice that had accumulated in front of the wheels. The whole business took four hours.

After many other adventures, we drove in through the beautiful city gate of Liang-chow-fu, and made our way to the house of an English missionary family, named Belcher, where we were warmly and hospitably received. The temperature of the chapel, however, in which I spent twelve nights, was not so warm. It was heated only on Sundays. On other days, the mercury would go down to 4° in there. I bought a *sho-lo,* or brass hand-stove, shaped like a teapot, in which a few pieces of charcoal, embedded in the ashes, would stay aglow a whole day or night.

My long stay in Liang-chow-fu was necessitated by the difficulty of securing draft-animals for Ning-sha. I used up the time exploring in and around the town. The most memorable excursion was one I made to the scholarly and kind Belgian missionaries in the village of Sung-shu-choang. It was strange to see Chinese peasants, of their own accord, leave their work in the fields, and enter the church, to cross themselves before a statue of the Virgin Mary. I was told that many families had been Catholics, from father to son, through seven generations.

At last we found a nice Chinese, who, for fifty *taels,* offered to take Islam, me, and all the luggage, on nine camels, over the two hundred and eighty miles that separated us from Ning-sha. Our road led through the sandy deserts of Ala-shan, Ulan-alesu (the Red Sand), and the capital of Wang-yeh-fu, in Ala-shan, where I spent an agreeable hour with jovial old Norvo, a vassal prince under the Emperor of China.

In Ning-sha, too, I was received with open arms by two good and benevolent missionaries, Mr. and Mrs. Pilquist, who, moreover, were countrymen of mine.

From Ning-sha, it was still six hundred and seventy miles to Peking.

IN THE ICE OF THE RIVER

Asia is indeed boundless! One rides for months, and years, before the continent is crossed! Our next stage included the crossing of Ordos, a steppe and desert, which, on the west, north, and east, was bounded by the curve of the Yellow River, and on the south by the Great Wall. The camels covered no great distance in a day; and it took us eighteen days of travelling to make the three hundred and sixty miles to Paoto.

At the point where we crossed the Hwang-ho on its thick ice, the river was 1,122 feet wide. A week later, we were riding through desolate stretches of desert, only rarely seeing Mongol tents. We camped at ancient, well-known wells, which were always very deep. The well of Bao-yah-ching was a hundred and thirty-four feet deep. The cold was penetrating, the lowest temperature being $-27.4°$. Inside the tent it was sometimes $-16.2°$.

Yet the worst of all was the constant, icy, dust-laden, northwest wind that swept across the land, and made us stiff with cold, where we sat between the humps of our riding-camels. I always kept my little *sho-lo* with glowing coals on my lap; otherwise my hands would have frozen during this trying ride. On January 31, we had a veritable hurricane, and travelling was absolutely out of the question. The entire desert-plain disappeared in thick clouds of whirling dust. We sat crouched in our miserable little tents, trying to maintain body-heat inside our furs.

It was delightful to cross the Hwang-ho again at a spot where the river measured 1,263 feet from bank to bank, and to ride into Bao-to, where again I was put up by Swedish missionaries, Mr. and Mrs. Helleberg, of the American Missionary Society of the Christian Alliance. These splendid and self-sacrificing people were killed, with innumerable others, during the Boxer uprising, in 1900.

Here I left Islam and the caravan, which was to continue to Kalgan, while I myself went to that town via Kwei-hwa-chung, travelling in a small, blue cart, with two Chinese. Along this road, there was a whole string of American mission-stations, with which sixty-one Swedes were associated. Thus I lived in Swedish homes during my entire journey to Kalgan. In that city, I was the guest of Missionary Larson. Little did I think, then, that twenty-six years later, in November, 1923, I would make a motor-trip with him from Kalgan to Urga, straight through all of Mongolia.

At Kalgan, I hired a *to-jo* (a palanquin), borne by two mules, and travelled down the Nan-kou valley to Peking in four days, a stretch that is now traversed by train in seven hours. On March 2, we got down into the lowlands northwest of Peking. I was a prey to the greatest excitement and impatience. For was I not in front of the goal which I had been approaching for three years and six months? The hours dragged slowly, and the mules tripped even more slowly, paying no heed to the calls of their two drivers.

We went through villages and gardens. I caught a glimpse at sunset, of something grey between the trees. It was the city wall of

Peking! I felt as if I were on the way to the greatest feast of my life. I was alone with two Chinese, with whom conversation was limited to the most common words of their language. But now, inside of half an hour, my voluntary wanderings in the interior of Asia would come to an end, and I would again embrace the comforts—and discomforts—of civilization.

My palanquin went, swaying like a boat, in under the arch of one of the south gates of the Tatar city. Advancing along the Street of the Ambassadors, I saw, on the left, a white gateway, outside which a couple of Cossacks stood guard. I called to them, and inquired whose

MY MULE-LITTER ARRIVING IN PEKING

house that was. "The Russian Legation," they replied. Splendid! At that time Sweden was not yet represented in "The Middle Kingdom." I jumped out of my rocking box, and crossed a large court to a house built in a noble Chinese style, and crowded with Chinese servants. A lackey announced me; and, within two minutes, M. Pavloff, Russia's chargé d'affaires, came out and received me. He congratulated me heartily upon the accomplishment of my journey, and told me that he had already long since received an order from the Foreign Office in St. Petersburg, that the apartment generally occupied by Count Cassini, the minister, who was now on leave in his home country, was to be placed at my disposal.

Aga Mohammed Hassan's palace in Kermanshah came to my mind! This time, too, I was arriving, weary and with an empty purse, and with no more luggage than I could carry myself, from the depths of the desert and from naked Mongol tents, to find a suite of drawing-rooms, dining-rooms, and bedrooms, adorned with Chinese carpets and silk embroideries, antique, costly bronzes, and vases and bowls from the days of Kang Hi and Chieng Lung!

I was really so destitute that it took me three days to rig myself out from head to foot with all that was required to turn a vagabond into a gentleman. And not until this had been done, could I call at the various legations, and throw myself headlong into the whirl of dinner-parties and feasts.

My most pleasant memory of Peking is my acquaintance with Li Hung Chang, the world-famous, wise old statesman. He was also considered to be one of the wealthiest Chinese of his age. Yet he lived very simply and unpretentiously in the midst of this hopeless labyrinth of houses and alleys. At that time, the streets of Peking were terribly narrow and dirty; and people did not, as now, use automobiles or carriages, or, what is even worse, trolley-cars. Even the rickshaw had hardly a foothold in Peking. It was out of the question to walk, because of the dirt in the streets, and the great distances. One had either to ride, or to be carried in a sedan-chair.

Smiling jovially, Li Hung Chang received M. Pavloff and me; and after inquiring about my journey and my plans, he invited us to dinner a few days later.

That dinner was really a wonderful affair! The small, round table was laid in the centre of an average-sized room, the walls of which were without decoration save for two photographs. Upon our entrance, the old man, with evident satisfaction, at once directed our attention to these photographs. One picture represented Li Hung Chang and Bismarck, the other Li Hung Chang and Gladstone. He smiled condescendingly, as if to intimate that the two European statesmen were veritable pygmies in comparison with himself, and that they might well have been grateful for the honour of being photographed on the same plates with him.

The food was European, and champagne flowed freely. We talked, through an interpreter, of Li Hung Chang's journey to the coronation in Moscow the year before (1896), and of his visits to several European countries and to the United States. We also talked about my travels through Asia. The conversation had several piquant points. To judge from Li Hung Chang's experience, all Europeans who visited Peking had selfish motives, and came there only for the sake of gain. He believed this was true of me also, and said quite frankly:

"Of course, you have come here to get a professorship in the University of Tientsin?"

"No, thank you!" I replied. "Should Your Excellency offer me such a post, with a minister's salary, I would not accept it."

Speaking of the King of Sweden, he used the title, *wang,* which means vassal prince.

Pavloff explained that Sweden had a most independent and very powerful king, who ranked with all the other European monarchs. Then I inquired:

"Why did not Your Excellency visit Sweden last year, when you were so near?"

"I did not have time to see all your countries over there. But tell me about Sweden and how people live in your country."

"Sweden," said I, "is a large and happy country. The winters are not immoderately cold there, the summers not too hot. There are no deserts or steppes, only fields, forests, and lakes. There are no scorpions or dangerous snakes, and wild beasts are scarce. There are no rich and no poor——"

At this point, Li Hung Chang interrupted me; and, turning to Pavloff, he said:

"What an extraordinary country! I should advise the Czar of Russia to take Sweden."

Pavloff became embarrassed, and did not know how to get out of this. He answered:

"Impossible, Your Excellency! The Swedish king and the Czar are the greatest friends on earth, and have no evil intentions toward each other."

Li Hung Chang then put this question to me:

"You say that you have travelled through East Turkestan, northern Tibet, Tsaidam, and southern Mongolia. Why did you really traverse those vassal states of ours?"

"In order to explore and map out their unknown parts, examine the geographical, geological, and botanical conditions, etc., and, above all, to find out if there were not some provinces suitable for the Swedish king to annex!"

Li Hung Chang laughed good-humouredly, put his thumbs in the air, and exclaimed: "Bravo, bravo!" I had got my revenge. But instead of pursuing the subject of an eventual Swedish conquest of China's vassal states, he thought he would get me into a quandary on another topic, and asked accordingly:

"So that's it! You study the geological conditions, too. Well now, if you came riding across a plain, and saw a mountain rise in the distance above the horizon, could you tell right off whether that mountain contained gold or not?"

"No, not at all! I would first have to ride up to the mountain and subject it to careful petrographic examination."

"Oh, thank you! That takes no skill. I can do that, too. The thing is to decide from afar whether or not there is gold."

I had to admit defeat on that score. Anyhow, the contest was an honourable one, considering that my adversary was China's greatest statesman in modern times. In this vein, our conversation went on during the whole dinner. And when it was over, we exchanged farewells, and left for home in our rocking sedan-chairs.

After a twelve-day stay in Peking, I returned to Kalgan, whither Islam had meanwhile gone with the luggage. I had decided to go home by way of Mongolia and Siberia. The Trans-Siberian Railway was then completed only to Kansk, east of the Yenisei, and consequently I had to travel by carriage and sledge for eighteen hundred miles.

Arrived in St. Petersburg, I paid my respects for the first time to Czar Nicholas II, at his palace at Tsarskoe Selo. In the years to come, I was to see him again frequently. I received a card through the Swedish Legation, giving the day and the hour that "His Majesty the Emperor had deigned to set for the audience," and all the other details as to train for Tsarskoe Selo and carriage to the palace. A lackey was to meet the guest at the station and accompany him to the palace. On the way from the station to the palace, I was stopped a couple of times by mounted Circassians or Cossacks, and had to prove by the card that I was the person expected.

The Czar wore a colonel's uniform, and produced the impression less of an emperor than of an ordinary man, being simple and unpretentious. He showed a great and benevolent interest in my travels, and revealed himself as very much at home with the geography of interior Asia. He spread out a huge map of Central Asia on a table, so that I might retrace my route on it. He underlined with a red crayon my principal stops, such as Kashgar, the Yarkand-daria, Khotan, Takla-makan, Lop-nor, etc., and knowingly referred to the regions where I had touched on territory explored by Przhevalsky. He was particularly interested to hear about the Anglo-Russian Boundary Commission at Pamir, in whose quarters I had spent some days. He asked me frankly what I thought of the boundary-line drawn between the Russian and the Anglo-Indian provinces on "The Roof of the World," and I could only answer, according to my conviction, that it would have been more natural and simple to let the border follow the main ridge of the Hindu-kush, which separates the waters, than to cut through the level tableland, where it had to be marked by artificial piles of stone, and where friction might easily arise because of the wanderings of the nomads.

The Czar knit his brows, stamped the floor, and exclaimed emphatically:

"That is just what I have pointed out all the time; but nobody has told me the plain and simple truth of the matter!"

Afterwards, when he heard of my intention of undertaking a new expedition to the heart of Asia, he asked me to inform him of the plan and details, when the time for my departure approached; for he wished to do all he could to assist me in my enterprise. He showed later on that this promise was not so many empty words.

A few days later, on May 10, 1897, I went, by steamer, from Finland to Stockholm. My parents, sisters, and friends were standing on the quay; and our joy at meeting again was indescribable. Had I not been within a hair's-breadth of never returning? That very same day, I called on the old King, my principal benefactor, and was royally honoured by him. But there was no trace of the triumphal procession that I had dreamt of as a schoolboy, that time when Nordenskiöld returned to Stockholm. The whole city was thinking only of the great exhibition which was then about to open.

On May 13, a couple of friends and I gave an intimate little farewell-dinner for Andrée, who, with two companions, was going to Spitsbergen, thence to sail across the North Pole to Bering Strait, in his balloon, "The Eagle." Andrée made a stirring speech, in which he congratulated me upon returning from my long years in Asia, and upon being privileged to bring back to Sweden all the accrued results. He himself stood on the threshold of an enterprise, the outcome of which was shrouded in uncertainty. I replied, expressing my warm hope that his flight across the seas and the ice-fields would be a brilliant success, and that we, who were now wishing him a happy journey, might be allowed to gather around him on his victorious return, bid him welcome, and be happy that the sadness which now moved us had been turned into rejoicing.

He left Stockholm on May 15. On July 11, he rose from the northern shore of Spitsbergen, and "The Eagle" disappeared beyond the horizon. He never returned; and to this day nothing has been learned of his fate or of that of his companions. But the memory of the glorious deed is still alive, and we are proud that the first men who attempted the daring feat of sailing over the North Pole through the air were Swedes.

On the evening of that same day, only a few hours after Andrée's departure, the King gave a supper, in his palace, for eight hundred persons, to celebrate the opening of the exposition. Fridtjof Nansen, having completed his journey across the Arctic Ocean, in the "Fram," had been received in Stockholm two weeks before my return home. Now it was my turn. The official toasts had been drunk. A contemporary account of the event reads: "Once more the King took the floor, and his voice, always so beautiful, rang with a particularly warm timbre." Tall and white-haired, he walked in among the guests, and made a speech for me. He said, in part: "At the risk of his life, and with indomitable energy, Nansen has searched for land among the ice-fields of the Arctic Ocean. Sven Hedin, a son of Sweden, at equal risk of life, and with indomitable energy, has searched for water—the water that does not flow very freely in the sandy deserts and steppes of interior Asia. A king's duties are often heavy, but his privileges are often precious. I am exercising one of these privileges when, in the name of the Swedish nation, I address myself to the political and social representatives of that people assembled here, and call on them to join with me as spokesman of the sentiments cherished by the Swedish people, when I cry aloud the name of Sven Hedin."

My aged father attended the party, and was at least as happy as I at the King's tribute to me.

It would be easy to fill an entire book with accounts of the receptions that were given me by almost all the geographical societies in Europe. Paris, St. Petersburg, Berlin, and London surpassed all other cities in that respect. I was showered with medals and royal distinctions. I remember with particular gratitude my old teacher, Baron von Richthofen, of the Berlin Geographical Society; Felix Faure, President of the French Republic; Milne Edwards and Roland Bonaparte, of the Geographical Society in Paris; old Semenoff, in St. Petersburg; the Prince of Wales (later King Edward VII) ; my old friend Sir Clements Markham, President of the Royal Geographical Society of London; and many others. The Royal Geographical Society of London presented me with one of its large, gold medals, The Founders' Medal, and elected me an honorary member.[1] During my stay in London, I was frequently at the house of Henry M. Stanley, the great explorer of Africa, who remained my friend for the rest of his life. Stanley was my best adviser at that time, when I received good offers, including one from Major Pond, to go over to America to lecture. That journey did not come off; for I had quite different plans in mind.

[1] Concerning my reception in London, see the *Geographical Journal*, Vol. XI, 1898, p. 410 *f.*

CHAPTER XXXII

Back to the Deserts!

O N Midsummer Day (June 24), 1899, when the lilacs were in full bloom, I set out for the heart of Asia for the fourth time. My chief backers were King Oscar and Emanuel Nobel. The instruments, four cameras, with twenty-five hundred plates, stationery and drawing-materials, presents for the natives, clothes and books, in short, all the luggage, weighed 1,130 kilos, and was packed in twenty-three boxes. A James Patent Folding-Boat, from London, with mast, sail, oars, and life-buoys, was to play an important part in that expedition.

The parting with my parents, sisters, and brother was, as usual, the hardest part of the whole journey. The joyous part came afterwards, as I experienced the ever-renewed charm of the unknown at every stage. I longed for the open air, and for great adventures on lonely roads.

I had been to see the Czar, and had shown him the plan for the new expedition, a few months before my departure. He did everything to facilitate my undertaking. Free transportation, free carriage, and exemption from customs-duties on all the Russian railways, in Europe and Asia, were accorded me; and the Czar himself offered me an escort of about twenty Cossacks, who were not to cost me one copeck. I told him that this was far too many, and that four men would do; so we decided on that number. The Cossack question was duly settled with General Kuropatkin, Minister of War.

I had to make 3,180 miles by rail, to Andishan, in Russian Turkestan. At Krasnovodsk, on the eastern shore of the Caspian Sea, the drawing-room car which was to be my home throughout my journey in Asiatic Russia, was prepared for me. I could stay as long as I liked in the various cities, and had only to specify the train to which I should like my car to be attached. My car was always at the rear end of the train;

and from its back platform I enjoyed a full view of the fleeting land-scape.

Islam Baï was waiting for me, when I arrived at Andishan. He wore a blue cloak; and the King's gold medal adorned his breast. We were happy to meet again, and to try our luck together once more. I ordered him to hurry to Osh, with all my luggage, and to make arrange-ments with the caravan-driver who was to help us to Kashgar. Mean-while, I stayed at the house of my old friend, Colonel Saitseff.

With seven men and twenty-six horses, and two puppies, Yoldash and Dovlet, each about a month old, I set out on July 31. In the two-hundred-and-seventy-mile trudge across the mountains to Kashgar, I had to cross the pass of Tong-burun, the watershed between the Aral Sea and the Lop-nor. All Asia lay before me! I felt like a conqueror before a whole world of discoveries, which lay waiting for me in the depths of the deserts and on the summits of the mountains. For the three years that this journey was to last, my first rule was to visit only regions where no one had been before; and the majority of my survey in 1,149 sheets actually represented hitherto-unexplored land.

It was delightful to listen again, in a tent, to the wind murmuring in the tops of the trees, and to the clangour of bells of large camel-caravans. The Kirghiz wandered in the pastures with their herds as of yore; and at a practicable ford they helped us take our horses across the dangerous, foaming Kizil-zu (the Red River).

In Kashgar, I met only old friends, namely, Consul-General Petrov-sky, Sir George Macartney, and Father Hendricks. Höglund, the Swedish missionary, with his family and assistants, had founded a Christian mission in the city. As before, Petrovsky helped me, both by word and by deed. For 11,500 roubles, I bought 161 Chinese silver *yambas,* which weighed 300 kilos. They were packed in several boxes, so as to reduce the chance of theft or complete loss. At that time, a *yamba* cost seventy-one roubles. Later on, when I needed more money, the *yamba* had risen in price to ninety roubles. We purchased fifteen splendid Bactrian camels, only two of which survived our adventures. Nias Haji and Turdu Baï were appointed caravan-leaders. The latter, a white-bearded old man, worth his weight in gold, stayed in my employ till the end of the journey. Faizullah, too, was a reliable camel-driver and young Kader was employed because he knew how to write, for occasionally letters in the East Turkestan language had to be sent. Two

of the Czar's Cossacks, Sirkin and Chernoff, of Semiryetchensk, I took
with me from Kashgar. The other two were to join me at my camp
on the Lop-nor.

At two o'clock in the afternoon, on September 5, we set forth, in
burning sunshine. To the clanging of large, bronze bells, the heavily-
laden caravan advanced between villages, gardens, and fields, away from
Kashgar. In every direction, the country consisted of smooth, yellow
loess. Yellow clouds of dust whirled about the camels and horses. It
grew dark above the mountains in the northwest. A gust of wind,
heralding a storm, swept the dust before it in thick clouds. The next

CROSSING A BRIDGE IN A SMALL VILLAGE OUTSIDE OF KASHGAR

moment, a violent rain whipped the ground, and peal after peal of
thunder resounded. We were deafened; the earth trembled; one might
have thought the end of the world was near. In less than a minute, we
were soaked. The clay softened, and became as slippery as soap. The
camels lurched as if intoxicated. When they slipped and fell, they
splashed mud in all directions. Piercing shrieks penetrated the air, as
new wreckages occurred. We had to stop continually, to free fallen
camels of their burdens, help them to their feet, and load them anew.
Had this severe rain fallen during our desert march in Takla-makan,

the caravan would not have succumbed! Now its effect was harmful. Night, with its darkness, set in, as we made camp in a garden.

After a walk of six days, across steppes and wilderness, we reached Lailik, situated on the Yarkand-daria, right opposite Merket, the village where we had begun our disastrous desert-journey. Not far from this village, on the right bank of the river, we found a barge for sale. It resembled the one at Yarkand, which conveyed caravans and carts across the river. We bought it for one and a half *yamba*. It was thirty-eight feet long, eight feet wide, and, when loaded, drew scarcely a foot of water. Having learned from natives that the river branched into several narrow arms near Maral-bashi, we built another, smaller boat. It was less than half the size of the other. This would enable us to continue the river-journey as far as to Lop-nor, regardless of conditions.

A deck was built in the bow of the barge, and my tent was erected on that. Amidships, there was a square cabin, covered with black blankets, intended as a photographic dark-room. It was provided with built-in tables and shelves, and two basins, with clear water, for washing plates. Behind this cabin, the heavy luggage and the food-supplies were stowed; and on the after-deck, my attendants had their mess, in the open, around a clay fireplace. Thus I could get hot tea during the journey. A narrow passage ran along the port side, which kept communication open between stem and stern.

In the opening of the tent, two of my boxes were placed, to serve as observation-tables, and a third, smaller box did duty as a chair. From this point, I had an unobstructed view of the river, and could draw a detailed map of its course. The interior of the tent was provided with a rug, my bed, and such boxes as I needed constantly.

The wharf presented a lively scene. Carpenters were sawing and hammering, smiths were forging, and the Cossacks supervised the whole affair. But autumn had already come, and the river was sinking daily. We had to hurry. When everything was ready, we launched the proud vessel, which, for almost three months, was to be my home, and was to take me nine hundred miles along a river that had never before been mapped out in detail. In the evening, I gave a party for our workmen and the people of the neighbourhood. Chinese lanterns glowed among the tents; drums and string-music vied with my music-box; barefoot dancing-girls, whose hair hung in long braids, and who were dressed in white, with pointed caps, danced around a roaring fire; and a festival spirit reigned on the shores of the Yarkand-daria.

On September 17, we were ready to leave. With the Cossacks in the lead, the caravan set out through the brushwood. Going by way of the towns of Aksu and Kucha, it was to meet me two and a half months later at a certain point on the river.

Islam Baï, Kader, and I embarked. The crew of the barge consisted of three men, Palta, Naser, and Alim. Two were placed in the stern, and one in the bow. They carried long poles, with which to stave the boat off, in case we got too close to the bank. A fourth man, Kasim, managed the smaller craft, which resembled a floating farm, with its cackling hens, fragrant melons, and vegetables. Two sheep were tethered on board the large boat. Here, too, Dovlet and Yoldash, the puppies, made themselves very much at home, right from the start.

At our starting-point, the river was four hundred and forty feet wide, and nine feet deep. Its velocity was three feet a second, and its volume 3,430 cubic feet a second. It was afternoon when I gave the command to cast off. We glided away gloriously between the woody banks. At the first turning, Lailik disappeared behind us.

The next bend found us in shallow water, quite close to the shore, where some women and children, who had been waiting for us, hurried into the water with gifts of milk, eggs, and vegetables, getting silver coins in return. They were the families of our crew, bidding us a last farewell.

Soon I was seated at my writing-table, the first sheet of paper, compass, watch, pencils, and field-glass before me, looking out over the magnificent river, which described erratic turns, as it wound through the desert. Like the snail, we carried our house with us, and were always at home. The landscape came gliding towards me, silently and slowly, without my having to take a single step, or rein in a horse. New prospects of wooded capes, dark thickets, or waving reeds opened at every turn. Islam placed a tray with hot tea and bread on my table. Solemn silence surrounded us. It was broken only where the water rippled around a bough, stuck in the mud, or when the crew had to stave the boat off from the banks, or when the dogs chased each other, or stood still in the bow, barking at a shepherd, who stood outside his tent of brush and branches, petrified, like a statue, watching our boats go by. I entered into the life of the river; I felt the beating of its pulse. Every day was to add to my knowledge of its habits. Never have I made a more idyllic journey than this one. I still cherish its memory.

A halt! We scraped something. The bow of the barge was fast on a poplar-trunk grounded in the river-bed, and the boat swung half-way around. It seemed as if the sun were rolling along the sky. I used the opportunity to measure the velocity of the current. But soon Palta and his comrades jumped overboard, and got us afloat. Then we glided along till twilight set in, and we camped for the first time on this river-trip.

The boat was moored, the men went ashore, made a fire, and prepared a meal. The puppies scrambled to land and pursued each other among the bushes, but returned afterwards to my tent on the boat, where I spent my nights, while the men slept at the camp-fire. Before I finished my notes for the day, Islam Baï served me with rice-pudding, broiled wild duck, cucumbers, sour milk, eggs, and tea; and the puppies got their fair share. The tent was open. The moon-path wound and twisted over the eddying river. Enchantment was in the air. It was hard to wrench myself away from the view of the dark forest and the silvery river.

To save time, we set out again as soon as the sun was up. Tea was brewed on the fire in the stern. I dressed and washed after we were on our way. Palta sat in front of me, with his pole, singing a song about the adventures of a legendary king. A shepherd on the bank answered some questions, as we slowly glided past his point of land.

"What kind of game is there in your forests?"

"Red deer, roe-deer, boars, wolves, foxes, lynxes, hares!"

"No tigers?"

"No, we have not seen a tiger for a long time."

"When will the river freeze?"

"In seventy or eighty days."

We had to hurry. The volume of water diminished quickly in the autumn. After two days' journey, it had already become reduced to 2,350 cubic feet a second. The wind was our worst enemy. The tent and the cabin acted like sails. In a head-wind, the speed of the boat decreased; and when the wind was behind us, we moved faster than we wished. One day, we had not gone far, when a violent wind forced us to make for shore. I then took the yawl, hoisted its sail, and flew up the river before a smacking breeze. The barge, together with the

shores and the forests, disappeared in a yellow-grey haze. I enjoyed
the peacefulness and solitude. Then I took down the mast and sail,
and lay down in the bottom of the boat, leaving the current to do the
rest.

The wind subsided, and we proceeded. Sometimes Islam had himself rowed ashore, to wander through the underbrush, gun on shoulder.
He always returned with pheasants and wild ducks, thus providing a
welcome variety to my bill of fare. Once he took the other men along,
and they stayed away seven hours. We saw them at length, stretched
out, on a point of land, sound asleep. The barge glided past them
noiselessly, and they did not awake. I sent a man ashore in the yawl,
to wake them up, and to bring them on board.

The wild geese had begun to stir, and were gathering for their
long flight to India. We had brought with us a captured wild goose
from Lailik. Its wings had been clipped, and it walked freely about
on the large boat. Now and then he would visit me in my tent, and
deposit his visiting-card (which looked like spinach) on the rug. When
we camped, he was allowed to swim about in the river at his pleasure;
and he always returned voluntarily. Upon hearing his cousins shrieking
in the air, he would cock his head and gaze up at them. Perhaps he
thought of the mango trees and the palms on the banks of the Ganges.

On September 23, we reached the critical place of which the people
in Merket had warned us; for there the river divided into several
rapidly rushing arms. The river-bed narrowed. We were carried
along at breakneck speed by the current. The water seethed and foamed
around us. We flew down a rapids. The passage was so narrow, and
the turns so abrupt, that the boats could not be steered off; and the big
boat struck the shore so violently, that my boxes were nearly carried
overboard. Before we knew where we were, we were swept down two
more rapids. The river had dug itself a new bed for a short distance.
There were no forests here; but the tamarisks were still standing in the
river, and the driftwood and poplar-trunks that had piled up against
them, formed veritable little islets. The water swirled all the way; and
we moved so swiftly, that the barge nearly capsized when we struck the
ground violently. At times, we got so thoroughly enmeshed in the driftwood, that we could work ourselves loose again only with great difficulty. The river had become shallower, for its several branches robbed
it of water. Finally, the bed that we followed became so shallow, that

the whole outfit got stuck in its blue-clay bottom. The crew were despatched to some near-by villages for aid. They returned with thirty men, who took all our luggage ashore, and then dragged the barge, inch by inch, across the shallow place. After that, only the last and steepest rapids remained. I stayed alone on board. The men held the barge in place by means of a long rope, thus preventing its turning crosswise and being upset in the torrent. It glided neatly over the brink of the rapids, and then tipped down like a seesaw. The current next showed itself in a narrow channel, where we were kept constantly on the alert, to avoid being wrecked, as we dashed along.

We were still in the newly-formed bed, where the shores were bare, and animal life was scarce. Only here and there were growths of reeds, with tracks of boars and roe-deer. An eagle sat watching us, and some ravens called across the river. The dogs amused me considerably. They dashed about, from stem to stern, like happy sprites. At first they barked themselves hoarse at grounded poplar-trunks, which lay swaying in the current like black crocodiles. But they soon got used to them, and left them in peace. Soon they invented another game. In the middle of the trip, they jumped overboard and swam ashore, in order to follow us along the bank, and stalk game. Wherever the river bent so as to cause the barge to leave the bank on which the dogs were running, they would swim across. This unnecessary move was repeated time after time. In the end, they grew tired, swam out to the boat, and were hauled on board.

The new river-bed ended, and we again drifted between old, majestic forests. The current was sluggish. The forests grew mightier. Autumn had come. The leaves were yellow and red, but the tops of the poplars were dense, and no sun-ray reached down to us. We glided along, as on a canal in Venice; only here rose the forest instead of palaces. The gondoliers slumbered at their poles. A mood of enchantment charged with mystery pervaded the forest. It would not have surprised me to hear Pan playing on his pipes, or to see roguish wood-nymphs peep out from the dense thickets. A breath of air passed through the forest, and the yellow leaves rained down over the bright surface of the river. They brought to mind the yellow wreaths which the Brahmins offer to the sacred Ganges.

The Yarkand-daria made the most crazy twists. At one point, only one-ninth was lacking for a complete circle. On another occasion, we had to drift 1,450 metres, in order to advance a distance of 180 metres. Another time, only one-twelfth of a complete circle was wanting. High water would soon cut through the narrow strip of land, and then the current would desert the old bend.

We went very slowly. The river fell. The air grew colder. I wondered if we were going to be caught in the ice, before we reached our goal.

CHAPTER XXXIII

Our Life on the Largest River in the Very Heart of Asia

O N the last day of September, the landscape about us became altogether different. The forest ended, the level steppe stretched all around, and the Masar-tagh rose above the horizon like a sharply-defined cloud. At times, the mountain was before us; at other times it was to starboard or port, and even behind us, when the bends took us southwest instead of northeast.

One day more, and to the north the snowy peaks of Tian-shan stood out like a faint background in the distance. The Masar-tagh became clearer; the contours grew sharper; and, when evening came, we encamped at the foot of the mountain. A tent stood there, and friendly natives came down to the shore to sell wild ducks, geese, and fish, which they had caught in their traps and nets. The chieftain of the place was commissioned to ride to the nearest village on the caravan-road, to buy furs and boots for my crew, and rice, flour, and vegetables to replenish our food-supply. He was given sufficient money for his needs, and was told where to meet us. We ran the risk of his stealing the money and not returning; for he was a total stranger to all of us. But he did not dare to deceive us. He came to the appointed place, with his task well performed.

Kasim, the pilot of our small boat, was skilful at catching fish. He made a fish-spear, and harpooned fish at a point where a small tributary formed a waterfall. After a few days more, we caught a glimpse of the Choka-tagh, being that part of the Masar-tagh from the southern end of which I had set out on my disastrous desert-journey. I wanted to see the place again, and to visit the lake from which we had taken too little water. The lake was joined to the river, and we were going to make the trip in the English yawl. Islam went with me. But he forgot to bring his rifle. In case we stayed away long, the men at home were to light a signal-fire at night.

With a smacking wind from behind, we sailed away from the

river, through a strait that led to a first lake, where reeds grew thickly. But there was open water, too; and fourteen snow-white swans were swimming there, watching our craft with amazement, wondering if our white sails were the wings of a huge swan. Only when we were quite close to them did they rise, with noise and bluster, but only to descend a little farther away.

A long strait connected this lake with its neighbour further south, called Chol-kol (the Desert Lake), at the southern end of which I had encamped on April 22, 1895. There we went ashore. Palta and two natives had followed us on land. Islam and the natives took charge of the boat, while Palta and I walked towards the Choka-tagh, later returning to the camp by way of the eastern slope of the mountain.

It took us a long time to reach the foot of the mountain and climb to its summit. By that time the sun was near the horizon. I stayed up there for a while. The view, from south to east, woke to life strange memories. The crests of the dunes, as far as I could see, shone with a red light, like glowing volcanoes. They rose like burial-mounds over my dead men and camels. Old Mohammed Shah! Could he forgive me, where he now refreshed his throat from paradisiacal springs, under the palm trees in Bihasht?

I was one of the three survivors; and over there, far away, was the place where we had last pitched our tents among the dunes. I did not notice that the sun had set. I seemed to hear a funeral-song from the heart of the desert. It grew darker. I had a vision of ghostly shadows rushing up to me from the darkening dunes.

Finally I was roused by a deer, which jumped lightly down a slope, and by Palta, who said: "The camp is far off, sir."

The descent was arduous. It was dark, and we had to exercise caution. We reached level ground, and stepped out northwards for a twenty-four mile walk. I was not used to walking, and felt dead-tired. At last the signal-fire appeared. It was baffling to walk towards the fire. It seemed to be quite near, yet it took hours to reach it. At midnight, I was again back in my tent, on board. It was my first strenuous day during that expedition. But later on there were to be others!

We left that memorable place on October 8, and continued our winding, tortuous way. Thenceforth we had always on board one or two shepherds who knew the country, and were able to give information. Directly before us, a deer swam across the river. Islam got out

his rifle in a hurry.   But the distance was too great; he was too excited, and missed.   With one jump, the beautiful animal was on shore,
and disappeared like a streak among the reeds.

At nightfall, we pitched camp in the woody region of More.
Dovlet, my pet dog, who for some days had been depressed, and was
acting strangely, ran ashore, and searched anxiously among the bushes.
Finally he fell in a cramp and died.   I felt his loss bitterly.   He had
been a wretched little puppy when we first got him, in Osh.   He had
grown, and promised to become a fine-looking dog.   Mollah, a priest,
who was a passenger of ours at the time, dug a grave, wrapped him in

A HERD OF WILD PIGS

the skin of our last sheep, mumbled a prayer, and filled in the little
grave.   It was lonely and desolate on the boat after Dovlet had left us.

The farther we advanced, the slower the current became.   The crew
did not have much to do.   All, except Palta, listened, when Mollah,
on the after-deck, read aloud of the day when the followers of the
Prophet conquered East Turkestan for Islam.   The green shades of the
forest-roof faded day by day, and the yellow and red became predomi-
nant.   We passed through what seemed an aisle, with high pillars on
both sides.   By way of diversion, Islam Baï set the music-box going,
and the stillness was broken by *Carmen,* the Swedish national anthem,
and regimental marches of the Swedish cavalry.   A wild duck came

swimming along the shore, and a fox skirted it stealthily. A herd of boars rooted in the reeds. The old ones were black, and the young ones brown. They stood still, and gazed at us steadily. Then they made a complete turn, and ran away noisily through the thicket.

I worked eleven hours a day, sitting at my observation-table as if fixed there. No gap must be permitted on the chart of the river. During the night before October 12, the temperature fell below the freezing-point for the first time; and after that, the last green spots in the forest soon vanished. When it was windy, the river was so closely covered with wind-driven leaves, that one might have imagined oneself gliding over a mosaic floor, done in yellow and red. Where the forest-belt was thin, we could sometimes see the nearest dune-crest in the Takla-makan Desert.

Four shepherds were tending their sheep on a point of land. They were sitting around their camp-fire, as the boats slipped by without a sound. They were struck dumb with terror, and got up and fled, swift as an arrow, into the forest. We went ashore, called loudly, and made a search for them. But they were gone, and remained so. They had probably mistaken the boat for a ghostlike monster that was stealing upon them to annihilate them.

A *sarik-buran* (yellow storm) raged on October 18 and 19, and whole Sargasso Seas of leaves floated on the river. We were compelled to moor, and I went afoot, through the forest, to the beginning of the sandy desert. At last the wind subsided, and we went on, during the night, by the light of the moon and lanterns. A log-fire was built at the camp, and four dry poplar-trunks gave us heat.

The next day, at a certain bend, Mollah declared that a *khaneka* (mosque), called Mazar Khojam, was to be found in the forest, at some distance from the shore. All of us, except Kader, went there. The small temple was of the most primitive kind, built of boughs and planks, driven vertically into the sandy ground, and surrounded by an enclosure. Streamers and rags fluttered on some poles. Solemn as a high-priest, Mollah read a prayer; and "Allahu akbar, la illaha il Allah" rang sonorously through the forest, so silent a moment before. When we returned to the barge, Kader, wishing to show an equal devotion to the Prophet, asked permission to go alone to the sanctuary, following our trail. He soon returned, however, as though a whole army of infernal spirits were at his heels. He had felt very uneasy in his loneliness, had mistaken every bush for a beast, and had been scared by the fluttering of the streamers.

Kasim drifted ahead of us, with the small boat, in order to sound the depth, and to warn us of shoals. He stood in the stern with his pole. Presently he pushed the pole so hard into the bottom, that he could not get it out again. He fell backwards into the river, while the rest of us nearly choked with laughter.

On October 23, things got lively on board. The river followed the caravan-road closely. A horseman appeared on the edge of the wood, and disappeared, but returned shortly with a whole troop of mounted men. They asked us to stop, and we went ashore. On a rug, they piled up heaps of melons, grapes, apricots, and freshly-baked bread. Afterwards, I invited the most prominent among them on board, and proceeded onwards, the other riders flanking us on the shore. New hordes appeared after a while. They were West Turkestan merchants, from Avat. But that was not all. Thirty more horsemen came dashing out of the forest. This time it was the *bek* of Avat himself who paid us homage. He and the merchants were likewise taken on board. Islam Baï served tea to all. The barge glided on. The mounted hordes on the shore increased. We landed, encamped, and stayed over one day. The whole population of the neighbourhood came to the shore to see our strange vessel. Eight falconers, and two horsemen with eagles, invited us to go hunting. The booty, one deer and four hares, was presented to me.

When we left this hospitable tract, fragrant bowls of fruit stood on my rug, and enough food to last several weeks had been added to our store. We had also procured a new dog, Hamra, whom it took some days to make fairly tame.

Two days later, the surrounding landscape changed completely again. We reached the spot where the mightier Aksu came flowing in from the north. Here the slow and winding journey on the Yarkand-daria ended, and the augmented river, now flowing eastward, was called the Tarim. The landscape unfolded magically. We left the last cape on the right bank of the Yarkand-daria, and moored on the left bank. There we stayed a day, to examine the eddies and the current where the two rivers met.

One day more, and we pushed off. The barge revolved once in the eddies, but afterwards it lay steadily on the strong current. The water was dirty grey. The river was broad and shallow. The turns were not abrupt, and for long stretches the river was almost straight. The shores flew past. To the south, the dry mouth of the Khotan-daria yawned. A few years before, that river had saved my life.

We encamped on the Tarim for the first time. Lots of wild geese flew past in flocks shaped like arrowheads. They were on their way to India. One flock settled down quite close to the boat. We did not molest them; for we had food enough. Early next morning, they continued their journey. Our tame wild goose, puzzled, gazed at them. One member of the flock stayed behind. He was probably tired. But he soon felt lonely; so he soared again, and followed the invisible trail of his comrades through the air. He knew their next halting-place, and was sure to overtake them. Our crew from Lailik knew the road less than did the wild geese. The ever-growing distance between them and Lailik bewildered them; and they did not know how they would find their way back. But I promised to help them, when the time came.

At this point, the Tarim carried 2,765 cubic feet of water, and the speed of the current was between three and four feet a second. During the night, the cold increased to 16°. The surface of the ground froze, but thawed again in the daytime. Whole blocks of earth and sand tumbled continually into the river from the perpendicular-terraced shores. Once this happened just as we were floating past. The entire starboard side of the barge got a cold shower-bath, and we rocked violently. At another point, a lone woman stood, with half a score of eggs in a basket. She asked us to buy them, just as our stern swept so close, that we could take the basket on board, while moving, and throw a silver coin to her.

The current was strong. Here and there, the water gushed, forming eddies, with funnel-shaped centres. Sometimes it looked as if we would surely bump against some jutting land, at full speed. All the poles were thrust in the water, but they were of no avail. The current helped us, however, and cleverly carried the boat away from the dangerous spot. For two days we were carried at breakneck speed through a newly-formed river-bed, almost straight, and bordered by perpendicular, high-terraced shores. Great masses of sand and earth were continually descending from these into the river. It looked as though the shores were smoking.

The greatest tension prevailed. Everybody was on the *qui vive*.

Kasim, who preceded us, called out in a desperate voice: "Stop!" A poplar-trunk was stuck in the middle of the current, causing an entire islet of driftwood and brush to accumulate. We were rushing straight towards this obstruction. Only a few hundred feet separated us. The water roared, foamed, and sizzled around us. Only a miracle could prevent us from being upset. When disaster seemed imminent, Alim jumped into the ice-cold water, with a rope, and swam ashore. He succeeded in checking our speed, so that the boat was got under control, and slowly passed the obstruction.

GOING FULL SPEED WITH THE STRONG CURRENT

The boat lay tossing and shaking all night at our camping-place.

We eventually got back to the old bed again, where the shores were wooded. We met shepherds, some of whom guarded eight thousand and ten thousand sheep. Some greyish-brown vultures clustered on a silt-peninsula. They sat there, fat and clumsy, not caring to turn their heads more than half-way, and following the boat with their eyes. Here and there, on the shore, the natives maintained nets, shaped like a goose-foot, or bat-wing. They were sunk in the river, the arms brought together, and the whole was then hauled up with the captured fish.

We purchased a new rooster at our next camp. Hardly was he on board, when he came to blows with our old rooster, and drove him into the river. After that, the two warriors had to be kept apart, each on his own boat. Then things went well. When one of them crowed, the other answered immediately. We bought a canoe, also, in which Islam and Mollah paddled ahead of the barge. And lastly we bought oil for the torches, which we would need later on. A new passenger came on board, namely, a small, brown dog, who inherited the name of Dovlet, and who instantly assumed command of the larger boat. At dawn, everything was white with hoar-frost. The forest was leafless and naked, and was awaiting the approach of winter. Thousands of wild geese were trav-

NATIVES WATCHING OUR BARGE ON ITS WAY DOWN THE RIVER

elling daily to warmer latitudes. Some of the flocks were very large. The leader flew well ahead of the arrow-point, the two wings of which were several hundred yards long.

The temperature at night was now about 12°. Sheltered inlets began to freeze. The boat-poles were ice-coated. We put on winter clothes and furs, and in the evenings warmed ourselves at big fires. I wondered how far we would get before the river caught us in its ice-fetters. We started drifting as early as possible in the morning, and kept going till nightfall.

During the night preceding November 14, all of the boats got stuck in the ice on the shore, and had to be dislodged with axes and picks. From that time on, we encamped where the current prevented the water from freezing. We drifted past a place where four men and four dogs were guarding some horses. The men fled at top speed, as though for their lives; but their animals followed us along the shore for hours, the dogs barking violently. They were answered by those on the boat, and there was a terrific din. The natives here seemed to be more shy than farther up the river. Once, everybody ran away from a hut, leaving the fire burning on the hearth, when we camped on the shore close by. We shouted after them for information. But all we could do was to catch a boy; and he was so frightened out of his wits, that we could not get a word out of him.

A few days later, we succeeded in getting a pilot from a hut made of boughs and reeds.   He was a tiger-hunter; and I bought a skin, which still decorates my study in Stockholm.

The forest-people in this region are not distinguished for bravery

CAUGHT IN AN IRON TRAP

in their tiger-hunts.   Having slain a cow or a horse, the tiger eats his fill, and then retires to the deep thickets in the woods.   But the next night he returns, to continue his meal.   In so doing, he always follows the beaten paths of shepherds or cattle.   Meanwhile, the shepherd and his comrades have dug a pit in the path leading to the spot where the felled animal lies.   In the opening, they have fixed a trap, the heavy, sharp frames of which snap around the tiger's foot, when he steps be-

tween them.   He cannot possibly free himself from the trap.   Nevertheless, he retires, dragging the trap after him.   Deprived of food, he
grows thin and miserable, and is doomed to die of starvation.   Only
after a week does the hunter dare go forth.   It is easy to follow the
trail.   The hunter approaches the tiger on horseback, and shoots the
last spark of life out of him.

While we were with the tiger-killers, we got in touch with the first
Lop people.   They lived in reed huts on the banks, fish being their
principal food.   One of them showed us how they caught the fish.   He
set out a net in the opening of a long, narrow inlet, between the shore
and a mud-bank that protruded from it.   The inlet was frozen.   He
rowed along the outer edge, smashing the ice with his oar as far as he

FISHING FROM CANOES THROUGH THIN ICE

could reach.   Then he removed the net to the new edge, and so on,
little by little.   The fish retired up the bay.   In the end, he broke up the
ice closest to the shore; and the fish, trying to make for the river, got
enmeshed in the net.   The whole manœuvre was carried out with speed
and skill.   We bought the plentiful catch.

On November 21, we came to a place where the river entered a new
bed.   The velocity was very great, as usual.   The *bek*, or head of the
district, came to warn us; but he was brave enough to go along with us
on the boat.   The forest had now been succeeded by bare sand-dunes,

towering fifty feet high on the shores.   Small groves of poplars were scattered about, some of them in the very bed of the river.   On several of our landings we saw fresh tiger-prints.

All this time, the Tarim was carrying us deeper and deeper into the heart of Asia.

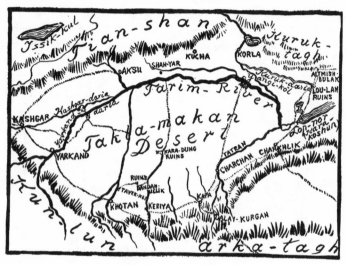

CHINESE TURKESTAN

CHAPTER XXXIV

Struggling with the Ice

ON November 24, we met with an adventure which might have had dire consequences. Contrary to the usual practice, the large boat was drifting in the lead, the smaller boats following. The river was narrow and the current very strong. We had rounded an abrupt turn, when a mighty poplar appeared not far ahead of us. Its roots had been dislodged by the river, and it had fallen. It was now lying like a bridge across one-third of the river, where the water flowed swiftly. The trunk lay horizontally about four feet above the surface of the water. It was easy enough for the small boats to pass underneath the trunk and between the branches trailing in the water. But the large boat, which was rushing at full speed towards the obstruction, would have had its tent and furniture, as well as the dark-room, swept away; or, what is more likely, the resistance offered by the dark-room would have made the boat capsize, with the result that my luggage and all my data would have been lost beyond recovery. The situation was extremely serious. Everyone shouted and gave orders. The poles would not reach to the bottom. The water eddied and boiled. In another minute we would be shipwrecked. In great haste, I packed my maps and all the loose articles that lay about. The Lailik men rowed for their lives, with the heavy oars they had improvised. The suction of the current kept carrying us in under the poplar. However, the men worked hard, and finally managed to get us out into the whirlpool that eddied about the crown of the poplar. Alim jumped into the icy water again, swam to the left bank, with a rope, and pulled us towards him with such force, that the tent and the cabin were only slightly damaged by the outermost branches of the poplar.

What if this adventure had happened at night! I hardly dared think of it.

Soon afterwards, Islam Baï came forward with some fresh, boiled fish, salt, bread, and tea. I had scarcely begun my meal, when piercing cries for help were heard from up the river. It proved to be the smaller boat, which had capsized over a grounded poplar-trunk, concealed be-

neath the water.   Pails, casks, boxes of flour and fruit, bread, cakes,
poles, and oars went spinning along the current, and were fished out
by the Lop men in the canoes.   Kasim had managed to hold onto the
treacherous poplar-trunk; and, straddling it, in ice-water up to his waist,
he called for help.   The sheep had swum ashore, and the rooster sat
soaking-wet on the overturned boat; but shovels, axes, and other hard-
ware had gone down.   No sooner was I informed that Kasim had been
rescued, than I busied myself again with the fish, which had grown cold

THE BARGE RUSHING FULL SPEED TOWARD A FALLEN TREE OBSTRUCTING
PART OF THE RIVER

meanwhile.   Large fires were made, and the evening was given over
to drying our things.

The next day, a *bek,* with two canoes, joined us.   Our fleet now
numbered ten boats.   We drifted down towards a spur of the great
desert called Tokus-kum (the Nine Sand-Mountains).   Dunes, two
hundred feet high, with no trace of vegetation, towered here on the right
bank.   At their base, they were parted by the river; and the sand slid
down, little by little, to be washed away by the water and form banks
and bars further down.

We stayed there an hour, and mounted the top of the dune, which
was not an easy job, as the sand gave way at every step.   The view over

the river and the desert was magnificent. The water and the sand contested for supremacy. There was life here. The river was rich in fish, and there were forests. But to the south was the desert, the land of death, silence, and thirst.

Our Lop men had said that from the day when the drift-ice began, it would be ten days more before the river would be frozen over. And on November 28, I awoke to a strangely tinkling and sawing sound from alongside the boat. It was the first porous drift-ice, that came dancing down the river.

"Cast off before sunrise! Light the fire on the after-deck, and put an iron brazier with glowing coals in my tent, so that my hands will not get frost-bitten at the writing-desk!"

At one o'clock, the ice was gone. But during the night it was 3°; and when I got out in the morning, the river was filled with ice-floes of all sizes. They were rounded, like white-edged discs, from their contact with one another. They made me think of funeral-wreaths, which had been presented to the river

A "BEK", OR CHIEF, ARRIVING WITH HIS CANOES

by invisible powers before Cold and Death stretched their hard shroud from shore to shore. The ice-crystals sparkled like diamonds in the light of the rising sun. They tinkled and rattled like china being smashed. They grated like a buzz-saw cutting through a block of sugar. Very soon, solid ice-borders began to form along the shores also. These grew wider, day by day. At our camping-places, the drifting floes struck the barge with such force that its frame shook. At first the dogs barked at the drift-ice and at the noise it produced. But they soon got used to it; and as we drifted, they would even run onto the floes that accompanied us on either side. But when the barge stopped on a sand-bank, it was odd and amusing to observe the ice continuing freely on its way.

Again we glided along the foot of huge dunes. Falcons, pheasants, and ravens were the only birds visible; the wild ducks and geese were gone. In the evening, Chinese lanterns and oil-torches on the small boats illuminated our way, and we proceeded on our journey till the night was well advanced. I, too, had a lantern for my writing-table to enable me to work at night. The sand ended, and was succeeded by dense yellow fields of reed. It was biting-cold, and we had to make camp. But the current was strong, and we could not see clearly enough to make a landing in the dark. One of the small boats was ordered to go ahead and set fire to the reeds. Soon the whole shore seemed to be afire. A fantastic, wild, and magnificent picture unfolded before us. The yellow-red light changed the river into melting gold; and the small boats and their oarsmen, silhouetted in raven-black, stood out against the background of dazzling light. The reeds crackled and cracked. We moored at a place that had not been touched by the fire.

On December 3, we passed a point where signal-fires and horsemen on the shore induced us to land. They had been sent out by the Cossacks to tell us that the caravan had encamped a few days' journey farther down.

The next day the velocity of the current was great, and the boat drifted gloriously among the floating ice-floes. At times, we brushed the bank, and ground against its icy edge. At Karaul, I saw Islam Baï on the shore, with a white-bearded man. This was our friend Parpi Baï, of 1896 memory. He wore a dark-blue cloak and a fur cap. We hove to, and took him on board. He greeted me with emotion, and was soon enrolled among my faithful retainers.

The Tarim still flowed at the rate of about two thousand cubic feet a second; but the ice-ribbons along the shore grew wider, and the open channel in the middle got narrower and narrower. At a shallow point, we ran up on a treacherously-concealed poplar-trunk, and would have stuck there, had it not been for the heavy drift-ice pushing us on from behind. The bow of the boat rose clear out of the water, and then fell back with a resounding smack.

December 7 was the last day of this glorious journey. We knew that the caravan had settled down at Yangi-kol, and that the river was frozen from shore to shore some distance below that point. Three *beks* and an immense troop of horsemen followed us along the shore, but only the *bek* of Yangi-kol was allowed on board. He sat smiling in front of my tent, and looked as if he were having the time of his life.

The river flowed due southeast. On the left there was a steppe, with sparse poplars and thickets.   On the right were enormous sand-dunes, with shallow lakes between.   The channel was so narrow in some places, that the boat broke up the edges of the ice on both sides, causing much noise and bluster.

Chernoff, Nias Haji, and Faizullah joined the rest of the horse-men.   At dusk, the lanterns and the torches were lit again, and we went on.   We were determined to reach the camp of the caravan.   At last a huge fire appeared on the left shore, and there the caravan was. We cast anchor for the last time, and hurried ashore to warm our limbs, which were stiff with cold.

The name of the place was Yangi-kol (the New Lake).   It became my headquarters for half a year.   It had a splendid location.   We had neighbours in several directions; it was only a three days' ride to the town of Korla; and south and west of us lay the great desert.

After I had had a thorough rest the next morning, and had inspected our camels and horses, we removed the two boats to a small, round, sheltered inlet, which froze to the bottom during the winter, making our boats rest as though in a bed of granite.   After that, we had a thousand things to do.   A post-courier had arrived from Kashgar, with a whole bundle of longed-for letters from home; and so my first occu-pation was to write letters, and to send the courier back.   We pur-chased provisions, candles, blankets, cloth and canvas, etc., in Korla. The crew were paid double wages, and I also saw to it that they got home safely.   Nias Haji, who had been guilty of theft, was dismissed. Islam Baï became *karavan-bashi* (caravan-leader); Turdu Baï and Faizullah were entrusted with the care of the camels; Parpi Baï, who, besides being falconer, looked after the horses, had sixteen-year-old Kurban for a messenger-boy; and Ordek, a Lop man, carried water, wood, and fodder, which we had bought from our neighbours.   The Cossacks supervised it all.   Sirkin, who knew how to write and read, was taught how to make meteorological observations.

During the following days, quite a nice farmyard was formed at Yangi-kol.   A stable was built of poles and bunched reeds for our eight horses, and their crib consisted of two canoes.   My tent was pitched on land, and the stove was installed; but, in addition to that, a reed hut was built for me, with two rooms, the floors of which were covered with straw and felt mats.   All my boxes were taken there.   What with the tents and huts of the men, the stables, the camel-burdens and woodpile, and my house, a veritable court, or square, was formed, with a lone poplar towering in its centre. At the foot of the tree, a fire burned continually; and around it we spread mats, where our visitors could sit and have tea. Sounds of chatter, laughter, and trading were always audible from there. Besides Yoldash, Dovlet, and Hamra, all of whom had been with us on the boat, and Yolbars, who had accompanied the caravan, we were presented by a chieftain from Korla with two uncommonly beautiful and intelligent wolfhounds, called Mashka and Taiga. They were tall, quick, and yellowish-white, but so sensitive to the nocturnal cold, that we sewed some felt coats for them. They became my favourites at once. They slept in my tent, and were extremely grateful when I helped tuck the felt coats tightly around them in the evenings. In comparison with the other dogs, they looked very slender-limbed and frail. But they assumed the leadership at once, treating everything in the shape of dogs, in the whole neighbourhood, as slaves. They were terribly ingenious in fighting. They sank their fangs quickly and agilely into one of the hind legs of their adversary, and whirled him round, releasing him again at the moment of greatest velocity, and letting him roll along the ground, howling.

Night-watches walked to and fro among the tents and huts, and kept the fire going. It did not go out, in fact, until May of the following year. Our village became known to people far and wide; and merchants and travellers came long distances to see this miracle, and to trade with us. The Lop men of the locality dubbed the place Turasallgan-ui (the Houses Built by the Lord). I fondly supposed that this name would remain attached to the spot for long years after we had left it. But already in the spring that followed our departure, the high water washed away all of that shore, and our abandoned huts with it. Only the memory of our transitory town would remain; and even that would gradually be effaced by the passage of time.

I longed for the desert in the southwest, and I had long discussions with the elder men of the region. Some of them told me monstrous tales about ancient cities and great treasures buried in the sand. How well I remembered those tales from Takla-makan! Others knew nothing of what the desert concealed, only that it was death to enter there. They had no other name for the mysterious waste than "The Sand."

Before setting out on the perilous adventure of crossing the desert with camels, I decided to make a little trial-trip of a few days. The river was frozen over now, but the ice was too thin to bear the camels. So we hewed a channel from bank to bank, and the animals were taken across in the large boat. The Cossacks, a few natives, Mashka, and Taiga went with us. We carried no tents. We examined the hard-frozen lakes, Bash-kol and Yangi-kol, and traversed a very large three-hundred-foot-high sandy promontory between them. These strange tributary lakes were very long (Bash-kol twelve miles) and narrow. Both of them extended from northeast to southwest, and were separated from each other by three-hundred-foot-high sand-dunes. They were connected with the Tarim by small channels. A sandy threshold, frequently quite low, rose at the southwestern end of each lake, and beyond that was another depression, like that of the lake, but without water. I hoped that, thanks to these depressions, we would be able to cross the desert without difficulty.

The ice-lid of the lakes was crystal-clear, and as shiny as window-glass. The water looked dark-blue when we gazed straight down, in the deep places; and we saw large fishes, with black backs, lolling among the algæ. Sirkin had made some skates for me out of a couple of knives; and the Lop men were amazed to see me cut white figures in the dark ice. They had never witnessed such a thing before.

TWO OF MY MEN ON THE ICE OF ONE OF THE LAKES

After my return to Tura-sallgan-ui, a native horseman came galloping one day up to the square in our village, and handed me a letter from Charles E. Bonin, the well-known French traveller, who was camping in a village six miles north of ours. I rode there at once, and brought him to Tura-sallgan-ui. We had an unforgettably pleasant day and night together. He was dressed in a long red coat and a red *bashlik,* and resembled a lama on pilgrimage. He was an uncommonly amiable and scholarly man, the only European I met during the entire journey. Except for him, I was the sole European in the innermost wilds of Asia.

CHAPTER XXXV

A Hazardous Journey Across the Great Desert

ON December 20, I began a new desert-trip, which, if ill-luck had accompanied us, might have turned out as disastrously as our terrible journey to the Khotan-daria, far away to the west. For the distance between our headquarters, on the Tarim, and the Cherchen-daria, to the south, was almost a hundred and eighty miles, and the sand-dunes were higher than those in Takla-makan.

I took with me only four men, Islam Baï, Turdu Baï, Ordek, and Kurban; also seven camels, one horse, and the dogs, Yoldash and Dovlet. A small auxiliary caravan, composed of four camels, Parpi Baï, and two Lop men, was to accompany us the first four days, and was then to return. These four camels carried nothing but large chunks of ice, in bags, and fire-wood. Three of my seven camels carried ice and wood; the others bore provisions, beds, instruments, kitchen-uten· sils, etc. I took no tent along, but slept in the open, throughout the winter. Our supply of ice and food was calculated to last twenty days. Should thirty days be needed for crossing the desert, we would surely be lost; for we could not hope to find a single drop of water in that region.

Again the camels were ferried across the river. They were then loaded, on the right or western shore, and led by Turdu Baï along the small lake of Tana-bagladi. At its southern end, holes were cut in the almost one-foot-thick ice, and out of these the camels drank their fill for the last time.

After this halt, we proceeded across the first low sand-ridge that separated the lake from the first dry depression southwest of it. These sand-free elliptical spots in the desert were called *bayir*. There were reed-growths still in the northern part of our first *bayir,* so that the camels did not have to go hungry.

The next day, we passed through four *bayirs*. Their bottoms consisted of soft dust, in which the camels sank more than a foot, and which, in a wind, whirled in light, grey clouds around the caravan. The lead·

ers of the caravan had the most difficult lot, and those who came last
had it the easiest, because the camels in front beat down a depressed,
hard track in the dust. Consequently, I brought up the rear of the caravan on my horse; and all day long the clanging of a bronze bell resounded in my ears.

The landscape was as dead as the surface of the moon. Not a
wind-driven leaf, not an animal-trail. Human beings had never before
been there. The prevailing wind was from the east. We were sheltered on that side by steep, mountain-like dunes, which stretched out
like a wall of sand, at an angle of 33°; but to the right, on the western
side of each *bayir*, the windward slopes of the dunes rose only gradually
to the next high ridge. The terrain continued like this all through the
desert. As long as we proceeded over level *bayir* ground, all went well.
It was the steep slopes of the dunes that tired the camels. Thus the
great question was, How far did this series of *bayirs* extend? From the
top of each new sand-ridge, at the south end of a *bayir*, we would anxiously look for the next one. Everything depended on that, success
or ruin.

We camped at the south end of the fourth of these hollows. We
had to conserve our fuel. Not more than two logs were spared for
the evening fire, and only one in the morning. It was cold enough inside
our fur wraps at night, but colder still when we crawled out again in
the morning. My horse drank the water that I washed in; and I refrained from using soap, so as not to spoil this for him.

In the next depression, we found white, fragile, porous fragments
of wild camels' skeletons. How many thousands of years had they
been covered with sand before being exposed by the moving dunes?

Early in the morning of the day before Christmas, the moon stood
looking down upon us. The air was almost clear. The sun glowed
blood-red when it rose, and by its light the barren dunes were coloured
like a welling lava-stream. Camels and men cast long, dark shadows
along the ground. Parpi Baï, with his subsidiary caravan, was sent
back, my seven camels accordingly became more heavily burdened.

I walked in advance. The ground became more difficult. The sand
increased, and the *bayir* depressions became smaller. From one of
them, I climbed a protrusion which appeared to be endless. At last
I reached its top; and, deep down among more high dunes, I saw the
next *bayir*, the sixteenth one, resembling a black, yawning, infernal hole,

surrounded by a white ring of salt.   I slid down through the loose sand, and waited for the caravan at the bottom.   The men were downcast. They thought that our difficulties would increase further on in the desert.   We camped.   No Christmas angel visited us this Christmas Eve.   We had sufficient water for fifteen days, and wood for eleven. But feeling the need for economizing, we soon rolled into our furs and went to sleep.

We were wakened by a heavy storm on Christmas morning.   The sand whirled like yellow plumes from all the dune-crests.   A universal grey prevailed.   Nothing was to be seen.   Everything became infiltrated with drift-sand.   And when, two and a half years later, I took out my notebooks, in order to elaborate them, desert-sand fell from between the leaves, and my pen rasped on the paper.

We saw the skeleton of a wild goose.   It must have grown weary on its journey to or from India, and had descended to die.   Mountain-high dunes surrounded our day-camp on every side; and the atmosphere was charged with depression.   It made one want to turn in early.

The cross-ridges between the *bayirs* increased in height.   Their southern slopes fell at an angle of 33° toward the depressions.   It was a strange sight when the entire caravan slid down the inclines.   The camels were wonderfully sure-footed.   They glided down, together with the surface-layer of sand, and remained erect on stiffly-spread-out legs.

We still had two and a half loads of ice left; but the wood was nearly all gone.   And when the last stick was burnt, there would be no more ice-melting.   As usual, in critical times, the pack-saddles were sacrificed, and their hay stuffing distributed among the camels.   The wooden frames were then used for fuel.

And we were not yet half-way.   But presently, on December 27, we received unexpected encouragement.   Having at last reached the crest of a ridge, after endless climbing, we perceived the thirtieth *bayir* depression, together with a faint straw-yellow colouration.   It was reeds!   That meant vegetation in the middle of the desert!   The next *bayir* also showed reeds, and we camped there for the sake of the camels. An entire load of ice was now sacrificed to the patient animals, so as to increase their appetite.   For did not everything depend on them?   Also, the camp-fire was fed with dry reeds, which helped to conserve our fuel.

There was a glorious sunset.   Against an intensely crimson back-ground, the clouds stood out, blue-violet fields, with a gold-shimmering upper edge, but the lower parts yellow as the desert-sand. The curved backs of the dunes, resembling the waves of the sea, formed an almost black silhouette against the flaming-red evening sky. And in the east, the deadly cold new night, black with twinkling stars, rose over the desert.

The temperature sank to −6°. I went on in advance, to act as pilot, and also to keep warm. All the beauty of the previous evening was gone. The wilderness, grey and sinister, surrounded us, and there was a strong wind. In a new *bayir,* I came upon a dead tamarisk, with which I built a small fire. One camel had tired, and was being led behind the caravan by Kurban. But when darkness came, Kurban showed up alone. Islam and Turdu went to carry straw to the tired animal in the evening. But they found him dead, with his mouth open; and he was still warm. Turdu Baï wept over him, for he loved the camels.

Again we came upon some tamarisks, and we dug a well on level *bayir* ground. Already at a depth of four and a half feet, it yielded water. It was quite fit for drinking; but it came forth slowly. We sank the well deeper, and got more water. Each of the camels drank six pailfuls. The place was so inviting that we stayed all of the next day. In that time, we saw the trails of foxes and hares. We also saw an almost black wolf, who stole over the crest of a dune before he disappeared. The camels drank up to eleven pails each, which made it possible for them to go without water for ten days.

On the last day of the Eighteen-Hundreds, we covered fourteen and a half miles, the longest record we had thus far been able to make in the heavy desert. The ground was difficult; but depressions free from sand helped us considerably. We camped at *Bayir* Number Thirty-eight. The sun set in the midst of clouds; and when it rose again, I wrote January 1, 1900, in my diary.

We did not proceed more than eight and a half miles, before the desert became sterile again. Snow fell during the night; and when we woke in the morning, the dunes were covered as with a thin, white sheet. The wind was from the south, and in the afternoon we had a real blizzard. The snowfall hung like white hangings from the dark clouds. All danger of our dying of thirst was past.

At a new tamarisk, the camels again had a day of rest. We had to spare them. Their days, indeed, were long. It snowed incessantly, and I was tentless. I lay by the fire, reading; but I had to shake the book continually, as the flakes fell on the text. We were quite covered with snow by morning. Islam swept my furs and blankets with a broom of reeds. The temperature was down to −22°. When sitting by the fire, washing and dressing, we had 86° on the side toward the fire, and −22° on our backs.

Once more camp was pitched, and the last log was sacrificed. We were stiff with cold, and dreamt of our autumn fires on the banks of the Tarim. The camels were white, in the morning, as though hewn out of marble; and their breath caused long icicles to hang below their nostrils. The snow-covered dunes had a strange bluish look in the now transparent air.

On January 6, the extreme northern ranges of Tibet appeared clearly and definitely outlined in the south. Our camping-place was wretched. All our fire-wood was gone, and no other combustibles were visible. The ink froze in my pen; so I had to write in pencil. The men slept close to one another, all huddled together, so as to retain as much of their body-heat as possible.

The next day's journey was in our favour. It took us to a region where lots of dead, withered poplars stood in the sand. We stopped there and made a fire big enough to roast an elephant. The hollow trunks writhed, crackled, and split. When evening came, the men dug holes in the ground, filling them first with glowing coals, then with sand. Afterwards, we slept on a slab as warm as those in the Chinese inns.

On the morning of January 8, I promised my men that our next camp-fire would burn on the Cherchen-daria. They doubted my words, for the dry forest had come to an end. But we had not advanced far in the barren desert, before a dark line appeared above the white dunes to the south. The men wanted to stop at the first forest, but I kept on. And before the shades of night began to fall, we arrived at the bank of the river. The river was three hundred feet wide at this point, and its frozen surface was covered with snow. That night we enjoyed a sparkling moonlight.

The perilous journey across the desert had been successfully accomplished in twenty days, and we had lost only one camel.

A few days more of marching, and we camped in Cherchen, a small town of five hundred families, where I slept under the roof of seventy-

two-year-old Toktamet Bek, my old friend from Kopa, who was now
the head of the place.

Having rested a few days, I started off on a small trip to the west.
I had not seen that part of the country adjoining the desert, but Pievtsoff
and Roborovski had been there; and this was almost the only place on
this journey which I was not the first to visit. It was a matter of two
hundred and ten miles, going and coming. I took with me only Ordek,
Kurban, and one Mollah Shah, who had formerly been in Littledale's
employ. We had seven horses and Yoldash, food and warm clothes,
but no tent.

We set out on January 16, in crisp, cold weather. Sometimes the
horses' hoofs would be clattering on bare ground; at other times the
snow would crunch under them. The road frequently wound like a corridor between entangled tamarisks that looked like huddled-up hedgehogs. Time and again we had to stop for half an hour, to make a fire
and warm ourselves.

Our way took us across the dry river-bed of Kara-muran, and
across the Molja, which was strong, higher up, at the foot of the mountain. We met a wanderer, with a dog that had been badly mutilated
by wolves. On January 22, we woke up quite covered with snow, and
then had a difficult ride in snow about a foot deep. Ordek had stretched
a blanket above my head for protection; but it was weighed down by
the snow during the night, and I woke with the sensation of a cold body
lying on top of my face.

We came upon some ancient ruins, and made measurements. Among
the ruins was a tower, thirty-five feet tall. In the vicinity of Andere, we
turned, and went back to Cherchen, where we had to endure a temperature of −26°.

The long way back to our headquarters took us, in the first place,
along the Cherchen-daria, now over the frozen river, now in abandoned
beds at its sides. Wolves howled outside our camp at night, and we
had to keep good watch over the horses. Our little band had been
strengthened by the addition of Mollah Shah, who remained in my
employ throughout the journey. We frequently came upon the trails
of tigers.

Upon one occasion, a shepherd showed us a weird burying-ground,
which was neither Mohammedan nor Buddhist. We dug out two old
coffins of plain poplar-boards. In one was an elderly man, with white

hair, parchment-like face, and a garment nearly fallen to pieces. In the other was a woman, whose hair was fastened at the back with a red ribbon. Her dress consisted of a blouse and skirt, in one piece, and the sleeves were tight. She had a bandanna around her head, and wore red stockings. The shepherd told us that there were many such graves in the forest. These were probably the remains of the Russian Raskolniki, who fled from Siberia in the Eighteen-Twenties.

At the riverside, there were poplars that measured twenty-two and a half feet in circumference, and twenty feet in height. Their branches were twisted in all directions, like the arms of a cuttlefish.

After leaving the Cherchen-daria, we entered the former bed of the Tarim, called Ettek-tarim, with wooded banks, and with dunes two hundred feet high toward the west. After that, we found better-travelled roads along the present course of the Tarim.

In a forest-region north of the village of Dural, we met, by chance, Abd-ur Rahim, a camel-hunter from Singer, in the north. He and his brother, Malek Ahun, had taken their sister and her trousseau to a *bek* in Dural, and he was now on his way home to the Kuruk-tagh (the Dry Mountains), which are the very extreme outpost of the Tian-shan toward the Gobi Desert. He was one of the two or three hunters of the whole country who knew the spring of Altmish-bulak (the Sixty Springs); and a few years earlier he had accompanied Kozloff, the Russian traveller, thither. My next project was to cross the Lop Desert, with a view to solving the problem of the moving Lop-nor; and for such a crossing there was no safer starting-point than the Altmish-bulak. Abd-ur Rahim and his brother had no objection to accompanying me; and we agreed that I should also hire his camels for the expedition.

On February 24, we entered our own village, Tura-sallgan-ui. Already a few miles outside the village, we were met by Sirkin and the two newly-arrived Cossacks, Shagdur and Cherdon, dressed in dark-blue uniforms, sabres in a hanger over their shoulders, high, black, lambskin caps, and shiny boots. They saluted, in military fashion, from up on their splendid Siberian horses. While saluting, they made a report of their journey. They had been four and a half months on their way from Chita, in Transbaikalia, and had come by way of Urumchi, Karashahr, and Korla. They were both twenty-four years old, Lamaists, and served in the Transbaikalian Cossack army. I bade them welcome.

and hoped that they would like being in my employ. I may anticipate by saying that their behaviour was beyond all praise, and that they, like the two Orthodox Cossacks, were two of the best men I ever had.

When we rode into our own village, a little later, I was surprised to see what looked like a live tiger standing in the middle of the square. But it was not as dangerous as all that. This tiger had been shot a few days before, and had then frozen as hard as stone in this position. His skin was added to my collection.

Our village had grown during my absence. Several new tents had been built. A merchant from Russian Turkestan had caused a shop of his own to be built, where he sold woven goods, clothes, cloaks, caps, boots, etc.; and the Mohammedans and the Cossacks had a sort of club under his roof, where they liked to foregather, for tea and a chat. Other merchants came from Kucha and Korla, with tea, sugar, teapots, china, and all manner of things useful to caravans. Smiths, carpenters, and tailors had opened their shops in Tura-sallgan-ui, which had developed into a trading-place known all over the country. The main road, even, was diverted from its course, and made a curve to our village.

Our menagerie had been increased by two new-born puppies, speckled black and white, and with shaggy furs. They were christened Malenki and Malchik, and they outlived all the other dogs in my caravan.

The horses and camels were now rested, and had become plump, strong, and healthy. The camels, being in their rutting-season, were half-wild, and had to be kept tethered, so as not to kick and bite. The dromedary in particular was dangerous. He had to wear a muzzle, and had all four of his feet fastened with chains to iron stakes. There was white foam round his mouth, as though he were ready for the barber.

During our absence, one of our camels had caused great excitement. Once, when he and his fellows were being driven in from pasture for the night, he broke away from the others, and ran away. Two guards and one of the Cossacks mounted their horses and pursued him. The trail was distinct. He had run across the frozen river into the desert east of the Tarim, and up towards the Kuruk-tagh. Our men stirred up some people, and organized a search. The fleeing camel had descended the desert-mountains again, and hurried like the wind, through the wastes, in the direction of Kucha. He had returned from there also, and had finally entered the Yuldus Valley. There the pursuers lost his trail. Nobody knew what eventually became of him. He was and remained a mystery, a veritable Flying Dutchman. A wise old man in our neighbourhood told me that the tame camel sometimes goes quite crazy, and becomes as shy as his wild brethren. At such times, he will run towards the desert, when he sees a man, and will keep on running day and night, as if haunted by evil spirits. He runs and runs, till his heart gives out, and he collapses from exhaustion. Another man thought that the camel had seen a tiger in the forest, and had gone crazy because of that.

Our tame wild goose was much better; for he patrolled the tents like a policeman, self-conscious and self-important. His wild kin returned soon, in big numbers, from their four months' stay in India. Day and night we heard them shriek in the air, and carry on a lively conversation, before settling in their old, ancestral breeding-places. One could not help believing that the laws and customs concerning the boundaries of grazing-grounds that prevailed among these winged communities held as firmly as those with regard to the fishing-grounds among the various families of the Lopliks.

CHAPTER XXXVI

We Discover an Ancient City in the Lop Desert

ON March 5, we were again ready to leave our headquarters. This time I took with me the Cossack, Chernoff; Faizullah, the camel-driver; Ordek and Khodai Kullu, the two Lop men; and the two brothers and huntsmen, Abd-ur Rahim and Malek Ahun, mounted on two of their camels, six others of which I also hired. Besides these, there were six of our own camels, Musa, and a Lop man, with some of our horses. The horses were to be sent back when the desert should prove too heavy for them. Two of the dogs were with us, Yoldash, from Osh, and Mashka, the wolfhound. We carried provisions, two tents, and seven goatskins to hold the ice.

The rest of the caravan was to remain at headquarters. Parpi Baï, well built and erect, stood among the Cossacks and Mohammedans. It was the last time I saw him. He died twelve days after I left our village, and was laid away in the burial-ground of Yangi-kol, at the foot of the desolate dunes, and on the bank of the large river.

Spring had returned. By day, the temperature rose to 55°, and at night it did not fall below 32°. We crossed the thick ice of the Konche-daria; and on the other side of the river, we found a row of cairns and towers, indicating the ancient road that once connected China with the Occident.

From the bleak, level steppe, we directed our course to the foot of the Kuruk-tagh. These withered, barren mountains, in brown, violet, yellow-grey, and red shades, extended eastward, and disappeared finally in the distant desert-haze. At long intervals, springs were encountered. One of these was in the gorge of Kurbanchik, which was a hundred and thirty feet deep. Another was named Bujentu-bulak. When I arose in the morning, Chernoff would light my little stove. But this morning, at Bujentu-bulak, the wind blew the canvas against the stovepipe, and in a moment the tent was ablaze. I just managed to save my precious papers. This mishap caused the tent to shrink considerably; but we pieced it together as well as we could.

We took leave of the Konche-daria and its forests. During the next few days' march, the dark belt of vegetation on the southern horizon was still visible, but soon it gave way to the yellow-grey desert.

One of the objects of this expedition was to map out the ancient bed, dried out more than fifteen hundred years ago, in which the Konche-daria used to flow. It had been discovered by Kozloff, but he had had no opportunity to do more than mention its existence at a certain point. At Ying-pen, an old station on the former Chinese road, we came upon two bends of the dry bed. There we measured and photographed the still-remaining ruins. One tower was twenty-six feet high, and its circumference one hundred and two feet. There was an enormous en-

CAMPING NEAR THE BANK OF THE KONCHE-DARIA

circling wall, with four gates, and many dilapidated houses and walls. From a terrace that had once been a burial-ground, skulls peeped out as from loop-holes.

On March 12, it was 70°; and as Musa was now to return with all the horses, except my Desert Grey, we also sent most of our winter clothes along. But we soon regretted it.

At Ying-pen, we still found live poplars; but not much farther east, the forest thinned out, and the remaining trunks stood like tombstones in a cemetery.

We advanced along the shore of the Dead River. The clay-desert extended all around us, without a trace of vegetation, and strangely sculptured by the driving-force of the winds. The sky was clear, the heat oppressive.

On the eastern horizon, a brown-black line appeared, which broadened rapidly, and seemed to shoot out arms and branches toward the zenith.

"Kara-buran! The black desert-storm! Halt!"

There was bustle and excitement. Our position was untenable. We looked for a more suitable camping-place. The first gusts of wind swept howling along the ground. The country appeared to be more level toward the southwest. I moved over a little in that direction. New gusts of wind stirred up whole clouds of sand and dust. I turned quickly, so as not to lose sight of the others. But at that moment the storm came like a shot, and swept the dry, warm desert with its unleashed fury. I was near to choking and suffocating, and at a loss which way to turn. But I had had the wind on my back a short time before; so I thought I would quickly return against the wind. The whirling sand scratched my face. Sheltering my face with my arm, I tried to see through the haze, which had changed daylight into twilight and darkness. But I could see nothing. I heard no calls. All other sounds, even those of possible rifle-shots, were drowned by the howling wind. I gathered up all my strength for a battle with the wind; but I had to stop continually and turn to leeward for air. I struggled for half an hour, and then believed I had walked past the caravan. Every trail had been obliterated.

"If I do not find them soon," thought I, "and the storm continues, I shall be hopelessly lost."

I was just about to stop where I was, when Chernoff grabbed hold of me, by chance, and piloted me back to the caravan.

My tent-poles were snapped in two, and only the half-poles could now be used. With great difficulty my men had managed to pitch the tent in the shelter of a clay-hillock. It was guyed with ropes, and heavy boxes were piled on its edges. The camels, freed of their loads, lay stretched out in the direction of the wind, their necks and heads flat on the ground. The men wrapped themselves up in their cloaks, and huddled under their tent-cloth, which could not be pitched. The velocity of the wind along the ground was eighty-six feet a second, and certainly twice as great a dozen feet above. The drift-sand beat against the tent-cloth, and the particles filtered through, and covered everything within.   My bed, which was always laid right on the ground, could no longer be seen; and the boxes were coated with yellow-grey dust. Every-thing was full of sand; and it tickled and scratched our bodies. A fire being out of question, it was impossible to prepare a meal. We had to content ourselves with pieces of bread. The storm lasted all day, all night, and part of the next day; and when at last it had shot past, hurrying westward, and calm was again restored, we felt queerly dazed, as after a long illness.

We wandered on eastwards. The grey, porous trunks on the banks of the dead river looked like tree-mummies. It was surprising that they had not long ago been worn away by the drift-sand.

On March 15, we left the river-bed, to go to the spring of Yardang-bulak.   Tracks of wild camels had now become frequent. This was the third region in the extreme interior of Asia in which I had encoun-tered this royal animal, the master of the desert, who lives almost in-violate in the least-accessible parts of the earth.   Chernoff shot a young female, whose meat was welcome; for what little we still had was bad, and Kirgui Pavan, the old Lop hunter, who was to have met us at Yardang-bulak with a number of sheep, had probably lost his way in the storm.

The wild camel became the general topic of conversation. Abd-ur Rahim had hunted it for six years, and had killed thirteen camels in that period, from which one may surmise that they are not easily caught. But our guide knew their habits as well as he did those of the tame ones. The wild camel requires water every eighth day in the summer, but only every fourteenth day in the winter; and he finds his way to the springs as surely as if he were crossing the sand-ocean with the aid of a nautical chart. He can scent a man at a distance of twelve miles, and then he flees like the wind. He shuns the smoke of camp-fires, and stays away, for a long time, from places where tents have been pitched. He flees from tame camels, but not from their young; for these have not yet been used by man, and their humps are not disfigured by burdens and pack-saddles. He drinks only at springs, but does not tarry; and he stays only three days, at the most, in places where reeds grow.   In the rutting-season, the males fight like mad. The victor takes all the females—sometimes as many as eight—and the defeated rival is left to mourn alone.   All the males have terrible scars, as a result of their love-battles.

Leaving the spring again, we had all the seven ice-filled goatskins and two large bundles of reeds loaded on one camel.   We headed south-east, back to the Kuruk-daria, the dry river-bed.   Abd-ur Rahim rode in the van.   All at once, he slid down from his camel, lithely and easily, and signalled for us to stop.   Chernoff and I followed him, as he stole, panther-like, to a vantage-point behind a small clay-ridge.   A few hundred paces away lay a dark he-camel, chewing his cud, and not far from him lay three females, while two other females were grazing.   The male stretched his neck in our direction, dilated his nostrils, and stopped chewing.   He rose suddenly and looked around.   He had scented us. I could see all the animals plainly through a field-glass.   A shot was fired.   The three reclining females rose like steel springs, and the whole herd galloped away at a pace that made the light-coloured dust whirl about them.   Within a minute the herd had shrunk into a little black spot; then we saw nothing more than the pale dust-cloud, on its way to the interior of the desert.   Abd-ur Rahim averred that the animals would not stop for three days.

After a while, we surprised a lone camel, evidently a male, who was probably played out.   At the first shot, he jumped, and disappeared as if by magic.

The Kuruk-daria, the dry river, was now nearly three hundred feet wide, and twenty feet deep.   On its shores we found millions of shells, fragments of clay vessels, axes of slate, and here and there withered poplar-trunks, still standing erect.   Once we came upon a large glazed and decorated clay vessel, and blue fragments, with small, round ears. Human beings must have lived on this river, when water passed between its banks, in bygone days.

Our supply of water was now exhausted.   But it was not far to Altmish-bulak.   After a long march back to the foot of the mountain, yellow reed-fields and dark thickets of tamarisk appeared through the haze.   While the caravan settled down near the enormous, white ice-floes on the water, Abd-ur Rahim, armed with a rifle, stole to the eastern edge of the oasis, where he had sighted a herd as large as the previous one, consisting of a dark male and five young ones.   I never tired of observing the life and characteristics of these glorious animals of the desert, and so I went with him.   But my sympathies were always with the camels, and I prayed silently that the bullets would miss them. When we needed meat, hunting was not forbidden; and, of course, Abd-ur Rahim, a camel-hunter by profession, was his own master. The wind blew in our direction from the grazing herd, and they did not suspect an ambush. But the distance was too great, and Abd-ur Rahim had to approach by a roundabout way to get within range unobserved. Meanwhile, I sat with field-glass at my eyes, and made mental notes of the shape and movements of these noble animals. They grazed quietly, raised their heads now and then, scanned the horizon, and chewed slowly, and with such pressure that we could hear the crackle of the reed-stalks as they were ground between the teeth.

When the shot was fired, the herd headed straight for me, quick as lightning; but they soon turned abruptly against the wind. One of the young ones, a four-year-old male, could go no further. He fell; but he was still chewing when we reached him. Then he tried to get up, but dropped on his side, and was slaughtered. A bullet from some earlier huntsman was found lodged in his front hump.

Now we had meat again for a while. The animals were to have a rest, before we next crossed the desert; and it was a joy to see their satisfaction over the pasture, as also, in the evenings, when they stood and crunched ice. The spring-water was salt; but the ice was sweet.

CAMEL BEING LED IN THE DEEP, WIND-CARVED FURROWS

Toward evening, a herd of eight wild camels came forth to drink; but fortunately they took alarm in time, and disappeared like shadows in the night.

We set out for the south on March 27, with all the goatskins filled with ice, and four of Abd-ur Rahim's camels laden with reed. He himself did not dare to accompany us further than two days' march; then he returned to his home. After a walk of eighteen miles, we were down in the yellow· clay-desert, ribbed into deep furrows and gullies, six to nine feet deep, by the unceasing northeast and east winds. All the time that we were walking in such depressions, clay-ridges obstructed our view on either side. Higher clay-ridges were also encountered.

No trace of life in any form was to be seen here. But the next day again disclosed dead forests and grey, porous, sand-eaten tree-trunks. In some furrows, the wind had collected shells, which crackled under our feet like dry autumn-leaves.

Chernoff and Ordek went ahead, in search of the most feasible route for the camels in this extraordinary land of furrows running southwest and south-southwest. At three o'clock in the afternoon, they stopped suddenly. I wondered whether they had once more sighted wild camels; but this time it was something quite different, and much more noteworthy. They were standing on a small clay-hill, on the top of which they had found the remains of a few wooden houses.

I ordered a halt; and while the caravan relaxed, I measured the three houses. How long had the sills maintained their present position? That I did not know. But the houses were standing on hillocks eight or nine feet high. It was evident that they had formerly been on level ground. The wind had eaten away the surrounding earth, while the houses protected the soil on which they stood.

A hasty examination revealed several Chinese coins, a few iron axes, and some wooden carvings, representing a man holding a trident, another man with a wreath, and two with lotus flowers. We had only one spade, but it was kept going all the time.

In the southeast, a clay tower rose at a considerable distance; and I went there with Chernoff and Abd-ur Rahim. From its top we discerned three other towers. We were not yet able to determine whether they had been built for defense, or for signal-fires in time of war, or whether they had a religious significance, like the Indian *stupas*.

It was pitch-dark before we reached camp; but Faizullah had made a beacon-fire.

I left this interesting place with regret on the following day. We could stay no longer; for the warm season was approaching, and our goatskins kept dripping alarmingly during the day's march.

Abd-ur Rahim was dismissed, after being generously remunerated. My servant, Khodai Kullu, was sent home to headquarters, with two camels and all the wood-carvings and other objects which we had found.

I continued south, through the clay-desert, with Chernoff, Faizullah, Ordek, four camels, one horse, and the two dogs. After a twelve-mile walk, we came to a depression, with a few live tamarisks. There must be subterranean water near by! We must dig a well! But where was the spade? Ordek promptly confessed that he had forgotten it at the ruins, and offered to go back at once and fetch it. I was sorry for him; but the shovel might mean life or death to us. The undertaking was not without risk, especially if a storm should arise.

"If you should not find our trail, just go on towards the south or southwest. Then you will be certain to get to the lake of Kara-koshun."

He had a few hours' rest. When he departed, at midnight, I loaned him my riding-horse. Both of them first took their fill of water.

Two hours after Ordek had disappeared in the dark, a heavy storm broke from the east. I hoped that he would return to us at once. But not hearing from him by daybreak, we set out towards the southwest. The heat was less oppressive than usual, thanks to the violent wind.

After crossing a belt of low dunes, we found a few pieces of wood in a sterile tract, where we encamped. To everyone's surprise, Ordek turned up there safely, not only with the horse, but with the spade as well. And this was his tale:

He had missed our trail in the storm, had lost his way, and happened upon a clay tower, near which he discovered the ruins of a number of houses, where beautifully-carved wooden boards were half-buried in the sand. Some coins, which he had found, as well as two of the carvings, he took with him. He also found our camp and the spade, after much searching. Then he tried to put the boards on the horse. But the animal shied, and threw off the burden. Then Ordek himself carried them to the place where we had left the shovel. He was not able to carry the heavy boards any further. The horse broke away, when fresh attempts were made to burden him with them, and was only caught with much difficulty. Thereupon Ordek left his plunder, and rode on till he reached our new camp.

So there were more ruins than I had seen! I first sent Ordek back to fetch the boards, a task which he finished before we were ready to depart. I grew dizzy, on seeing these artistically-carved scrolls and leaves; and having learned from Ordek that there were more of them, though he had been able to bring only two samples, I wanted to go back. But what folly! We had water for only two days. All my travelling-plans were upset. I must return to the desert next winter! Ordek took it upon himself to guide me to the place where he had discovered the carved boards. How fortunate that he had forgotten the spade! Otherwise I should never have got back to the ancient city, to complete this most important discovery, which was destined to spread a new and unexpected light upon the ancient history of the very heart of Asia.

But just now we had to think of saving ourselves and our animals. We hurried south, now across clay-soil, now over twenty-foot-high dunes. I walked barefoot. The sun, of course, made the ground hot; but the sand was cool in the track of the camels. When camping in the evening, the camels got a pail of water apiece, and the last bag of straw. They had had nothing to drink for five days. We had water now for only one day more; and that was foul-tasting after its contact with the goatskins.

The next day I walked on ahead. It was supposed to be thirty-eight miles to the Kara-koshun. I ascended a dune and scanned the distance through field-glasses. Nothing but low dunes. But what was that shining in the southeast? Water, or a mirage over a salt-field?

I hastened thither. It was pure, clear water, which had a rank taste, but was good enough to drink. It was a joy to see the camels drink! But now we had also to find pasturage for them. And we must find something eatable for ourselves. All that we had left was a bag of rice and a little tea.

We proceeded along the shore; and on April 2, we reached the Kara-koshun (Lop-nor), in which stretches of reedy growth could be seen toward the south, extending from east to southwest. Here the water was altogether sweet. Wild ducks, wild geese, and swans swam there; but were too far from shore to be killed.

The following day was devoted to rest and grazing. A fresh north-easter was blowing; and I had an irresistible desire to get out on the lake and to cleanse myself of all the desert-dust. But what about a boat? Well, we would build a boat. It is the will that counts! Where there's a will there's a way. I walked far to the northeast with Chernoff and Ordek. There were no trees, nor was there any driftwood. But we took along the goatskins and the wooden ladders that had been fastened to the pack-saddles.

We halted at a long spit of land. Ordek inflated the skins till they were taut as drumheads. We made a frame by lashing the ladders together with ropes, and fastened the skins underneath. The northeast wind blew steadily. We could drift over a wide expanse to the camp, and so I ought to be able to take a series of soundings. The sun was hot. It would be nice to get out where it was cool. When Chernoff "went aboard," the float nearly upset. We sat on the edge, with our feet dangling in the water.

The wind caught us in the back and started us from shore. Foam-crested waves rolled by, every one of which soaked us up to the waist, while the spray rose as high as our caps. I found no greater depth than twelve feet. Wild geese and swans rose with noisy flapping; and wild ducks flew so close to the surface, that the tips of their wings touched the waves. The trip took two and a half hours. The tent loomed large. We were blue with cold, and anxious to land. And when, at last, Ordek met us at the camp, we were stiff to the bone, and could hardly walk up to the fire. I was half-dead, and fell into a violent trembling. Only after I had had several cups of hot tea, and had gone to bed, did my body-heat return.

Sky, earth, and lake were suffused with wonderful tints at sunset. The sun spread a scarlet light over the dunes; but the dust-clouds, that were now racing southwest, glowed underneath with a dark flame-colour. It was a splendid, almost awe-inspiring sight. The lake was blue-black, and the whitecaps were empurpled by the reflection of the sun. But the waves thundered so violently against the shore, that we had to move my tent farther inland.

CHAPTER XXXVII

Our Final Weeks on the Branching Tarim

FOR two days more, we skirted the desolate shore, without seeing a trace of human beings. We were short of everything, and were downright hungry. A cloud of smoke appeared to the south, on the evening of the second day. Ordek, quick as a lizard on land and as a fish in the water, walked and swam across the reed-grown lakes, and returned with eight fishermen, three wild geese, two-score goose-eggs, fish, flour, rice, and bread. And then all danger of starvation was past.

At Kum-chapgan, we came across old friends. Kunchekkan Bek was dead; but his son, Tokta Ahun, became one of our trusted men. Numet Bek was entrusted with our four camels and the horse, and was to take them to the pasture-grounds at Miran, where one of our caravans would soon call for them, on its way to Tibet.

I returned by canoe to headquarters, with Chernoff, Faizullah, and Ordek. But before that, I made a quick canoe-trip out on the Kara-koshun. The lakes—or marshes, rather—were more overgrown by reeds than upon my visit four years before. The greatest depth was hardly seventeen feet. We skimmed over a large, open expanse, where we took part in a dramatic episode, which I shall never forget. A dead swan lay on the water near the edge of the reeds, and her mate swam near by. My oarsmen put their blades in the water, and the canoe shot swift as an arrow towards the swan. He did not rise, but swam with increasing speed, aided by his wings. He reached the border of the reeds, and broke through the dry stalks. But once there, he could no longer spread his wings. One of the Lop men jumped into the water and swam after him. The swan dived; but, because of the reeds, rose again at the same spot. The man caught him with one fell swoop, and wrung his neck. The whole thing was over in a minute. The swan had not been able to bring himself to abandon his dead mate; and it was only the knowledge that his sorrow was ended, that consoled me for his death.

A new branch, the Shirge-chapgan, had formed north of the lower Tarim. I wanted definitely to chart that arm of the river, and record its dimensions. But there were no boats there. Our four camels had not yet departed; so they were harnessed in pairs to the two canoes, and dragged our boats overland to the new channel.

On we went, northwards, along new water-routes and lakes. One day, at the Tarim, we met Cherdon, who took our thirty-five horses, six mules, five dogs, men, and provisions up towards the mountains in northern Tibet, where our various divisions were to meet in the valley of Mandarlik.

Everything at headquarters was shipshape. The barge lay ready. My tent on the forward deck was converted into a cabin, made of ribs and blankets. We had a thousand things to do. Our headquarters had become a veritable new capital in the Lop country. The natives brought their disputes to us as to a court, and we administered justice.

Our remaining camels were now to start for the rendezvous in northern Tibet. Chernoff, Islam Baï, Turdu Baï, and Khodai Kullu rode horses. Yolbars, whose side had been badly torn by a boar, was one of the dogs to accompany them. In spite of his wound, he was the only dog who survived the journey through the desert, up to the foot of the mountains.

The departure of that caravan made a colourful and beautiful scene. With bronze bells clanging, it passed out through the sparse forest. Tura-sallgan-ui lay empty and desolate after that. All the merchants and craftsmen had packed their goods and departed. Only some crows croaked in the square; and smoke still issued from the last fire in the kitchen-hut.

Sirkin and Shagdur, the Cossacks, alone of my faithful men, were still with me. Accompanied by them and four new Lop men, I left these headquarters forever, on May 19. The entire population of the district gathered on shore to bid us a kind farewell, as the barge was carried off by the current to continue its journey down the Tarim, which had been interrupted for half a year.

We stopped time and again to survey the lakes on the right bank of the river. I measured a dune between two such lakes, and found it to rise 293 feet above the river-level. Other dunes near by were as much as forty and fifty feet higher. The Lop people occasionally dam up the channels that link the river with the lakes. This closes the fish in; and the water, becoming slightly salt, renders the fish more palatable. They are caught in a seine, sixty fathoms long, which is hauled along by two canoes.

Kirgui Pavan, our old friend the hunter, came aboard after a few days. He summoned men, and a whole fleet of canoes, to help us across new lake-formations and reed-growths so thick that we had to burn them before we could proceed.

On May 25, we made an adventurous trip on the large lake of Beglik-kol, one of those situated on the right bank of the Tarim. We had two canoes, one carrying Shagdur and two boatmen, and the other one me, Kirgui Pavan, and another oarsman. It was a perfectly quiet day; the lake lay like a mirror; and the reflections of the dunes in the water were as sharply outlined as their originals. For three hours we rowed south, making soundings. The sun was burning-hot, and we had to sprinkle water on our clothes, in order to keep cool.

In the evening, we reached the middle of the west shore, and rested for a while. Then Kirgui Pavan pointed to the dune-ridge on the east lake-shore, and uttered those most depressing words: "Kara-buran!" (black storm).

Dark streaks and yellow-red clouds rose above the entire dune-expanse, and soon merged into one single curtain. Our boatmen wanted to stay overnight where we were. But I had to get back to the barge, to wind the chronometers.

"Out again, and row for dear life!"

If only we could reach the opening of the channel, we would be out of danger. But in order to get there, we had to cross the mouth of a wide bay, extending toward the west.

The air was still calm, and the lake was like glass. The men were kneeling, and their oars bent like bows. If the oars did not snap, we would escape the storm. Otherwise, the canoes would fill inside of two minutes, and we could not swim ashore.

"Ya Allah!" (O God!), cried Kirgui Pavan, in a dull voice.

"Now it has reached the dune," he added, as black plumes of whirling sand were swept out over the lake by the gale.

In the next moment the dune and the entire eastern shore disappeared in the dust.

A roaring sound was heard in the distance. It approached at a terrific speed, and became a deafening roar. The gale was already out on the lake. The first gusts of wind reached us.

"Row, row!" Kirgui shouted. "There is a God!"

Our speed increased. The canoes cut through the water like knives. The water sizzled and foamed about their stems. We sat in tense expectation. It was still a mile to the northern shore. But in less than a minute, that, as well as the western one, was enveloped in the haze.

Presently the storm was upon us. The wind struck us a terrific blow. Had we not thrown ourselves over to windward in time, the canoes would have capsized.

The waves rose with terrific rapidity. There was a whipping and sizzling foam from their crests. They lifted and tossed the canoes. One wave after another broke over us. We sat as if in tubs, and the water splashed back and forth with our careenings. Kirgui tried to get the best of the waves, by steering the canoe into them. I could see nothing except our boat and the nearest whitecapped waves, which were nearly black. Everything else had disappeared in a thick haze. It was dark and uncanny about us. And night was approaching. I wrapped up my notebooks and instruments, and started to undress. A few more waves would be enough to sink us. The long, straight gunwales of the canoes were hardly two inches above water.

But suddenly a miracle occurred! The waves suddenly became quite small, and the rocking stopped. Aha! Something dark appeared close to starboard. It was a tamarisk-thicket on a point of land jutting out from the northern shore: a natural breakwater! We were saved! We disembarked long enough to empty the canoes, and then continued on through the channel. But it grew pitch-dark, and the stalks of the reeds whipped our faces. After much groping about, we beheld a storm-lashed fire, and were soon back in the barge.

We drifted on, with the current. Kirgui Pavan sat with his pole in front of my work-table; and he was an inexhaustible source of funny remarks and strange tales. The demons of the air had once more been appeased. Silence reigned. Then a canoe approached at full speed, and pulled up alongside our boat. Quick steps were audible on board. Musa, the courier from Kashgar, came up to my table, and placed on it a large bundle of letters from my home, as well as newspapers and books. That night I lay reading until three o'clock.

On the following days, we were often delayed by storms. We had to move at night, when there was less wind. At these times, torch-bearers, in the canoes, went ahead of us.

Again we were surprised by a courier. He brought only *one* letter, and that was from Petrovsky. Surely it was something important. The Governor-General at Tashkent had ordered the two Cossacks, Sirkin and Chernoff, to return to Kashgar, as there was some disturbance on the frontier between Russia and Asia. Chernoff happened to be in northern Tibet, and nothing could be done until he returned to my camp. I therefore sent a courier after him.

At Chegelik-ui, a fishing-place, we had to abandon our old barge, as the waterways were too narrow for it. So we made two smaller vessels. Each consisted of a platform resting on three long canoes. On each platform we erected a framework, and covered it with blankets. I lived in one of them. The other became the home of Sirkin and Shagdur. Meanwhile, I developed the plates which I had exposed during the past weeks, in the cabin of the large boat. This vessel, having drifted nine hundred miles on the river, had certainly done good service. I gave it to the people of the place, for their own uses.

The new boats were easy to manage; but when the water was rough, we had to bail the canoes out all the time. Yet we succeeded in reaching Abdal, an old fishing-village, the final point on our river-journey.

A few days later, Chernoff, Turdu Baï, and Mollah Shah arrived, with four camels and ten horses, to take me and the rest of my luggage to our new headquarters, up in the mountains. The beasts had to rest a few days before we could start. The heat was terrible; the temperature rose to more than 104° in the shade, and the air was full of big, bloodthirsty gadflies. They were the worst sort of plague for the camels and horses. The animals, if left free to graze, in the daytime, would be covered with tens of thousands of these gadflies. The flies sucked the beasts' blood and destroyed them. In consequence, the animals had to be kept inside of thatched huts, as long as the sun was up. After sunset, they would be bathed in the river, and afterwards permitted to remain out all night. One night, our camels disappeared. It was plain from their trail that they had gone back to the mountains, to escape the gadflies. Turdu Baï mounted a horse, and chased them back. The gadflies tortured us, too. A walk from one hut to another was like venturing out in a shower of bullets. We all longed for the fresh, highland air.

On June 30, at five o'clock in the evening, my remaining belongings were loaded onto the four camels and two of the ten horses. While the camels were being laden, four men stood beside each beast, simply to kill gadflies. When everything was ready, the caravan proceeded. Shagdur had charge of the dogs that were still with us. These were Mashka and Yoldash, together with the puppies, Malenki and Malchik. Turdu Baï was ordered to take the caravan to a point on the south shore of the Kara-koshun, from which point the road went southeast to the nearest spring in the mountains. It would take us a whole night to make this point on the shore. I preferred to go that distance by canoe; and thus, after the caravan had disappeared in the twilight, I was alone with Sirkin, Chernoff, and the last of our friends among the natives.

The Cossacks took all my post with them, and were generously rewarded for their excellent service. After a final hand-shake, they mounted their horses, and disappeared in the dusk, with their small caravan, riding to Kashgar by way of Cherchen and Khotan. We parted with sadness and mutual regret. I felt companionless in the heart of Asia, with never a servant, and with no more baggage than I carried in my pockets. Therefore I did not stay one minute after the Cossacks had left me. I bade farewell to the Abdal people, got into a waiting canoe, and two Lop men took me down the river at a spanking pace. As long as the moon was up, we could see the shores. But the moon went down after a while; the river opened out into reedy marshes; and it became pitch-dark. How the men found their way was a puzzle to me. They did not talk. They just rowed towards the goal, without the slightest hesitation. The stars twinkled above the moving waters. The hours passed; and the canoe, never stopping, glided on and on. I dozed off, now and then, but was unable to sleep. This last journey of mine on the Tarim waterways was too exciting for that.

Darkness still reigned, when the men touched the bank, saying that here was the meeting-place. We walked ashore and waited. After a while, shouts were heard in the distance. It was Shagdur arriving with the horses. We made a fire, prepared tea, and had breakfast.

At dawn, Turdu Baï turned up with the camels. He merely saluted with "Salam aleikum," and went on, without stopping. We said good-bye to the boat, mounted our horses, and followed in his track.

The sun rose. Light, colours, and heat spread over the wilderness.

Thin violet clouds, with edges of molten gold, floated above the horizon. The outermost mountains of Tibet, bordering on the desert, looked very much like a sharply-outlined back-drop, done in light shades. Millions of gadflies awoke, and whizzed past us like shots, gleaming, with their stolen blood, like red rubies, when seen against the sun.

At Dunglik, our first camping-place, where we were already 650 feet above the lakes, there were no human beings; but we found a spring and pasturage for our horses and camels.

MAP OF ASIA SHOWING POSITION OF TIBET

CHAPTER XXXVIII

Adventures in Eastern Tibet

A FEW hours before daybreak, we began preparations for a tedious day's journey across barren country. After the animals had quenched their thirst, we filled the copper vessels with water for ourselves and the dogs. The ground was hard. It consisted of gravel and coarse sand. The lakes in the north looked like a faint, dark ribbon. All else was yellow-grey. The mountains became more distinct. Protruding rocks, entrances to valleys, and clefts became visible.

After seven hours' forced march, we passed a cairn.

"Now we are half-way," Tokta Ahun declared.

Mashka and Yoldash were quite used up, from the heat and drought. We halted a few times to give them water. Yet they lagged behind. We stopped once more, and waited; but there was no sign of them. Had they gone back to the lakes? Shagdur rode back with a can of water. He returned with Yoldash on his saddle. Mashka had drunk the water, and had then died, as if from a stroke. Yoldash was wrapped in a blanket and fastened to a camel. He was absolutely helpless. The little puppies lay in a basket, on another camel, who tossed them to and fro as he swayed.

At last we reached the opening of a valley, with a small, rippling brook, and rested there for a while. The first thing we did was to release the three dogs. They could hardly stand on their legs; but upon hearing the rippling water, and slaking their thirst, they revived. They drank, coughed and hawked, drank again, and finally lay down in the brook, rolling about voluptuously. It grieved me that beautiful Mashka had not been able to get there. A little higher up in the valley, where there were fine, large tamarisks, we encamped at the well of Tatlik-bulak. We were now 6,300 feet above the sea.

During the following days, we crossed the Astin-tagh and Akato-tagh, the first two mountain-ranges. From the pass, at the latter range, we perceived a third mountain-range to the south, the Chimen-tagh;

and between it and us there was a long, open valley, with a small lake, on the shore of which we pitched our camp.

At the well of Temirlik, we were 9,700 feet above the sea. We were rising to ever greater heights in desolate Tibet. During the day which we spent there, resting our animals, a whole caravan arrived, with maize, which we had ordered from Charkhlik, a small town southwest of the Lop-nor.

Messengers from headquarters, at Mandarlik, also arrived, to say that all was well. One of the men had been employed by Islam Baï because he knew the region better than anyone else. This Aldat was of Afghan descent. He spoke Persian. He had an eagle nose, a short beard, and eyes full of melancholy. He was a yak-hunter by profession, and lived alone in the mountains all year round. His food consisted of the flesh of the wild yak, and his drink was snow-water. His possessions were limited to the clothes on his body, a fur robe, a rifle, and ammunition. In the summer, his brothers would come up, with donkeys, to fetch the skins of the yaks he had killed. These they sold at the bazaar in Keriya.

Aldat always walked by himself, his head held high, and with a regal carriage.

"What do you do if the hunting fails?" I asked.

"I go hungry till I find a yak again."

"Where do you sleep during the cold winter nights?"

"In ravines and caves."

"Are you not afraid of wolves?"

"No. I have my rifle, fire-steel, flint, and tinder; and in the evenings I make a fire."

"Don't you ever get snowed in during the violent blizzards?"

"Yes; but I always manage to get out in some way."

"Isn't it gloomy to be always alone?"

"No; I have nobody to miss but my father and brothers, and they come up for a few days every summer."

Aldat was charmingly mysterious. He was like a disguised prince in a fairy-tale. He answered all questions briefly and correctly, but did not speak unless questioned. He was never seen to smile or laugh, or to talk with the other men. It was as though he were fleeing from a great sorrow, and sought solitude, danger, and the hard, adventurous struggle against the wolves and the storms. Yet he was a human being, and probably had a craving to see other people once in a while. Thus, when I asked if he would go along on my first journey into wild Tibet, he answered yes! He was to be my huntsman, and show me the secret paths across the mountains.

On July 13, we were all again assembled at the springs and brakes of Mandarlik, where we established our second large headquarters, the starting-point of our future expeditions.

On July 18, we set out on the first of them. I planned to map out parts of the tableland of eastern Tibet that had not heretofore been explored. We took food sufficient for two and a half months, and for not more than eight men. Cherdon became my body-servant and cook. Turdu Baï led the seven camels, and Mollah Shah eleven horses and a mule. Kuchuk, a capable Lop man, was to be my boatman on any lakes which we might discover. Nias, a gold-miner from Keriya, had our sixteen sheep in charge. Aldat was guide and huntsman, and Tokta Ahun helped with the horses. Yoldash, Malchik, and a big Mongolian dog—a deserter from some nomad camp in the east—were also among those present.

Already at our first camping-place, after crossing two passes, we had attained an altitude of 13,000 feet. Wild yaks, wild asses, marmots, and partridges were our immediate neighbours. The glowing summer, which we had left behind us so recently, had now changed to winter. The temperature sank to 23°. We broke camp on July 22, in a snow-storm, and rode through snow and a blizzard that raged all night.

I was awakened at dawn by a great commotion in the camp. Cherdon reported that Nias and twelve sheep were missing. Only the four sheep that had been tethered were left. Everybody hurried out to search, Cherdon on horseback. About ten o'clock, Nias came back, deeply grieved, with only one sheep. He had found all the others done to death by wolves, and lying in their blood, here and there, in the snow. Only one sheep remained unaccounted for. Nias had been sleeping under a blanket-mat. In the middle of the night, awakened by pattering steps and bleating, he started up, and saw three wolves, who had stolen up on the sheep against the wind. The stupid animals had run out towards the fields. Nias dashed after them, but forgot to awaken the other men. The wolves intercepted the sheep and tore them to pieces. Only one had escaped. The sly wolves had taken advantage of the blizzard, which roared and howled so loudly, that the dogs had not noticed anything.

The wolves probably stayed at the scene of carnage after we went away. Now we were more dependent on Aldat's rifle than ever before. We had not gone far, when we saw the missing sheep, crazed and frightened out of its wits, running down a snow-covered hill. We rejoiced more over that single sheep than we had mourned over the loss of those that were killed.

During the days that followed, we made long, hard marches across the snowy ranges that were called Chimen-tagh, Ara-tagh, and Kalta-alaghan by gold-seekers and yak-hunters. The last-named range we crossed through a pass 15,700 feet high. From there we beheld, in the south, a number of peaks with perpetual snow, belonging to four different ranges, and, farthest away, on the horizon, the Arka-tagh, whose conquest a few years previously had cost me such great pains.

On the south slope of the Kalta-alaghan, we got down into a wide, open valley, which we followed westwards. We were still in regions that had been explored by Russian travellers, and also by Bonvalot and Littledale. We kept in the middle of the valley. The place swarmed with marmots, who would whistle before their holes and dive into them when the dogs darted after them.

A herd of thirty-four wild asses was grazing in the valley. Cherdon and Aldat, on horseback, went after them. They all fled, except a mare, with her scarcely four-day-old colt. At last the mother fled, too; and Aldat gathered the colt up on

WILD ASSES AT THE AGE OF A WEEK OR TWO

his saddle. Later on, we caught another colt. They were both wrapped in blankets and loaded on a camel. We intended to feed them with flour-porridge until they could be put out to pasture. And they did actually lap it up. But when they showed signs of pining away, I told the men to let them loose, on the steppe where they had been caught, so that their mothers might find them again. Tokta Ahun assured me that the mothers abhorred their colts after human hands had touched them. If that was so, these colts would fall prey to the wolves. We decided, therefore, to kill them; and we found their meat to be tender and palatable.

A well-defined field of drift-sand, with dunes of considerable height, extended along the entire base of the southern mountain enclosing this large valley. A horse-fly, called *ila,* was common in this valley. It had the bad habit of lodging in the nostrils of the grazing animals. Our horses were terrorized by these tormentors. They would snort, jerk their heads, lie down on the ground, and writhe, regardless of burdens and riders. The wild yaks, wild asses, and antelopes go up among the sand-dunes, where they are safe, in the daytime, and graze in the valley at night. Quite a while before sunset, we noticed thirty fine yaks wandering on the sand-field, on their way to the valley. At the sight of the caravan, they halted on the top of a high dune. The pitch-black yaks made a splendid and impressive picture against the yellow-grey sand, as they stood in a long line, sniffing, with heads raised, and with the perpetual snow-fields for a background.

We approached the shore of the Bash-kum-kol (the Upper Sand Lake), a small lake, discovered by Przhevalsky. Fourteen yak were grazing there. Cherdon stole up to an old bull in the herd. But the bull refused to be frightened. He gazed steadily at the hunter, and even advanced a few steps towards him. Indeed, Cherdon was the one to turn and flee, much to the amusement of the caravan. To save his reputation, he pursued a wolf-cub instead, and brought it back to the camp. A halter was put around the neck of the little beast, and we kept him a prisoner overnight. Tokta Ahun believed that if harm came to the youngster, the mother would surely take revenge on our last sheep. But the cunning wolfling gnawed through the rope during the night, and in the morning he was gone. The men hoped that he would grow till the noose choked him; but I suspect the mother wolf knew how to free him from the rope.

New, long, and difficult marches took us up toward the heights of the Arka-tagh. We marched through stupendous labyrinths of mountains. Now it rained, now the hail lashed the hills, now the sun shone so warmly that huge bumblebees, dressed in furs and buskins, hummed in the air like organ-notes.   In the valleys, we sometimes surprised large herds of antelope.   It is hard to imagine a more beautiful spectacle than these agile, elegant animals presented, with their shiny horns sparkling like bayonets in the sunshine.

Aldat's knowledge of the country ended here; so Turdu Baï rode up towards the heights of the Arka-tagh to look for a pass.   Yoldash went with him.   The dog caught sight of an antelope, and ran in pursuit

A HERD OF "ORONGO" ANTELOPES

of the animal across a defile.   When Turdu Baï returned, Yoldash was missing.   We went on, thinking that the dog would find his way back to us.   A heavy rain began to fall.   We stopped at once, but failed to get the tents up in time to prevent a soaking.   Yoldash was still missing. He was separated from the caravan by a pass, as well as by the pouring rain.   Turdu Baï rode back, crossed the ridge over which the antelope and dog had disappeared, and finally came upon Yoldash, who, quite beside himself—he having lost his own trail—was searching for us in a side-valley where we had never been.

Thereupon we crossed the Arka-tagh by way of a pass 17,000 feet high, and descended to the large, elongated valley in which I had discovered the twenty-two lakes, four years before. Now we had virgin country ahead of us to the south, and we were to cross the routes of only two previous explorers. It was with a sense of satisfaction that I entered this new *terra incognita,* where there were no paths except those beaten by wild yaks, wild asses, and antelopes. Aldat shot two antelopes; and so we had meat for several days, without having to have recourse to our last three sheep.

The night, too, possessed a sublime grandeur. Scattered clouds, with luminous borders, sailed across the moon; and silvery snow shimmered gloriously on an enormous expanse of glacier in the south. Majestic desolation and loneliness surrounded us.

The caravan-animals began to tire. The pasturage was miserable at these great heights. The camels, who shed their hair in summertime, were freezing in the snow, hail, and rain which the bulky clouds, formed by the strong western winds, let fall daily. Induced by the severe climate, however, the winter coats began to grow on the camels.

Crossing the Tibetan highland from north to south, as we did, we had to traverse all the parallel mountain-ranges running west and east. Ever-new ranges in the south, and mighty, broad, endless valleys between them, were visible from each pass. Again a range lay before us. It looked flat and smoothed-off. I rode on ahead. The barren ground was soaking-wet, and as soft as mush. I dismounted, and led my horse, who sank one foot deep in the mud at every step. The camels followed lumbering and slow. Their feet made deep holes, which immediately filled with water. We were unable to proceed in this treacherous muck; and after vainly working our way up to an altitude of 17,200 feet, we turned back. The animals were given two days' rest, in a valley in which there was a sparse growth of grass. We covered the camels with blankets at night, to keep them from freezing in the snow and wind. Cherdon's horse died, and my splendid Cossack was unconsolable. He had taught the horse all sorts of tricks—to lie down, to come when called, and to walk daintily and carefully when the Cossack stood on his hands in the saddle.

On August 12, we tried to cross the nasty stretch of mud by another pass. The ground was as treacherous as before. It cluck-clucked and swished under the feet of the camels and horses. Everyone went on foot. Our hearts thumped as though they would burst. We finally reached the summit, 16,800 feet high.

A lone wolf was lurking up there. At the same moment that we reached the top, the day's hailstorm came driving along, with roaring, rattling thunderclaps. The ground shook. It sounded like salvos from a warship, or like a whole army of giants playing skittles. We were so high up, that the clouds were partly below us in the valleys. We were in the very heart of the storm. Nothing was discernible in the beating hail, and we did not know which direction to take to get down from this terrible ridge. There was no alternative but to pitch the tents in the wet, herd the camels close together in a semicircle, and cover them with blankets. Everything was splashing-wet; and the tent, blankets, and impedimenta were all dripping with water. One of the camels had collapsed on the way up. The others made a feast on the hay of his pack-saddle.

The next day brought fine weather; and in the valley at the southern base of this ugly range, we found pasturage on sandy soil, and rested for two days. All our clothes and blankets were spread out on the sand to dry.

We left one more range behind, and then the highland opened out into a vast plateau, with a soil well suited for travel. A salt-lake appeared far away to the south, and we camped on its northwestern shore. Late one evening, the men heard strange sounds in the distance. They had an uneasy feeling; for it sounded like human beings calling. Aldat suspected wolves. He had wounded an antelope; but it had escaped. Later on, he found the victim eaten by wolves down to the bone. We needed meat; but there was still enough rice and bread.

On August 22, Kuchuk and I rowed across the lake, to a hillock on the south shore, where the caravan was to meet us in the evening and make a bonfire. The weather was glorious. The lake was so shallow, that for hours Kuchuk could propel the boat simply by pushing his oar against the bottom, which consisted of a hard layer of salt. Further out, we found the greatest depth, which was only seven and a half feet. The lake was nothing more than an extremely thin sheet of water in a shallow basin. The day was beautiful and calm. Absolute Sabbath stillness reigned over the lake. The colours were wonderful in the sunlight. Close to the boat, the water was light-green; farther away it was marine-blue. The sky, the water, the clouds, the mountains, everything stood out in ethereally light and fleeting shades. The weather was quite warm; and we got thoroughly dried out, after all our wettings in the mountains. The water was so salt that everything it touched became white. It was for all the world like the Dead Sea, except that we were here at an altitude of 15,600 feet. Throughout the first few hours, we could see the caravan on the left shore; but later on, the distance became too great.

The day passed, twilight fell, and we were still on the lake. No fire was to be seen, nor camels nor horses. We landed, and looked about us, from a hillock. Here lay the skull of a wild ass, and there was the fresh track of a bear. We shouted, but got no answer. Something had happened to the caravan. Otherwise, a couple of horsemen, at least, would have met us, with food, warm clothes, and bedding.

Before it got absolutely dark, we gathered fuel, which was only the droppings of the yak and wild ass. At nine o'clock we made a fire, and sat talking for an hour. Then we went to sleep. Kuchuk wrapped the sail around me. A life-preserver served for a pillow; and half of the collapsible boat was inverted over me like a bell. There I lay, like a corpse in its coffin. Kuchuk shovelled sand all around me, with his hands, so as to keep the draught out. It reminded me of a grave-digger filling up the grave. He himself crept in under the other half of the boat. A heavy shower battered noisily on the tightly-stretched canvas bottom. That might well have been the roll of the drums in our funeral-music. However, I soon fell asleep in this tomb of mine, and did not arise again from the dead until the sun stood well above the horizon.

A fresh breeze set in from the east. That suited us splendidly, as we were going westwards along the southern shore, to find out what had become of our people. We put the two halves of the boat together again, stepped the mast, hoisted sail, and had a lovely three hours' trip across the salt-waves. There was considerable pitching, and Kuchuk became seasick. At last we saw the tent. Cherdon and Aldat waded into the shallow water, and pulled us ashore. We were hungry, and were longing for breakfast. Aldat had shot a wild ass; and once more we had meat.

The caravan had been checked by a river, one hundred and ninety feet wide, and ten feet deep, which emptied into the salt-lake. We went to the bank of the river. We stretched a rope across the river, and in fourteen relays the baggage was transferred. The horses swam across, but the camels gave us trouble. They had to be hauled along by the boat; and they lay in the water like dead, until they felt solid ground again under their feet.

This done, we continued southwards, arriving in a few days at still another salt-lake, which derived its supply from two beautiful freshwater lakes to the south. This region was extremely charming. I willingly sacrificed a week, during which our camels and horses grazed on the shores. I myself employed the time in crossing the lakes in different directions, sounding their depths, mapping their shores, and catching fish under perpendicular cliffs. Kuchuk and I had many wild adventures here in heavy storms, but we came through safely.

On September 2, I rode seventeen miles southwards, through a country full of wild yaks, wild asses, antelopes, hares, field-mice, marmots, wild geese, wolves, and foxes. Some slopes were quite thickly dotted with yaks.

When we were once more all together in the camp, we found we had sufficient meat for two weeks; for Aldat had shot a yak calf and four antelopes. But we had been away from our headquarters at Mandarlik one and a half months, and had taken along provisions for only two and a half months. We had fed to the caravan-animals part of the flour, and were now living principally on meat. So far we were all right. But we would have to go back by a more westerly route, still in unexplored country. It was not a part of my plans to penetrate deeper into Tibet; for I purposed visiting the ancient town in the Lop Desert once more, before the coming winter should end.

CHAPTER XXXIX

A Death-Strewn Retreat

I ORDERED Turdu Baï to take the caravan westward, on the north side of a huge mass of glaciers, while I skirted it on the south side, with Cherdon and Aldat. We took enough food to last the three of us one week.

A lone yak was grazing on a hillock close to our second camp. Aldat sneaked like a cat through the ravines and depressions, till within thirty paces of the yak. I followed the hunt through my field-glasses. Aldat calmly rested the rifle on a notched stick, and fired. The yak gave a start, took a few steps, stopped, fell, rose, swayed to and fro, fell again, and remained prostrate. It had been a fatal shot. Aldat lay motionless with his rifle. Cherdon and I advanced to the place with knives. Having made sure that the yak was dead, we joined in skinning him and removing the best parts of his flesh, including the tongue, kidneys, and heart, which were usually reserved for me.

On the next morning, Aldat returned to the fallen yak to fetch more meat. We were at an altitude of 16,870 feet. There was a strong west wind. In the west, a high pass was visible, which we had to traverse, in order to meet Turdu Baï and the caravan. There being no sign of Aldat, Cherdon went to search, and found him lying ill beside his victim. Cherdon helped him down to the camp. The young huntsman was suffering from headache and nose-bleed. Cherdon and I loaded our horses, wrapped Aldat up in his fur, and helped him into the saddle.

The soil yielded under the weight of our horses, and they worked their way with difficulty up towards this terrible pass, 17,800 feet high. Aldat was delirious. He swayed to and fro in his saddle so much, that he had to be lashed to it.

A day later, we came upon Turdu Baï and Kuchuk, who were on the lookout for us. They took us to their camp. When we continued westward, in a body, afterwards, we made Aldat a bed of bags and blankets on the back of a camel. He, who was usually so taciturn, now lay singing Persian songs. For quite a while, an old coal-black yak, whose sides were adorned with long fringes, walked ahead of us. He looked like a tournament-horse dressed in mourning.

We proceeded toward the northwest for several days. The weather was cruel to us. There was wind and snow every day. The snow was a foot deep, and treacherously concealed marmot-holes. The horses would step into them frequently, and stumble. Where we camped, the animals vainly sought the sparse grass under the snow.

Aldat grew worse. His feet turned black. I rubbed them for hours to induce circulation; and we gave him warm foot-baths, which afforded relief. We ought to have stopped for his sake; but our food-supply was perilously near its end, and Aldat was the hunter who should have provided us with fresh meat. Cherdon was an excellent shot, too; but he had taken too few cartridges with him. With his last one he brought down a young yak, which gave us meat for some time.

One evening, Aldat asked to be laid outside, between two camels; for he thought the warmth of their bodies might be beneficial. His wish was granted. Mollah Shah and Nias watched over him.

On the morning of September 17, I was awakened by shrieks and noises in the camp. I rushed out just in time to see a bear, that had been nosing among the tents, trot off, pursued by the dogs.

Two days later, we came back to the ugly, muddy range which we had crossed with so much difficulty far eastwards. A camel sank deep into the mud, fell over, had to be freed from his load, and would have been lost, had we not managed to dig out his legs, one by one, and put blankets under them. By means of tent-poles and ropes, we finally got him on his feet again. He looked like a clay model. His dark-grey armour had to be scraped off with a knife.

We had seen no sign of human beings for two months. We were still two hundred and forty miles from Temirlik, where the caravan had been instructed to await our arrival. Everyone longed to get there, away from this uncanny, murderous highland.

At one camping-place, Aldat became so sick, that we tarried there for a day. With Aldat's rifle, Cherdon shot a yak, and, near the camp, an antelope. The Mohammedans then tried a new cure on the patient. They skinned the antelope, undressed Aldat, and wrapped the still-warm skin, hairy side out, closely around the sick man's body.

Yoldash cut off a marmot's retreat to his hole; and one of the men caught the little fellow, and tied him to a pole between the tents. We tried to tame him, hoping thus to acquire a nice new playfellow. But he never became quite tame. If a staff or tent-pole was held out to him, he would bite large chunks out of it with his sharp front teeth. At every camp, he would begin digging a new hole, in which to take refuge; but before the hole was even a foot deep, we would be off for a new camp.

In the evening, Aldat grew still weaker. He breathed rapidly; his pulse was imperceptible; his temperature was low. When we were ready to depart, the following morning, the sick man was made as comfortable as possible on his camel. Just as the beast was about to rise, a strange, grey pallour passed over the sunburnt face of Aldat, and he opened his eyes. He was dead. We stood there, silent and grave, around his living bier. He lay there, regally straight and proud, his broken glance directed upward to the Tibetan sky.

Notwithstanding the wishes of the men, I could not bring myself to have Aldat buried at once. His body was still warm. Part of the caravan had already begun the day's march. Aldat's camel, too, was allowed to rise and follow the trail. It was a sad and gloomy journey. No singing was heard, nor any conversation. Only the bronze bells tolled, like church-bells for a departing funeral-cortège. Two ravens circled above us. Yaks, wild asses, and antelopes gazed at us, and approached closer than usual. They seemed to be aware that the Nimrod of the wilderness was dead.

We halted, and pitched tent, in a small valley near a salt-lake, on the shores of which no European had ever before set foot. A grave was dug. The dead man was lowered, on his coat, into this grave, and covered over with his fur rug. Then the grave was filled, and the heavy soil of Tibet rested on his breast. His face was turned toward Mecca. A post, to the top of which we tied the tail of the last yak he had shot, marked the head of his grave; and a small head-board, nailed to the post, gave his name, date of death, and the fact that he had sacrificed his life in my service.

On September 24, everyone wanted to leave the valley of Death's shadow as early as possible. When the camels were laden, and everything was ready, we went to the grave, where the Mohammedans knelt down in prayer. Then we departed. On a ridge near by, I turned in my saddle. The yak-tail was fluttering in the wind. Aldat was sleeping

his last sleep in majestic peace and solitude. I wheeled my horse rou...
and the grave vanished from my sight.

No grass! No wild animals! One horse fell down for good; and
the others were in bad shape. The camels walked with half-closed eyes,
as if affected by sleeping-sickness. We had only enough maize for two
days; and we sacrificed a portion of our rice to the animals. We
encamped at an altitude of 16,800 feet. After I had put out my candle,
in the evening, the flap of the tent burst open violently, and in came—a
new blizzard, with whirling clouds of snow.

In their regular order, we traversed once more the same mountain-
ranges that we had already crossed, far to the east. One of them

THE GRAVE OF ALDAT IN THE SOLITUDE OF TIBET

towered now right across our path. We mounted slowly to its pass,
which was more than 17,000 feet high. But the northern slope was
very steep. From the top of the ridge, it looked as if solid ground
had come to an end, fathomless space yawning below and before us.
A blizzard was raging in the valley, and the snow whirled along the
mountain-side as if in a witches' cauldron. The horses slid on their
haunches, but the camels had to be carefully piloted through the snow.

We slaughtered our last sheep at the next camp. It was like mur-
dering a fellow traveller. We continued northward. Yoldash overtook

l killed it; and we had meat once more. We
er pass. Two horses died on the way, and two
the top. One of them was the little grey horse
through the desert to Cherchen, and across the Lop
to the sixty wells and the ancient city. In the morning, one
more horse lay dead between the tents.

Again we were in familiar country. On October 8, the temperature
sank to −1°. Our provisions had dwindled down to six pieces of bread
and enough rice for four days. The way led through a valley, enclosed
by granite cliffs, and with some abandoned gold-workings in its centre.
We were all on foot. A camel died the next night. He had held out
to the very end, proud and resigned. Now he was giving up all hope
of pasturage, and had no choice but to die. His pack-saddle was consumed by the surviving veterans.

The valley sank. We approached lower regions, and pitched our
tents at an altitude of 13,300 feet. On the face of a rock, I discovered
some petroglyphs, which represented bowmen pursuing antelopes. There
was also a Mongolian *obo,* with *mani* (stones). Cherdon shot a wild
ass with Aldat's rifle, and we were saved once more. But the most
wonderful thing that happened at this camping-place was that Mollah
Shah, while tending the grazing animals, perceived two mounted hunters
from East Turkestan, and hailed them. They were brought to my tent.
We had not seen a human being for eighty-four days, and were greatly
cheered by this chance encounter. I began by purchasing their two
horses and a small batch of wheat-flour. Next, one of the men was
commissioned to ride to Temirlik, personally to bear my order to Islam
Baï to hurry to meet us with food and fifteen horses. I gave him two
empty tins to serve as credentials. Togdasin—that was his name—
might well have stolen the horse, which I had already paid for. But
I trusted him; and he executed his commission faithfully.

After two more days of travel eastwards, we broke camp, on October
14, in a hopeful mood; for on that day we were to meet Islam Baï's
rescuing-party. We marched all day. It grew grey and dark; yet we
walked on.

"A fire in the distance!" someone shouted.

We increased our speed. Everyone was hungry. The fire disappeared. We shouted, and fired some revolver-shots, but got no
answer. The night-cold chilled us. We stopped for half an hour, and

made a fire. Then we continued eastward, hour after hour, through the same large valley in which Temirlik and our headquarters were situated.

The fire reappeared. We kept on for a while; but when the light finally vanished again, we found ourselves exhausted. Our animals were tired to death. They were naught but skin and bones. Perhaps we had seen only a phantom fire. There was some tea-water left in a jug; and I had a piece of broiled wild ass's meat with it for supper.

Grass and fuel were plentiful; and we stayed here for a day. A well was discovered near by. Yesterday's fire had evidently been built by hunters who wished to avoid us. Perhaps, after all, Togdasin had failed us.

Later in the day, Cherdon came to me in my tent, and said he thought he saw a troop of horsemen approaching from the west. I went out with my field-glasses. Was it wild asses or a witch-dance that I saw in this enchanted valley? Whatever it was, the shimmering atmosphere caused me to see an undulating swarm of some kind, floating above the ground. But they grew larger; they came nearer; I saw the clouds of dust they stirred up. They were indeed horsemen! Presently Islam Baï rode up to my tent, and reported that all was well at headquarters. He brought fifteen horses; and a Lucullian dinner was soon prepared for us, who had been hungry for so long. They had ridden past us, during the night, after our fire had gone out, and had continued west until they were set right by the trail of our camels.

Kader Ahun, a brother of Aldat, was among Islam's men. He told of having dreamt one night that he was out walking in the waste and had met our caravan. All except Aldat were there. When he awoke, he understood that Aldat had died; and he told Islam and the others about it. We figured out that he had had his dream on the very day that Aldat died. He got his brother's rifle, the wages due him, and the equivalent of his clothes and of the skins of yaks he had killed.

Two horses out of twelve, and four camels out of seven, remained, when we reached Temirlik, two days later. And Aldat was dead.

After a rest, and after I had developed the exposed plates in a cave, I started out, on November 11, on a month's expedition, the large salt-lake of Ayag-kum-kol being my objective. I took with me Cherdon, Islam Baï, Turdu Baï, Tokta Ahun, Khodai Verdi, the hunter, Togdasin, thirteen horses, four mules, and two dogs.

New, unknown country was mapped out. The eternal mountains were crossed by new passes. Once Cherdon and Togdasin went to hunt wild sheep. They caught sight of a herd, tied their horses, and pursued the sheep on the precipices. The sheep escaped. Togdasin suddenly collapsed like a rag, complaining of pains in his heart and head. They

remained out in the open all night, and reached camp the following morning, much exhausted. From that time on, Togdasin was an invalid. I sent him down to Charkhlik, after we got back to our Temirlik headquarters. He lost both his feet; and the compensation that I could give him in silver was nowise proportioned to his loss. But even as a cripple, he was always cheerful, content, and grateful.

Tokta Ahun and I made some long trips on the wide waters of the Ayag-kum-kol, to sound its depth. We found the greatest depth to be seventy-nine feet. Thereupon we returned over new roads to the headquarters in the valley of Temirlik.

WILD SHEEP OF TIBET

A large Mongolian caravan of pilgrims, from the district around Kara-shahr, had arrived at Temirlik during our absence, and had stopped there for some days. It consisted of seventy-three Lama priests and two nuns, with a hundred and twenty camels, forty horses, and seven fine horses intended as a gift to the Dalai Lama in Lhasa. They had held long conversations with Shagdur, who spoke their language, and had shown a marked interest in our headquarters. They told of having with them a hundred and twenty silver *yambas* (about 5,500 dollars), which were also to be presented to the Dalai Lama. That was the Peter's pence which the pious had to render to the highest chief priest of Lamaism, for the favour of being blessed by his holy hand and seeing his face. Their provisions consisted of dried meat, roasted wheat-flour, and tea. They were going to travel over the high mountains, across the range of Tang-la, and down to the river of Nakchu, where they intended to leave their camels, continuing to Lhasa on hired horses. They told Shagdur that the Governor of Nakchu required a passport of every pilgrim, and exercised the most rigorous control, in order to prevent disguised Europeans from penetrating to Lhasa. This caravan of pilgrims harmed us considerably. My plan, which I had not yet confided to any of my men, was to attempt to approach the Holy City in disguise, the following year. The pilgrims would be in advance of us, and would report in Lhasa what they had seen and heard about us; and the roads leading over Nakchu would be guarded more strictly than ever. For a while, I thought of outstripping the pilgrims, and riding with a light horse-caravan to Lhasa by a more westerly route. But between the alternatives of Lhasa and the ancient desert-city, I chose the latter. Grueber and D'Orville, two Jesuits, had visited Lhasa in 1661; and in the eighteenth century, the Capuchins maintained a mission-station there for several decades, the most famous members and chroniclers of which were Orazio della Penna and Cassiano Beligatti. The Jesuit priests, Ippolito Desideri and Manuel Freyre, had been there in 1715, and Van de Putte, a Dutchman, two decades later. In 1847, Huc and Gabet, two French Lazarists, visited Lhasa, and gave an account of it. Indian pundits and Russian Buriats had been sent there, time and again, with instruments and cameras. And thus we have a fairly good knowledge of Lhasa.

But ever since Noah stepped out of the Ark, no European had set foot in the ancient desert-city, until I discovered its towers and houses, in March, 1900. Thus a hazardous journey to Lhasa, in disguise, was rather a whim, a sporting-feat; whereas a systematic examination of the desert-city might be of incalculable importance to science. I therefore devoted the winter to the desert and its mysteries. The Lhasa expedition was postponed to the next summer. In a later chapter I will tell how the Mongolian pilgrims succeeded in thwarting my designs.

CHAPTER XL

Through the Gobi Desert Without Water

BY my orders, Cherdon, Islam Baï, Turdu Baï, and a few more
of my men moved our headquarters to the small town of
Charkhlik, there to await my arrival in the following spring.
I was accompanied by the Cossack Shagdur, the Mohammedans Faizullah, Tokta Ahun, Mollah, Kuchuk, Khodai Kullu, Khodai
Verdi, Ahmed, and another Tokta Ahun, a Chinese-speaking huntsman
whom we called Li Loye, in order not to confuse the two like-named
men. We had eleven camels, eleven horses, and Yoldash, Malenki,
and Malchik, the dogs. All the animals were thoroughly rested and in
excellent form. It was my plan to march two hundred and forty miles
between the parallel ranges of the Astin-tagh to Anambaruin-ula (a
mountain-mass in the east), then northward through the Gobi Desert,
thence westward to Altmish-bulak, and finally southwestward to the
ancient city and by way of the Lop-nor to Charkhlik.

We left on December 12. In the beginning we had some
troublesome days, pushing our way through the narrow valleys of the
Akato-tagh, with their soft slate-clay. Nobody had ever been there
before, and not even the natives knew the glen which we hoped would
lead to a pass across the range. The lateral mountains were perpendicular, and several hundred yards high. The bottom of the valley
was dry as tinder and absolutely barren. The bronze bells echoed
wonderfully in the yellow passage. There had been landslides in various places, but the rocks did not stop us. We were, however, always in
danger of being buried by new landslides. The valley became narrower.
Eventually the packs scraped the walls on both sides; and the camels,
squeezing their way through, made the dust fly. I hurried ahead to
reconnoitre, and found that the valley shrank to two feet, and that
at the very end there was only a vertical crack, which not even a cat
could have squeezed through.

There was nothing to do but turn back. We hoped there had not been a landslide meantime; for in that event we might very well have been entrapped like so many mice.

After a thorough reconnaisance, we finally succeeded in surmounting the ranges; and thereafter we walked east and northeast over good terrain.

New Year's Eve, the last night of the century, was cold and clear, and the moon shone like an arc-light. I read the texts that were being listened to in every church in Sweden that evening. Alone in my tent I awaited the approach of the new century. There were no bells here other than those of the camels, no organ-music but the roar of the continual storms.

On January 1, 1901, we encamped in the valley of Anambaruin-gol, and I decided to encircle the entire mountainous bulk of that name, a stretch of a hundred and eighty-six miles. On one occasion we surprised twelve beautiful wild sheep climbing the steeps of an almost perpendicular mountain-wall with the agility of monkeys. They eyed us steadily, the while Shagdur managed to steal in below them. A shot rang out, and a dignified ram tumbled two hundred feet down the precipice and received a death-blow on the round pads of his twisted horns.

A week later, we were at the lake of Bulungir-gol and visited some *yurts* of the Mongolian Sartang tribe on the surrounding steppe. The road back to Anambaruin-gol took us north of the mountain-group, and we had to cross its deep valleys, which stretched toward the Gobi Desert. There were countless springs and ice-cakes. The pasturage was good, and we encamped under old willow trees. It did not matter much that the cold dropped to −27°, for fuel was plentiful. Partridges were abundant, and they gave pleasant variety to my dinners. Two old Mongols, of whom we inquired our way, sold us grain for our camels and horses. And at last we camped on the Anambaruin-gol, on the same spot as before.

From there, I sent Tokta Ahun and Li Loye to headquarters, in Charkhlik, with six tired horses and the specimens I had collected thus far. Also, they took a written order to Islam Baï to send a relief-party to the northern shore of the Lop-nor (or Kara-koshun), to establish a base of supplies there, and to light a bonfire every morning and evening, from March 13 on, for at about that time we would be on our way from the ancient city through the desert.

The rest of us, carrying six bags full of ice, started north into the desolate Gobi Desert. We walked through stretches of high sand-dunes, across small weather-worn granite mountains, across a clay-desert and a steppe, and came out on a very ancient road, identifiable only by the heaps of stones that had withstood Time. Wild camels, antelopes, and wolves appeared now and then. We dug a well in a welcome depression. It yielded potable water, and the camels and horses quenched their thirst.

With enough ice to last men and horses ten days, we marched northward through an unknown desert. Wild-camel prints were now exceedingly frequent. The desert was as smooth as a lake. After a while, the terrain rose; and we crossed some small weather-worn ridges. There was not a drop of water. And it would have been useless to dig for any. We accordingly turned southwest and west, and I made for Altmish-bulak by compass.

We made long marches for the next week or so. Our friend Abd-ur Rahim, who had showed us the way to Altmish-bulak the year before, had mentioned three salt-springs situated east of that place. The camels had had no water now for ten days, and only a few mouthfuls of snow from a crevice. On February 17, our situation began to be critical, and it became imperative to find one of Abd-ur Rahim's three springs. All day long and the entire next day we searched in vain for water. The terrain, too, was now against us. We reached those parts of the clay-desert where the wind had ploughed furrows, twenty feet deep and thirty-five feet wide, between long, perpendicular clay-ridges. They ran from north to south, and we had to explore endlessly before we got past them. There was not a stick of fire-wood at the camp that evening, and so we sacrificed one tent-pole.

By February 19, the camels had not drunk for twelve days. They would soon die of thirst, if water was not found. I moved on in advance. My horse followed me like a dog. Yoldash was with me. A small mountain-ridge made me swerve to the southwest. I walked in a dry bed, in the sandy bottom of which I discerned the fresh trail of about thirty wild camels. A small glen opened on the right. All the camel-tracks radiated from there like a fan. There must be a well there. I walked up the valley and soon found a cake of ice, forty feet in diameter and three inches thick. Thus the camels were saved. When they got into the valley, we broke the ice-cake into pieces and fed them to the animals. They crunched the ice like so much sugar.

During the following days we discovered the other two springs also. They were surrounded by reed-fields. Eighteen wild camels were grazing near the last spring. Shagdur stole upon them; but he shot at too great a range, and the camels vanished like the wind.

We were scheduled to be twenty-eight kilometres from Altmish-bulak on February 24. The little oasis should be situated S. 60° W. Consequently, in the morning, I promised my men that before evening came we would pitch our tent among the tamarisks and reed-thickets of "The Sixty Springs."

There was a strong northeast wind, which helped us along. But an enveloping haze rested on the waste; and what would become of us, if we should inadvertently pass the little oasis? I was headed for a certain point in the desert, but the dust-haze obstructed my view.

I had already covered twenty-eight kilometres and began to fear that the oasis was behind me. But what was this? Something straw-yellow gleamed right in front of me. It was reeds. And I caught sight of fourteen wild camels. I stopped, while Shagdur stole upon them. He succeeded in bringing down a young female, who was still on her feet when we got to her; also an older specimen, a male, whose skeleton we prepared during the following days, and which now reposes in the Zoological Museum of the Stockholm High School.

According to my calculations, our distance from the spring should have been twenty-eight kilometres; but it proved to be thirty-one. This miscalculation—three kilometres in 1450, or two-tenths per cent—was not great.

We indulged in a thorough rest after these forced marches. Then I left one man, the horses, and some tired camels in pasturage, and went south with the rest of the caravan. We took all of our luggage and nine bags of ice.

On March 3, we camped at the base of a clay tower, twenty-nine feet high. We stowed our ice in the shadow of a clay-ridge and sent a man back to the spring with all the camels. These were to return to us again in six days, with a further supply of ice. We promised to have a beacon-fire burning on the sixth day.

We were now cut off from the world. I felt like a king in his own country, in his own capital. No one else on earth knew of the existence of this place. But I had to make good use of my time. First I located the place astronomically.   Then I drew plans of the nineteen houses near our camp.   I offered a tempting reward to the first man who discovered human writing in any form.   But they found only scraps of blankets, pieces of red cloth, brown human hair, boot-soles, fragments of skeletons of domestic animals, pieces of rope, an earring, Chinese coins, chips of earthenware, and other odds and ends.

Nearly all the houses had been built of wood, the walls of bunched osiers or clay-covered wicker.   In three places the door-frames still remained upright.   One door actually stood wide open, just as it must

BUDDHAS CARVED IN WOOD, FORMERLY DECORATING A TEMPLE IN LOU-LAN

have been left by the last inhabitant of this ancient city, more than fifteen hundred years ago.

Shagdur succeeded in finding the place which Ordek had discovered the year before, when he went back for the shovel.   There we came upon the remains of a Buddhist temple.   This, in its day, must have presented a charming sight.   Originally the town was situated on the old Lop-nor, which, because of the altered course of the Kuruk-daria, had since moved south.   No doubt the temple stood in a park, with wide waters extending to the south. Houses, towers, walls, gardens, roads, caravans, and pedestrians were then to be seen everywhere. Now it was the habitat of death and silence.

Our excavations yielded the frame of a standing image of Buddha, three and a half feet high; horizontal friezes, with seated Buddhas, and vertical wooden posts, with standing Buddhas artistically carved thereon; lotus flowers and other flower ornaments; also sections of breast-works, all carved in wood and very well preserved. It was Shagdur who finally found a small wooden board with inscriptions (Karoshti, India), and won the prize. A similar amount was promised for the

THE REMAINS OF A HOUSE, IN LOU-LAN, ABOUT 1,650 YEARS OLD

next discovery. My men worked as long as there was a trace of day-light on the waste land.

The days went by. Dawn found us already at work. We made excavations in every house. At last there remained only one house, of sun-dried clay, in the shape of a stable, with three cribs opening out-ward. Mollah found a slip of paper, with Chinese ideographs, in the crib on the extreme right; and he got the reward. The paper lay two feet deep under sand and dust. We dug deeper and sifted the sand and dust between our fingers. One piece of paper after another was brought to light, thirty-six in all, every one of which bore writing. We also discovered a hundred and twenty-one small wooden staffs, covered with inscriptions. Aside from these ancient documents, we found only some rags, fish-bones, a few grains of wheat and rice, and a small fragment of rug, with a swastika design and colours still quite clear. For all I knew, it may have been the oldest rug in the world. The whole collection looked like a rubbish-heap. Yet I had a feeling that those leaves contained a slight contribution to the history of the world. We found nothing in the other two cribs.

March 9, our last day, was due. I completed the plans and measurements of the houses, and examined a clay tower, finding it solid. We found two hair-pencils such as the Chinese write with to this day; an unbroken earthenware pot, two and a third feet high; a smaller pot; and a great number of coins and small objects of various kinds. The tallest post still standing in a house measured 14.1 feet.

At dusk the two men returned from the spring, with all the camels, and ten bags and six goatskins filled with ice. The sun sank, and our work in the ancient city came to an end.

PART OF THE GOBI DESERT AND EASTERN TIBET

CHAPTER XLI

Lou-lan, the Sleeping Town

IT would take a whole book to describe Lou-lan and the discoveries I was fortunate enough to make among its ruins, but I can devote only a few pages to my ancient desert-town.

Upon my return home, I handed over all the manuscripts and the other relics to Mr. Karl Himly, of Wiesbaden, who made the first report on them, stating that the name of the town was Lou-lan, and that it flourished in the third century A. D. After Himly's death, the material was taken over by Professor A. Conrady, of Leipzig, who translated all the documents, recently publishing a voluminous work about them.[1]

The most ancient of the papers is a fragment from the historic work, *Chan-Kuoh-ts'eh,* and dates from the later Han dynasty (25-220 A. D.). The Chinese invented the manufacture of paper, in 105 A. D. The document referred to was written between 150 and 200 A. D., and is thus the oldest piece of paper in existence, and, consequently, the oldest handwriting on paper known, antedating by at least seven hundred years the handwritings on paper which Europe had hitherto cherished as the oldest.

All the other documents on paper and wooden staffs date from about 270 A. D. Many of them are dated, and we can therefore tell their age to a day. They reveal the official and epistolary style, in China, on administration, commerce, reports, products, agriculture, army organization, political and historical events, and warfare, and give a clear picture of life in Lou-lan, 1,650 years ago.

The letters on paper had been folded and enclosed between two wooden boards, which were tied together with a string, and marked, as, for example, "Letter sealed by Ma Li."

[1] Die chinesischen Handschriften und sonstigen Kleinfunde Sven Hedins in Lou-lan. (191 pages text, 53 full-page facsimiles of Chinese manuscripts on paper and wood, and a few illustrations in colour.) Lithographic Institute of the General Staff of the Swedish Army, Stockholm.

Letters, reports, notices, and receipts from the military administration, the bureau of food-supplies, and the post-office were written on wooden staffs. Such staffs were also used as symbols of official authority. The finding of two hair-pencils proved that such articles were in use in China as early as the second century A. D.

That the reader may form some idea of how people used to write in those parts, 1,650 years ago, I reproduce two of Professor Conrady's translations.

A private letter runs thus: "Chao Tsi says: (T), Chao, and the others are (here) far away; my younger brother and my sister and the children are at home, and we cannot meet at will; and thus there is a dearth of raiment and food there. I now inform you that those at home have sent (a messenger) to Tien-ki Wang Heh in Nan-chou (?) to get permission to receive fifty bushels of grain so that they may have enough to eat. I beg (you) to intercede with Heh and to induce him to give (it) in time. I hope most respectfully for your high-minded sympathy and benevolence, and therefore need not use many words; (thus) says Chao Tsi!"

Written upon receiving a message of sad news: "Tsi Ch'eng answers: Miss Yin having been without any previous illness, the misfortune that so suddenly befell her was quite beyond expectation. I received the sad news and so much greater is (therefore) my deep-felt sympathy and regret. But a deep wound cannot be endured. What then can help?"

A little leaf shows the existence of Lop-nor and of the river that paid tribute to it. "Shi Shun probably waits. . . (as) the Ta-choh Lake is of great depth (and) also the counter-current is weak. I figure that he will have arrived at Lou-lan about the end of the month."

A receipt from the Government warehouse, concerning deliveries of provisions, ends with these words: "In the second year of T'ai-shi (i. e., 266 A. D.) on the 11th of the 10th month, Ts'ang-ts'ao-shi Shen Chuan and Kien-ts'ang-shi Tih T'ung and K'an Hi have delivered (this receipt?) to Shu-shi Lin Ngo."

A wooden staff reads: "The military office. Concerning the roster of common soldiers dispatched in the 6th month of the 4th year of T'ai-shi (i. e., 268 A. D.), those arrived at camp in Kao-ch'ang deserted, dead," etc.

The collection of smaller objects that we dug out in Lou-lan contained many coins which bridge a gap in the monetary system of the Wei and Tsin dynasties. One bears the date of the year 7, another 14 A. D., years when Christ still trod the earth.

There were also hunting-arrows, battle-arrows, and fire-arrows, "to which fire could be tied"; sinking-weights of lead and stone, for fishing-nets; cowry shells; ear-pendants; necklaces; an antique gem, with an image of Hermes; glass from Syria or Rome; spoons, tweezers, and hair-pins of bronze; an iron chain; spoons and other wooden articles; pieces of silk, in various shades, for clothes; a bed-cover; a woolen rug; linen; shoes; etc.

The written documents, and the objects themselves, show that the Lou-lan government had its warehouses, that there were an inn, a hospital, a post-office building, a temple, private dwellings, and huts where the poor people lived, huts which have as surely disappeared as will the modern reed huts in the Lop country. References to imports, particularly that of Chinese silk for local consumption, are evidence that the population was rather great. In the better houses, hard earthen floors were covered with reed mats, on which lay the precious woven rugs. Large clay jugs, with water for the household, stood in the yards. Bowls and dishes decorated with Indo-Persian lion-heads, were in use; also, glass from Syria, the nearest country in those days which under-stood the manufacture of glass.

The educated classes possessed famous works of literature. Accord-ing to Conrady, a barbarian-Chinese-international mixed culture, of present-day character, flourished in Lou-lan; for the town was a frontier citadel, a gateway or barricade to ancient roads in the heart of Asia, principally to the great "silk road" between China in the east and Persia, India, Syria, and Rome in the west. Travellers from far and near came there. The peasants took their products there on burden-animals and in carts, the Government purchasing and paying for the goods. There the soldiers received their pay in grain, and, in its market-places, bought felt for their winter clothes. At times the city was crowded and all inns were filled.

The documents allude to tax-evaders and their punishment; to post-couriers; to Ma, the chief inspector, who proceeds on his round of duty, with outriders and escort; to hostile tribes of nomads; to silk-caravans, flying the Government banner at their head, and with sturdy Tibetan asses in their train; to cavalry, lancers, archers, war-chariots, apparatus for siege and defense; to military baggage-trains; to all sorts of weapons; to the military high command; to a general; to a general staff-officer; to the inspector of war-chariots; to the inspector of military supplies; to the staff-surgeon and other officials. Because of Lou-lan's significance and location, it was heavily garrisoned. Mention is also made of the officials of the civil service, the chancellor, district commissioners, secretaries, the mayor or city prefect, the chief of dikes, the inspector of agriculture, the director of posts and his four deputies, various administrators of warehouses and depots, chief supervisors, etc. Here are references to the administration of law, criminal statutes, taxation, domiciliary right, recruiting, passports, the barter of grain for silk (though there was a regular system of coinage), and to many other matters.

Professor Conrady points out that the social organization and administration in Lou-lan, which was extraordinarily precise and efficient, implies a process of evolution which extended over many centuries—nay, thousands of years—before the third century.

It is also plain from the Lou-lan texts that unsettled conditions prevailed in and about the little town. They tell of serious revolts, of war-expeditions and battles. The structure of the Chinese dominion was tottering to its fall. The cord around Lou-lan tightened more and more. The "hooting of the owls," as the war-clamour is called in one of the letters, came nearer and nearer. Weakened by internal party-strife, China finally succumbed to the barbarians, fell to pieces, and was ruled by its conquerors for centuries.

Lou-lan fell in the beginning of the fourth century, a symbol of the fall of China itself. The little ruin is, therefore, as Conrady says, a monument to a catastrophe of universal import. The authors of the letters which I found have, each in his own place, contributed to the account of these historic events.

But the authorities never flinched in their duty to the state, in spite of the ominous cloud that hung over the town. Everyone did his part. When the drums outside the walls sounded the call to arms, and the fires burned on the towers, these officials remained steadfast in their places, finishing their reports as if nothing unusual had happened. They sent New Year's greetings and letters of condolence to their friends, not allowing themselves to be disturbed by the impending danger. We read with admiration and emotion of the strength of character and the courage with which these Chinese did their duty, and we understand how it is that this remarkable people could keep the control of Asia in its hands.

And this is not fantasy or myth. It is the naked truth. The letters, resting silently under the earth for 1,650 years have again delivered a message. They were written by human beings who once lived on earth, and whose troubles, sorrows, and joys have finally been brought to the light of day.

The same realism as in Pompeii is found here in simple handwriting exercises and the scribbling of children's hands, practising the multiplication-table, "2 × 8 = 16, 9 × 9 = 81," etc.

Conrady calls the story of the Lou-lan texts an idyll, a *genre* picture seen against the mighty, stormy, dark background of the world's history.

In connection with the discovery of my first two desert-towns, I have already pointed out that I am no archæologist. I was fortunate, therefore, in being able to entrust my material to such hands as those of Professor Conrady. His interpretation fully proves the importance of the discovery of Lou-lan. Corroboration lies in the fact that after my discovery in 1900, and my second expedition to the town, in 1901, it was visited, in 1905, by Ellsworth Huntington, the American geographer; in 1906 by Sir Aurel Stein; in 1910 by the Japanese, Dr. Tachibana; and again, in 1914 and 1915, by Dr. Stein. The latter, in particular, did much to develop my discoveries during his three visits. It was with the help of my maps that it became at all possible for the travellers to find the ruins in the middle of the desert. Thus Stein says in his great work, "Serindia" (Vol. I, p. 362):

"I felt grateful, too, for Dr. Hedin's excellent mapping, which, notwithstanding the difference of our route-lines and the total absence of guiding features, had enabled me to strike the ruins without a day's loss. When, subsequently, the results of our own plane-table survey for these parts, checked by astronomical observations and triangulation as far as the mountains southwest of Cherchen, came to be completed, I was much gratified to find that Dr. Hedin's position for the site differs from ours by only about a mile and a half in longitude, the astronomically observed latitude being identical." A reviewer in the *Geographical Journal* (Vol. XXXIX, 1912, p. 472), calls this "a real triumph of geographical science."

The reader will not fail to understand why I considered it less important to reach Lhasa than to make a thorough investigation of Lou-lan, the city of my dreams.   To this day I like to dream of its past greatness and its glamour in about 267, the same year in which the Goths attacked Athens and were driven back by Dexippos, the historian, and when the Roman emperor Valerian was a prisoner of the Persian king Sapor. I recall the marvel that not a single one of our ancient Swedish rune-stones is older than the fragile wooden staffs and paper fragments that I found in Lou-lan.   When Marco Polo made his famous journey through Asia, in 1274, the sleeping city had already lain a thousand years unknown and forgotten in its desert.   And after the great Venetian's journey, it was to slumber six hundred and fifty years more before the ghosts of its past were roused to life, and their ancient documents and letters made to shed new light on bygone days and mysterious human fates.

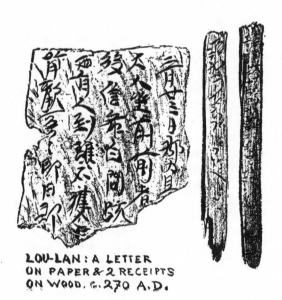

LOU-LAN : A LETTER
ON PAPER & 2 RECEIPTS
ON WOOD. c. 270 A.D.

CHAPTER XLII

Back to High Tibet

ON March 10, in the morning, I divided the caravan into two sections, taking with me Shagdur, Kuchuk, Khodai Kullu, and Khodai Verdi, also four camels, of which one carried the baggage and food needed for eight days, the others bearing ice and reeds. Faizullah took the rest of the caravan—camels, horses, all the heavy luggage, and the entire find from Lou-lan—southwest across the desert to the Kara-koshun marshes and Abdal, where we were to meet.

It was my intention to survey the desert with a levelling-rod and telescope, and thus map out the northern depression definitely. With three of my men I proceeded on foot, making my calculations. Khodai Verdi was to follow with the four camels, and be at hand when we made camp at dusk. But when we had finished our day's work, he was missing. Shagdur went back to look for him. Khodai Verdi appeared during the night, guided by the great fire we had lit. He had lost his way and had been misled by Faizullah's fire, far to the west. A fierce sand-storm set in the next morning, and Shagdur was missing. But as if by a miracle he returned about noon.

During the following days, my levelling, often rendered difficult by the storms, was continued. Notwithstanding the furrows made by the wind, the desert was almost level. By March 15, we had made nine miles and descended one foot. We were approaching the Kara-koshun, but searched in vain for the fire that Tokta Ahun was to have kept going on the northern lake-shore on and after March 13. On the seventeenth, we reached the shore safely and encamped. We had fallen 2.272 metres in a distance of 81½ kilometres, or 7½ feet in scarcely 50 miles. In this northern section of the desert I had clearly proved the existence of a one-time lake. It was still filled with reed-stubble and mollusc-shells. Lou-lan had been situated on the northern shore of this lake. The old Chinese maps, and Baron von Richthofen, who relied upon them to support his theory, were right, after all.

Our next task was to get in touch with Tokta Ahun and his relief-expedition. Our food-supply had come to an end. Kuchuk did some fishing, without luck; and it was Shagdur who saved us by shooting wild ducks every day. As soon as we had encamped, I sent Khodai Kullu southwest along the lake-shore to look for Tokta Ahun's party. A raging storm began in the evening, and continued for three nights and two days. We waited all this time; but on the twentieth we started off southwest.

We had not gone far when we were stopped by a mass of water, which had inundated the sterile desert; and we had to walk around this newly-created lake. Twice we saw Khodai Kullu's footprints. At one point he had swum across an arm of the water.

On March 23, I sent Shagdur out to search. After a while we espied him again in the distance. He signalled to us to come; and when we got there, he pointed to the southwest shouting, "Horsemen, horsemen!" Two mounted men were seen galloping in a cloud of dust.

We stopped to wait for them. Great was my surprise to see Chernoff, my faithful Cossack, who, the previous summer, together with Sirkin, had been ordered by the Governor-General of Tashkent to return to Kashgar, because of disturbances on the Asiatic frontier. His presence here was readily explained. The Governor-General had no right to withdraw any of the four Cossacks given me by order of the Czar, and so I had written in protest to the Czar himself. The Cossacks took the letter with them when they went to Kashgar. No sooner did the Czar receive my letter, than he telegraphed Consul-General Petrovsky to send the Cossacks Sirkin and Chernoff to my camp immediately. Chernoff now told me of their joy, that Saturday evening, when they got the order to look me up in the heart of Asia. They had asked for permission to stay over Sunday, but the Consul said an order from the Czar could not be postponed. So they saddled their horses and brought my post, camera, plates, and twenty-seven silver *yambas*. When at last they reached headquarters at Charkhlik, Tokta Ahun was already there. Islam Baï thereupon organized the relief-expedition, which, led by Chernoff and Tokta Ahun, was to seek me on the northern shore of the Kara-koshun.

Carrying provisions, they marched in a large body along the lake-shore, until they were stopped by the newly-formed bodies of water. There they built huts and established their base of supply. A veritable

farmyard, with sheep and poultry, canoes and fishing-nets, enlivened
that solitary shore. Every evening they made a huge fire on a hillock;
but the air being hazy, we did not see its light. Khodai Kullu turned
up suddenly, one day, half dead from hunger, having had nothing to
eat for five days. They started off immediately with him as a guide.

And now they had found us. It was a great joy to me to see
Chernoff again. The men's bags contained all the good things in the
world, even packets of letters from my home. We were in a Chinese
province, and yet my first news of the year-old Boxer uprising in China
came via Stockholm.

On we went together toward Abdal, crossing the trail of Faizullah's
caravan, and finding a dead horse, whose meat he and his men had
doubtless eaten, when their provisions gave out. From Abdal it was
only a three days' march to Charkhlik, our new headquarters.

Now came a period of work and preparation. We hired a pleasant
caravansary, with a garden, where my *yurt* was pitched under mulberry-
trees and plum-trees. A tame deer strolled about there, a gift from
the governor, Jan Daloy. Whole rows of horses and mules stood at the
stable-cribs; and I bought twenty-one new camels to add to the eighteen
we had before. But three of the new ones were cubs, the youngest
one being only a few days old and hardly able to stand on his feet. He
became everyone's favourite; and when he died, in Tibet, his two
comrades had long since departed.

We purchased stores to last ten months—rice, flour, and toasted
flour. The bags were arranged on light pack-ladders, which were easy
to attach to the camels' pack-saddles. We bought an adequate supply
of furs for the men and felt mats for the camels.

I developed a great many photographic plates and wrote letters.
The longest one, to my parents, covered two hundred and sixteen
pages. I wrote also to the King, the Czar, Nordenskiöld (who received my letter a few days before his death), and Lord Curzon, Viceroy of India. All my specimens were packed in cases—the discoveries
from Lou-lan, skeletons, minerals, plants, etc. This material made up
eight heavy camel-loads. I sent them to Kashgar by Islam Baï and
Faizullah. They left on May 5, enveloped in a howling sand-storm.

A few days later, the main caravan departed, in command of Chernoff and Turdu Baï. They had about twenty-five men. Going by way
of Abdal, where they were to buy fifty sheep, they would take the most

comfortable road to the western shore of the Ayag-kum-kol.   It was my largest caravan so far, and it looked quite imposing, as it wended its way from Charkhlik, to the sound of tinkling bells.   Only one-fifth of this caravan reached Ladak alive, and not a single one of the animals was with us when we finally reached Kashgar.

From Dovlet, a caravan-man from Bokhara, we hired seventy mules, which, laden with maize for our caravan-animals, were to follow Turdu Baï's section, and return in two months, by which time most of the maize would be eaten.   He left with ten men, and took a short-cut toward the mountains.

Thus I was fully occupied during the rest-period.   Visitors arrived continually, not the least of them being the sellers of live-stock and provisions.   One little gentleman, who often came to see me in my *yurt,* was the six-year-old son of Jan Daloy, a charming child, polite and well-mannered, as Chinese etiquette required.   He presented me with sweetmeats, and my saddle-horse with clover.   I learned with pain and regret, one evening, that he had died of smallpox the day before his grieved father returned from an official trip.

Our large caravans having left, only Sirkin, Li Loye, and Mollah Shah remained with me; and only twelve of our horses were in the yard. Eight dogs had gone with the caravans, but Yoldash stayed with me. Our yard, so recently the scene of life and commotion, now looked empty and deserted.

Soon after our arrival in Charkhlik, I charged Shagdur and Cherdon, the two Buriat Cossacks of Mongol descent, with an important commission.   They were to ride to Kara-shahr and buy a complete outfit of clothes, furs, caps, boots, packing-cases, cooking-utensils, jugs, etc., all genuine Mongol products, in quantities sufficient for four men.   These articles were designed for my intended journey, in disguise, to Lhasa. They were also to engage a lama who spoke Tibetan, one who could interpret for us.   I looked for their return within a month.

They performed their task beyond my expectations; and Shagdur returned half of the money as not being needed.   On May 14, they arrived with the entire Mongol outfit, and with Shereb Lama, of Urga, twenty-seven years old, in the red robe of a lama, with a yellow girdle and a Chinese cap.   We became friends right off, and began immediately with lessons in the Mongol language, which, in the interim, I had forgotten. The lama had described the wonders of Lhasa to Shagdur. He had studied in that city and was desirous of returning there.

Shagdur also brought our friend Ordek, who begged to accompany me to Tibet. Cherdon was to join the large caravan speedily.

On May 17, we were ready to depart. A group of ten Mongol pilgrims, from Tarbagatai, had arrived at Charkhlik the day before. They were headed for Lhasa, and became suspicious on learning that we, too, were on our way to the high mountains. Like the pilgrims of the year before, these, too, were destined to work us harm. Now, just as I was setting out with Sirkin, Shagdur, Mollah Shah, Li Loye, Shereb Lama, a guide, twelve horses, and ten mules bearing maize, the pilgrims were there, following us with their eyes.

We rode up through the Charkhlik-su valley—a road hitherto untravelled by me—left the glowing summer of East Turkestan behind us, crossed a difficult pass, and were soon again on the Tibetan table-land, where we were received by shy, wild asses, frost and falling snow. In one valley we met eighteen shepherds, from whom we purchased twelve sheep. At that point we hired new guides.

During a day of rest, I confided to Shereb Lama my plans to reach Lhasa. He was greatly amazed, and declared that a lama who took a European to Lhasa would be decapitated. He would never have joined us had Shagdur told him all the facts in Kara-shahr. I told him I had cautioned Shagdur not to reveal anything of my plans, which had to be kept secret. We discussed the matter, not only for hours, but the entire day, and in the end Shereb Lama agreed to go along to the Ayag-kum-kol. From there he might return to Kara-shahr, if he so wished. He was to tell me of his decision when we got to the large salt-lake; and, in any case, he was perfectly free.

On June 1, we reached the left shore of the Ayag-kum-kol, where we spent a few days waiting for our large caravans, which, their route being much longer than ours, had not yet been heard from. On June 4, Shereb Lama sighted something that looked like a huge caravan, in six divisions, at the foot of the mountain in the northeast. He was right. The dark lines slowly grew larger. First, the two Cossacks came to report that all was well. Then the asses trudged to the camp, and the bronze camel-bells were heard in the distance. Afterwards, Dovlet from Bokhara appeared, with his seventy maize-mules. A wild ass happened to join them; but he discovered his mistake in time,

and dived like an arrow into the interior of the desert.   The horses
and the fifty sheep brought up the rear.   The bell-wether, a ram called
Vanka, from Kucha, was the only one of the flock that entered Kashgar
with me a year later.   The other sheep would follow Vanka, and he
displayed an authority and assurance unusual in a sheep.

Our camp presented a splendid sight, especially at night, with the
fires blazing on the shore.   The superfluous men were sent back; for the
fewer mouths there were, the longer the food would last.   But a
sufficient number remained to give colour and variety to the camp-life.
The Mohammedans were in the majority.   Mingled with them were
Buriat and Orthodox Cossacks, and a lama in a bright-red robe.
Among the animals, the three young camels and Vanka attracted most
attention.   The deer died, and we kept his skeleton.   In Charkhlik
we purchased the beautiful large camel that I had had, in 1896, on our
journey along the course of the Keriya-daria.   He was my particular
favourite, the ranking veteran.

Once assembled and off to the south, our train looked like a small
invading army.   Each man had his job, and the Cossacks maintained
excellent discipline.   The camps were pitched according to a fixed plan,
exactly as in the days of Xenophon.   The camels' loads were deposited
in long rows, and next to them Turdu Baï and his men had their tents.
Nearby was the kitchen-tent where Cherdon prepared my meals.
Sirkin, Shagdur, and Shereb Lama shared a small *yurt*.   The last named,
a doctor of theology, had no other duty than to be my teacher; yet
he always did more than his share, whenever there was need for it.
Chernoff and Cherdon lived in a small tent, next to my own, which,
at the extreme end of one flank, was policed by Yoldash and Yolbars.
Shereb Lama made up his mind at the Ayag-kum-kol.   He declared
himself willing to go with me to the end of the world.

Again we approached the Arka-tagh, passing over wet and slippery
ground that sapped the strength of the animals.   Two of the camels
were exhausted; and one, refusing to go further, was left behind, alive,
in a grassy place.   Dovlet of Bokhara was to have him, in case the
animal should still be alive when the asses went back.   But the out-
look was not a bright one.   One day, nine asses collapsed; another day,
thirteen.

One evening, we encamped at the gate of a valley, covered by a thick layer of ice. When camp was made, Chernoff pointed in the direction of the ice-floor, and said: "A bear is heading straight for the camp."

We tied all of the dogs. Bruin trotted slowly across the ice. He looked old and tired. He stopped to rest a few times; then he walked to the edge of the ice, straight towards death. The Cossacks were lying in wait. Three shots were fired. The bear made off, galloping past the tents and up a slope. Two more shots, and he rolled down to the bottom. We kept his skeleton, too. He had big cavities in his teeth, and must have suffered terribly with toothache. His stomach contained a marmot, which he had eaten, skin and all. Rolling the

AN OLD BEAR HEADING FOR OUR CAMP

skin into a ball, with the hair inside, he had swallowed it at a single gulp.

The next days were terrible. We constantly sent men in advance to reconnoitre. The pasturage was miserable. We were battered by hail and snow, and were driven across the highland by westerly storms. One camel, otherwise satisfactory, had the bad habit of flatly refusing to ascend steep slopes. We called him the "Pass-Hater." Even when the men united to push him uphill, he remained immovable. He delayed the whole train, and finally had to be left behind.

I now told Dovlet of Bokhara to go back with the surviving asses.

We allowed them liberal rations, in order to lighten the burdens of our animals.

Five of our camels had dropped out by the time we reached the desolate valley that rises to a pass of the Arka-tagh, more than 17,000 feet above sea-level.   And on the way up to the pass, a most violent tempest burst upon us.   First there was a rattling hail, then came blinding, whirling snow.   I could see nothing but the nearest camel plodding ahead of me.   Time and again the ghastly call was heard, "A camel is exhausted!" and we could see him, with his groom, looming behind, like a spectre in the whirling snow.

I rode to the top of the pass with Shereb Lama.   At last the heavy, slow train came dragging along.   We waited till all passed by; but of the thirty-four camels, only thirty reached the top.   The rest were either worn out, had died or had been killed.

As a result of these casualties, the animals' burdens again became too heavy.   They were accordingly given as much maize as they could eat.   The two young camels were fed on white bread.   There was always some sickness among the men.   I gave them quinine, and they recovered immediately.   The medicine-chest was in requisition at every camp.   It is not easy to travel in High Tibet; it is not a flower-strewn pathway.

On June 26, we camped on the very spot that we had occupied the year before, on the shore of a lake.   Charred wood from our fire was still there.   The ice had not yet broken up; but at noon it was 68°, and a lovely summer breeze swept the ice-covered lake.

We ascended a pass, 17,500 feet high, in a region of brick-red, weathered sandstone.   By the time we got to the top, all the men were dead-tired and dropped to the ground.   Everything was red—mountains, hillocks, valleys—and Shereb Lama, in his red robe, harmonized with the red background.   At a pool, Yoldash overtook a female antelope and her calf, and killed the latter.   I asked Sirkin to shoot the mother, so as to put an end to her misery.   But she escaped.   Hunting was permitted by me only for the sake of meat. The Cossacks had only a hundred and forty-two cartridges left; hence the need for economizing ammunition.   In the evening a fog lay over the highland.   The full moon shed a yellow light on the black clouds.

We traversed the valley where, far to the east, Aldat slept under his mound.   Then we crossed a high pass, and after that, for several

days, we were in open country.   Every evening I would call at Sirkin's
tent to check up the meteorological readings and to try on the Mongolian
attire that Shereb Lama and Shagdur were making for me.   Shereb
Lama drew a plan of Lhasa, and showed me the location of the various
monasteries.   The leaders of our different caravans also came to that
tent for orders concerning the next day's journey.   Our tired animals
rarely could make more than twelve miles.

The veteran from the Keriya-daria was exhausted; and he wept,
which was a sure sign of approaching death.   He stood on shaking
legs when I took a last picture of him, and threw a philosophically
indifferent glance over the land that would soon claim his life.

On July 8, only twenty-seven camels were able to reach camp.   I
picked out eleven of the weakest, and also six horses.   They were
to be led in our rear, slowly and cautiously, in charge of Chernoff and
five Mohammedans.   With the rest of the caravan I continued south.
Wild leeks grew abundant here, to the satisfaction of all, the camels in
particular.   The rainy season had set in.   It poured steadily; and the
dripping and streaming from the animals, loads, and tents made everything heavier, while at the same time making the ground as soft as a
marsh.   At one camp, where the water was salty, Shagdur took a jug
in search of water, and was attacked by a wolf.   He hurled the jug
at the wolf, and returned to the camp, much upset, to fetch his rifle.
But the wolf escaped.

We took a fine old yak by surprise, in a broad glen.   The dogs
attacked him.   He lifted his tail in the air, planted his horns in the
ground, and made for his assailants, now for one, now for another.
I forbade the Cossacks to shoot him.   But then Turdu Baï pronounced
the death-sentence.   He needed meat, and we had to save the last six
sheep.

On another occasion, Yoldash started a hare, which took refuge
in its hole, but not deep enough to prevent Shagdur from pulling the
poor creature out with his hand.

"Hold on to Yoldash, and let go of the hare," I shouted.   The hare
made off like an arrow, but had not gone a hundred yards, when a
falcon swooped down upon him.   We hurried to his assistance, but were
too late.   His eyes were already plucked out, and he lay in death-
convulsions.

At our camp of July 16, next to a brook, a yellowish-grey wolf paid for his boldness with his life. A bear, too, came splashing across the brook, and was chased by the Cossacks. They returned in an hour. The bear had escaped, but they themselves had ridden straight into a Tibetan camp. There were three yak-hunters there, with horses and rifles. The Cossacks returned to fetch Shereb Lama, the only one of us who could speak Tibetan. I sent him and Shagdur to the place. But the Tibetans had gone. The rumour of our approach would now pass from mouth to mouth to Lhasa, which was still three hundred and thirty miles away. The nomads and hunters knew that a reward awaited him who warned the authorities of approaching Europeans. We gave up all thought of pursuing the three men. We would have gained nothing thereby, and our animals were too worn out. Shereb Lama, perceiving that discovery was now very likely, became anxious.

Next day we left an exhausted camel behind in a field where the grazing was good. In an empty tin, fastened to a tent-pole, I placed a written order to search for the camel, if it was not to be seen. But as it happened, Chernoff and the rear-guard made a detour at this place and saw neither camel nor can. Hence we remained ignorant of the abandoned animal's fate.

On July 20, we crossed an immense snowy range, where three hundred yaks were wandering on the edge of a glacier. The ground was dotted with them. On the other side, in a valley, there were seven yaks, which the dogs routed. All fled but one, and so the dogs concentrated their attack on him. He walked quite unperturbed, and planted himself in the valley-brook, the water coursing around him, the baffled dogs on the shore, barking.

A partridge lay motionless in a field, sparsely covered with grass, where we intended to camp. One of the Cossacks shot at it. She started up, but fell dead, while the three little chicks she had been keeping warm ran about unhurt, looking for their mother. The destruction of such earthly happiness was like murder. The deed pained me for a long time. I would willingly have surrendered my partridge-dinner, if I could have granted life to the unfortunate family. I tried to console myself with the thought that I myself was not a hunter.

Pouring rain, marshy ground, quicksand! Detestable! Again we had to negotiate a muddy range. Two tired camels were being led behind. One of them reached our camp. The other sank so badly

into the mud at the top of the pass, that every effort to pull him out
failed. A few of the men stayed with him through the night, hoping
that rescue might be more feasible when the ground had frozen. But
during the night he sank in deeper and deeper, and when morning
came he was dead. Quicksand is the greatest difficulty to be overcome
in northern Tibet. But this was the only time that one of my camels
literally sank into the mud. It is a hard way, this one through northern
Tibet, a veritable *via dolorosa*.

During our march, on July 24, we caught sight of better pasturage,
in a distant valley, than we had seen for many days. We directed
our steps thither and made camp. It was the last occasion, for some
time, on which I had the company of the caravan.

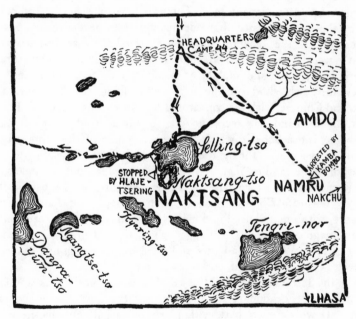

THE DASH FOR LHASA

CHAPTER XLIII

Toward Lhasa Disguised as a Pilgrim

OUR new headquarters, 16,800 feet high, was designated Number 44. From there we were to start our wild ride toward Lhasa. I had intended to rest a week, for the sake of the animals, but Sirkin having noticed, near by, fresh footprints of a man leading a horse, I decided to break camp immediately. Were we already being watched? I also decided that only Shereb Lama and Shagdur should accompany me. This was hard on Cherdon, who, too, was of the Lamaist faith; but our headquarters needed every possible defense in case the Tibetans should use armed force against us.

We were three Buriat pilgrims, bound for Lhasa. Our caravan was to be as light and mobile as possible, only five mules and four horses, all newly shod for the trip. Rice, flour, toasted flour, dried meat, and Chinese brick tea constituted our provisions. My Mongolian cloak, ox-blood red, had secret pockets for my aneroid, compass, watch, note-book, and a book in which I sketched a map of the route. In my left boot was a pocket for the thermometer. I also took shaving-utensils, a lantern, some candles, matches, an axe, Mongolian pots and pans, and ten silver *yambas*. Two Mongolian leather cases held most of these things. I wore a Chinese skull-cap, with ear-laps, and round my neck a rosary, with one hundred and eight beads, and a copper case containing an image of Buddha. A dagger, chop-sticks, a fire-steel, etc., hung in my girdle. We also had furs and blankets of Mongolian make, but no beds. The smallest of our tents was to shelter us.

On the last evening I addressed the men. Sirkin was appointed commander of headquarters, and received the keys to the boxes of silver. If we were not back within two and a half months, he was to return to Charkhlik and Kashgar with the whole caravan. Twenty ravens circled round our tents. Night came and we went to bed.

At sunrise, on July 27, Shagdur roused me. I shall never forget that day. Off for Lhasa! Whether we succeeded or not, the experience would be something extraordinary. If successful, we would see the

Holy City, unvisited by Europeans since Huc and Gabet, two French abbés, had spent two months there, in 1847, or fifty-four years before. And if we failed, we would be entirely at the mercy of the Tibetans, becoming their prisoners, with no inkling of how that captivity might end. However, when Shagdur woke me, I rose eagerly to the great adventure; and in less than a quarter of an hour, I was a thorough Mongol, from head to foot.

At the last moment, it was decided that Ordek should accompany us for a day or two, in order to guard our animals at the camp, and thus allow us a good sleep before our night-vigils began. I rode my white horse, Shagdur his yellow one, Shereb Lama the smallest mule, and Ordek one of the other horses. Malenki and Yolbars were to go along. Yolbars had once been lacerated by a boar; he was the largest and the wildest of our dogs.

When everything was ready, and we were already in the saddle, I asked Shereb Lama if he preferred to stay at headquarters.

"No, never!" was his answer.

We said our farewells. Those we left behind thought that they would never see us again. Sirkin turned away and wept. It was a solemn moment; but, secure in the protection of the Eternal, my calm was unshaken.

We went down the valley at great speed. Hunters had recently been camping on the shore of its stream. The skeleton of a yak lay there. A bear had been foraging about. We rode southeastwards. At an open spring we made our camp. The animals were released to graze, and Ordek tended them. We gave our blessing to the moon that illuminated the silent wilderness, but went early to sleep in the narrow tent.

On the second day, we rode twenty-four miles across fairly level ground, as far as two small lakes, one of them salt, the other of fresh water. Tent was pitched on the narrow strip of land between the lakes. It was a lovely evening. Seated outdoors before the fire, I underwent treatment by Shagdur and Shereb Lama. The former shaved my head, and even my moustache, till I was as smooth as a billiard-ball; the latter rubbed a mixture of fat, soot, and brown pigment into me. I became almost frightened at the sight of myself in my polished watchcase, my only mirror. We were in high spirits, laughing and chatting like schoolboys.

We ate and had tea by the fire, and went to rest early. The animals were grazing on the shore, two hundred paces away. Ordek watched over them. In the evening a storm blew up. At midnight Ordek put his head inside the tent, and said: "There is a man."

We rushed out with the two rifles and revolver that constituted our arsenal. The tempest howled. The moon spread a pale light amid dark, flying clouds. On a small hill to the southwest, we perceived two galloping horsemen, urging two free horses before them. Shagdur directed a few shots at them, but they disappeared in the dark.

What was to be done? First we counted our animals. There were seven of them. My white horse and Shagdur's yellow one were missing.

ATTACKED BY ROBBERS, WHO STOLE TWO OF OUR BEST HORSES

It was evident from the footprints that one of the thieves had stolen upon the outermost horses and frightened them down to the shore, where two mounted Tibetans had taken them in charge. They had been lying in wait for us like wolves, and were assisted by the storm. I was furious at this skulking attack, and my first impulse was to pursue them night and day. But could we leave our camp and the rest of the animals? Perhaps we were surrounded by a whole band of robbers. We lit the fire, and our pipes, and sat in conversation until dawn. Peace was gone. Our hands were on our daggers. Sunrise found Ordek weeping.

He was to go back to headquarters alone. On a leaf torn from my note-book, I wrote Sirkin to strengthen the guard.

Afterwards we learned that Ordek had arrived half dead at head-quarters. He had sneaked like a cat in hollows and river-beds, taking every shadow for a robber, and two docile wild asses for hostile horse-men. And when at last he reached the camp, he came near being shot by the guard. When the others heard that we had been attacked by robbers, after only two days' journey, their fears grew, and they were convinced we would never come back alive.

We continued southeast; and the lone Ordek, after helping us load the beasts, disappeared. We came upon a huge herd of yaks on a plain. Were they tame? No; they fled. We pitched our tent in open terrain, and I gathered yak-droppings for the fire. From this moment on, not a word of Russian was to be spoken, only Mongolian. Shagdur was ordered to act the part of our leader. I was his servant, and he was to treat me as a servant in the presence of Tibetans.

I slept till eight o'clock in the evening. Then Shagdur and Shereb Lama came driving our seven animals up to the tent. They were in a serious mood; for they had seen three Tibetan horsemen, who were on the lookout. The animals were immediately tethered in the lee of the tent, the entrance of which was open. Yolbars was tied beyond the animals, and Malenki to windward of the tent. The night was divided into three watches. Mine was the first, from nine o'clock to twelve; Shagdur's the second, from twelve to three; and Shereb Lama's the last, to six o'clock.

Thus my two comrades went to sleep while I stood watch. I walked from Yolbars to Malenki, and back, and alternated between playing with them and stroking the exhausted horses and mules. At nine-thirty an infernal storm broke—coal-black clouds, lightning and thunder, and a rattling, pouring rain. I took refuge in the entrance to the tent. The rain battered the canvas, and a fine drizzle sifted through. I lit my pipe and the candle in the lantern, and took out my note-book. But every ten minutes I patrolled the space between the dogs. The rain splashed dully and monotonously. It ran in jets from the animals' manes and tails, and from the pack-saddles. It ran from my skin-coat. The Chinese cap stuck to my bald head like glue.

I heard a plaintive sound in the distance, and hurried out. "Oh," thought I, "that is only Yolbars, expressing anger at the rain." My eyelids grew heavy. A thunderbolt roused me. The dogs growled, and I went out again. There was a clacking and swishing, as I trod in the mud. The hours seemed endless. Would my spell never come to an end? But at last the midnight-hour struck. I was just about to wake Shagdur, when the two dogs began to bark furiously. Shereb Lama woke up and rushed out. We took our arms, and all three of us stole away to leeward. The tramping of horses was audible. There were horsemen near by, and we hurried in their direction. But then they disappeared, and again all was quiet. The rain beat the ground. I lay down in my wet clothes. For a while, I heard the splashing steps of Shagdur in the wet; but then I fell sound asleep.

RIDING THROUGH THE POURING RAIN

We broke camp at daybreak, crossed a ridge of the pass, entered a beaten path, saw many old camping-places, but no people, and halted again on a strip of land between two small lakes. As soon as camp was made, two of us lay down to sleep. We tethered the animals as on the night before, and I began my watch. Merciless rain fell all night long. One mule tore herself loose, and trotted off to the pasturage. I followed. At least she kept me awake. After many vain attempts, I managed to seize her halter, and tied her up.

On July 31, we set out in a pouring rain. It made us and our animals glisten. It dripped and spouted in streams. The road became wider. No doubt it led to Lhasa. We followed the trail of a large yak-caravan across five small passes. The yak-caravan was encamped on the roadside. Shereb Lama went up to them. The travellers were Tanguts from Kum-bum on their way to Lhasa. They questioned Shereb Lama about us and our errand. Meanwhile, our dogs and theirs began to fight. I felt sorry for the dogs that got into a scuffle with Yolbars.

A little further on, we encamped in a glen, quite close to a Tibetan tent, where a young man and two women were living. The owner came home soon. We invited him to our tent, and he gave us an armful of yak-droppings and a wooden vessel, with milk. His name was Sampo Singi, and the place was Gom-jima. Sampo Singi was black with dirt, bareheaded, had long hair, no trousers, yet sat down, right in the wet, outside the tent. He took snuff offered by Shereb Lama, and after sneezing about a hundred times asked whether there used to be pepper in our snuff. He thought it was nice of us, who lived so far away, to make a pilgrimage to Lhasa. We were still eight days distant from there.

All of a sudden Shagdur roared at me to drive our animals in, and I obeyed straightway. The sun went down and the moon peeped out. But during the night it poured again. I felt secure in the vicinity of the nomads.

The next morning, Sampo Singi and one of the women brought us sheep-fat, sour and sweet milk, cheese-powder and cream, and a sheep. He would not accept money; but we had a piece of blue Chinese silk, over which the woman nearly went crazy. The man killed the sheep by choking it; he wound a strap around its nose, and thrust his thumb and index-finger in its nostrils. Then he slaughtered it. We allowed him to retain the skin. Thereupon we took leave of the kind nomads, threw ourselves into our saddles, and rode on.

At the same moment the rain began again. It poured from the sky in jets, and it was like riding through dense clusters of glass. A big body of water was dimly seen through the mist. At first we believed it to be a lake; but upon reaching the shore, we found a gigantic river, the yellow-grey, thick, muddy water-masses of which rolled southwest with a hollow and sinister roar. I knew at once that it was the Sachu-tsangpo, which Bonvalet and Rockhill had once crossed. The opposite (left) bank was not visible at all. The road to Lhasa had taken us down to the right bank. But where was the ford? Before one could say Jack Robinson, Shereb Lama led the way into the river, leading the pack-mules. Shagdur and I followed.

In the middle of the river we halted for a minute on a sand-bank, in water about a foot deep. From there, neither the right nor the left bank could be seen. The water rolled by in great volume, seething and rumbling. Owing to the constant rain, the river was rising rapidly. If we stayed too long, we risked being cut off in both directions. Shereb Lama went on. It began to look bad when the water rose above the

CROSSING A BIG RIVER IN POURING RAIN

root of his little mule's tail. And now one of the pack-mules slipped. The two Mongol boxes tied to her back acted as cork-cushions and kept her afloat. The swift current swept her along at breakneck speed. I thought she was lost. Only her head and the edges of the boxes were visible above the water. She swam, however, and after a while touched ground again. Far away she righted herself and scrambled up on the left bank.

Lama rode on alone. The water got deeper and deeper. We called out to him at the top of our lungs; but he continued, bold and fearless. The rain beat the river; all was water. I rode last, and

my horse fell behind. I saw the other two, and the pack-animals,
rising above the surface of the water. I had a glimpse of the left
shore. They managed to make it safely. I dug my heels into my
horse. But we happened to strike a little below the ford, and sank
deeper and deeper. I felt dizzy, as the water filled my boots. Presently it rose above my knees and the saddle. I loosened my girdle and
pulled off my skin coat. Lama and Shagdur shouted and pointed;
but in the roar of the water I did not hear them. Now it reached
my waist. Now I saw no more of my horse than his head and neck.
I prepared to throw myself from the saddle and let go of the horse.
But at that very moment he began to swim. Involuntarily I grasped
his mane. He was carried along by the current, and almost choked.
But the next moment he touched bottom, got his footing, and heaved
himself onto the shore. I never experienced a worse river-crossing in
Asia. It was nothing less than a miracle that no one was drowned.
Neither Shagdur nor Shereb Lama could swim.

Our little caravan looked tragi-comic in the teeming rain. Lama,
who always led the way, continued as though the river had not existed.
I pulled off my boots, poured the water out, and hung them behind
my saddle. It rained heavily, and everything was soaking-wet. The
water streamed out of the two boxes.

At last our honourable monk stopped in a field, where there were
yak-droppings. By scraping away the wettest layer, we managed after
much trouble to ignite the cakes. And when the fire was burning
properly, in spite of the rain sizzling in the flames, I undressed, bit
by bit, and wrung the water out of my Mongolian clothes. Had any
Tibetans happened by, they would have been dumbfounded at the sight
of my white body.

Night came, with its cloak of darkness, its rattling rain, and its
mysterious sounds. I heard steps, the tramp of horses, human voices,
shouts, and rifle-shots. I waked Shagdur at twelve o'clock sharp,
slipped into the tent, and lay down in my still-wet clothes. I was so
tired that I almost longed to be captured and get a thorough rest.

On August 2, it did not rain. We entered populated regions. We
rode past two nomad-tents, where there were sheep and yaks, and
passed a caravan of three hundred yaks, laden with brick tea for the
famous Tashi-lunpo monastery. The drivers built their fires close to
the roadside; and as we rode past, the men approached us, asking

many questions. One old man pointed at me and said, "peling" (European). The region was called Amdo-mochu.

We proceeded to a spring and a field, and spread our clothes out on the ground in the evening sun. But then came a hail-storm and a downpour, and we stowed everything in the tent. The thunder pealed with a ringing sound, strangely reminiscent of church-bells.

The next morning I enjoyed a complete rest. I was waked at nine o'clock by the other two, who advised me to take a look at the tea-caravan. It was really amusing. The men were all afoot, their rifles on their shoulders. They looked like robbers, every one of them black, men as well as yaks. They whistled, shouted, and sang.

We stayed there all day to get dry. I filled my boots with warm, dry

THE GREAT TEA CARAVAN. EVERYTHING WAS BLACK, THE MEN, THE YAKS, THE RIFLES

sand, to get the moisture out of them. While the animals grazed, we took turns in sleeping. The night was clear, the moon was up, and the stars twinkled.

The fourth of August saw us on the main road to Lhasa. We were constantly passing nomads' tents and herds, meeting large caravans, and riding past others. And now we also passed cairns of holy *mani* stones. We stopped for the night, and a young Tibetan dropped in to see us.

On the fifth, we rode twenty and a half miles, brushing past the Tso-nek (the Black Lake), where tents and herds were numerous, till at last we reached a plain, on which there were twelve tents. There we established our Camp No. 53, having covered one hundred and sixty-two miles since leaving headquarters.

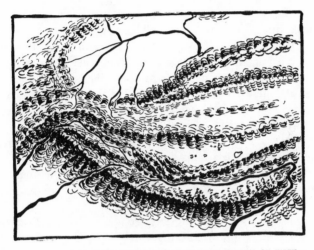

A PLASTIC REPRESENTATION OF THE MOUNTAIN SYSTEMS OF TIBET

CHAPTER XLIV

A Prisoner of the Tibetans

AT dusk, three Tibetans came walking toward our tent, and Shereb Lama and Shagdur went out to meet them. They conversed for a long time, and it was dark in every sense when my two comrades returned. One of the Tibetans had told them, in a magisterial tone, that three days before a messenger had come from a yak-hunter in the north, who reported having seen an enormous caravan proceeding toward Lhasa.

"Are you associated with them?" he asked. "Tell the truth. Remember that you are a lama."

Shereb Lama's knees trembled, and he stated the facts, without mentioning my presence. But Shagdur assured me that the magisterial Tibetan had several times used the expression "shved peling," or "Swedish European." The pilgrims from Temirlik or Charkhlik had probably ascertained my nationality through their questioning, though none of them had the slightest knowledge of Sweden. They had only very hazy ideas about China, British India, and Russia. Shagdur thought that Shereb Lama had betrayed us, but I could not share his suspicions. And even if it were true, all is now forgotten and forgiven. The Tibetan had finally said: "You will stay here to-morrow."

We sat up long, pondering over our prospects. All through the night, watch-fires surrounded our tents at a little distance.

Shortly after daybreak, three other Tibetans came to our tent. I always wore blue Mongolian eye-glasses. The newcomers asked to see my eyes, and were much surprised to find them as dark as their own. Their wish to see our weapons was granted with pleasure. After that lesson they backed towards their horses.

A while later, an old white-haired lama and three other men visited us. The former asked a number of questions about our headquarters, and informed us that couriers had been sent to Kamba Bombo, the Governor of Nakchu. We were prisoners until his instructions came.

The next number on the day's program was not reassuring. Fifty-three horsemen, in red, black, or grey cloaks, wearing high white hats or red bandannas around their heads, and armed with spears, lances, swords, and muskets, decorated with streamers, gathered at a tent-settlement a few hundred yards away.   They dismounted, held a consultation by a fire, right in the rain, and then sprang into their saddles. Seven of them rode east on the road to Nakchu, two went south along the main road to Lhasa.   The rest galloped off, making straight for our

tent, emitting wild war-cries, and swinging their swords or muskets above their heads.   Shereb Lama believed that our hours were numbered.   We took our stand in front of the tent, with finger on trigger.   Like an avalanche the Tibetans rushed forward.   The hoofs of the horses smacked in the wet.   When so close that the nearest horses splashed us, they divided into two squads, and swung back in two wide curves to their starting-point.

Having repeated this warlike manœuvre twice, they dismounted and shot at a target.   They evidently intended to inspire us with awe.   Finally they rode toward the northwest, and I wondered if they would dare to attack our headquarters.

THE TIBETANS CHARGED STRAIGHT DOWN UPON US

All day long new visitors came.   They brought us little gifts of fat, milk, or sour milk, and none of them would accept payment.   During a shower we had four fellows in our tent, where we sat packed like sardines.   But when a small stream of rain-water found its way into our shelter, I sent them out to dig a ditch around the tent.   In the evening we counted thirty-seven watch-fires around us, faintly gleaming through the rain.

The next day new spies arrived.   One of them presented us with an armful of yak-droppings and a bellows, and told us that Lhasa was five days off, but that the mounted postman made the journey in a day.   The district where we were was named Yallok.   Our seven pack-animals had been led away, probably to prevent our flight.   We saw horsemen in every direction, riding singly or in squads.   At times the place swarmed with mounted, armed men.   It looked like a mobilization.   We were but three against this superior force.   We were prisoners and in the midst of a great adventure.

On the morning of August 8, five men came up and presented us with a sheep.   A message had arrived that Kamba Bombo, the All-Highest, was himself on his way to see us.   Shereb Lama was afraid that the Governor would recognize him.   By way of punishment for a dereliction, a lama had once been sentenced to travel the entire distance from Urga to Lhasa in a prostrate position, i. e., he had to measure the road with the length of his body.   It had taken him six years.   Shereb Lama believed that he would suffer a like penalty.

We could not take fifty steps from the tent without spies coming forth to watch us.   Ben Nursu seemed to be a sort of chief spy.   His tent was close to ours.   He sat with us for hours, and ate his meals with us.

In the afternoon we were seated with seven Tibetans around our fire in the open, when a troop of horsemen came galloping straight up to us from the east.   It was Kamba Bombo's interpreter, who spoke a poorer Mongolian than I, but was otherwise a decent fellow.   He questioned us thoroughly, and was most interested in our headquarters. Apparently they had illusions of a Russian invasion, with thousands of Cossacks.   The interpreter told us that the Dalai Lama received daily reports about us.   I asked him harshly how they dared to detain peaceful pilgrims from the Buriat provinces of the Russian Czar.   "Your subjects steal our horses at night; but you treat us, who do you no harm, like robbers."   The interpreter looked pensive, but answered that the road to Lhasa was closed to everyone who had no proper passport.

On the ninth, in the morning, the scene became animated.   The whole plain swarmed with horsemen and pack-animals, and a new tent-village was growing up not far away.   So much ado because of us, three poor pilgrims!   One large tent was white, with blue ribbons.   None but a chief could lodge thus.

Accompanied by a squad of horsemen, the interpreter came to our tent, and announced that Kamba Bombo had arrived, and was expecting me to a feast.   Everything was prepared.   Each of us was to receive a *haddik*, a long piece of thin white gauze cloth, symbolizing welcome.   There were viands, including an entire sheep.

I answered stiffly: "People of good manners first pay a visit before inviting guests to a party. If Kamba Bombo wants anything of us, let him come here. We have nothing to withhold from him. All that we wish to know is whether the road to Lhasa is open to us or not. If not, Kamba Bombo will have to take the consequences on himself."

The interpreter was in despair. For two hours he sat begging and imploring us to come to the feast.

"I shall be dismissed if you do not come," he pleaded.

Even when he was in his saddle, he continued his persuasion. Finally he rode off.

Another two hours passed, when a troop of sixty-seven horsemen

KAMBA BOMBO, ACCOMPANIED BY 67 MEN ON HORSEBACK

came dashing up from the new tent-village. They presented a splendid picture in their deep-blue and dark-red attire, their swords in scabbards ornamented with silver, coral, and torquoises, their cases holding an image of Buddha, their rosaries, and the rattling silver accoutrement at their sides. Kamba Bombo rode in the centre on a milk-white she-mule. He was a small, pale man, perhaps forty years old, with eyes that blinked roguishly; and he wore a red cloak and red *bashlik* over a yellow silk robe, with skunk sleeves, green velvet boots, and a blue Chinese cap.

He dismounted in front of my tent. His servant spread a rug on the ground and placed cushions on it. Here he and another high official, Nanso Lama, a monk, settled down.

I invited the two gentlemen into my tent, where each found a seat on a bag of flour.

Kamba Bombo was polite and kind, notwithstanding that we had tried to deceive him, had responded uncivilly to his invitation to a party, and were in his power. The interrogations were renewed, the Governor's secretary recording all my answers. To my request for permission to continue, see the Holy City, and then return to headquarters, Kamba Bombo answered with a significant gesture of his hand toward his neck.

"No; not one step further toward Lhasa. That would cost your heads—and mine, too. I do my duty. I get orders from the Dalai Lama every day."

He was immovable, inexorable. He did not lose control of himself for one moment. He was at once dignified and jovial. When we spoke of the two horses that had been stolen, he laughed and said: "You shall get two others from me. When you return to your headquarters, you shall be escorted to the border of my province, you shall have provisions, sheep, and everything you need. You have but to give your orders. But not *one* step farther toward the south."

In those days it was impossible for a European to travel to Lhasa. Przhevalsky, Bonvalot, De Rhins, Rockhill, Littledale, all had met with the same insurmountable resistance. Two years later, Lord Curzon sent his Anglo-Indian army to Lhasa. It opened the southern road to the Holy City by force, and four thousand Tibetans were killed. That was called war. But the Tibetans had asked nothing but to be left in peace. When the Tibetans under Kamba Bombo outwitted me, they too used peremptory means, but no violence, and they made their will effective without staining their hands with blood. On the contrary, they treated me with the utmost consideration. As for myself, I had the satisfaction of going to the limit of the adventure without capitulating until the opposition proved absolutely unconquerable. In the end, Kamba Bombo rode back to his tent. I told him it was my purpose to start off for headquarters already on the following day.

Early in the morning, I mounted my horse, and rode—much to the dismay of Shagdur and Shereb Lama—quite alone to Kamba Bombo's tent. But I had not gone half-way, when twenty horsemen surrounded me and asked me to dismount. After some waiting, Kamba Bombo appeared with his escort. Rugs and cushions were spread out, and we settled down to converse on neutral ground. I asked him jokingly how it would be if he and I should ride to Lhasa, only we two together? He laughed, shook his head, and said that it would be a pleasure to him to travel in my company, provided the Dalai Lama gave his permission.

"Well, let us send a courier to the Dalai Lama. I am willing to wait a couple of days."

"No," he answered determinedly. "I should be dismissed immediately after such a question."

Kamba Bombo screwed up his eyes, and pointing at me, said: "Sahib!"

I asked him how he could think that an Englishman from India could come from the north with Russian and Buriat Cossacks in his service, and I tried to explain to him where Sweden was.

Presently two horses were brought forth as compensation for the stolen ones. They were poor stock, and I said that I did not want them. Thereupon two perfect animals were produced, and I declared myself satisfied.

Finally I asked Kamba Bombo why he came with sixty-seven men, when we were only three, nay, I was quite alone now. Was he afraid of me?

"No, not at all, but I have orders from Lhasa to treat you as we treat the highest dignitaries in our own country."

We mounted again, and Kamba Bombo and his gentlemen accompanied me to my tent. There our weapons were examined and the escort was introduced to us. It consisted of two officers—Solang Undy and Ana Tsering—a non-commissioned officer, fourteen men, and six men for the Tibetans' belongings. They brought ten sheep for themselves. Kamba Bombo gave us six besides; also fat, flour, and milk. Thereupon I said farewell, and we parted, the very best of friends.[1]

[1] Edmund Candler, Reuter's correspondent in the British-Indian military expedition against Lhasa, relates in his book, "The Unveiling of Lhasa," that a small British force was attacked unexpectedly in the beginning of May, 1904, by one thousand Tibetans under the command of that same Kamba Bombo who, three years earlier, had checked my advance near Nakchu. After ten minutes' violent shooting, the Tibetans retired, leaving behind one hundred and forty dead. The British lost five. It is probable that my friend Kamba Bombo was among those killed. On that occasion as when we met him, he did only his duty to his country. I was not angry with him in 1901. After what happened in 1904, I admire him and honour his memory.

Our procession looked like the transfer of prisoners. We were flanked by Tibetans, and they rode before us and behind us. When we encamped, they pitched two of their tents immediately next to ours, and kept watch during the night. We slept the whole night, and gave no thought to our pack-animals. Yolbars inspired them with the greatest awe, and had constantly to be held in leash. The escort included two lamas, who constantly swung their prayer-wheels, mumbling "om mani padme hum."

The day's journey was divided into two stages, with an interval for tea. Then the Tibetans cut three chunks of earth out of the ground, with their swords, and made a triangular support for the saucepan over a fire. Their lunch consisted of boiled mutton, *tsamba,* and tea. Their horsemen looked handsome, with queues rolled round their heads, and red turban-like sashes. Their right arms and shoulders were bare, the skin coat being allowed to slip half-way down their backs. All the horses wore bell-collars, and they made the valleys gay with their tinkling.

A BEAR DIGGING UP A MARMOT-HOLE

After we had ridden across the Sachu-tsangpo, which had fallen considerably, the escort bade us farewell, and we were once more left to ourselves. It seemed lonely and desolate after they abandoned us, and our night-watches began again. Once Malenki stood barking on a small hillock by the roadside. I rode thither and saw a bear digging up a marmot-hole. He was so absorbed in his work that he did not notice me until I was quite close upon him. Then he left the hole and slunk away. The dogs chased him, he turned round and held his ground, and there was a gay dance before both sides tired.

On August 20, only a few miles remained to be covered. We heard rifle-shots in a glen, and beheld two horsemen—Sirkin and Turdu Baï—who were out getting meat for the caravan. They wept with joy on seeing us.

And then we rode up to the camp, where everything was quiet. Chernoff had arrived with the rear-guard, having lost only two camels and two horses. To me it was like coming back to civilization. Using the caravan-buckets, I took a hot bath. I had not washed in twenty-five days, and the water had to be changed several times. Afterwards it was pleasant to lie undressed in one's clean, dry bed, while some of the men gave a concert with a *balalaika,* a flute, a temple-bell, my music-box, and two improvised drums. We had not reached Lhasa, but we had tasted the enchantment of the great adventure as never before.

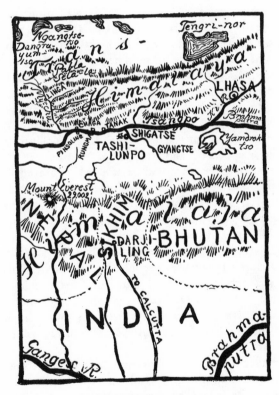

LHASA AND ROUTE TO INDIA

CHAPTER XLV

Stopped by an Armed Force

IT was now my plan to cross Tibet and reach India in one way or another. I decided, therefore, to push south with the entire caravan until confronted by insurmountable obstacles, and then to head westwards to Ladak, and, by way of Kashmir and Himalaya, eventually reach warmer regions on the banks of the Ganges.

This was a difficult march. Several high passes had to be crossed, and new belts of treacherous quicksand negotiated. Several horses died. One of our men, Kalpet of Keriya, being sick, had to ride. The region was rich in game, and the Cossacks kept us in meat. Once they shot a wild goat and an antelope, and allowed them to freeze bone-hard in their fleeing posture, so that they looked quite lifelike. Another time, a poor hare was chased by seven dogs. Yoldash caught him; but then Yolbars appeared, and ate him up.

That sooner or later we would be stopped, appeared certain. The Tibetans, being warned, had increased the guard on the north. By September 1, after one week on the road, we again encountered nomads. From the top of a pass, we viewed the plain to the south, which seemed dotted with horses; and there were thousands of sheep grazing there. Shagdur and Lama rode up to a tent to buy milk and fat, but the inhabitants declared they were forbidden to sell us anything. Shagdur displayed anger, whereupon the frightened Tibetan sold us what we wished. Three Tibetans were brought to our camp, where we treated them to tea and bread. When we let them go, they were in a terrible hurry to get into their saddles; and they rode away as if pursued by evil spirits.

On September 3, six armed horsemen appeared on the left of the caravan, and seven on the right, all at quite a distance, every one wearing a tall white hat. There were many tents, and we looked into some of them. The women wore their hair in small plaits; and on their backs they had red ribbons, with coral, turquoises, and silver coins.

We reached the Sachu-tsangpo again, far below the point where we had crossed the river before. Here the water was crowded into one very deep channel. The Tibetans, seated on the shore, expected to see a free show. When we assembled our boat and launched it, they stared blankly. At the camp, a chief with his band ventured forth and said:

"We have orders to prevent you from continuing south."

"All right, prevent us."

"We have sent messengers to Lhasa. If you proceed in that direction, we shall lose our heads."

"That would serve you right."

"All the nomads have been forbidden to sell you anything."

"We take what we need. And we have firearms."

I took Ordek along, and we sailed down the river, for two days, to the point where it emptied into the large salt-lake of Selling-tso. The Tibetans followed on shore, occasionally letting out wild shouts. We met the caravan near the mouth and encamped. Our Cossacks forced some people to sell us four sheep.

We continued along the lake-shore; and on September 7, sixty-three horsemen were at our heels. On the following days, we skirted the western shore of the lake, and then the northern shore of a fresh-water lake quite close by. The Tibetans increased in number. It looked again as if the tribes were being mobilized. The chief implored us daily to turn off toward Ladak, or to await orders from Lhasa. But we did not allow ourselves to be diverted. I wished to map out the two lakes, and viewed the situation calmly.

The fresh-water lake, called Naktsong-tso, was extremely beautiful, with its steep shore-rocks, bays, and isles, and its blue crystal-clear water.

Kalpet's sickness grew worse, and the poor man had to be transported, reclining on a camel. Time and again we made short stops to minister to him. Once during such a pause, near a tent-village, on the eastern shore, he asked for a cup of water. The next time we halted, he was dead. He was laid in a tent overnight, the Mohammedans keeping vigil. At the grave, Rosi Mollah spoke of the dead man and his faithfulness, and the others repeated prayers for the dead. A black cross, with an inscription, was raised on the hillock. His tent, clothes, and boots were burned. During the funeral, the Tibetans observed us from a little distance. Afterwards they expressed their surprise at the amount of trouble we had taken with a dead man. "It would be simpler to throw the body to the wolves," they said.

We returned to the cares of every-day life and the uncertainties of a new day. As we moved southwards, the Tibetan crowds grew larger; and presently new groups appeared ahead of us, gathered about some black and two blue-white tents. A band of horsemen surrounded us and asked us to stop, as the two Governors of Naktsang, the province in which we were, had arrived. They had received important

A HERD OF "GOA" GAZELLES

information from the Devashung, or the government in Lhasa. I concluded to encamp a hundred and fifty paces from their tents. Our largest tent was adorned with a rug from Khotan, and was used as an audience-chamber.

After a short time, the two governors rode up, wearing gorgeous red robes and button-caps of Chinese cut. I went out to receive them. They dismounted, greeted me politely and friendly, and entered the tent. The more eminent of the two, Hlaje Tsering, was an elderly, beardless man, with a queue; the other one was Yunduk Tsering. We began a palaver that lasted three hours. Hlaje Tsering began:

"You rode to Lhasa with only two companions on a road further east, but you were stopped and escorted over the border by Kamba Bombo of Nakchu. You have now come to Naktsong, and you may not proceed a single step along this road."

"You cannot prevent me," I replied.

"Yes, we can; we have millions of soldiers."

"What does that signify? I am able to use force, too."

"Either you or we will have to lose our heads. We will be decapitated, if we let you through. We might as well fight first."

"Do not worry about my and my men's heads, you will never get hold of them. We are supported by higher powers, and we have terrible weapons. We intend to continue south."

"If you have eyes, you will see to-morrow how we can stop your caravan," they cried, beside themselves with excitement and anger.

"If you have eyes, you had better look out to-morrow, when we go south," I retorted, most coolly. "But keep your muskets ready, for it will be hot about your ears. Before you have time to load, we will have you down, your noses in the air, all of you."

"No, no; there is no talk of killing," they answered, persuasively. "If you will return by the way you came, you shall have guides, provisions, caravan-beasts, and everything you need."

"Listen, Hlaje Tsering, do you really think that I am so mad as to go back to the wastes in the north, where I have already lost half of my caravan? Wherever we may go, I shall never go *there!*"

"Very well," he said, "we will not fire at you, but we will make your journey impossible."

"How will that happen?"

"Twenty soldiers will hold each one of your horsemen and camels. We will keep your animals till they collapse. We have special orders from Lhasa."

"Show them to me," I said. But I had realized from the first that we could not proceed.

"With pleasure," they replied; whereupon the paper was produced. It was dated, "In the year of the Iron Cow, sixth month, twenty-first day." It contained an account of the reports of the Mongol pilgrims concerning our large caravan, and concluded thus:

"Let writings be quickly sent to Namru and Naktsong so that it may be known to all and sundry, from Nakchu unto the limits of my (the Dalai Lama's) land, that Europeans are forbidden to travel southward. Let writings be issued to all chieftains. Guard the borders of Naktsang; it is necessary to keep the whole country foot by foot under surveillance. It is quite beyond any need for Europeans to enter the land of the holy books to look about them. They have no affair in the province which you two command. If such should declare that it is necessary to do so, then be it known unto you that they shall not travel southward. If despite that they should proceed, your heads will be forfeit. Oblige them to turn and to retreat on the path over which they came."

Thereupon they said hard words to poor Shereb Lama, because he "had shown us the way." But then the latter became furious, and asked what right they had to scold a lama who was a Chinese citizen. When the quarrelling became too violent, I took out the big music-box and placed it between the disputants. Then the Tibetans were baffled, and did not utter a sound for a long while.

In the evening, I returned the visit, and had tea in the Governor's large tent, which was adorned with rugs, cushions, low tables, and a house-altar, with sacred images, oil-lamps, and offerings. We had an agreeable time, and talked till midnight.

Kuchuk and I had two divine days in the boat on the lake of Naktsang-tso. The lake was circular, and of fairylike beauty, where steep cliffs rose from the water. We rowed into narrow, picturesque bays, where golden eagles soared among the cliffs. Nomads, tending their herds in the fields along the shore, were amazed at our silent approach on the water. They had never before seen a boat, and they hurriedly drove their animals away from the lake. On the northwest shore we found our people again, and rode on to the eastern shore of the Chargut-tso, another beautiful lake, with its mountains and hillocks, its isles and fjords. The camel that had borne Kalpet when he went to his last sleep, died on the way there; and the superstitious Mohammedans found that quite natural.

Our camp was magnificent. We had five tents, the Tibetans twenty-five, and their force had increased to more than five hundred men. The shore swarmed with horsemen, men afoot, horses, yaks, and sheep; and the red streamers fluttered from the soldiers' muskets. Military displays and wild equestrian feats were performed in my honour. It was a brilliant scene when the sun shone on the variegated garments and the gleaming weapons. There was an interchange of hospitality. Hlaje Tsering presented me with two horses and placed forty yaks at my disposal. They were to be in constant readiness for the long journey to Ladak. I gave the two Governors watches, revolvers, daggers, and other articles, and we became the best of friends.

On September 20, I set out with the boat, Khodai Kullu being my oarsman. We were a good way out on the lake, when a full western storm broke. The waves rose increasingly high, and our light bark was hurled violently back toward the camp. When we rose on the crests, the tents were in sight; but down in the troughs the shore disappeared from view. We approached the shore rapidly. The surf roared. Soon we would be dashed ashore, and the boat smashed to pieces by the waves. The Tibetans gathered in dark groups on the shore to witness our destruction. But the Cossacks were ready. They undressed and sprang into the water, Khodai Kullu jumped overboard, and strong arms carried the boat, as well as me, across the foaming surf to dry land. The Tibetans were dumbfounded.

The evening was calm, and I was able to conduct a successful sounding-expedition by lantern-light. When we returned, the shore, as seen from the lake, resembled an illuminated city. The moon shed its light over the camp. The tents resounded with mirth and the music of stringed instruments.

The following day I made another excursion on the lake, with Kuchuk. The caravan and the Tibetans were to go to the end of the lake. It extended far in a westerly direction, and a rocky island rose in the middle. We steered toward the isle. The north shore disclosed the long black lines of our caravan and its attendants, moving westward.

The wind rose. It increased. We pulled on the oars. The isle had to be reached. After desperate efforts, we landed in the lee of its eastern shore. We drew the boat up and went to explore the land.

"How about it?" I asked Kuchuk. "Did we tie the boat properly?"

"I think so," was his amazed reply.

"What if it should drift away from us? We have food for three days. But what then? If the boat should fill, it would sink; and the others could not then get out to us. We would have all the lake to drink from, but no rifle with which to shoot water-fowl."

"I guess we would have to try to catch fish," Kuchuk suggested.

"Yes, but it would be three months before the lake froze."

"There is plenty of fuel, evidently yaks graze here in the winter."

"We would have to build a stone hut and dig in for the autumn."

"And we could make a signal-fire at the top of the cliff, which our people could see, in case they went in search of us."

"Oh, don't talk nonsense, Kuchuk. Better go and see if the boat is still there."

It was still there.

We walked to the western shore. The storm hurled the waves among huge cliffs, where they were turned into spray. We went to our camp beside the boat, lit a fire, made tea, and had dinner. Afterwards we lay listening to the roar of the storm among the cliffs. Dusk and dark came, and the moon rose.

"Let us row westward, later on in the night, when the storm subsides."

But the storm continued violently. We went to sleep. The sun rose brilliantly, but the storm was as noisy as before. We strolled about on the isle, gathering fuel. For hours I sat on the western shore, dreaming to the song of the waves. At the top of the cliff I took farewell of the sun. And again we sat waiting by the fire.

The storm subsided suddenly during the night. We put out and steered west, where I had taken the bearings of another small rocky island. It was dark; so we lit the lantern. The boat rolled in the swell. At last we struck the shore of the island, pulled the boat up, and went to sleep.

The next morning was again windy, and so we tarried. Then the weather improved and we pushed off. But we had not gone far, when a new storm broke, and forced us ashore. In the afternoon it quieted down, and we made another attempt. We had the largest area of open water still before us; and the lead sank 157 feet, where the depth was greatest. The sun set in light clouds. The sky grew dark over a mountain-ridge in the southwest. We rowed with one oar each. The new storm fell upon us. We rowed like galley-slaves against the wind. The waves grew and we shipped a lot of water. Mountainous walls rose in the southwest. We longed for the security of their lee. The boat was already half full of water.

"Be ready with your life-belt, Kuchuk; I have mine."

We were soaked with spray. A point of land appeared near by. Straining our muscles, we reached it just in the nick of time. Half dead from exhaustion, we threw ourselves down on the shore. There were big blisters on my hands. We prepared our evening meal over a small fire, and slept soundly.

In the morning we ate our last piece of bread. We rowed on across the most westerly part of the lake; and, sighting none of our people, we continued through a very short strait, which brought us to a new lake, the Addan-tso. We had not gone far on its crystalline waters, when a fresh storm literally heaved us onto the shore. The boat was swamped, and we were upset in the surf. We were so soaked, that we had to undress on shore, drying our clothes in the wind. I was just setting off for a near-by nomad-tent, when Kuchuk cried: "There are Cherdon and Ordek on their horses!"

Within a few minutes they were with us. They had ridden around the Chargut-tso and the Addan-tso, looking for us; and failing to find any sign, they feared we had drowned. While searching, they encountered several Tibetan patrols and eight sentry-tents, guarding the main road to Lhasa. Later on I learned that the two Governors suspected a stratagem, and feared that I had escaped their vigilance by means of the horses kept in readiness on shore, and that I had hurried to Lhasa, mounted on them.

During our absence, another camel had succumbed, and one of our Tibetans had died. On the way to the camp we passed his abandoned corpse, already disfigured by birds of prey.

Hlaje Tsering and Yunduk Tsering were enchanted at my return, and invited me to a feast.

The next morning our roads parted. I was entrusted to the escort that had been commissioned to accompany me westward, while the two Governors returned to the capital of their province. Little did I dream, as I saw them depart, with their magnificent train, that Hlaje Tsering was to figure conspicuously in a later episode of my wanderings in Asia.

CHAPTER XLVI

Through Tibet to India, and Back to Tibet

ON September 25, we began a journey through the entire interior of Tibet, that lasted three months. Our first escort numbered twenty-two men, and was under the command of Yamdu Tsering. We were provided, too, with a sufficient number of yaks. As we went on, men and animals were renewed repeatedly. The escort's task was to restrain us from proceeding too far south, to "the land of the holy books." But on several occasions I violated this restriction, principally because I wished to shun the routes of the pundit Nain Sing and the Englishmen, Bower and Littledale, hoping thereby to make new additions to the maps of that region.

Although most of our equipment was now being borne by the yaks which had been placed at our disposal, scarcely a day passed without the loss of a camel, mule, or horse. Mohammed Tokta, an old camel-driver, headed the sick-list, and we let him ride one of the last horses. He was always cheerful, jovial, and uncomplaining. He was generally the last to reach camp. But once his horse arrived at our tents without its rider. I sent two men for him with a mule. They found him asleep in a hole at the side of the path; and he declared that he had become so sleepy, that he had fallen off the horse, and had remained lying where he fell. He was carried to the camp, and went sound asleep in the hospital-tent. From that sleep he never awoke. We buried him in the morning, following the rites of the Prophet as far as circumstances permitted.

We came to Lakor-tso, a salt-lake that was drying up, on October 20. It was still four hundred and eighty miles to Ladak. We would never have been able to make our way thither without the help of the Tibetans. Of forty-five mules and horses, only eleven were left; and of thirty-nine camels, only twenty. The cold season was approaching. The temperature had already sunk to $-2°$. Food was everywhere obtainable. We bought sheep from the nomads, the Cossacks followed the chase, and the Lop men set nets in the Bogtsang-tsangpo, a river which we followed for several days. At Perutse-tso we encountered the first bushes since entering Tibet; so we stayed there four days, because of the pasturage, and had gorgeous camp-fires.

On the border of Rudok, a province of Tibet, we were met by a bold and imperious chieftain, who asked to see our passport from Lhasa.

"We have no passport," I answered. "I should think it was sufficient that we are being escorted by Tibetans."

"No; you may not take a step to the west without a passport, nor travel through my province. Stay here and wait, while I send couriers to Lhasa."

"How soon will the answer be here?" I asked.

"In two and a half months."

"Excellent," I exclaimed, roaring with laughter. "That suits me perfectly. We will go back to Perutse-tso, where there is pasturage and fuel, and establish a base of supplies. When the spring comes, and you get your silk rope from Lhasa, you will know how I spent the winter. Have a care, and don't blame me when your head falls."

He became exceedingly polite, recalled his men from the border, and opened Rudok to us. The Tibetans, too, grew bolder, as our distance from Lhasa increased. Once, when we were to change men, the new relay was missing, and the old gang was preparing to return and leave us in the lurch, without guides and yaks. We took their yaks, loaded them, and proceeded, whereupon the men thought it prudent to come along.

On November 20, there were still two hundred and forty miles to be covered. The thermometer dropped to −18.8°. One of the veteran camels died. He had been with us through the large desert, to Charchan, and twice to Lou-lan. Every day I had to part from one of the friends who helped me to conquer vast territories of innermost Asia. One of the horses that Kamba Bombo had given me fell into a hole in the ice on the Tsangarshar River. He was rescued with great difficulty, dried by the fire, and covered with blankets. The next morning the animal lay dead beside the embers. Another day, four horses died. And now only a last one was left, the one that I still rode.

Having passed the temple-village of Noh, we reached the beautiful fresh-water lake of Tso-ngombo (the Blue Lake), narrow and endlessly long, walled in by high, steep mountains, where the clangour of the bronze bells evoked a melodious echo. The lake consisted of four basins connected by short straits. The fourth basin was not yet frozen over, and the mountain-wall on its northern shore descended abruptly into the lake. We were thus confronted with an obstacle as fierce as the Tibetan hosts.

It was the third of December. Large parts of the lake were covered with thin ice, but the deep water was open directly in our path. The air was cold, clear, and calm. During the night, the ice-film extended itself over the entire lake, to the foot of the mountain. The next afternoon it was five centimetres thick. I decided to build a sort of

TESTING THE STRENGTH OF THE ICE

sledge, or float, of camel-ladders and tent-poles, cover it with felt mats, and then haul the camels, one by one, across the thin ice.

We first of all subjected the sledge to a test. As many men as equalled the weight of one camel got on the sledge. Two men pulled it around the projecting land with ease. But the ice was still so thin that it undulated under this weight, and one after another, the men jumped off the sledge. As each hero proved craven, he was greeted with shouts of laughter. The ice glistened, and was transparent as glass. We saw the backs of the fishes, in the depths, as in an aquarium. One night more, and the ice was two centimetres thicker. It was now possible to transport our entire burden around the promontory. Finally, the camels, too, were hauled across, on ice nine centimetres thick.

A short arm extended from the western end of the Tso-ngombo to the Panggong-tso, a salt mountain-lake, which, cradled between noble, rocky walls, resembled an enormous river-valley. The landscapes that unfolded at every peninsula cannot be described in words; they were among the most magnificent on earth. With perpetual snow on their ridges and tops, the shoulders of the mountains extended like scenic wings, becoming dimmer and dimmer until they merged into the distance in the northwest.

On the north shore, which we followed, the ground along the base

CAMELS CROSSING THE BIG BOULDERS ALONG THE NORTHERN SHORE OF PANGGONG-TSO

of the mountains was generally quite level. But at times we had to traverse low, steep ridges; and sometimes a mass of large boulders was piled at the foot of the mountain. Because of its great depth, and the high percentage of salt, the lake was open; and we often had great difficulty in getting the last camels across.

I had sent two couriers to Leh, the capital of Ladak, announcing our approach; and on December 12, we had the pleasure of meeting a relief-expedition on the boundary between Tibet and Ladak. Headed by Annar Joo and Gulang Hiraman, two Ladakis, it brought us twelve horses, thirty yaks, and an abundance of flour, rice, maize, fruit, preserves, and live sheep. The last Tibetans were paid and dismissed, and a new era began for us.

There was animation and gaiety in our camp that evening. Only Yoldash was disgruntled. It is true, he slept at my feet, as usual, in the tent. But when morning came, he shook himself, dug his nose in the ground, and ran eastward as fast as he could, along the shore of the Panggong-tso. He ran back to Tibet. He had indulged in *liaisons* with bitches belonging to the nomads. He never returned. He had been my tent-mate since the day I left Osh.

Immediately west of the Panggong-tso, we crossed a low ridge, from which we beheld the region of the Indus. We had spent two and a half years in territory that was without an outlet to the sea.

On December 17, I left the caravan and rode rapidly to Leh, so as to be able to send telegrams home for Christmas. Piles of letters awaited me in the little town. I had not had a word from home for eleven months. Lord Curzon sent me a most kind invitation to visit him in Calcutta.

I spent Christmas with the kind Moravian missionaries, Ribbach and Hettasch, Dr. Shawe and Miss Bass; and the sight of Christmas-candles, twinkling in a Christian mission-room, seemed strange.

Sirkin and nine of my Mohammedan men returned home by way of the Kara-korum pass. The others stayed in Leh, awaiting my return. I took only one man to India with me, namely, Shagdur. It was two hundred and forty-two miles to Srinagar, and we rode there in eleven days. We departed on January 1, 1902, and crossed the dangerous, ice-covered pass of Zoji-la on foot. From the capital of Kashmir, we drove to Ravalpindi, in a *tonga,* in three days.

Space forbids my dwelling on fabulous India. In Lahore, I was fitted out from top to toe by an English tailor, whereupon I went to Calcutta by way of Delhi, Agra, Lucknow, and Benares. Each of these cities is like a dream that haunts one through life. In Government House and Barrakpore, Lord and Lady Curzon overwhelmed me with hospitality. Few students knew Asia better than he did; and his wife was one of the most beautiful and most charming women of America. Sir Ernest Cassel was also their guest for a few days.

Shagdur, my splendid Cossack, wandered about, as if in a dream, and could not trust his eyes for all the lovely sights. How different from the quiet forests of eastern Siberia! He fell ill of typhoid fever, however, and was conveyed back to Kashmir by special arrangements.

As for myself, I visited Colonel McSwiney at Belarum, near Hyderabad, in Dekkan; was then a guest of Lord Northcote, Governor of Bombay; rode on elephant-back from Jeypore to the ruins of Amber; stayed a few days with the Maharajah of Kapurthala; and finally returned to Srinagar. Shagdur, having recovered somewhat, was able to go back with me to Leh. The Zoji-la was so thickly covered with snow at this season, that a winter road led through the deep, narrow valley at its foot. Avalanches slid down into the gorge almost daily from the overhanging mountains, rendering the way perilous. The most dangerous part is always traversed before sunup. It took sixty-three men to carry our belongings. It took us four days to negotiate the pass and that region. After walking, we rode yaks; and, later on, horses.

On March 25, we were in Leh, where Shagdur, suffering a relapse, was treated at the mission-hospital. I could not leave until he was out of danger. The nine surviving camels, after enjoying a three and a half months' rest, were fat and round. They were sold to a merchant from East Turkestan. On April 5, with the rest of my caravan, I left, to cross Tibet once more. But why? Why not rather go home by steamer from Bombay? No; I could not leave the Cossacks and the Mohammedans adrift. Was I not responsible for them? Shagdur was the only one I had to leave behind. He needed a two months' rest. I gave him ample travelling-funds and credentials. When I said good-bye, thanking him and invoking God's blessing, he turned away and wept. Much later, I learned that he had reached his home safely, by way of Osh.

I spent May 13 in Kashgar, with my friends, Petrovsky, Macartney, and Father Hendricks. The ram Vanka accompanied us to this point. He was as devoted to us as a dog. He and all the faithful Mohammedans stayed in Kashgar. I left Malenki and Malchik in Osh. Later on, I parted with good old Chernoff, who was to return to Vernoye. In Petrovsk, on the Caspian Sea, I parted from Cherdon and Shereb Lama. They were going to Astrakhan, at the mouth of the Volga. The ultimate goal of the former was Chita, in Transbaikalia; the latter intended to settle down in a lama monastery, with the Kalmucks. These various partings with men and beasts upset me greatly.

At last, again all alone, I travelled through Russia to St. Petersburg. I saw the Czar in Peterhof. He was delighted to hear my praise of the Cossacks, and decorated them with the order of St. Anna and gave them two hundred and fifty roubles each. He also ordered that an imperial order of the day be issued to all the army-posts of Siberia, stating how the four Cossacks had honoured themselves and their country on a long and perilous expedition. Later they also received gold medals from King Oscar.

June 27 proved to be one of the happiest days of my life: it was the day of my arrival home!

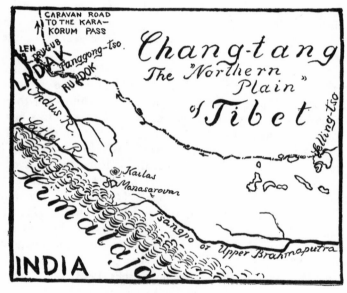

THE ROAD TO LADAK THROUGH TIBET

CHAPTER XLVII

Fighting Four Governments

I STAYED at home in Stockholm for three years. Most of the time was devoted to the preparation of a scientific account of my latest journey, "Scientific Results of a Journey in Central Asia," six volumes of text, with two volumes of maps.

During the progress of this work, my head teemed with wild plans for new journeys of conquest to unexplored parts of Asia; and the desert-winds lured me with the call, "Come home!" But this time it was especially Tibet that lured me. Three large white spots still yawned like blank pages, north of, in the centre of, and south of the highest and most extensive mountain-region on earth. Most important of all was the territory north of the Tsangpo, or the upper Brahmaputra. Two expeditions had traversed this immense valley to the north of, and parallel with, the Himalayas—those of the pundit Nain Sing, in 1865, and of the Englishmen, Ryder and Rawling, Wood and Bailey, in 1904. But neither they nor any others had ever crossed the white spot north of the Tsangpo River. That an enormous mountain-system existed in these regions was almost certain; for the few travellers who explored western and eastern Tibet had to conquer sky-high passes. No doubt, too, towering, gigantic ridges lay in the opening between the two wings. A few high summits had even been triangulated on Ryder's route. But nobody had been there, and Sir Clements Markham, president of the Royal Geographical Society, was right in saying of the mountains north of the Tsangpo: "In the whole length from Tengri-nor to the Mariam-la pass, no one has crossed them, so far as we know, . . . and I believe nothing in Asia is of greater geographical importance than the exploration of this range of mountains.[1]

The main purpose of my new journey was to advance to that unknown country, and, while there, to discover the source of the Indus. On the latest map of Tibet, published in 1906, in the *Geographical*

[1] *Geographical Journal,* Vol. 7, p. 482.

Journal, by the Royal Geographical Society, the white spot north of the river bore only the one word, "Unexplored." It was my ambition to obliterate that word from the map of Tibet, to supplant it by the correct names of mountain-ranges, lakes, and rivers, and to cross and recross the white spot in as many directions as possible.

I held a strong trump-card in the warm interest which Lord Curzon of Kedleston, Viceroy of India, took in my plan. Answering a letter of mine, he wrote me, on July 6, 1905, from Simla:

"I am very glad that you propose to act upon my advice and to make one more big Central Asian journey before you desist from your wonderful travels. I shall be proud to render you what assistance lies in my power while I still remain in India, and only regret that long before your great expedition is over I shall have left these shores. For it is my intention to depart in April, 1906. Now as regards your plan. I gather that you will not be in India before next spring, when perhaps I may still see you. I will arrange to have a good native surveyor ready to accompany you; and I will, further, have a man instructed in astronomical observations and in meteorological recording, so as to be available for you at the same time. . . . I cannot say what the attitude of the Tibetan Government will be by the time that you reach India. But if they continue friendly, we will, of course, endeavour to secure for you the requisite permits and protection. Assuring you that it will give me the greatest pleasure in any way to further your plans, I am, yours sincerely, Curzon."

Conditions could not have been more propitious. There it lay, in the silence of mystery, the vast unknown territory north of the Himalayas, untouched by the British during the hundred and fifty years that the keys of India lay in their hands. And, in India, a Viceroy most amiably promised every assistance in furthering my plans. The necessary funds had been placed at my disposal by generous backers, notably King Oscar and Emanuel Nobel. With an equipment more complete than ever before, the only dark cloud hovering over me was the separation from my beloved home.

On October 16, 1905, I wrenched myself from parents and family, and travelled through Europe to Constantinople, and across the Black Sea to Batum, so as to make Teheran by way of the Caucasus and the Caspian Sea. But revolutionary disturbances were raging in Batum, as in several other places. Railway-bridges on the road to Tiflis had been blown up, and I had to change my route. Choosing the road via Trebizond, on the shore of Asia Minor, I went from there by carriage, escorted by six Hamidieh cavalrymen, whom Abdul Hamid lent me, by way of Erzerum and Bayazid to the Persian border. Thence I continued, without escort, to Teheran, by way of Tabriz and Kazvin.

Mussaffar-ed-din Shah, the new king, received me hospitably, and did everything to help me in my long journey through his great domain. I purchased sixteen splendid camels, engaged attendants, bought tents, boxes, and provisions, and on January 1, 1906, began a journey on camel-back that took four and a half months. During that time I crossed the perilous Kevir Desert twice, spent one week in Nasretabad, in Sistan, the scene of a ravaging plague, and then proceeded, by fast dromedaries, through the whole of Baluchistan, to Nushki, where I came to the Indian railway. Space forbids me to dwell on this exciting and interesting journey. We must hurry on to unknown Tibet.

In a burning heat (107° at the end of May), I crossed the plains of India; and in Simla, 7,000 feet high, I revelled in the fresh mountain-air, in dark forests of royal Himalaya cedars. Sir Francis Young-husband met me at the station. I was received with exquisite hospitality by Lord and Lady Minto, and was their guest in the Viceregal Lodge. An atmosphere of the greatest cordiality surrounded me, and everybody wanted to help me toward success. Three native assistants awaited me at Dehra Dun; and Lord Kitchener of Khartum, the Commander-in-Chief of the Indian Army, offered me twenty armed Gurkhas. From my window I saw the eternal snow-fields on the Himalaya ridges, but only on the first day. On the other side was Tibet. Then the curtain of impenetrable clouds descended and concealed the Promised Land in the north.

A new government, headed by Sir Henry Campbell-Bannerman, was at the helm in London, and Lord Curzon had left his post in India. Lord Minto, his successor, did all that could be done to fulfill the promises of Lord Curzon. But a very powerful man, John Morley, the Secretary of State for India, blocked my path effectually. Sir Louis Dane, the Foreign Secretary in India, imparted Morley's verdict to me: the Government in London refused me permission to enter Tibet by way of the Indian border! Surveyors, assistants, armed escort, all that had been promised was withdrawn. I had survived revolutions, deserts, and plague; but at the very threshold of the unknown country, I met an obstruction harder to surmount than the Himalayas.

I cabled the Premier and was met with refusal. Lord Minto sent several telegrams to Morley and was refused. Lord Percy interpellated Morley in Parliament, only to be answered: "The Imperial Government has resolved to keep Tibet isolated from India." He thought, with Kipling:

> "*The gates are mine to open*
> *And the gates are mine to close,*
> *And I set my house in order,*
> *Said our Lady of the Snows.*"

God, how I hated Morley at that time! The gates would have opened at a single word from him; instead, he slammed them right in my face. The English were worse than the Tibetans. But they stirred my ambition. "We shall see who is more at home in Tibet, you or I," I thought. In an address to me, a few years later, Sir Cecil Spring-Rice said: "We closed the doors to you; but you climbed in through the windows." I did not understand then how grateful I should have been to Lord Morley; but subsequently I got the opportunity to tell him so in public.

All these negotiations and futile endeavours took time. But I was all right. I won a lifelong friend in Colonel Sir James Dunlop-Smith, private secretary to the Viceroy. My correspondence with him would fill a fat volume. I spent two unforgettable weeks with the charming family of Lord Minto. He told me about his life. His great-grandfather had been Viceroy of India a hundred years before. The journey being arduous, he had left his family in the mother country. When his term was up, he sailed for home, but died of a stroke when only one station from his castle, Minto, in Scotland. On the packet of letters that passed between him and his wife during his Indian years, she wrote these words: "Poor fools." Lord Minto, the younger, served as a young officer in the military expedition into Afghanistan. In 1881, during a visit to St. Helena with Lord Roberts, they were strolling with Governor Johnson on the road to Longwood. Two old ladies approached, and the Governor whispered to the two lords: "Observe carefully the lady nearer to us." The ladies having passed, the lords remarked: "Her profile was the image of Napoleon's."—"Yes," the Governor replied, "she is a daughter of Napoleon." Lord Minto, who was a great admirer of the Corsican, told another anecdote of him. Lord Russell, one of Lord Minto's forbears, visited Napoleon in Elba, and used very strong words in condemnation of the war and its terrible cruelty. Napoleon listened with a smile, and, when Russell finished, said: "Mais c'est un beau jeu, c'est une belle occupation."

However, Minto rose in rank, and became Governor-General of Canada, when Roosevelt was President. Minto spoke much of him, and of his simple habits. The two men were as different as night and day. The President was the more powerful of the two. But Minto was an unusually fine and noble man; and when Curzon retired, he was appointed Viceroy of India, over its population of three hundred and twenty millions.

Lord Kitchener, too, was an acquaintance not easily forgotten. He was furious at the unyielding attitude of his Government toward me. The public dinners and parties given by him and the Viceroy surpassed anything that can be attained in that line in Europe and America; and the Maharajahs shimmered with pearls and precious stones. The entrance-hall of Lord Kitchener's house was hung with flags he had taken from the Mahdi and the Dervishes at Omdurman, and trophies from the Transvaal and Orange Free State. His apartments were decorated with busts of Alexander and Cæsar, and portraits of Gordon Pasha, not to mention the magnificent collection of china from the Kang Hi and Chien Lung periods. Townshend, his chief of staff, was also a friend of mine. He was head of the campaign in Mesopotamia, in 1916, when I met him as a prisoner of the Turks in Bagdad, after the fall of Kut-el-Amara. I could tell much about that—but we are on our way to Tibet.

All attempts proving vain, I decided to reach Tibet by a road over which Morley had no authority, i. e., from Chinese territory in the north. I said farewell to my friends in Simla, and went to Srinagar. Officially it was said that I was on my way to East Turkestan. The Maharajah of Kashmir received me very cordially; and Daya Kishen Kaul, one of his trusted adjutants, personally assisted me in organizing my caravan. We bought forty mules from the Maharajah of Poonch, modern rifles and ammunition, tents, saddles, tools, provisions, etc. Two Rajputs— Ganpat Sing and Bikom Sing—and two Pathans—Bas Ghul and Khair-

ullah Khan—were to take the place of the unmaterialized escort from
India. A Eurasian, Alexander Robert, was to be my secretary; and
Manuel, a Catholic Indian from Madras, my chef. I took with me
9,000 rupees in gold and 22,000 in silver. The latter all bore the
likeness of Queen Victoria. Tibetans do not accept rupees that bear
the King's portrait. The queen wears an imperial crown and a pearl
necklace and looks like a Buddha; while of the King, no more is shown
than his head, and that without a crown.

I had a collapsible boat from London and a very beautiful, silvery
aluminum chest, with hundreds of different medicines in tabloids, the
gift of Burroughs Wellcome, in London. The boat, as well as the
chest, was to figure importantly in Tibet.

No sooner had I arrived in Srinagar than I received this written
message from Colonel Pears, the Resident: "The Indian Government
advises that the border between Kashmir and Tibet is closed to you.
You may go to East Turkestan, provided you have a Chinese passport;
otherwise not." Fresh annoyances! Of course, I had no Chinese passport to East Turkestan, for I had been prepared to enter Tibet from
India. By cable I requested the Swedish Minister in London, Count
Wrangel, to negotiate with the Chinese envoy for a passport to East
Turkestan. It was granted and forwarded immediately. I found it
upon my arrival in Leh; and, upon showing it to the British agent there,
he telegraphed the Indian Government about it. This was the situation:
Here was I, in Leh, with a passport to East Turkestan, to which the road
via the Kara-korum pass was open. But my intention was *not* to go to
East Turkestan, and thus the passport was actually not necessary. As
soon as I had gone far enough to be out of reach of the Anglo-Indian
authorities, I planned to leave the caravan-route that leads over the
Kara-korum, and turn east toward the interior of Tibet. This eventu-
ality, too, was foreseen by the British authorities; and more than a week
after I left Leh, the Joint Commissioner was notified from Simla that
the Viceroy had orders from London to stop me, by force, if necessary,
should I head for Tibet. The failure of this message to reach Leh
in time was due to the "negligence" of one of my friends. He withheld
the telegram for days, releasing it only after I was safely across the
border. He is dead now, and I hold his name in grateful remembrance.
But the Joint Commissioner replied something to this effect: "He has
long since disappeared among the mountains. One might as well look

for a needle in a haystack." And as for me, I might as well have burnt the Chinese passport to East Turkestan. Fortunately I did not.

Now just a few words about my journey to Leh.

I departed from Srinagar on July 16. My first camp, at Ganderbal, seen in the light of the fire at night, might have been taken for an Orientalist conference. There were men from Madras, Lahore, Kabul, Rajputana, Poonch, and Kashmir. In a Srinagar street we had picked up three wretched little puppies. We dubbed them simply White Puppy, Brown Puppy, and Manuel's friend. We went over Sonamarg in several sections, one of which was composed of a long string of hired horses from Kashmir, and got to Kargil by way of Zoji-la. By that time I was able to measure the calibre of my men. The two Pathans were persistent trouble-makers, the men from Poonch and Kashmir a motley riff-raff, wholly without discipline. I got rid of the whole crowd; and only Robert, Manuel, and the two Rajputs remained of the entire Orientalist conference.

Making a radical change in my plans, I engaged seventy-seven horses and a gang of new men; and thus organized, our caravan made its festive entry into the monastery of Lamayooroo, where the monks entertained us with dances of exorcism and music.

In Leh, where the British, the German missionaries, and the natives all received us warmly, we were to complete our equipment for the forbidden advance on Tibet. Younghusband had counselled me to secure the services of Mohammed Isa. He had accompanied many famous Europeans on their travels into interior Asia. He had been with Carey and Dalgleish, De Rhins and Grenard, with Younghusband to Lhasa, and with Ryder to Gartok. He spoke Turki, Hindustani, and Tibetan. He was a big, strong man. In his presence all trembled. He maintained strict discipline, but could nevertheless be gay and jocular.

Mohammed Isa met me with:

"Salaam, Sahib!"

"Salaam! Do you want to come along to lead a caravan? It will be a hard trip."

"Certainly. But where to?"

"That is a secret."

"But I have to know how much food we will need."

"Get enough for three months for men and beasts. Buy as many horses as necessary, and hire experienced people."

Mohammed Isa set to work, and that speedily. He got invaluable assistance from powerful Haji Naser Shah's great firm, and particularly from his son, Gulam Razul. Twenty-five men were employed—nine Mohammedans and sixteen Lamaists. Mohammed Isa himself was a Mohammedan, but his brother Tsering was a Lamaist. Then there were two Hindus, one Roman Catholic, and two Protestants (Robert and I). When the whole body was lined up in my court, Captain Patterson, the joint-commissioner for Ladak, addressed them. They were to receive fifteen rupees a month, half a year's wages in advance, and at the journey's end fifty rupees each, provided they worked satisfactorily. Sixty-two-year-old Guffaru was the dean. He had served with Forsyth on the way to Kashgar, thirty-three years before, and had seen the great Yakub Bek. He took his son and his shroud along, so as to insure ceremonial burial, should he die during the journey. Shukur Ali I had seen in 1890, in Younghusband's tent. The others will be introduced as my story unfolds.

My doughty caravan-leader also purchased fifty-eight horses— thirty-three from Ladak, seventeen from East Turkestan, four from Kashmir, and four from Sanskar. Each one was numbered; and, in due course, each one had to be entered in the casualty-list. They all died in Tibet. Our caravan thus included, at the outset, thirty-six mules, fifty-eight horses, thirty borrowed horses, and ten borrowed yaks.

When provisions had been purchased, and tents, saddles, and all the other things were ready, the major part of the caravan, with Sonam Tsering as leader, was ordered ahead to the fields of Muglib.

CHAPTER XLVIII

Stormy Journeys by Water

SHORTLY before leaving Leh, I called on the Rajah of Stogh, a middle-aged, kindly visionary, who, but for its conquest by Kashmir, in 1841, would have been king of Ladak. The solid castle of the former kings towered above the small town, and was visible a great distance. On August 14, its high façade disappeared from our sight, behind wild crags, as we headed for the Indus. Not long afterwards, we left the flowing waters of the royal river; and I prayed silently that I might one day pitch my tent at its source, where no European had hitherto set foot.

Our camps looked grand. They swarmed with men, horses, and mules. It was an itinerant community. Sadly I looked on our fine, fat, and flourishing beasts of burden, standing at ease, munching grain out of their bags; for I knew that it would not be long before one after another would die of exhaustion. Every evening a sheep was slaughtered. My men sat in congenial groups around the fires, having their meal; and when all had gone to sleep, nothing was heard but the song of the night-watch.

In long, slow-moving columns we ascended the Chang-la pass (17,600 feet). I was now crossing it for the third time. On its other slope were Drugub and Tanksi, small villages that I knew of old. After leaving Tanksi, we saw no trees for six months. Here we made a large tent, of Tibetan design, for the men, and made a close inspection of all the pack-saddles, to make sure that they would not bruise the animals; and in the evening we had a party, with music and women dancers.

We reached the last human habitations in Pobrang, beyond the Panggong-tso. There we purchased thirty sheep, ten goats, and two dogs. Nine fires burned in our camp. Under our scheme of organization, Sonam Tsering was charged with responsibility for the mules, Guffaru for the horses, and Tsering, Mohammed Isa's brother, was chief of the small section that cared for my tent and kitchen. The boat was borne by one of the borrowed yaks. We took stock of our provisions. The grain and maize would last sixty-eight days, the flour eighty, and the rice four or five months. The first snowfall aroused the indignation of the puppies. They barked at the flakes and snapped at them. The Indians were equally amazed, for they had never before seen falling snow.

The snow lay a foot deep around the pass of Marsimik-la, and the caravan looked like long, winding, black ribbons in the dazzling whiteness. The first horse succumbed before we reached the ridge (18,300 feet). Then we descended again into wild valleys, between mighty snow-crowned ranges. We had a delightful camp in the Chang-chenmo valley, where bushes provided excellent fuel for our fires. It is true that I was unrestricted now; but in Simla I had given my word of honour not to go eastward through this valley to the pass of Lanek-la, five days distant, and thus to a comfortable road into western Tibet. The animals might have been spared hardships, and I would have saved considerable time and money, had Lanek-la never been mentioned. But under the circumstances, I was forced to make the long, roundabout way through northern Tibet, with its murderous climate and its immense uninhabited areas.

In the Chang-chenmo valley, we bade adieu to the fleeting summer, and mounted the heights to face winter. We camped in a valley at the foot of Chang-lung-yogma pass; and as it had no name, we called the camp "No. 1." Before this journey ended, I would reach Camp No. 500. Mohammed Isa erected a stone man at the gateway to the valley, to indicate our trail to the last post-courier we were expecting from Leh, but who was never to find us.

Making hundreds of turns, we zigzagged up the steep hills, where each horse had to be supported by several men. Cries of warning and urging resounded among the mountains. Riding past the caravan, I reached the saddle of the pass, at the immense height of 18,950 feet. I rode a few hundred feet higher, so as to get an unobstructed view.

My effort was rewarded by a view that no doubt is one of the most magnificent in the world. I was surrounded by an agitated sea, composed of the highest mountain-ranges on earth. The snowy tops of the Himalayas towered dazzling-white in the south and southwest, and the glacier-surfaces shone like green glass beneath enormous snow-caps.

The sky was brilliantly clear, with only here and there a small white cloud sailing by. The main ridge of the Kara-korum, on which we now stood, extended northwest and southeast. All the water that flows south from here is collected by the Indus, and reaches the warm, salt sea. I mounted my horse again, and headed northwards, leaving the Indian world behind me. For two years and one month I was to live in Tibet, in spite of the prohibition of those in power.

We were in the wild, desolate Tibetan tableland, which has no outlet to the sea. We crossed a region bare of pasturage. The trail of the caravan in the soft, moist, yielding soil looked like a highway. In the southeast, the Kara-korum ridge was still visible under a dome of blue-black clouds, heavy as lead. Time and again these clouds were illuminated from within by flaming flashes of lightning, and the thunder roared among the mountains. It began to snow; and soon we were shrouded in a thick, whirling fall. Riding behind the mules, I could see only the nearest animals, while most of the others were very faintly visible; but those at the head were not discernible at all. The wind was strong, and the snow swept horizontally along the ground. Our camp that evening was silent and cold. One mule died during the night.

We saw the first antelopes here. The weather was fine, as we passed over the plains of Aksai-chin, searching for water. After marching eighteen miles, we found good pasturage at the foot of a rocky point of fossiliferous sandstone and conglomerate. On its top, Mohammed Isa erected a cairn. Here we dug for water. This was Camp No. 8. Little did I know that I would camp there again.

On we went, eastward, to Lake Aksai-chin, and pitched our tents on its shore. We were still in territory hitherto visited by only a very few white men, Crosby, the American, being one of them. The country to the east was level and open, a longitudinal valley bounded on the north by the gigantic mountain-system of the Kun-lun, with its cupola-shaped snowy summits. The ground was sandy and afforded tolerably good pasturage. Yet three horses died in one day. A wolf lay in wait. As was the case in the desert, all the pack-saddles were stuffed with hay, to be consumed by degrees, as the animals succumbed.

After crossing a small ridge, we beheld east thereof the large lake which Captain Wellby discovered in 1896 and named Lake Lighten. Camp No. 15 was established on its western shore. Certain changes were made in the caravan. I dismissed the two Rajputs, of whom

Mohammed Isa said, not without reason, that they were of no more use than the puppies. These men from India could not stand the cold climate and the greatly rarefied air. We were enabled to send them home from this remote place, because our hired Ladakis, having lost four of their thirty horses, asked leave to return. I sent a large post with them. The most important letter I wrote was one to Colonel Sir James Dunlop-Smith. All my post from Sweden went to the headquarters of the Viceroy, and I requested that it be sent by a reliable messenger to the southern shore of Dangra-yum-tso, a lake that I expected to reach at the end of November. It was a long chance. There was no certainty that I would be able to make my way so far. We were five hundred and ten miles from the lake. My friends in India understood very well that I would try to reach southern Tibet from the north, notwithstanding prohibitions. What happened to the post I shall soon relate.

However, our company was considerably reduced at Camp No. 15, where also seven of our own horses died. The rest were treated to an abundance of maize and grain, so as to lighten the burdens. Our resting-place was arranged in the following way. Mohammed Isa, Tsering, and my kitchen were housed in a large tent, where my twenty-two boxes were piled up. The Ladakis had their black Tibetan tent beyond an enclosure of bags of provisions. Robert lodged in quite a small tent, and I in another.

Our next camp fronted on the northern lake-shore. Mohammed Isa was to proceed with the entire caravan to the eastern shore on September 21, and light a signal-fire in the evening. With Rehim Ali as oarsman, I crossed the lake, heading straight south. It was a lovely, calm day; the lake was like a mirror. A mighty mountain-range towered on the southern shore, red and flame-coloured, and topped by changeless snow and ice. I sounded the depth of the water. The line was only two hundred and thirteen feet long; and as the lead failed to touch bottom in the middle, the lake proved to be one of the deepest I examined in Tibet.

"This lake has no bottom," my trusty oarsman complained. "It is dangerous; let us turn!"

"Row on; we will soon reach the shore."

The lake was of the same colour as the sky, and the red-yellow mountains were reflected in its surface. The picture that surrounded us was beautiful beyond words. Most of the day had passed before we landed. And it was after half-past three when we pushed off again, to row eastwards to the rendezvous.

We kept a fair distance from the shore. The lake was still as a mirror. Rehim Ali looked apprehensive, and suddenly said: "A western storm, and a hard one!"

I was at the tiller, and turned round, to see the yellow dust-clouds scampering along, over the pass in the west. They grew denser, darkened, and rose toward the zenith. They tussled with one another and merged into angry clouds. Far away in the west they went chasing out on the lake, which was still mirror-like.

"Up with the mast and the sail," I shouted. "We'll land if it gets bad."

Hardly was the sail set, when the storm was howling about our ears. The next moment, the clear surface was shattered like a pane of glass; and with a crack of the wind, the sail bellied out. The billows rose into foam-crested waves, and the light boat flew across the lake like a wild duck. The water boiled at the bow, and millions of air-bubbles seethed in the path of foam that was our wake.

"A sandy spit ahead!"

"Shallow!" cried Rehim Ali.

"The boat will be ripped if it grounds here. It's only canvas!"

I put all my weight on the tiller. We touched upon the tip of the spit, right in the roaring surf. In case of accident, the boat would sink like a stone; for it was weighted with a zinc centreboard. But we had two life-cushions.

The storm increased. The mast was strained like a bow. The sheet cut into my hand; but to fasten it would have been foolish.

"Another cape ahead!"

"We must try to land on the lee shore!"

Now we perceived that the lake beyond that cape was endless. No shore was visible in the east. The sun was setting. Flame-coloured like a glowing ball, it shed a wonderful light over land and water. All the mountains shone like rubies. The waves and foamy ridges were red. We sped across a lake of blood. Even the sail shone purple. The sun set. Soon the last reflection on the highest mountain-tops died out, and the landscape resumed its ordinary twilight hues.

Now we were close to the second cape.

We swept past its roaring breakers. I intended to force the boat to leeward; but before I knew where I was, we had shot beyond it. We flew along on our stormy course, carried by wind and wave. It would have been a pity to have put an end to our winged flight. The moon was up, and in our path another cape projected. Rapidly we approached its extremity. I was ready to shift the helm to port and make for the lee shore. But it proved to be impossible in this sweeping storm. We dashed past the cape. It was too late. We were hurled out over new, vast waters.

The day had died in the west. The night reached over the eastern

SAILING ACROSS A STRANGE LAKE AT NIGHT

mountains and extended its black rings over the lake. The wave-crests shone chalky-white in the moonlight, like snow-fields on the mountains. Rehim Ali was beside himself with fear, and cowered in front of the mast. We shot across the growing waves on our mad ride to death. Only three wave-crests could be seen at a time, the one that lifted the boat on its back, the one that rushed past us, and the one that came rolling behind us. Sailing in a canvas boat at night in such weather was a dangerous thing.

The moon went down, and darkness kept vigil over us. The stars twinkled; it grew cold. I loosened the thwart and sat down in the bottom of the boat, so as to obtain some shelter. Only a canvas separated us from the foaming waves beneath which unknown depths yawned.

The hours were long. The lake had to come to an end sooner or later. If steep cliffs descended into the lake on the eastern shore, we were lost. I called out to Rehim Ali to warn me as soon as he discerned the breakers on the shore. But he did not hear me. He was paralyzed with fear.

Now I heard a dull rumbling ahead, through the howling storm.

WE HAD TO JUMP INTO THE WATER AND HAUL THE BOAT ASHORE

It was the surf. I yelled at Rehim Ali, but he did not move. The white, foamy ribbon was dimly visible in the dark. The boat bore off. In a second it would be sucked out again, filled by the next wave, tossed up, and smashed to pieces. Then I grasped the mast with my left hand, to keep my balance; and with my right I seized Rehim Ali by the collar, and hove him overboard. That helped. The wave came rolling like thunder; and the next time the boat bore off, and the wave half filled it with its foamy crest, I too jumped into the water. Then, by united effort, we hauled it up on shore.

We emptied the boat and saved our drenched belongings. Our

clothes had frozen to ice, and were as hard as wood. We tilted the boat against the oars, to provide a shelter for ourselves. The wooden roller, round which the lead-line was wound, as also its frame, was broken into small pieces beyond repair. And so we got a fire. The matches in my breast-pocket were dry. I undressed, thawed out my clothes, wrung the water out of them, and tried to dry at least my under-wear. It was 3°. Feeling that my feet were nearly frost-bitten, I let Rehim Ali rub them. Would we survive this night?

The splinters were consumed, and I was just about to sacrifice one

WE USED THE BOAT AS A PROTECTION AGAINST THE WIND

of the thwarts from the boat, when Rehim Ali said: "A light to the north."

Yes, really! It appeared, faintly, and vanished; returned, and grew larger. We heard the tramp of horses. Three horsemen came trotting up to us, Mohammed Isa, Robsang, and Adul. We jumped up and rode through the dark to the camp, where the tea-kettles were singing on the fires.

Two days later we crossed another ridge and entered a new basin without an outlet. In the centre lay a turquoise-blue, shimmering salt-lake, known to the East Turkestan population as Yeshil-kul (the Green Lake). On this water, too, we made an adventurous trip, and again we were to be brought to safety by a beacon-fire. Robert and

Rehim Ali were my crew. We provided ourselves with clothes. Steering northeast, we stopped for lunch on the northern shore, and headed south to the meeting-place agreed upon.

We put off and poled the boat about a stone's-throw from the shore; for this lake, unlike the other, was shallow. Observing yellow storm-warnings in the southwest, we held a council. Would it not be wiser to spend the night on the northern shore, and let the storm blow over? Scarcely had we turned the bow of the boat back toward the land, when we saw two big, dirty-yellow wolves, awaiting our arrival, at the very edge of the water. They did not retreat one

WOLVES WAITING ON THE SHORE

step. Rehim Ali thought that they were outposts, and represented a whole pack. We had no firearms with us. Now the question was: "Which is worse, the wolves or the storm?" We were just discussing the situation, when the storm broke, filling the sail and nearly upsetting the boat.

"All right, then, let's go! We will land before it gets dark."

Once more the bow cut through the hissing breakers. The sun went down, yellow-red; and with the rising of the moon, the serpent-like formations were transformed into silver dust. We had the wind on our quarter, and the men used their oars, too. We warded off the waves as best we could. But at times they broke over the gunwale, and eventually we sat in a splashing foot-bath. Yet nothing disastrous happened. Two large signal-fires appeared in the south. Darkness fell. Suddenly an oar touched the bottom, and we found ourselves under the lee of a small cape. We landed and spent a wretched night on a moist salt-patch. But we got tea; for we had with us two jugs of fresh water, as well as food. At dawn, Rehim Ali gathered fuel, and soon afterwards Mohammed Isa arrived with horses.

Sonam Tsering, having been in the service of both Captain Deasy (1896-99) and Captain Rawling (1903), was able to show us where these Englishmen had camped, and where the former had buried some boxes after his animals died. We dug them up, but found nothing of value. I took only a couple of novels and books of travel. I was eager to leave the routes of these explorers behind me, and strike out on the large triangular spot of unknown land in northern Tibet, alluringly described on the English map as "unexplored."

After another two days on the road, we found ourselves on the western shore of the fresh-water lake of Pool-tso. It was a pleasant camp; and Tundup Sonam, the hunter, shot a wild yak, which provided us with meat for several days. I got the kidneys and the marrow-bones, a real tidbit. After nightfall, the men sat by the fires, over their meal, while I worked in my tent. Then, like a blow, came a raging storm—from the east, for a change. Two tents toppled over, and the glowing embers blew away like fireworks. The surf beat heavily and dully against the shore, and its spray fell over the camp like rain.

The next day was beautiful. We crossed the lake by two routes, sounded the depth, and camped on the southern shore, while the caravan, after a day's rest, made for the eastern shore. One more day was devoted to the lake, and we reached our new camp without any storm. The distance from the abandoned camp on the western shore was not great. Presently a fire and bulging clouds of smoke were visible there. All were amazed and puzzled. They had left the camp eight hours before, and the fire had died down then. Were there already Tibetans ready to pursue us and to interfere with our expedition? Or was it a post-rider from Leh? No; that was inconceivable. That ghosts were wont to walk on the shore, was the belief of my men. They said it was a phantom fire lit by the lake-spirits. I suspected it to be a pile of dry yak-droppings that had been forgotten, and that had caught fire in the wind.

The caravan dwindled. One horse lay dead in the camp; and the next day I rode past three candidates for death, who were being led. Our provisions shrank proportionately; and the walled grain-bags that served the Ladak-men as a windbreak, diminished progressively. Three of our horses ran away, at night, near a small, open lake; and I sent Robsang in search of them. After three days he returned with two of the horses. The trail of the third one revealed an episode both sad and dramatic. Pursued by a flock of wolves, the horse had run for dear life, straight toward the lake and out into the water. The wolves

ATTACKED BY WOLVES, ONE OF OUR HORSES RAN OUT INTO THE LAKE AND WAS DROWNED

turned back, but not the horse. He had evidently kept on, in the hope of saving himself by swimming; but he must have drowned from exhaustion, for no trace of him was discernible on the other shore.

The caravan, too, was followed by wolves and ravens. The former always appeared when our horses died; the latter were half-tame, and we could identify some of them.

On October 6, the temperature was down to −13°. Some of

the mules came up to my tent during the night, and in the morning one of them lay dead at the entrance.

Until now, our course had been east-northeastward. We now turned to the southeast, across the large triangle which no European had ever entered. It was still 396 miles to the Dangra-yum-tso. The Lamaists chanted prayers every evening, that we might succeed in making our way to the large monastery of Tashi-lunpo; and should we succeed, they would make an offering of an entire month's pay to the holy Tashi Lama. Two days later we had lost twenty-nine horses and six mules, twenty-nine horses and thirty mules being left. Eighteen sheep still remained. On the same day, Tundup Sonam shot two fine *Ovis Ammon*. He was invaluable. Whenever the meat-supply gave out, he would shoot a yak, a wild sheep, or an antelope. One day he preceded us, surprised a herd of grazing yaks in a glen, and killed a bouncing specimen, that rolled headlong down a slope, and fell stone-dead at his feet.

MOUNTAIN RANGE AND PHYSICAL FEATURES OF TIBET

CHAPTER XLIX

Marching with Death Through Northern Tibet

WINTER had come. All the men wore sheepskin jackets. They tanned the skins of the slaughtered sheep for *bashliks* and footgear. I slept on one half of a large, square, silky, white goatskin, and covered myself with the other half. Tsering tucked me up at night with furs and blankets. I had a soft skin *bashlik,* and at night I lay as if in a den. As long as I remained awake, Robsang kept my brazier hot with glowing dung. Even the puppies had sleeping-jackets of felt. Brown Puppy, having been fitted out with such a garment, walked slowly about for a while, making desperate attempts to free herself from it. We doubled up with laugh‑ ter, especially when White Puppy joined the sport, and tore at her coat. Then Brown Puppy squatted down and looked reproachfully at her tormentors.

Tundup Galsan was the chief cook and story-teller for the men. Tsering, my cook, also never tired of telling stories to a small select group. But he was most amusing when he sang. It sounded like a pig caught in a gate.

On October 17, it was —18°. I now had twenty-seven horses, twenty-seven mules, and twenty-seven men; but two horses and one sheep froze to death two days later. We had not seen a trace of human beings for fifty-nine days. Our apprehensions increased. Would we be able to keep enough animals alive until we met nomads? Or would they die, and require us to abandon our belongings, while pro‑ ceeding on foot in search of people?

The terrain was obstructive; we were caught in labyrinthine moun‑ tains and valleys. At Camp No. 44 we were struck by a heavy blizzard, and were at a loss which way to turn. Our scouts suggested a pass in the east, and Mohammed Isa went there the next day, through snow a foot deep. On my arrival there (18,400 feet above sea-level), I found the main ridge to be quite close by, southeast of the pass; but Mohammed Isa had descended northeastwards by a snow-covered, deso‑

late valley, in the lower part of which he had encamped. Neither fuel nor pasturage was in evidence, and our fire was kept alive with empty boxes. Heavy cloud-masses lowered upon the white mountains and again snow fell. Right above the camp was a small ridge, hardly forty feet high. One of the men directed my attention to it. There stood two fine wild yaks, observing us. They were as amazed as we, but they certainly looked impressive in the whirling snow.

During the night, the horses chewed one another's tails and pack-saddles. Two of them lay dead. The next camp was just as forlorn. Mohammed Isa went to reconnoitre, and returned with the news that there was open land three hours away. At twilight he had the unfortunate impulse to continue on to the level, grassy plain. I stayed behind, with Robert, Tsering, and Rehim Ali. The others departed, in three sections, the shepherd and his sheep bringing up the rear. They disappeared like phantoms in the dark. It was terribly cold, but that did not matter; for we were buoyed up by the expectation of better times the next morning.

We had two poor mules with us. One of them died at midnight; the other one was so far gone by morning, that we released it with a knife-cut. Its glistening eyes looked toward the sun, and shone like diamonds. The red blood looked lurid against the white snow.

We followed in the trail of the others. Soon we met Tundup Sonam, who told us that the caravan had lost its way in the darkness of the night, that the several sections had missed one another, and that four mules had died. We continued with him as guide. There lay a dead mule, the two bags of rice that it had borne lying near by. In the distance, Mohammed Isa appeared; he was out reconnoitring, with two men. At last we reached the plain, where the grass was fairly good. We dismounted, and, half dead with cold as we were, built a fire. By and by, the various sections came together in our sad Camp No. 47. Sonam Tsering turned up first, with the surviving mules. He wept at our losses. That night had claimed seven mules and two horses. The shepherd had lost complete track of the others, and took his sheep into a ravine, where he settled himself in the centre of the herd, to keep warm. It was a miracle that the wolves did not find their way to the place.

We made a rough estimate of our train. Thirty-two loads, twenty-one horses, and twenty mules remained, four of the latter being useless.

Only I and Robert continued to be mounted.   I decided that five of the remaining seven loads of rice should be sacrificed to the animals. Everything depended on them.   Tundup Sonam brightened this sad state of affairs by shooting three antelopes.   When some of the men went to cut up the quarry and prepare the meat, one antelope had already been devoured by the wolves.

Two mules and one horse succumbed during the march on October 24.   Our situation became graver every day.   Silence reigned around the fires.   We made camp on a small lake, on the shore of which we found dried grass and an open spring.   At ten o'clock in the evening, a flock of wild geese, bound for the south, flew toward us.   The landscape was illuminated by the most brilliant moonlight, and the weather was calm.   From the quacking conversation of the wild geese, we learned that they intended to descend and rest at the spring.   But perceiving that the spot was occupied by human beings, the goose leader screeched a new word of command to his troops, and, with lively chatter, they rose again and continued southward to the next spring.   Doubtless such communities follow the same routes over Tibet for thousands of years, on their way to and from India, in the autumn and spring.

The big dapple horse that I rode when we left Leh, was tired; and so I mounted a small white Ladaki, a friend of mine.   He bit and kicked as I touched the saddle; but once I was up, he walked with sure, steady steps.   In two places we saw the common stone tripod on which yak-hunters cook.   We were approaching human life after sixty-five days of isolation.   Everybody was on the lookout for black tents. The longer it took to get in touch with nomads, the later would rumour of our approach reach Lhasa.   And yet we longed for people, for our surviving horses and mules could not hold out long.   Water was scarce. Sometimes we were obliged to melt ice in the pans, so that the animals could drink.

We made a short march to Camp No. 51, in stormy weather and bitter cold.   I was so exhausted that I could hardly sit in the saddle, and we stopped twice to make fires of dung.   As soon as the tent was ready, I crawled in and lay down on the bed as I was.   I developed the most violent ague, a throbbing headache, and a temperature of 106.6°. Robert produced the Burroughs Wellcome medicine-chest, that blessed store, which the same firm had also given to Stanley, Emin Pasha, Jackson, Scott, and others.   Robert and Tsering undressed me and kept watch during the night. In my delirium I was far from Tibet. Thus I lay crushed for eighty-four hours. Robert would read aloud. For six days a storm raged. The dust blew into my tent, in which a candle flickered at night. The wolves were bold, and Tundup Sonam shot one of them. A raven that pecked the horses' manes also had to be killed. Many of the men were sick. Of the fifty-eight horses, sixteen survived.

On November 3, I was able to proceed, well wrapped up. We frequently came upon old camping-places and pot-stones for cooking. Two days later we found traces of gold-mines and indications of

THE WOUNDED WILD YAK CAME DOWN FROM THE STEEP GLEN

digging for the metal. There was a path apparently beaten by human beings. A herd of wild yaks grazed in a narrow glen. Tundup Sonam led the way. Except for an old bull, as big as a young elephant, the yaks fled up the glen. The bull advanced with lowered horns toward the huntsman, who hardly had time to betake himself to safety on a terrace. From there he brought the yak down with two well-aimed balls. I took several photographs of the beautiful animal.

On November 7, we had an unusual adventure. Occupying myself with collecting mineral specimens, charting the route, and sketching and photographing, I was always at the tail-end together with Robert on horseback and Rehim Ali on foot. The latter used to hold my horse when I dismounted. We were riding along a lakeshore, with a steep mountain-wall on our right. Two herds of wild sheep appeared. Here and there were cairns built by prospectors. We emerged on a plain, and fifty yaks that were grazing there fled. A herd of twenty *Pantholops* antelopes appeared before us, and vanished like the shadow of a cloud, as we approached. Presently we sighted Camp No. 56, half a mile ahead of us. In a few minutes we would be there. The smoke was already rising from the fires. A big black yak was grazing scarcely two hundred paces from the camp. Mohammed Isa came out of his tent and sent a bullet into the animal. The

wounded beast became furious; and, catching sight of us and concluding that we were enemies, he made straight for our little group.   Rehim
Ali uttered a cry of despair and ran for dear life toward the tents.
But he changed his mind and turned.   Our horses shied and started
to gallop off.   Rehim Ali caught Robert's horse by the tail.   The yak
was quite close.   He foamed with rage.   He rolled his blood-red eyes,
his blue-violet tongue hung out, his breath issued from his nostrils like
clouds of vapour, the dust whirled behind him.   He rushed forward
with lowered head; and as I was riding on the extreme right, it was
my horse that he would first impale, and throw it and me in the air,
after which he would trample us to a pulp.   In imagination I could
already hear the crunching of our breaking ribs.   The yak was within
fifty feet of us now.   I threw off my *bashlik* to distract his attention.
He took no notice of it.   I unfastened my girdle, intending to throw

IN ANOTHER MOMENT HE WOULD HAVE TAKEN ME AND MY PONY ON HIS HORNS

the sheepskin coat over him, and thus blind him, when he was close by.
I felt like a toreador at a bull-fight.   Only a tiny step separated me
from death.   Before I could get free from the coat, a piercing shriek
was heard.   It was Rehim Ali, who had stumbled, and he was now
prone on the ground.   The yak, diverted by this, turned to Rehim Ali.
With horns lowered, he rushed upon his victim.   But whether the
yak thought the man was already dead, or considered him to be harmless—for Rehim Ali never so much as budged—the yak contented

himself with prodding Rehim Ali with his horns, and then continued his wild career across the plain, and took himself rapidly off.

I turned at once, dismounted, and hurried to Rehim Ali, believing him to be dead. He lay still, tattered and dusty. Upon my asking how he was, he made a comical gesture with one hand, as if to say: "Never mind me. I am already stone-dead." Presently help arrived from the camp. Poor Rehim Ali really looked most miserable. He had a long, but harmless gash along one leg. He was lifted up on a horse, his wound was dressed, and he was cared for in a tent. Hence-

THE FIRST NOMADS WE MET

forth he was to ride. But the event certainly made him a bit queer, and it was long before he became normal again.

At the next camp, we lost a day by having to retrace our steps to the north, because of a pack of wolves that chased our horses back. On November 10, we saw the fresh tracks of a man and a tame yak on a lake-shore; and, while prospecting for game, Tundup Sonam came upon an isolated tent, in which a woman and three children lived. And two days later, after we had lost three horses and still possessed only thirteen, our mighty hunter brought two mounted Tibetans to our camp. These were the first men we had seen in eighty-one days.

They might have been fifty and forty years old, respectively. The elder was named Puntsuk, the younger Tsering Dava. They were half nomads, half yak-hunters, and called themselves *changpa* (northerners). All of northern Tibet is known as Chang-tang, or the North Plain. They called me *bombo-chimbo* (the Great Chieftain). They were dirty, their hair was long and untidy, their caps were made to protect their cheeks and chins, they wore warm sheepskin coats and felt boots, and they were equipped with rude swords, fire-steels, and rifles, but were entirely destitute of—trousers!

Did they want to sell us some of their yaks and sheep? Yes, with pleasure! They would come back the next morning. But we did not quite trust them, and kept them prisoner in Mohammed Isa's tent overnight. In the morning, a few of my men accompanied them to their camp. The whole party soon returned, with five fine yaks, each of which was to bear the loads of two of our worn-out horses, and also with four sheep and eight goats. We paid them generously; for they had indeed saved us.

They told us all they knew about the region and about their own wanderings. They lived on old, hard, dried, raw meat, butter, sour milk, and brick tea. Hiding behind small stone walls, next to springs, they would lie in wait for their game. Tsering Dava swore that he had shot three hundred wild yaks in his day. They made boots and straps of the wild asses' skins, and thread from the tendons of the wild beasts. They and their women took care of the tame yaks, the sheep, and the goats. Thus their lives passed monotonously from year to year, but healthily and actively, on the dizzy heights, in killing cold and storms and blizzards. They erected votive cairns to the mountain-gods, and venerated and feared all the strange spirits that dwelt in the lakes, rivers, and mountains. And in the end they died, and were borne by their kin to a mountain, where they were left to the wolves and the vultures.

On November 14, we went on, Puntsuk and Tsering Dava acting as guides. They gave me the geographical names, and we verified their statements, Mohammed Isa questioning Puntsuk, and I Tsering Dava, identical questions being put to each. They told of gold-seekers (*topka*) who work two or three months a year, and bring home loads of salt, which they trade for grain. They would count and play with the shiny silver rupees that I gave them every evening. Their small horses amused me. When I and Tsering Dava got to the camp, Puntsuk had already put his horse out to pasture. But upon our arrival, he came galloping to meet his comrade, neighing joyfully, and then they exchanged greetings by rubbing noses. The Tibetan horses took a genuine interest in our horses, and did not seem to understand that our emaciated, wretched animals were of their own species. It was interesting to observe the delight with which these little ponies ate dried meat, cut in long strips. In a country where pasturage is so meagre, the nomads have to train their horses to become meat-eaters.

One day Tundup Sonam shot two wild yaks. We took with us as much meat as we needed. The rest we left for Puntsuk and Tsering Dava; but as likely as not, the wolves got it first.

Then we rode across the Chakchom-la pass, the altitude of which is identical with that of Popocatepetl in Mexico (17,950 feet). It was crossed by the usual gold-seekers' trail. At our camp, south of this range, our new friends begged me to let them return; for they had never been farther south. They were granted their release, and generous tips besides, and seemingly they had never dreamed of the existence of such kind people as we were.

One day later, from another pass, we sighted six tents, surrounded by grazing herds. We camped on the shore of Lake Dungtsa-tso. The tents housed forty persons, who owned a thousand sheep, sixty yaks, and forty horses. Lobsang Tsering, a lame old man, offered us three fine-looking yaks, at twenty-three rupees apiece, and one of his comrades offered us two at the same price. Thus we had ten yaks in all, and were able to relieve our other beasts considerably. Lobsang Tsering looked handsome in his red skin coat and red turban-like headdress. He told of the gold and salt deposits in this region, which were exploited by people from Lhasa. He himself, and all the other nomads there, were from the district of Gertse, in the southwest. They seemed desirous of assisting us, but were afraid of one another. Yet it was evident that they had not received any special orders from Lhasa.

With our fourteen mules, twelve horses, and ten yaks, we came upon a highroad, on November 22. Its existence was attributable to the gold-seekers and their yaks, and to the salt-caravans with their sheep. The daily storms were a torment. Wrapped up like Arctic explorers, we rode through clouds of whirling dust. Our skin cracked, especially around the nails, where we developed chronic sores. And at night there was a rumble and a roar, as of great trains rolling into covered railway-stations, or of heavy artillery rushing at full speed over cobbles.

Four mules died the next day. The temperature at night dropped to −28°. Once more we made camp, near a village of six tents, enclosed by stone walls. The dwellers belonged to the Province of Naktsang, and took their orders from the Devashung, or the government in Lhasa. Mohammed Isa tried to negotiate the purchase of some yaks and sheep; but some official or other entered the tent and forbade the people to sell us anything. He knew that a European was concealed in our caravan, and advised us to go back at once.

"Here is where it begins," thought I. "Now a swift messenger will be dispatched to Lhasa, and then will follow the usual espionage and charges, and finally the mobilization of the mounted militia."

Not far from this critical place, we met a caravan of thirty-five pilgrims from Nakchu, who, with six hundred sheep and one hundred yaks, had been to the holy mountain of Kang Rinpoche (Kailas), and were travelling so slowly that the round-trip took two years. At our next camp we found two spies on watch. A mule died during the night, and was immediately half eaten by five wolves, who did not run off, even when I rode quite close by them.

We hurried on as fast as our exhausted animals could walk. One evening, when we were camping among wild rocks, two horsemen approached our tents. Their queues were coiled round their heads, which were adorned with red fillets. Red and green ribbons ornamented their coats, their sword-sheaths were set with semiprecious stones, and their boots were made of many-coloured felt. They said they belonged to the caravan of the Nakchu pilgrims, and this statement sounded more plausible when they said:

"You are the *peling* (European) who came to Nakchu with two companions five years ago. The name of one of them was Shereb Lama."

"That is correct."

"You had camels and Russians in your caravan. The whole province talked about you."

"That's nice," thought I. "Now the governors will soon know that I am on my way, and then they will stop us."

"Have you any yaks to sell?" I asked.

"Yes. We will be back, early to-morrow morning; but nobody must know that we sell to you."

"All right, you come; we will not tell anybody."

And before sunrise they arrived with yaks, butter, brick tea, and tobacco from Bhutan.

"I will give you three rupees a day each, if you will come with us," said I.

"No, thank you!" they replied. "Word is being sent south to stop you, and to force you westwards, the same as last time."

And so they were off. And we, owners of eighteen yaks now, went southwards, by way of a pass, on the other side of which we found the country covered with snow. With Robert and Haji, I rode far behind the caravan, as we crossed a plain. Pointing toward the pass behind us, Haji exclaimed: "Three galloping horsemen!"

"Now we are really in for it," I thought. The horsemen headed straight for us. A heavily-built man demanded authoritatively that we give an account of ourselves. We, in turn, asked who they were. After further questioning, they went on to the caravan, which had already encamped, and there they subjected Mohammed to a severe examination, and rode westward.

On December 4, we rode through a stretch where hundreds of wild asses were grazing. When we got to the Bogtsang-tsangpo, a river that I knew from my former journey, we were only 15,600 feet above sea-level, which was unusually low for us, but actually higher than the top of Mt. Rainier. We lost no time in establishing friendly relations with the natives, who willingly sold us food. And it was high time; for our own supply of rice, flour, and toasted flour was gone. I was still getting my daily small roll of white bread, but the men subsisted on meat and tea.

We had not yet been deprived of liberty. This was the very road I had passed in 1901, and just south of the Bogtsang-tsangpo was the beginning of the large white spot, the main objective of my expedition. But again a cloud fell on our expedition. The next day, six men came riding up to our camp. The highest among them was *Gova*, or head of the district. He said:

"I have got information from the north about you. And now I want to know everything. Last time you passed through this area with camels. I am now going to send a messenger to the Governor of Naktsang, otherwise he will cut my throat. Bombo Chimbo must stay here till the answer arrives."

"When will that be?"

"In twenty days."

"No, thank you! I have not the time. We will go on to-morrow."

The old man was kind and pleasant. He accompanied us down the river, pitched his tent next to ours, and offered no objection to our being assisted by the nomads. The latter assured me that all Naktsang knew of my present journey.

It was December 13, when, from a pass, we sighted the long-looked-for lake of Dangra-yum-tso. I had ordered the post-courier to its southern shore, and we were already half a month late. Nevertheless, I decided to go first to the Ngangtse-tso, a lake a little further east.

Near the camp was the opening to a gorge so narrow, that in spots we were able to touch the two mountain-walls simultaneously. I and two of the men took a walk there. Robsang was to call for us with yaks. He looked very downcast when he met us at the appointed time, and told us that twelve armed horsemen had come to stop us.

We had advanced only a few days' journey into the unknown country, and now my path was obstructed as before. All our suffering during the winter, all the dead animals—all had been in vain. I rode back to my tent in a gloomy mood. When Tsering entered with the glowing brazier, I said:

"Now you see that I was right when I said that we would be stopped."

"Stopped!" he exclaimed. "Nobody has stopped us."

"Robsang says that twelve horsemen were here."

"He misunderstood; that was only a rumour."

"Good! Then we will slaughter the leanest sheep and have a feast to-night!"

CHAPTER L

Through the Large White Spot—"Unexplored"

IN the evening, three more Tibetans rode up to our camp. They were decidedly friendly, told us that a robber-band from Nakchu was abroad in the north, and declared they had taken us for the robbers. They were pleased to meet nice people instead. One of them had seen me five years before, and remembered my being escorted by Tibetans on that occasion. They did not mind selling us some yaks, and also provided us with a guide.

We bought three splendid yaks; and so our last ten horses and two mules were now without burdens. Upon entering the Province of Naktsang, we met a big band of horsemen, with a great number of yaks. "They will stop us at the very border," was my thought. But not so; they were only harmless nomads from the Bogtsang-tsangpo, who had been south to buy goods. A few days later, however, we came upon some tents, the inhabitants of which shouted impertinently at Mohammed Isa: "Go back. You have no right to travel here." Upon which Mohammed Isa drew himself up, and let the most insolent of them have a taste of his riding-whip. After that they were as meek as lambs.

On the morning of December 24, I was awakened by a lugubrious song. An itinerant beggar and his old woman sat outside my tent, singing and swinging their magic staff. A small boy was our guide, and took us across a pass. A man led my dapple horse over the summit. I patted the faithful animal as I passed it, hoping that his strength would hold out to our next camp. The horse sighed heavily, and gazed after me, when I rode on. But he never reached the camp.

The Christmas Eve trudge was a long one; and the evening shadows were already stealing over the foot of the mountains, as we descended into the circular valley, where the Dumbok-tso, with a small rocky island in its centre, gleamed white with ice. The Christmas-fires showed their yellow flames some distance from the shore. The day's work done, I wanted to do something to celebrate Christmas. Robert had saved about forty candle-stumps; so we arranged them in rows on a box, and lit them. I summoned all my men, and had them seat themselves before the closed tent. All of a sudden we threw back the tent-flaps and surprised the men with this unexpected illumination. They fetched flutes and pots and pans, and started to play, sing, and dance. The nomads in the neighbourhood probably thought that these rites and incantations were part of a witches' service. But our young guide believed that we had gone mad, and asked permission to go home to his tent. The Lamaists sang a song in honour of Tashi-lunpo; and, when the noise subsided, I read the Biblical passages, appropriate to Christmas, that were being read that evening in every church of Sweden and the rest of Christendom.

Camp No. 97 was pitched on the northern shore of the Ngangtse-tso, a large, shallow salt-lake discovered by Nain Sing, an Indian pundit. At this very place we crossed his route. The pasturage was fair, and I wanted my animals and men to have a good rest. Some of the strongest men, however, were to work with me. We were going to sound the depth of the Ngangtse-tso, which was thickly frozen over. It certainly was taking chances to spend time here, when we should have been penetrating the forbidden country by forced marches. But the animals had to rest, and the lake had to be sounded and charted.

We made a sledge, on which I sat cross-legged, muffled up in my sheepskin coat. Robsang and Haji pulled. Seven other men carried our provisions and a small tent across the ice. At suitable intervals we pierced the ice and dropped the lead through the holes. Our first camp was made on the southern shore. The second trip took us northwestward; and we had great difficulty crossing open water in a fissure almost five feet wide. On December 31, we made Camp No. 100, on the western shore. There a shepherd was tending five hundred sheep. On seeing us, he ran off at full speed, and left the sheep to their fate.

On January 1, 1907, we crossed the lake diagonally, south-south-eastwards. A strong wind swept the powdered salt along on the shiny dark-green ice. We sighted tents, tame yaks, and wild asses on the southern shore. A severe storm broke. My Ladak men sat round their fire in the open, making a picturesque group in the flying dust and the diffused moonlight.

On January 2, we crossed the lake, going southwest against a strong head-wind. I remained seated on the sledge at one of the holes, when it was carried off by the storm-wind and blown along over the lake like an ice-yacht. Had it not been that a crack caused me to capsize, I probably would have been driven across the entire lake at that wild speed. At the camp, we fastened the sledge securely. Finding some sheep-dung in a pen, we made a fire; but it took us an hour to thaw out. We looked a sight. Our faces were as white as those of a miller, from all the salt-powder.

We drove northeast after that, a glorious wind being with us. The powdered ice spurted from the runners. We bought food from the nomads. White Puppy was with us, and kept me company. On January 4, we saw a black spot on the ice in the distance. It was Islam Ahun, who, with a letter from Robert, had been looking for us for two whole days. The letter said that a troop of armed horsemen had arrived, in order to stop us, and that they insisted on speaking with me.

So they really did mean to stop us, as in 1901. I had now reached my southernmost point, and the gates of the land of the holy books were being slammed ruthlessly in my face; for,

> "The gates are mine to open
> And the gates are mine to close,
> And I set my house in order,
> Said our Lady of the Snows."

The next day, we made soundings along one more route, which disclosed the deepest spot in the whole lake, only thirty-three feet. Another messenger arrived, with this message: "The governor him-self is expected in four days. We are strictly guarded." Was it Hlaje Tsering, as before? Why had I not gone to the Dangra-yum-tso, as I had first intended, and thus avoided the Naktsang region?

On January 6, we made soundings along the final route. While we were thus engaged, Mohammed Isa himself came. He told me that twenty-five Tibetans were tenting at our camp, and that mounted messengers were coming and going. Nobody had heard of any courier with post for me. I had appointed November 25, at the Dangra-yum-tso, and now it was already January 6. But then, why should Colonel Dunlop-Smith comply with my request to send my letters to Tibet, when he knew that the British government had done every-

thing to prevent my journey, and I had eventually gone to East Turkestan on a Chinese passport?

On January 7, we were called for with horses, and rode to Camp
No. 107, a short distance from the northeastern lake-shore. I sat
down in Mohammed Isa's tent and received the Tibetan chiefs. They
bowed deeply, their tongues hanging out. One of them had been
present when Hlaje Tsering intercepted me on my former expedition.

"Is Hlaje Tsering still Governor of Naktsang?"

"Yes; and he knows that it is you who have come back. He has
sent word about you to Lhasa. He will be here in four days, and
you must wait till then."

In the evening of the eleventh, troops on horseback arrived, and
a large blue-white tent was pitched. The next day the Governor, with
a young lama, called on me. The Gov-
ernor wore a Chinese cap, with two fox-
tails and a white glass button, a silk
caftan, with wide sleeves, otter-skin collar, earrings, and velvet boots. He
greeted me warmly; in fact, we were
not far from embracing each other.
But he was inflexible in his command:

"You must not travel through Naktsang, Hedin Sahib. You must go back
north. Though we are old friends, I
don't want any fresh trouble on your
account."

"Hlaje Tsering," I replied, "I started
out on this journey with one hundred
and thirty beasts of burden. I have
eight horses and one mule left. How
can you ask me to go back to that
murderous Chang-tang with such a caravan?"

"I AM VERY GLAD TO SEE YOU AGAIN,
HEDIN SAHIB," SAID HLAJE TSERING

"You may go wherever you wish, but not through my province."

"The Dalai Lama has fled. There is a different régime now than
when I was in Tibet before. The Tashi Lama is expecting me."

"I only take orders from the Government in Lhasa."

"I am expecting letters from India that are to come to me through
the Tashi Lama."

"I have no proof of that. I shall not leave this place before you are on your way north."

"And I shall not depart until I have got my post from India."

I saw now that I ought to have gone to the Dangra-yum-tso, which is outside the Province of Naktsang, and that the only thing I could do now was to go back to the Bogtsang-tsangpo and from there to the Dangra-yum-tso.

Upon returning to his tent, Hlaje Tsering sent me rice, butter, and other victuals as a gift of welcome; and I gave him two pieces of goods and two Kashmir knives. Then I returned his call in his large, beautifully-decorated tent, where we continued negotiating. He did not object to my sending two couriers to Captain O'Connor in Gyangtse. Rub Das and Tundup Galsan were to be ready by the following evening. But nothing came of that; for the Governor visited me again the next day, and this time he had changed his mind. To my extreme amazement he said:

"I have discussed the matter with my trusted men, and we have agreed that the only thing for you to do is to leave and go south to the region of Labrang (Tashi-lunpo). I ask that you resume your journey to-morrow."

What had happened? What did he mean? Had he received orders from Lhasa? I did not trust my ears, but kept my countenance, and said quite coolly:

"All right; I will go south, if you will get me some new beasts of burden."

"You may buy them from the nomads. Your road runs east of the Ngangtse-tso."

After the customary return-call, we repacked our luggage carefully. Hlaje Tsering was greatly interested in that procedure, and asked for the empty boxes that were left over. He got a lot of leather boxes and several other odds and ends. He deserved them all; for he had opened the land of the holy books for me to pass through.

January 14 was a memorable day. When the sun was near the meridian, there was an eclipse of nine-tenths of its surface. For three hours I observed the phases with the theodolite, and noted the temperature, direction of wind, etc. The sky was perfectly clear. It grew half dark, and general silence prevailed. The Tibetans hid in their tents.

The Ladakis mumbled prayers. The sheep returned from pasture. The ravens perched, inert and drowsy, as though night were near.

As soon as the phenomenon had ended, I went to Hlaje Tsering's tent.

"There you see," I said, "that the gods of the Dangra-yum-tso are angry because you wanted to close my way to their lake."

But he smiled superiorly, and replied:

"It is the big dog roaming about the sky, who sometimes obscures the sun."

As we sat talking, the tent-door burst open, and in came Robsang, his heart in his mouth.

"The post has come!" he shouted.

"Who brought it here?" I asked, with imperturbable calm.

"A man from Shigatse."

"What has happened?" asked Hlaje Tsering.

"Oh," I answered, "it is only the Tashi Lama, who has sent my post here."

Hlaje Tsering sent one of his confidential men out to verify my statement. The man questioned the courier, who told him that Duke Kung Gushuk, brother of the Tashi Lama, had ordered him at all hazards to go and find me. He had learned from the nomads where I was.

Now it was Hlaje Tsering's turn to be astonished. He opened his eyes and mouth wide, and just stared. At last he said:

"Well, I have nothing more to say, now that I know the holy Tashi Lama himself is expecting you. The way is open to you. The day after to-morrow I shall go home to Shansa-dsong."

"Did I not tell you that my letters would come from the Tashi Lama?" I replied.

I took my leave, hurried to my tent, and received Ngurbu Tundup, the splendid courier. The precious post-bag had been sent from Calcutta to Gyangtse, and on to the Tashi Lama, with the request that he forward it to the Dangra-yum-tso. Fortunately it had been delayed, as we had been.

Piles of letters! Good news from home, newspapers, books! Relations with the outer world were re-established. I devoured the letters and papers. The Ladakis arranged for dancing and music in the evening; and I went out to them for a while, and made a speech in

Jaggatai Turki, thanking them for their steadfastness and faithfulness during the past winter. Now they would get their wages, and soon they would see Tashi-lunpo and the holiest man in Tibet.

With —13° inside the tent, and wolves howling outside, I lay reading half the night. All day long, on the fifteenth, I went on reading. On the sixteenth, good old Hlaje Tsering departed. We exchanged gifts once more, he mounted his horse, and after mutual adieus of real regret, he disappeared with his escort over the nearest hillocks.

This was a great victory for me. I would cross the eastern portion of the vast white spot which no European or pundit had yet traversed. All the obstacles in my way were as if swept away.

We purchased three new horses from the nearest nomads, and proceeded to the southeastern shore of the lake. A wild ass that had been torn by wolves lay there. The cold went down to —30°.

We had a splendid view of Lake Marchar-tso from our next camp, in a valley. White Puppy and a black dog from Pobrang were absent, having remained with the wild ass. I sent two men to fetch them; but the dogs were gone, and never came back. Two days later, two stray dogs joined our wandering band. One of them was old, lame, and shaggy, and the men tried to drive him off with stones; but he followed us to the next camp, and after that, for hundreds of miles; he became everyone's favourite. He kept fierce watch over the tent-city, and was simply called "The Lame."

We rode through a labyrinth of winding valleys with frozen water-courses and dark ranges that had never before been recorded on a map, nor even been seen by a white man since Noah left his ark. The nomad name for the main ridge was Pabla. We approached it in stormy weather, with frequent whirling snows. In every pass, we found cairns, with streamers, bearing the six holy syllables, fluttering from clusters of votive poles. The Sela-la, 18,060 feet high, was the highest and most important pass on the whole way. It is situated on the great watershed that separates undrained interior Tibet from the Indian Ocean. All of the water that flows south from its ridge empties into the Tsangpo, the upper Brahmaputra.

Descending the pass, we met three men, with seven horses, presumably stolen, for the men made a great detour upon seeing us. A day later we encountered seven heavily-armed men, who asked if we had seen any robbers with stolen horses. Upon hearing that we had, they spurred their mounts and went up the pass.

We hired twenty-five fresh yaks, so as to cover the ground more quickly. The terrain was very unfavourable. It became evident that we would have to cross a series of passes, situated in reaches of the Pabla, all of them almost as high as the Sela-la. Running westward among them were frozen affluents of the My-chu, a tributary of the Raga-tsangpo, which empties into the upper Brahmaputra. The Shib-la was the first of these secondary passes. The road was a very important highway. We were often met by caravans of yaks, horsemen, nomads, hunters, pilgrims, and beggars. There were votive cairns and *mani* walls all over. We approached a large religious centre. The nomads were all friendly; for Ngurbu Tundup, who had rapidly preceded us, had given us a good character.

After crossing the Chesang-la pass, I left the exhausted yaks from Chang-tang that belonged to us in the care of Tundup Sonam and Tashi, whom I instructed to follow us slowly. Had I had any idea of that which I learned later, I would have left the *entire* caravan behind, and pressed on to Shigatse with three or four men. But we had no apprehensions, and took things calmly.

Every step here led to a discovery; every name was a new addition to our knowledge of the earth. Until those days in January, 1907, this section of the earth's surface had been as little known as the other side of the moon. Familiarity with the visible side of that satellite was far greater than with this complicated mountain-land.

A steep road led to the pass of Ta-la, 17,800 feet high. Before its cairn and pennants, both Tsering and Bolu prostrated themselves, their foreheads touching the ground, and worshipped the mountain-spirits. The view to the southeast was magnificent. The reaches of the mountains, of various colours and shades, stretched like bears' paws down toward the valley of the Brahmaputra; and on the other side, or south of the gigantic valley of that river, the ridges and peaks of the Himalayas appeared dazzling-white beneath a light-blue sky, with fleecy white clouds. Were we to succeed, after all, in cutting all the way through the unknown country down to the great Holy River?

On February 5, we passed a village. From out of its reed tents, forty Tibetans came to greet us. They stretched their tongues out as far as possible, held their caps in their left hands, and scratched their heads with the right. These various manœuvres were performed simultaneously.

The following day found us at the cairn on the pass of La-rok, 14,560 feet high. Thus we had dropped 3,300 feet since leaving Ta-la. The river resembled a narrow ribbon in the distance, and we were closer to the Himalayas. But Mt. Everest, the highest mountain on earth, was not to be seen: it was shrouded in clouds.

CHAPTER LI

The Pilgrims' Journey on the Holy River

FROM La-rok we rode down a steep road to Ye-shung, where the valley widened. We were now no higher than 12,950 feet. The houses about us were white, with streamers on the roofs. The monasteries Tashi-gembe and Tugdan beckoned to me. Here ran the great highway to Shigatse, Tashi-lunpo, and Lhasa. Hundreds of Tibetans surrounded our tents, to sell us sheep, fat, butter, milk, radishes, hay, barley, and *chang* (beer made from barley). And here, too, splendid Ngurbu Tundup presented himself, with greetings of welcome from Kung Gushuk, the Duke.

Should we rest a day? No; we could recoup in Shigatse. So, onward!

And on we went, past villages and barley-fields. Not the smallest part of the heavy traffic on this road was due to pilgrims on their way to the New-Year festivities in Tashi-lunpo. The road ran down along the north bank of the Brahmaputra, or Tsangpo (the River). The water, transparent and noiseless, glided in its bed. It was holy. We drank of it. In the village of Rungma, we saw our first trees since leaving Leh. Here we stopped, and had camp-fires that were fed with real wood.

On February 8, the narrow, picturesque way ran along the mountainous northern bank. The river was full of clattering drift-ice. Situated on a high terrace of detritus, the village of Tanak afforded a magnificent view up and down the valley.

Our last day dawned on the journey to the famous monastery. I gave Mohammed Isa orders to stick to the road with the caravan. Robert, Robsang, and I went by way of the river. We hired a boat, one of those funny, simple craft that can originate only in a country where wood is scarce. Only the gardens contained a few trees; and no wild forests grew at these altitudes.

The boat, of a rectangular shape, was made of four yak-hides, sewed together, and fastened to a framework of light boughs. A triangular piece of leather was fastened in the forked end of the oar, making it look like a duck's foot. After the boatman has taken his passengers, say, from Tanak to the opening of the Shigatse valley, he takes the boat on his back, and returns along the road to Tanak. The current, running four or five feet a second, is too swift for anyone to row up the river.

Guffaru was to wait for us, with horses, where the highway crossed the river. My journey on the Tsangpo was a strategic move on my part. It permitted me to pass unobserved by spies; and, in the event

IN A YAK-HIDE BOAT ON THE UPPER BRAHMAPUTRA

of last-minute instructions from Lhasa to stop me, the soldiers would only be able to capture Mohammed Isa and the caravan. It would have been quite a futile task to search for me on the river.

We embarked. My eyes took in the approaching landscape, and I drew a map of the river's course, the banks, and their surroundings. This was the Tsangpo, or simply "the river," as the Tibetans call the upper Brahmaputra (Son of Brahma). I rubbed my eyes, hardly believing that I had crossed the forbidden land. The water was transparent and light-green. We seemed to stand still, and the shores apparently moved past us at great speed. Looking down over the side of the boat, I could see the gravel and the sand-banks, at the bottom, rapidly unrolling beneath me. On the right, toward the south, the furthest ranges of the Himalayas towered high. In the north appeared the last offshoots of the immense mountain-system that we had just crossed by the Sela-la, and which had hitherto had no name. I called it the Transhimalaya, because it was on the other side of and beyond the Himalaya (Winter's Abode). Every moment revealed the landscape in a different aspect. Owing to the sharp bends, we moved in all directions. At one moment the sun was right in our faces; at the next, on our backs. Now we skirted the foot of the north mountains, now those on the south. Wild geese, in long, grey bat-

PILGRIMS ON THEIR WAY TO THE NEW-YEAR FESTIVAL IN TASHI-LUNPO

talions, watched us from the bank. They screamed as we passed them, but they did not stir. Nobody ever killed them, and so they were very tame.

But entrancing and magnificent as these scenes were, I yet could not remove my eyes from the pilgrims' boats, which, in long files, came gliding down the royal river. Now we rowed past them, now we paralleled one and the same boat for a long while. Occasionally we hugged the shore, to let new strings of boats pass. They were frequently lashed together, in twos or threes; and they carried peasants, villagers, and nomads, with their women and children, going to the imminent New-Year festivities in Tashi-lunpo. They were in holiday-attire, red, green, or dark-blue. The women wore high, arched frames, like aureoles, on their heads, adorned with coral and turquoise; and the long, red, green, and yellow ribbons hanging from their braids down 'to their heels were covered with ornaments and silver coins. Here and there a bareheaded lama, in his red monk-gown was seated. The occupants of the boats all seemed to be congenial. They gossiped, smoked, had tea and food. Rods, with prayer-streamers at the top, were fixed to the gunwales. These appeased the river-spirits and assured a happy journey to the pilgrims. Groups of boats were seen up and down the river, strewn about like coloured islets. They did not detract from the beauty of this malachite-green waterway that lies between the highest mountain-ranges of the globe.

Once in a while the shore disclosed a cairn with a streamer-decked pole. These indicated the points at which the river could be crossed, and at which ferries—always the light boats made of yak-hides—were available for travellers and their caravan-beasts. Living, the yaks carry the nomads across the mountains; after death, they serve to transport human beings on the Holy River.

Sheer black granite mountains, close by, descended into the river. We flew past one promontory after another. Along a path at the foot of one of them, on the southern shore, some men were advancing up the river, their boats on their backs. From behind they resembled strange-looking, gigantic beetles. We observed fishermen busy with their nets. Their catch was placed on sale by Chinese dealers. We asked them to bring us some of the fish intended for the next day's market in Shigatse.

"How far have we still to go?" I enquired of our good skipper.

"Oh, it is still far! Behind the farthest point is the road to Shigatse."

I lost myself in reverie. No spies, no soldiers were in sight. The water rippled in narrow streaks, but did not eddy. I was thinking of the nine hundred miles on the Tarim. This time we could employ the motive power of the water only for one day. Or—the thought entered my head for a moment—should we continue down the valley, to the point where the Ki-chu River joined the Tsangpo, go ashore at the junction, buy three horses, and ride to Lhasa?

No! The longing I had had, in 1901, to penetrate the Holy City in disguise, was completely gone. The charm of the unknown had passed. A whole corps of officers, and thousands of Tommy Atkinses, had been there with the Younghusband and General MacDonald expedition, only three years before. Ryder, Rawling, Bailey, and Wood, the correspondents of the big newspapers, and, above all, Colonel Waddell, the learned connoisseur of Lamaism, had been with them.[1]

Some villages appeared on the right bank. Rows of newly-arrived rowboats were lying there; and heaps of hay, dung, and produce were piled up, awaiting transport to Shigatse by caravan-animals. And in the midst of the crowd of Tibetans stood Guffaru, with four of our horses.

Our boatman received his pay and a little more. We mounted our horses and rode up the Nyang-chu valley, which led to Shigatse. The sun went down; the shadows grew longer. We had no guide, but found our way easily. The pilgrim-procession and the caravans showed us the road. We were the objects of much attention, but nobody made a move to interfere with us. I rejoiced in the twilight and dark. Nobody noticed us then. A tall white *chorten* stood on our right; and a little further along, on an isolated hill, rose the Shigatse-dsong, the mighty citadel of municipal authority. Would we be halted and apprehended, as we entered the city? No. Presently white houses were seen faintly through the dark, on both sides. We were in a street in the city of Shigatse.

A man approached me. Ah, it was our own Namgyal! He led us to a gate in a wall, behind which lay Kung Gushuk's garden. Here Mohammed Isa and the other men met us. There were also some Tibetans there, Kung Gushuk's servants. They took me to a house just inside the gate. It had been prepared and tidied up for my use. But I preferred my tent in the garden. Our airy dwellings were already

[1] Two years ago, another Englishman went to Lhasa. His achievements are criticized in the *Geographical Journal*. He lectured in Europe and America, and published a book. A San Diego newspaper that was sent me advertised him in these terms: "Lecturer with real story will tell how he entered city closed to 'heathen dogs!' Said to be the only white man who ever entered Lhasa, the capital of Tibet." But shortly before him, Mr. Bell had lived a year in Lhasa, and General Edward Pereira had just been there. Major Bailey had visited the city. Dr. H. Hayden, a geologist, had lived for six weeks in Potala, the Dalai Lama's palace. Two mechanics had spent one and a half months installing telephones in that palace, and two English officials were for some years employed in the telegraph-office in Lhasa; not to mention Younghusband's military expedition to Lhasa, or the succession of Catholic missionaries who had been there in years gone by.

set up. A fire was burning in front of them. I sat down by my tent and asked myself if I was dreaming.

Late in the evening, a member of the Tashi Lama's secular staff called at my tent, put a number of questions to me, and made notes. Afterwards, I had my supper, and went gloriously to sleep in the city of Shigatse.

The next morning, I looked about and inspected our extraordinary camp. We had arrived here with six horses and one mule from Leh. One of the horses now lay dead in his stall, and was dragged away. His tragic fate made me grieve. For half a year he had endured innumerable hardships in Chang-tang, only to succumb at the very goal. He had crossed passes at almost 19,000 feet; and now he had died in front of his filled crib, at a height of 12,700 feet. The last six veterans were cared for with the greatest solicitude. We made them beds of straw, so that they might lie soft, in case they wanted to rest. They were to have their fill of barley and clover, be watered, and lightly exercised, so as not to become stiff. Among them was my little white Ladaki that had carried me through so many storms. I went into his stall and stroked him, but he only bit and kicked.

CHAPTER LII

With the Tashi Lama at the New-Year Festival

I HAD hardly finished my round of inspection, when a plump, jovial Chinese called on me. He was an officer, in command of the *lansa* of a hundred and forty men garrisoned there. I invited him to my tent, and offered him tea and cigarettes. His name was Ma. Ma could not understand where I had come from. He said he believed I had fallen from the sky. He had not heard a sound.

"Had I known that you were approaching Shigatse," he said, "I would have stopped you with an armed force; for this city, like Lhasa, is closed to Europeans."

I laughed and joked with Ma, and asked him what in the world we were to do, now that I was actually safe and sound, right in Shigatse.

On February 11, early in the morning, I was visited by Lobsang Tsering Lama and Duan Suen, a Chinese. They, too, had been without the slightest knowledge of my approach; and they probably thought that I had risen from the ground. They, too, made inquiries and notes.

"I know," said I, "that the New-Year festival begins to-day. It is my desire to witness it."

"That is impossible for a European."

"I also wish to meet the Panchen Rinpoche (the Tashi Lama)."

"Only a very few mortals may appear before his face."

It occurred to me to disclose my Chinese passport, for the benefit of Duan Suen. He read it through attentively and with increasing interest. His eyes grew larger and larger, and finally he said:

"But this is a wonderful passport! Why did you not show it to us at once?"

"Because it is made out for East Turkestan, and I have come to Tibet instead."

"That does not matter. This paper is of great importance."

They withdrew. Soon I received a token of welcome from the Tashi Lama, in the shape of a *kadakh*, or *haddik*, a long piece of light-blue gauze, the delivery of which implied respect, blessing, and welcome. And what was more, I was solemnly bidden to the monastery to attend the New-Year festival. Now I blessed the Indian government which had insisted on the Chinese passport. Without it I should probably never have gained permission to see Tashi-lunpo. To this day I am puzzled at having made my way unnoticed to Shigatse. It may have been due, in part, to the Tibetans' respect for European weapons since the English military expedition to Lhasa, in 1903 and 1904; perhaps, also, to the fact that so many chiefs and others had betaken themselves to Tashi-lunpo for the New-Year festival, and were thus absent from their posts when I passed with my caravan. Another possible reason was my travelling by water on the last day, and arriving after dark. I was fortunate, also, in getting there two days before the New-Year festival began; for it gave me the opportunity to witness the greatest annual rite of Lamaism, and this in the monastery that was the most important in the entire world of Lamaism, because the Dalai Lama was away in Urga.

Losar, or the New-Year festival, is celebrated to commemorate Buddha's victory over the six false prophets, and the triumph of true religion over unbelief. A feast of the whole people, it celebrates the return of spring and light, the victory over cold and darkness. The seeds sprout once more; the grass shoots up for the nomads' herds. For fifteen days the festival goes on. Pilgrims from far and near flock to Tashi-lunpo, and on every hand is heard the buzz of the six holy syllables, "Om mani padme hum."

Tsaktserkan, a chamberlain, appeared with further messages of welcome from the Tashi Lama, and informed me that he and Lobsang Tsering Lama had been commissioned to attend me during my sojourn in Shigatse.

I dressed in my best, and Mohammed Isa put on his gorgeous, red, festive robe and gold-embroidered turban. Robert, Tsering, and two other Lamaists were allowed to accompany me. We rode to the monastery in about twelve minutes. Pilgrims swarmed in all directions. Along the road were small stands, where sweetmeats and other edibles were offered the guests from afar.

We dismounted at the gate of the lamasery, and left our horses. Then we ascended a steep street, paved with large, dark flagstones, smooth and shiny from the feet of innumerable pilgrims throughout the centuries. On either side were tall dormitories; and above it all rose the beautiful white-façaded "Vatican," the Tashi Lama's private residence, with dark window-frames, a black-and-red-striped frieze at the top, and small balconies. We were taken through a labyrinth of dark rooms and passages, up slippery wooden steps that were almost vertical, through galleries and halls, where daylight began to filter in, and where clusters of red monks were silhouetted against the light. At last we were led out to a gallery, on the very edge of which a chair was placed for me.

From there I had a fine view of the courtyard where the festival was to be held. Verandas, or open galleries, ran along its four sides, and columns rose in several tiers. There were uncovered balconies at the top. Immediately below us there was such a balcony. There sat the pilgrims, gossiping and eating sweets, strangers from Ladak, Bhutan, Sikkim, Nepal, and Mongolia crowding together. The officials, in their beautiful, variegated dresses and pompous hats, formed a group by themselves. In another balcony were their ladies in equally festive attire. Everywhere, even on the temple-roofs, people were crowded. Deep down was the paved court, with a tall pole, hung with multicoloured ribbons, erect in the centre. From the courtyard, stone stairs led to the Red Gallery, concealed by heavy black curtains, woven of yak-wool.

Two monks appeared on one of the uppermost roofs, and produced a hollow sound on sea-shells. Then the monks drank tea. From the interior of the Red Gallery came the tones of a melodious chant of choristers. It rose and fell in waves. The gallery of the Tashi Lama, above the Red Gallery, was marked by a wide hanging-curtain of yellow silk, gold-fringed. Through a small square opening in that hem, the holiest of all the priests of Tibet was to witness the festivities.

BLOWING THE SHELL TRUMPETS TO START
THE RELIGIOUS PLAYS

Great, hollow trumpet-blasts announced that the Tashi Lama had left the Labrang. A murmur passed through the waiting crowd. The procession arrived. It was headed by the chief monks, carrying the insignia of the Holy One. And then he himself appeared. All rose and bowed low. His robe was of yellow silk; and his headgear, of heavy, woolly material, resembled a Roman helmet. He sat down, with crossed legs, on some cushions, his mother, his brother (the Duke), and several high prelates seated on his right and left. They all moved slowly, with deliberation and dignity.

Some monks set a table before me. It bent underneath its burden of sweetmeats, tangerines, and tea. They informed me that I was

THREE TOMBS OF TASHI LAMAS IN TASHI-LUNPO

the Tashi Lama's guest. My eyes met his. I rose and bowed, and he gave me a friendly nod.

Now the ceremonies began. Two masked lamas moved down the stairs of the Red Gallery, with dancing steps, and went in mysterious circles about the quadrangle. Eleven others followed, each carrying a folded flag. Each flag was unfolded and elevated on a long, forked pole, in salute to the Grand Lama. The flags were of various colours, and three strips of a different colour hung from each one.

This strange procession received new accessions. Now came a group of lamas in white, bearing various religious symbols. Some had swing-ing censers of gold, from which blue-grey smoke arose. Others were arrayed in harness and other accoutrements; and still others in cloaks of gold-embroidered silk. Then followed the church-music. This con-sisted of six copper trumpets, ten feet long, and bound with yellow brass, their bells resting on the shoulders of novices. The trumpet-blasts resounded solemnly and sonorously in the courtyard, and mingled with trilling flutes, clashing cymbals, bells, and the dull beats of forty

THE DEVIL DANCE

drums, carried vertically. The musicians, wearing yellow mitres, seated themselves on one side of the court.

A lama came out on the stairs of the Red Gallery, bearing a bowl brimful of goat's blood. Gyrating in a mystic dance, he poured the blood over the steps. Was it a survival of the superstitious human sacrifices of ancient pre-Lamaist times?

Twelve lamas, in masks, simulating devils, dragons, and monstrous wild beasts, entered the courtyard, and began their circling, demonic dance. The music continued unceasingly. The tempo increased; the dancers accelerated their steps. The magnificently gold-embroidered, multicoloured silk vestments stood out like open umbrellas. They wore square collars, with a hole in the middle for their heads; and these, too, stood out horizontally from their necks. They held fluttering ribbons and streamers in their hands. And all the time the music grew wilder, and the dancing became more furious. It was more than enough to make one giddy. The enthusiasm of the pilgrims rose. They pelted the dancers with rice and barley. The monastery pigeons rejoiced at that.

A fire was lighted in the court. A large sheet of paper was held close to it. On this paper was written all the evil of the past year of which one wished to be purged. A lama advanced with a bowl, containing an inflammable powder. He recited some incomprehensible formulæ of incantation, and described mystical motions with his arms. The paper was brought closer to the flames. The lama emptied the contents of the bowl into the flames, causing the fire to blaze up and consume the paper and all the evil which had tormented the children of man during the previous year. The multitude shouted with joy. The last number on the program was an ensemble dance of sixty lamas.

The Tashi Lama then rose, and retired as slowly and solemnly as he had entered. The pilgrims dispersed like chaff before the wind.

On my return home, a whole caravan of mules, laden with rice, flour, barley, dried and fresh fruit, and other viands, entered my garden. It was all a gift of welcome from the Tashi Lama, and indeed a valuable one; for those supplies were sufficient for me, my men, and animals for an entire month. In the end, Tsaktserkan appeared and announced that His Holiness expected me the following morning.

Accompanied by my interpreter, Mohammed Isa, and two high lamas, I traversed the apartments, passages, and stairs of the Labrang. One of the highest dignitaries of the monastery, a small, fat man, with a head as shiny as a billiard-ball, received me first. His cell was resplendent with solid and splendid luxury, altars, bookcases, tables, and stools, all of shining lacquer. Images of Buddha, of silver and gold, stood in precious cases of the same metals, and the perpetual lights flickered in their bowls. He presented me with an idol, and I gave him a dagger in a silver sheath.

After an hour, a message arrived, saying I might proceed toward the highest regions of the "Vatican." Little knots of lamas stood whispering in the corridors and halls. We arrived. None but Mohammed Isa could accompany me. We entered the room, which was larger but much plainer than that of the fat man. Half of it was exposed to the sky; the other half, a step higher, had a roof. In a small alcove, on the right, the Holy One was seated, with crossed legs, on a bench fastened to the wall. He was looking through a small, square window, that opened out over Shigatse and the valley. Before him stood a table, with a teacup, a telescope, and some printed

STEEP STAIRCASES AND OPEN ALTARS ON THE WAY TO THE
TASHI LAMA

sheets. His garb was that of an ordinary lama, differentiated only by the yellow gold-embroidered vest. His arms were bare.

With an expression of the utmost kindness and amiability, he gave me both his hands, and motioned me to the European chair beside him. Now I could observe him at close quarters. I forgot that he was not good-looking, according to our standards; for his eyes and his smile, his great unpretentiousness, his soft, low, almost shy voice, captivated me all the while. He begged pardon for the simplicity of the reception; but I assured him of my happiness merely to be in Tashi-lunpo, and to be *his* guest.

Then we conversed for fully three hours. It would be banal to relate in detail what we talked about—my journey, Europe, China, Japan, India, Lord Sahib (Minto), Kitchener, and a thousand other things. He told me of his visit to Lord Minto a year before, and of his pilgrimage to the places that had been sanctified by the events of Buddha's life and wanderings. Two lamas of menial rank stood bolt upright in the roofless part of the chamber. Twice the Tashi Lama dismissed them with a wave of his hand. That was when he wished to say or to ask something he did not want them to hear; as, for instance, when he requested me not to let the Chinese know that I had been *his* guest, or that he had disclosed the secrets of the temple to me. He said that I had full freedom, and that I might go about, photograph, draw, and take notes, wherever and whenever I wished to do so. He was my friend; and he himself would give orders to the brethren who were to guide me through the monastery.

At the age of six he had come to Tashi-lunpo, and for nineteen years he had held his present high office. In Tibet he was called Panchen Rinpoche (the Precious Teacher), while the Dalai Lama in Lhasa was called Gyalpo Rinpoche (the Precious King). These two titles themselves indicate the difference between the spiritual and the worldly power. The Dalai Lama has greater political power, for he rules over all Tibet, with the exception of the Province of Chang, which is under the rule of the Labrang in Tashi-lunpo, i. e., of the Tashi Lama. But the latter is regarded as holier and more proficient in the holy scriptures. The Dalai Lama, who had fled during the British campaign, in 1903, was still absent at the time of my visit; and the Tashi Lama was therefore the mightiest man in Tibet. This explains why England tried to win his friendship and confidence by inviting him to India, where he received a lasting impression of the power and splendour of empire.

The two prelates stood in a certain reciprocal relationship to each other. The Tashi Lama acted as a tutor to the infant Dalai Lama, instructing him in the religion and the contents of the sacred scriptures. Similarly, the Dalai Lama cared for a new Tashi Lama. The Tashi Lama was an incarnation of the Dhyani Buddha, of the present age of the world (Amitabha), but represented also the supernatural rebirth of the reformer Tsong Kapa; for the latter, too, a contemporary of Tamerlane, was an incarnation of Amitabha Buddha. The Dalai Lama, on the other hand, was an incarnation of the Bodhisattva Avalokiteshvara, whose Tibetan name is Chenreisig, the representative of Sakyamuni Buddha, the patron in our age of all living things and of the Buddhistic church, and the patron saint of Tibet.

The Tibetans thus believe in the transmigration of souls (metempsychosis). When a Tashi Lama dies, and his soul—i. e., the soul of Amitabha Buddha—begins its wanderings, it lodges in a boy born simultaneously with the death of the Holy One.

Inquiries are made all over the Lamaist world. Several years may pass before all the replies come in. The parents must particularly give information as to whether any miracles or omens accompanied the birth of their boys. Hundreds of replies come to Tashi-lunpo, and are investigated. The most plausible ones are selected, and tested again. In the end, there remain only a few, among which the true, new Tashi Lama must certainly be. The names of the boys are written on strips of paper and placed in a covered golden bowl, and a high Lama picks out a strip at random. The name thereon indicates the holy successor to the throne of Amitabha Buddha.

The audience came to an end at last, and I bade Mohammed Isa produce the Burroughs Wellcome aluminum medicine-kit. We had polished it till it shone like silver, and had wrapped it in yellow silk cloth. It pleased the Grand Lama. I had great difficulty, later, in explaining to two medical lamas how to employ the remedies in various illnesses. Everything had to be written down in Tibetan. We retained a sufficient supply of the more valuable medicines for our own needs.

Finally, the Tashi Lama bade me farewell, with the same friendly smile. Neither he himself nor I believed he was a god. But it was a noble and gentle human being who followed me with his eyes, until the door closed behind me.

Thereafter, all Shigatse talked of the unusual honour that had been bestowed upon a stranger. And upon returning to their homes, the pilgrims told of it in their valleys. It proved to be of great use to me at times, of greater value even than a passport. And I blessed the good Grand Lama, when the nomads, more than once, exclaimed: "Ah, you are the friend of the Tashi Lama!"

CHAPTER LIII

Our Experiences in Tashi-Lunpo and Shigatse

TASHI-LUNPO is a *gompa*, an "abode of solitude," or monastery. It is a cloister-and-temple town of at least a hundred separate houses, a labyrinth of whitewashed stone houses, with bands of red and black colour along the roofs. The houses are separated from one another by narrow lanes and steps. The Labrang, the "Vatican," with its beautiful façade, rises above them all, against a background of wild mountain-ridge, at the foot of which the monastery lies. In front of and below the Labrang is a row of five gilt-roofed pagodas, in Chinese style, mausoleums of departed Tashi Lamas. The monastery was founded in 1445. The mortuary pagoda of the first Grand Lama rises above the court where festivals are held. Its interior is dim. One can see the high pyramid-like *chorten* of silver and gold, set with precious stones, the sarcophagus of the late prelate. The dead man sits embedded in salt, for lamas must die in a sitting position, like that of Buddha.

From this tomb we went to the last resting-place of the third Tashi Lama. His name was Panchen Lobsang Palden Yishe. Amitabha Buddha dwelt incarnate in his body between the years 1737 and 1779. It was he who conducted lively negotiations with Warren Hastings, Governor-General of India, and in consequence was invited by the suspicious Emperor Chien Lung to Peking, where he died. A plate over the entrance of the tomb bears his name in brilliant colours.

The tomb of the fifth Tashi Lama, the gift of pilgrims, stands open. A string of nomads pass there and prostrate themselves on the wooden floor, before the row of idols, holy offering-bowls, and lighted tapers on the altar-table in front of the sarcophagus.

Outside each mausoleum is a court, from which a wooden staircase, in three flights, leads up to an open veranda, or entrance-hall, the walls of which bear paintings of the four spiritual kings. They are pictured as wild beasts and dragons, surrounded by flames and clouds, their hands holding weapons and religious symbols. Solid doors, of red-lacquered wood, with yellow brass-work, open from this hall into the sepulchral chamber.

A jovial old man kept watch in the temple of Tsong Kapa. A carved representation of the reformer, smiling and many-coloured, as if rising from the petals of the lotus flower—indicative of his divine origin—was displayed in the large chamber. Tsong Kapa was the founder of the *Gelugpas,* the "sect of the virtuous," the "Yellow Caps," a large sect, to which all the most important monasteries and the chief lamas belong. He founded the Galdan, Brebung, and Sera, the large

PILGRIMS WORSHIPPING AT THE TOMB OF THE FIFTH TASHI LAMA

monasteries near Lhasa; he introduced celibacy; and he rests in Galdan, in a sarcophagus that is suspended in the air. The monks chant and mumble their religious hymns before him, beat drums, and tinkle brass bells. Two lamas appeared and offered me tea and present-greetings from His Holiness, who hoped that I would not tire myself.

It would take too long to relate all my experiences in Tashi-lunpo. I look back on that wonderful time with wonder and delight. One day, the Tashi Lama, seated on his pontifical throne, along the narrow side of the court of ceremonies, was listening to a theological disputation, in which he himself occasionally joined. After that there was a feast, for which the tables had been set. The Holy One was served tea from a pot of gold, the others from pots of silver. Then he descended the staircase to the Red Gallery, supported by two monks, a third one holding a yellow sunshade over him.

We looked into the dormitories, to see how the monks lived in their plain cells. And we descended into the kitchen beneath the Red Gallery, where tea for thirty-eight hundred monks was brewed in six enormous cauldrons. Loud signals were made with seashells as the hour for tea arrived. During my saunterings in the monastery-town, I sometimes saw the Tashi Lama walking in a procession to or from some sacred function. Once we entered the Kanjur-lhakang, a large hall, with an impluvium, in which the *Kanjur,* or holy scriptures, in a hundred and eight volumes, was housed. At long benches and tables, young lamas were being instructed by a Kampo-lama. There were four lamas of that degree in the monastery, but only two of the Yungchen degree. The young monks intoned rhythmically. Time and again a handful of rice was cast over them. For a few rupees they would chant an extra prayer for the peace of one's soul—and I did not fail to avail myself of the opportunity to buy such a song.

On February sixteenth, the Tashi Lama asked me to come to the Labrang to photograph him. He was just giving his blessing to a procession of pilgrim nuns. Again we conversed for nearly three hours, mostly on matters of geography. When we parted, he presented me with piles of goods made in Tibet, gold-embroidered cloth from China, gorgeous red hangings that still decorate my rooms, bowls and teacups of copper and silver, and finally a gilded image, wrapped in yellow silk, representing the Amitabha Buddha, "he who has an immeasurably long life." This last gift was a symbol of his wish that I might long survive.

Thus I wandered about daily in the monastery, making sketches and taking photographs. All the lamas were friendly and courteous. In all the corners and under the eaves there were bells. Falcon-feathers were attached to the tongues of these bells; and as the wind passed over the cloister-city, melodious chimes were heard.

The New-Year festivals are not limited to religious ceremonies; for the pilgrims are human beings, and they must be amused. One day the crowds betook themselves to a field outside Shigatse, where seventy gaily-attired horsemen galloped at full speed on a race-course, shooting at small targets with arrow and bow, all the while riding at a furious pace. After the game, I invited all the competitors to tea in my garden. One evening, my friend Ma celebrated the Chinese New Year in his *yamen,* with fireworks; and there were lanterns of tissue-paper, in the shape of big dragons and horses, which wound their way through the crowds.

The houses in Shigatse are white, with red and black bands at the top. The flat roofs are guarded by parapets. Like the temple-roofs, they are adorned with bundles of twigs and stubble, dressed up in cloth. These are supposed to drive away demons. In the yard, a large, red-eyed watch-dog, savage as a wolf, is tied by an iron chain.

THE WIFE OF DUKE KUNG GUSHUK AND SISTER-IN-LAW OF THE TASHI LAMA

The house of Kung Gushuk, the Duke, was the nicest we saw. There were rugs, couches, bookcases, altars, and tables in its rooms. The duke's wife was a handsome woman; and I had the honour of drawing her portrait.

When I was not in the monastery, I was busy sketching types from far and near. All kinds of persons came to our garden—mendicant nuns and friars, dancing-boys, and spies. One day a *lagba,* or corpse-cutter, paid me a visit. The despised caste of corpse-cutters live in the village of Gompa-sarpa, not far to the southwest of Tashi-lunpo. When a lama is dying, prayers are said. When death has come, the prayers for the dead are said. For three days the deceased is left in his cell. Then one or two brethren carry him to Gompa-sarpa. They strip the corpse and divide the clothes among themselves. The monks then hurry off, while the *lagbas* take charge of the body. They pass one end of a cord around its neck, the other end being fastened to a post in the ground. Then the corpse is pulled straight and skinned. The vultures are waiting for that moment, and in a few minutes the skeleton is laid bare. The bones are then crushed to powder in a mortar, and the bone-dust is mixed with the brains. The *lagbas* knead the mixture into balls, to be thrown to the vultures. Many monasteries keep sacred dogs, who take the place of the vultures. Laymen are treated about the same way. When my *lagba* related these customs, Mohammed Isa paled, and asked leave to retire.

I stayed in Shigatse forty-seven days. Gradually the warmth and hospitality toward me cooled. Many lamas were displeased with my frequent visits to the monastery; and the Chinese were ill-disposed toward me. The worst center of gossip in Shigatse, one where there was much talk of me, was the square where the Tibetan merchants had booths, and women vendors, in red head-dresses, were seated on the ground, with the Chinese, Ladakis, and Nepalis doing business in their own establishments. Spies in disguise would appear in my garden and lounge there all day long. Already on the fourteenth of February, I received a visit from a lama and an official from Lhasa. They told me that a scout-patrol of spies had sought me around the Dangra-yum-tso and the Ngangtse-tso for twenty-two days, finally getting on our track, and arriving in Shigatse thirty-six hours after us. That meant that we had been within a hair's-breadth of failure. Another party had been sent from Lhasa to intercept us.

Now the two gentlemen from Lhasa were seated in my tent. They declared that according to the treaty between Tibet and Great Britain, only three frontier-towns in Tibet were open to the "Sahibs," under certain conditions. These were Gyangtse, Yatung, and Gartok. I replied: "To begin with, I never signed that treaty. Secondly, I *am* already in Shigatse, thanks to your negligence. And, thirdly, I am the friend of the Tashi Lama, and thus inviolable."

They left, baffled. But they returned frequently, to keep informed about us, and to report to Lhasa. Or they would send their spies to watch us. But we ourselves kept disguised Ladaki spies spying on the spies of the Lhasa spies.

I heard no more from the Tashi Lama. For political reasons he had to be cautious. In the end, I had only one friend left in the country, Captain O'Connor, in Gyangtse. He was above political intriguing; but he helped me privately in every way. He exchanged my gold for silver; he sent me boxes of provisions; he forwarded my post to and from India; and he gave me a whole library of highly welcome literature. Our acquaintance was maintained solely through correspondence; but I shall never forget the gratitude I owe him.

I was burning with impatience to be off. Yet I stayed, day after day, in order to extort the most favorable conditions for my subsequent movements. One day I received a laconic letter from Gaw Daloi, China's representative in Gyangtse. He simply sent me a copy of a few clauses in the Anglo-Chinese treaty, one of which read: "No representatives or agents of any foreign power shall receive permission to visit Tibet." My reply ran something like this: "If you want information about me and my plans, you had better address yourself to Captain O'Connor, instead of sending me impertinent letters."

A new letter from Gaw Daloi said: "Under no condition may you go to Gyangtse."

"Certainly not," thought I; "I'll take good care not to!" But I answered: "Whatever treaties may have been made between Great Britain and Tibet do not concern me in the least; for I *am* in Tibet, and *our* arrangements must proceed from *that* point." Gaw Daloi answered: "I have received orders from my government to send you immediately across the Indian frontier, should you come to Gyangtse. My government would be greatly obliged to you for being so good as to return the same way you came."

If I had gone to Gyangtse, I should, of course, have stayed at O'Connor's house. A Chinese official threatening to arrest a guest of the British agency! In a letter to me, O'Connor treated the thought with derision.

Ma was in despair. He had been reprimanded by the Amban, Lien Darin, in Lhasa, for not having stopped me. The Lhasa authorities advised the monks of Tashi-lunpo to treat me coolly. An exchange of notes was now going on between Lhasa, Shigatse, Tashi-lunpo, Gyangtse, Peking, Calcutta, and London. I was hard pressed, the quarry of four governments. Yet I won out in the end.

On March fifth, Gaw Daloi advised me to write to Tang Darin, the Imperial Chinese Chief Commissioner in Lhasa, and to the Amban, Lien Darin, requesting, as a favour, to be allowed to travel through Gyangtse. This right-about-face implied a stratagem. I, therefore, wrote to Tang that because of my disinclination to act contrary to the wishes of the Chinese Government by travelling to Gyangtse, I would go toward the northwest, as soon as they provided me with yaks.

And, to Lien, I wrote: "If you want to get rid of me, you should facilitate my return. I shall never go to India. My servants are mountaineers, and they would die there. They are British subjects, and I am responsible for them."

On March fourth, I made my last visit to Tashi-lunpo. The monks *asked* me not to come any more. After March twelfth, a heavy silence fell upon us. Ma, Tsaktserkan, and all our other friends had disappeared. No one visited us now. We were isolated. All intercourse with us was forbidden. I felt like a prisoner in my own tent. As long as I was in Tibet, I was tabu to the English; and no one could touch me, as long as I kept still. But as soon as I moved, I would actually be a prisoner; for then I would be surrounded by an armed escort. The longer I tarried, the more amenable they would finally become. Thus a week passed; and at last Ma, the two gentlemen from Lhasa, and some officials from Shigatse-dsong came to me, desiring to know by which road I would return. "Along the Raga-tsangpo to its source, and through the country north of the Tsangpo," I answered. After a conference, they decided to accept my conditions and to take the responsibility upon themselves.

After more conferences, and after the receipt of a polite letter from Tang and an equally polite document from Lien, the old men softened. They visited me frequently in my garden, and equipped us with all that we needed. In the end, they also handed me a new passport for Tibet, asking me to indicate the points at which I intended to touch. But I took good care not to reveal my actual plans.

On March twenty-fifth, the number of inhabitants in my tent was suddenly augmented by Brown Puppy's delivery of four black puppies. I competed with the mother in the bestowal of affection, and rejoiced in the thought of future agreeable companions. The next day, I bade adieu to Ma, and gave him three poor horses, as a reward for his pains and as a token of my gratitude for his not having prevented my progress. After that, only two horses and one mule remained of the hundred and thirty animals with which we had left Leh. We also had a few mules and horses, purchased in Shigatse. But the bulk of our baggage was to be carried by hired yaks. An escort of two Chinese and two Tibetans, one from the Labrang and the other from Shigatse-dsong, was to accompany us. They brought their own men, mounts, and beasts of burden.

Early on the morning of the twenty-seventh, I sent Mohammed Isa with a farewell message to the Tashi Lama, who returned hearty greetings and regrets that the superior power of the Chinese had prevented him from being of such service to me as he had wished.

When we departed, a severe storm was coming from the west. No doubt the Tashi Lama was sitting at his small window, with field-glasses to his eyes. The waves of the Tsangpo were white-capped, and we had no easy time taking our horses across in the hide-boats.

THE HOLY LAKE AND THE DEVIL'S LAKE

CHAPTER LIV

Strange Monasteries—Walled-in Monks

I AND my men soon got to be on very friendly terms with our escort, and I did my best to weaken the vigilance of the four guards. I gave them cigarettes, trifling gifts, and silver coins.

The first result of this was that they made no objection to my advancing to the monastery of Tarting-gompa. Its *lhakang* (large divine hall) was most picturesque, in its subdued light, with its forty-eight red pillars, rising from a floor of large stone flags. The hospitable lamas of Tarting-gompa belonged to the heterodox *Pembo* sect. They

FOUR LAMAS READING THE PRAYERS FOR THE DEAD

had certain characteristics of their own. They swung their prayer-mills contrary to the prescribed direction; and when pilgrimaging to temples and holy mountains, they moved in a direction opposite to that of clock-hands. This, according to the *Gelugpas* (the Yellow Caps), was quite improper. However that may be, the view from their monastery, over magnificent mountains and wild valleys, was glorious.

It was in 1832, or seventy-five years before, that Yundung Sulting, a five-year-old nomad boy, came to Tarting-gompa, entered as a novice with the religious name of Namgang Lama, and rose, step by step, until he had attained the highest degree, when he became known as Namgang Rinpoche. The evening before our arrival, he had passed away, and his corpse was still in its cell. I went there with two of my men. An old couple sat in the court, splitting wood for the funeral-pile. He was to be cremated in the valley, after which his ashes were to be taken to Kang Rinpoche, the holy mountain of Kailas. We entered the cloister-cell. Four monks were seated there, reading the prayers for the dead all through three days and nights. The deceased old man, a cloth around his forehead, and a many-coloured crown on his skull, sat on his bed, stooping slightly. Before him on the bed stood a stool, with images and two lighted candles.

The four monks were dumbfounded at our entrance. Such sacrilege was unheard-of. But they said nothing. They mumbled their prayers without interruption. I stayed for a good while. I received a strange impression of the majesty of death. For seventy-five years Namgang Rinpoche had heard the chime of bells in the wind, and had seen the days and nights, winters and summers, come and go among those royal mountains. And now, at this very moment, his soul was liberated from the flesh, and had begun its migrations. And this moment, the one of supreme importance to his fate, had been disturbed by our arrival.

THE GOD OF THE DEAD

In Gandan-chöding, a convent with sixteen nuns, the dark, desolate temple-hall, with its six mighty, red pillars, afforded greater pleasure than observing the poor and dirty sisters, who were robed like lamas, and, like them, wore their hair short.

A most beautiful sight was the monastery of Tashi-gembe, the white town at the southern foot of the Transhimalaya. In its main court stood a throne for the Tashi Lama, who visits the temple once a year. The divine halls were rich in precious images of Buddha and gold ornaments. The library contained the hundred and eight folios of the *Kanjur* and the two hundred and thirty-five huge tomes of the *Tanjur,* enough to burden at least fifty mules. The big prayer-mill measured eleven feet in height, and its circumference was four times the span of my arms. A peg at the upper edge of a smaller prayer-

NUNS IN THE CONVENT OF GANDAN-CHÖDING

cylinder caused a bell to ring at every revolution of the cylinder. Year in and year out, two monks sat, from sunrise to midnight, and turned the prayer-mill. It made ten thousand revolutions a day; and it was covered with millions of prayers, written on thin paper. The monks themselves were saying prayers. They were in a trance. They roared, closed their eyes, threw themselves down, and were deaf to all remarks.

On the pillars hung cuirasses, suits of armour, standards, and temple-pennants, with tastefully-painted scenes from the lives of Buddha and the saints. On the altar-tables stood offering-bowls and

lighted tapers; and behind them sat Sakyamuni Buddha, dreaming, unfathomable, full of love of mankind. He seemed to have risen from
the petals of the lotus flower.

I found it hard to tear myself away from this enchanting temple.
Most of the day passed. The setting sun shed its luxuriant red light
through the windows of the
main temple-hall, the best-
lighted one I ever saw in Tibet.
The pillars were, as usual, red-
lacquered. The sun transmuted
them into transparent rubies.
Red-garbed monks sat on red
divans, and the shadows fell
dark behind them. The golden
images and the leaves of the
lotus flowers sparkled.

We continued our journey toward the west, along the northern shore of the Tsangpo, to the
village of Chaga, where a funny
iron-chain bridge, now dilapidated, spanned the river to the
monastery of Pinzoling. Immediately west of this point, the
Raga-tsangpo flowed into the
main river, the Tsangpo, or upper Brahmaputra. The latter
flowed from the south, through
a black, yawning portal in the

THE GIGANTIC CYLINDRICAL PRAYER WHEEL IN
TASHI-GEMBE

valley. I wished to obtain some measurements of the rivers at this point;
but the caravan had continued to the village of Tangma, on the Raga-
tsangpo. There the boat was assembled; and, with a Tibetan as oarsman, I drifted on the wild current, down to the confluence, whither some
of our people had proceeded with horses and provisions. My oarsman was a skillful hand, and wide-awake. He steered through seething foam, along narrow channels, between threatening cliffs. The escort,
uncertain of my purpose, followed along the bank. A few of the men
became sufficiently interested to ask permission to make a boat-trip

on the Tsangpo, which I willingly granted. We stayed there the entire day, and did not return to camp until dark. The bells on the Chinese horses, and the singing of the Ladakis, resounded melodiously in the narrow valley.

We rode on up the valley to the village of Lingö, where the My-chu River flows into the Raga-tsangpo. Two gigantic representations of Buddha are there hewn out on the face of a perfectly smooth, per-pendicular granite wall. I was astonished that the escort took us, not up the valley of the Raga-tsangpo, but northwards through that of the

SOME OF THE GOLDEN, RED AND YELLOW LACQUERED GODS IN THE
MONASTERY OF TASHI-GEMBE

My-chu. It extended from the main ridge of the Transhimalaya, just where I wanted to go. We went higher and higher. Almost daily we obtained a new set of yaks to carry the baggage. We passed *mani* chests, cairns, and streamers continually. We were on a pilgrim-route, a road that led to a monastery. There was much traffic. We met caravans, merchants, peasants, pilgrims, horsemen, mendicants. They all saluted us politely, with their tongues.

Riding among granite and slate rocks, and through the infinitely beautiful and wild My-chu Valley, we arrived at the large monastery, resembling a town of white houses, in the village of Tong. There our

Shigatse escort was replaced by a new set of guards. In the village of
Sirchung we were at a height of 13,700 feet. Among the inhabitants
was a twenty-year-old married woman, named Putin. She was unusually pretty and well set up.
Jealousy does not exist in Tibet.
It cannot arise where a wife generally has two or three husbands,
usually brothers. Marital fidelity
consequently does not amount to
much.

The rapids of the My-chu intoned their rushing songs in the
deep, beautiful valley. Eagles
soared between the mountain-walls,
rock-pigeons   cooed,   partridges
burred in the gravel, and wild ducks
quacked on the banks. I spent several hours at every new monastery.
That   of   Lehlung-gompa   was
among the largest. An account of

A GIGANTIC GRANITE BUDDHA NEAR LINGÖ AND
A MAN SITTING BELOW

all these monasteries would fill a book. Now and then we passed
picturesque bridges. The valley contracted to a narrow corridor, and
the dangerous road ran about two hundred feet above its base. Forced
into the cracks of the steep mountain-wall were iron and wooden plugs,
upon which slabs of schist were laid loosely. This shelf was only a foot
wide in spots, the abyss yawning below. All the tributary valleys that
we crossed on the way down from the Sela-la, broke through the
mountains on the eastern side of the valley.

We encamped in an expansion of the valley, where a bridge, built
on caissons, crossed the My-chu. In a small, steep glen, among the
mountains, west of the river, lay the strange monastery of Linga-gompa.
It consisted of about forty separate houses; and, like everything else
in this region, it was absolutely unknown to Europeans before my visit.
I rode up to it with two of my men. The sacred words, *om mani padme
hum,* were outlined in huge stone slabs on a dark slope. In the chief
temple-hall, or *dukang,* where mysterious twilight prevailed, where
temple-banners, standards, drums, gongs, and trombones adorned the
walls and pillars, and a faint light from an opening in the ceiling fell

on the images of gods, the monks were seated on divans, chanting a song that rose and fell in rhythmical waves.

On the point of a platform-like ridge of rock, the temple of Pesu towered. From its roof-terrace and windows we saw the abyss beneath us on three sides. The panorama seen from this roof was of a wild, bold beauty that resists any attempt at description. In the interior, too, there was an air of mystery. I ascended a steep flight of steps into a Hall of divine images, where the light, from an opening on the left, with a shutter creaking in the wind, fell on a whole row of medium-sized Buddha-figures. My companions had remained in an entrance-hall, and I was alone with the gods. Now and then a mouse ventured out of the dark, to feast on the contents of the offering-bowls on the altar-table. As the painted banners on the left stirred in the draught from the window, the features of the gods changed; and the sight of the squatting images, grinning at the marauding mice, was enough to make one fear ghosts.

MRS. PUTIN, IN THE VALLEY OF MY-CHU, WHO WAS SUPPOSED TO BE A BEAUTY

I found Linga-gompa so attractive that I tarried for several days. One day we walked up to the section of the monastery known as Samde-puk, and to the *dupkang* (hermit-cave) higher up, at the foot of a mountain-wall. It was really a hut, built of fair-sized stone blocks. It had no windows, and its entrance was walled up. A small chimney was visible on the roof; and near the ground there was an aperture in the wall, through which food was pushed in on a piece of board.

In this pitch-dark cell, a lama had been walled in for three whole years, cut off from communication with the world during all that time! He had come to Linga three years before, unknown and nameless. As the cave was unoccupied, he made the most binding and terrible of all monastic vows, namely, to let himself be immured there for the rest of his life. Another hermit had died shortly before, after spending twelve years within its walls. And before that, a monk had lived in its darkness for forty years! Indeed, in Tong, where there was a similar grotto, the monks told us of a hermit who had entered the darkness quite young, and who had lived there for sixty-nine years. Sensing the approach of death, this hermit could not resist the longing to see the sun once more; and so he gave the signal that required the monks to restore him to freedom. But the aged man was stone-blind; and he had hardly got out into the sunshine, when he crumpled up like a

SINGING LAMAS IN ONE OF THE TEMPLE-HALLS OF LINGA-GOMPA

rag and died. Not one of the lamas then present had been among the living when he had entered the cave.

And now we stood outside such a cave at the monastery of Linga. The hermit who dwelled therein bore the honorary title of Lama Rinpoche (the holy monk). He was thought to be a man of about forty. He meditated and dreamt of Nirvana. In return for his voluntary penance, his soul would be absolved from the pains of transmigration, and would enter the everlasting rest—annihilation—directly.

Every morning, a bowl of *tsamba,* and perhaps a small pat of butter, were shoved in to him. He got water from a spring that bubbled in the interior of the cave. Every morning, the empty bowl was withdrawn and refilled. Every sixth day, he got a pinch of tea, and twice a month a few sticks, which he could ignite with a fire-steel. Should the lama who brought him his daily food address him through the opening, he would bring down upon himself eternal damnation. He was therefore silent. Should the immured man speak to the serving-brother, he would sacrifice all credit for his years of solitary meditation. If the serving-brother found the bowl untouched when he pulled it out, he understood that the recluse was either ill or dead. He would then push the bowl back again and walk away in dejection. If the bowl remained untouched the following day, and altogether for six days, the cave was broken open; for then it was safe to assume

SAMDE-PUK, A PART OF LINGA-GOMPA, SITUATED HIGH UP IN THE VALLEY

that the recluse had died. The dead man was then carried out, and his body destroyed by fire, like those of the saints.

"Can he hear us?" I asked the monks from Samde-puk.

"No," they replied; "the walls are too thick."

I could hardly tear myself away from the place. In there, only a few feet away from me, was a man, possessed of will-power compared to which all else became insignificant. He had renounced the world; he was already dead; he belonged to eternity. The soldier going toward inevitable death is a hero; but he does it once. The Lama

Rinpoche's physical life persisted through decades, and his sufferings lasted until death liberated him. He had an unquenchable longing for death.

The Lama Rinpoche fascinated me irresistibly. Long afterwards, I would think of him of nights; and even to-day, though eighteen years have passed, I often wonder if he is still alive in his cave. Even if I had had the power and the permission, I would not for the life of me have liberated him and led him out into the sunshine. In the presence of such great will-power and holiness, I felt like an unworthy sinner and a coward.

I imagined seeing him before me, as for the first, last, and only time in his life he walked in a solemn procession, accompanied by the lamas of Linga, up the valley along the road we had just taken. Everybody was silent. He felt the sun's heat and saw the bright fields on the slopes. He saw his own shadow and those of the other marchers on the ground. Nevermore was he to see a shadow move; for he was going to live in impervious, solitary shade, until he died. For the last time he saw the sky and the drifting clouds, the mountain-peaks and their shimmering snow-fields.

He beheld the open door of the cave. He entered, with the rag mat which was to be his bed. Prayers were offered. The door was locked; and outside the door a wall of large stones was built, reaching to the roof of the grotto. Was he standing in there, catching the

THE SACRED LAMA WALKING TO THE CAVE WHERE HE IS TO BE IMMURED FOR THE REST OF HIS LIFE

last glimpses of light of the fleeting day? And when the last crevice between the blocks of stone had been filled, darkness descended inexorably upon him. The serving-brothers, having accomplished their labour of love, walked down to Linga, silent and grave.

The walled-in man heard no sound but that of his own voice, as he uttered his prayers. Nights were long. But he did not know when the sun went down and the night began. For him there was only darkness unrelieved. He went to sleep; and when he was rested, he awoke, knowing not whether the day had dawned. Summer would

near its end. He would become aware of that, because of the falling temperature and the moisture. Winter came, and he froze; spring and summer approached, and the rising temperature afforded him a sensation of well-being. A new year began its course, and one year succeeded another. He was constantly saying his prayers and dreaming of Nirvana. Gradually his grasp on time relaxed, he was not aware of how slowly days and nights wore on, for he was always seated on his mat, lost in dreams of Nirvana. He knew that the Kingdom of Heaven could be entered only at the cost of tremendous self-control.

A LAST GLIMPSE OF DAYLIGHT

He grew old, unconscious of the fact. For him, time was static; and yet his life seemed to him like a second, in comparison with the eternity of Nirvana. Nobody visited him, except perhaps a spider or a centipede that sometimes ran over his hand. His clothes disintegrated, his nails grew, his hair became long and tangled. He did not notice that his complexion turned quite white, and that his vision weakened, until the light of his eyes went out. He yearned for deliverance. And one day there would come a knock on his door, made by the only friend that could visit him in the cave. It would be Death, who had come to lead him out of the dark and to take him away to the great light in Nirvana.

CHAPTER LV

New Transhimalaya Passes—Mohammed Isa's Last Journey

ON April seventeenth, we rode to the village of Govo, the last one where people still lived in stone huts. Then the black tents, the grazing black yaks, and the white sheep on the lofty alpine fields were seen once more.

On the left rose a mountain, with a strange, vertical cave, in the lower opening of which dwelt two mendicant lamas and two nuns from Nepal. They were the servitors of two hermits whose caves were higher up in the mountain. A natural, spiral flight of stairs, slippery and dangerous, led up to the alcove-like grotto, where Gunsang Ngurbu, a centenarian hermit, had dedicated himself to meditation. To approach him, we had to remove a thin slate plate, that barred the entrance to his cave like a shutter. But the Nepalis begged me, by all that was holy, not to disturb the aged man; and so I contented myself with peeping into the hall of the cave through a chink beneath the shutter. Nothing was visible but two images. I heard the old man mumbling his prayers. It must have been cold for him up there in winter. But at least he saw the sun, the stars, and the whirling snow; for his rocky dwelling opened out upon the valley. But he might never speak to a soul; and he was not even aware of the fact that he had a neighbour in another cave.

Not far from there we came to the pass of Chang-la-Pod-la, 18,270 feet high, a pass of first importance on the Transhimalayan continental watershed, forty-three miles west of the Sela-la. This was a significant new discovery. We crossed the Transhimalaya and the large white spot north of the Tsangpo for the second time. It was my dream to fill it out, step by step, as far as its western end.

We proceeded toward the northwest. I could not discover the intentions of the escort. They merely led us in that direction. But I could not have wished for a more favourable route. One of the chief members of the escort had been a lama in Tong, but had been expelled from the brotherhood because of his love for a woman.

On the other side of the pass, we were again in regions that have no outlet to the Indian Ocean. The waters here emptied into the lake of Dangra-yum-tso. I hoped to penetrate to its shores. A cairn with streamers stood at the point from which one could first see the holy mountain of Targo-gangri, which Nain Sing, the Indian pundit, sighted from the north. No European had ever seen it. The Tibetans prostrated themselves there, in worship of the mountain.

At the next change of escort, we got five old men and a large number of others as guardians. They wanted to take us back toward the Raga-tsangpo, but I induced them to continue northwestward. They had eleven tents and about one hundred yaks. I used to look in, to make sketches of the old men.

We approached the sacred mountain, with its enormous, snowy peaks and its five visible glacier-tongues. A new, unknown range, of grandiose dimensions, and with perpetual snow on its ridge, towered in the west-southwest. We pitched our Camp No. 150 at the foot of the Targo-gangri and on the shore of the Targo-tsangpo, which flows into the Dangra-yum-tso, two short days' march further on. So far everything had gone well. But at this very point, twenty armed men appeared, Hlaje Tsering having sent them to check our progress to the Holy Lake. Their leader was Lundup Tsering, known to us from Ngangtse-tso, where he had been in Hlaje Tsering's suite. They declared that on no condition were we to go to the lake. But not very far from our camp, on the right-hand side of the valley, there was a red, rocky promontory, from the crest of which the lake was said to be visible. I promised to refrain from visiting its shores, provided they let me climb the red promontory. They did not object to this. But when, on April twenty-eighth, we were on the point of departing, the district (Largäp) chieftain appeared, with sixty horsemen, in red and colourful attire, and mounted on white, black, and bay horses. They gathered round us, brawled and shrieked among themselves, and would not allow me to take one step from the camp. We negotiated the whole day, and in the end they yielded. I rode to the lake with two companions, and saw it shimmering blue in the north, like a sword-blade.

Thereupon we walked toward the southeast, in order to cross the Transhimalaya a third time. On the way there, we discovered the Shuru-tso, a lake of moderate size, that was still frozen. On May sixth, we crossed the Transhimalaya again, this time by the pass of Angden-la (18,500 feet). It was situated fifty-two miles west of the pass of Chang-la-Pod-la. I had once more succeeded in making a part of the large white spot mine. The view in both directions was magnificent. Behind us, in the north, we could still see the Targo-gangri, and in the south the chalk-white crest of the Himalayas.

We were on our way to the Raga-tsangpo. One evening, old Guf-faru was reported ill. He was lying in his tent, and appeared to be dying. He had already asked his son to be ready with the shroud. The old man had terrible stomach-pains; but when I prescribed fomen-tations, he told me to go home and lie down. Mohammed Isa nearly choked with laughter, and the others squirmed in paroxysms of mirth around the death-bed. At length I gave him opium, and the next morning he was as lively as an eel.

On May the eleventh, we reached the Raga-tsangpo in a whirling snow. The little puppies, travelling in a basket, snatched surprisedly after the snowflakes. We were on a route that Ryder and his com-panions had previously mapped down. But during the eighty-three-day journey to the Manasarovar, I was able to travel the entire distance, except for two and a half days, over new, unknown routes.

The two chiefs in Raga-tasam were obdurate. They showed me the orders received from the Devashung. The gist of them was that from here I was to go by no other route than the *tasam,* i.e., the main caravan-road to Ladak, as the Ryder expedition had done. I wrote to Tang Darin and Lien Darin in Lhasa for permission to go, by way of the Teri-nam-tso, Nganglaring-tso, and Manasarovar, to India. I entrusted Tundup Sonam and Tashi with the difficult task of taking my letters, on foot, to Ma, in Shigatse, two hundred miles distant. They were then to rejoin us.

We did not hurry, not wishing to get too far ahead of them. We stayed in the place one week. As late as May fifteenth, the tempera-ture at night sank to −15°. Contrary to the wishes of the Tibetans, we wended our way to the huge mountain-group of Chomo-uchong, with its wild nature and icy winter cold. Coming to its other side, we stayed one day in the entrance to the Basang Valley. From there, it was but one day to Saka-dsong, the residence of the Governor. Instead of going that way, I wished to make a more southerly detour to the point where the Chaktak-tsangpo emptied into the large Tsangpo.

This wish was granted by the Tibetans, on condition that Mohammed Isa, with the bulk of the caravan, travelled to Saka-dsong by the main road.

On the evening before we separated, the Ladak-men danced around their fire, and Mohammed Isa played the guitar. On the morning of May twenty-seventh, the caravans departed in their respective directions. Mohammed Isa and I were the only ones left. We were on horseback, and as usual I gave him my orders. Then we said good-bye. My splendid caravan-leader appeared to be in the best of condition, as he galloped off to catch up with the others. It was the last time I gave him orders.

I myself overtook the section in charge of Robert and Tsering. Our excursion turned out very profitable. Using our boat, we measured the volume of water in the two rivers, and encamped in the region of Takbur, after four days' work. On May thirty-first, we were to make the last day's journey to Saka-dsong. But early in the morning, a savage and hard-hearted chief arrived at the camp, with a group of hirelings. He flogged the Tibetans who had served us, and ordered them to depart, together with their horses, which we had hired. We ourselves were to be detained three months as his prisoners, and were not to get any provisions. I sent one of my men secretly to Saka-dsong, with a message to Mohammed Isa, to send us five horses. Then I called the chief to my tent. He declared that I had no right to travel by any other road than the *tasam*. I warned him not to put on airs. I could, if it pleased me to do so, commend his head to my friends, the mandarins, in Lhasa. That aroused his fury, and he rushed up and drew his sword to deal me a blow. But as I remained seated, without displaying any fear, he desisted, and took himself off. He returned in the evening, with men and yaks, declaring that the way to Saka-dsong was open to us.

On June the first, in the morning, a few of our men arrived, with five horses, and a message from Mohammed Isa that all was well in his camp. We broke camp. It was a long way. Being detained by my work, as usual, I arrived at the camp long after the others. Guffaru and the whole crowd welcomed me.

"But where is Mohammed Isa, who is generally on hand?" I inquired.

"He lies in his tent; he has been ill all day."

I knew that he frequently had headaches; so I went calmly to my tent, to have supper. It was already dark, when Robsang came to tell me that the sick man did not reply when spoken to. I then hurried to his tent. His mouth was distorted; and his pupils, too, showed that he had had a stroke. The others, whom I now questioned thoroughly, told me that he had collapsed at noon, and had lost his speech after a few hours. An oil-lamp was burning at his head, where his brother Tsering sat weeping. I spoke his name, and he made a weak attempt to move his head. I whispered to Robert that he would not live to see another sunrise, and Robert was terrified. The only thing we could do was to put ice on his head and hot-water bottles at his feet.

But it was all in vain. His hour had come. At nine o'clock in the evening, the death-struggle began. His feet and hands grew cold; his body shook with ague. His rattling breathing grew fainter, and stopped; but after a minute, the last breath came, and Mohammed Isa was dead.

I uncovered before the majesty of death. The Lamaists mumbled their prayers in their own language, and the Mohammedans said their *La illaha il Allah.* Guffaru bound the dead man's chin, to keep the lower jaw in place, and covered his face with a white cloth. Tsering wept without restraint, beat his brow and threw himself to and fro. I tried to quiet him; but finally we had to carry him to his tent, where at length he fell asleep.

The Mohammedans converted the tent into a chapel, and five of them kept vigil. At midnight I repaired thither. There he lay, the giant, royally straight, and with a quiet smile on his lips. His face was pallid, but bronzed from all the storms of the Chang-tang and the sunny Tibetan days.

June the second was a Sunday. That day the corpse was washed, wrapped in Guffaru's shroud and a grey blanket, placed on a rude bier, and carried by eight Mohammedans to the funeral-place which the Saka-dsong authorities had placed at our disposal. My men of the Lamaist faith were still working at the grave. The procession was a simple one. I walked immediately behind the bier, then came Robert and a few of our retainers. Tsering stayed in his tent, lost in sorrow. Some Tibetans were abroad to watch us. They had never before witnessed such a ceremony, their custom being to throw their dead to wild animals. The pall-bearers sang a funeral-dirge. They walked very slowly, and rested twice—their burden was so heavy.

The corpse was lowered into the grave, with its face toward Mecca. It was deposited in a side-chamber, so as not to be unduly weighed down by earth and sand. When the grave was filled, I stepped forward and thanked Mohammed Isa for his constant fidelity.

Then we returned to our tents, silent and sad. I wrote on a slate slab the English names of the Europeans[1] whom Mohammed Isa had served for thirty years before he came to me to die on June 1, 1907, at the age of fifty-three. This writing, together with his name in Arabic characters, and an *om mani padme hum* (in order to make the grave sacred to the Tibetans, too), was then incised in the stone erected over his head. A small slab was placed at the side, where Mohammedans happening by could kneel to offer a prayer for the dead.

Already, on June third, the Mohammedans and the others asked for a sheep, for a feast in honour of their caravan-leader. And then came the realization of our loss. We missed him bitterly.[1]

Nostalgia seized everybody; and it was moving to see the ardour of the Ladak-men, as they sat by the camp-fires, fashioning shoes for their wives and children back home. Robert, too, longed for his mother, wife, and brothers. But, more than anybody else, I longed for the unknown country north of the Tsangpo, the upper Brahmaputra. If we had only been permitted to depart at once; But a whole week was needed for negotiations with the Tibetans about my route. After many "ifs" and "ands," they granted my request to take the northern route to Nyuku.

Guffaru was appointed successor to the late leader; and I told my men that whoever did not show him the same obedience as that accorded to Mohammed Isa, would be dismissed instantly. The dead man's belongings were sealed in two boxes, to be delivered eventually to his widow. Of money we found only ten rupees. This was proof of the honest handling of the funds with which he had been entrusted.

On June seventh we departed. I rode up to the grave and paid my last respects. Soon the hillocks obscured our view of the grave, and it was left in the care of the great solitude.

[1] Captain Rawling, who died as Brigadier-General at the eleventh hour of the World War, wrote an epitaph for Mohammed Isa in the *Geographical Journal*, 1909, p. 442.

CHAPTER LVI

The Discovery of the Source of the Brahmaputra

OUR road led us past the monastery of Targyaling-gompa. The imperious monks declared they would receive us with bullets, if we dared to visit their sanctuary. I sent them word that they need not worry, we had seen Tashi-lunpo and had no use for their trumpery monastery.

Nyuku was ruled by a decent *gova*, who, without fuss, permitted me to ride up to the Kilung-la, a pass 17,400 feet high, in a range that branches off from the Transhimalaya. From there we viewed several of the high, snowy peaks of the Lunpo-gangri, the same that the Ryder expedition had triangulated from the Tsangpo Valley. I was tempted to continue to the main ridge. But I had promised the *gova* not to proceed beyond the pass; and, with aching heart, I again had to forego exploring great reaches of the unknown country.

On June seventeenth, we encamped in the valley of Dambak-rong. Then we heard bells tinkling out on the road. A horseman came galloping up to my tent, dismounted, and handed me a letter. On the seal I read with a beating heart the English words: "Imperial Chinese Mission, Tibet." Thus I held my sentence in my hand. All my men, who were longing to get home to Ladak and hoping that we would not be delayed by any extensive excursions, gathered before the tents. The letter was from Tang Darin. It was polite in form, but its contents may be summarized thus: "You go straight to Ladak without excursions to the north or in any other direction!" I imparted this message to my men. They walked back to their tents in silence. Now the return home seemed nearer than before. These inexorable mandarins excited my anger, and I decided to exercise all my ingenuity to outwit them. The farther we moved west, the larger were the stretches of the unknown land we left behind us. But in some way I would manage to get there.

Tundup Sonam and Tashi, who had gone to Shigatse, happened to return that very evening. Having fulfilled their mission, they hurriedly began their return journey. But one evening, not far from Shigatse, they were attacked by robbers, who, covering them with guns, robbed them of everything but the clothes they wore. By mere chance the bandits overlooked thirty silver coins which one of my men had concealed at the back of his girdle. Terror-stricken, they afterwards imagined seeing a robber in every shadow, every stone. They finally reached us, tired out, but happy. I gave them large rewards for their service. Rumours of Mohammed Isa's death had already come to them on the way.

A strange sickness gripped the four little puppies, which had just about become pleasant tent-companions for me. Within one week they died, all four; and Brown Puppy and I were again alone in the tent.

At the monastery-village of Tradum, we touched again upon the main road (*tasam*). The authority there lay in the hands of a *gova* who had once been a lama, but had been expelled from the fraternity of the Yellow Caps because of a love-affair. He was a great rascal. But sometimes it pays to have rascals as friends. I promised him a big sum, in silver, if he would let me have a little peep into northern Nepal. "With pleasure," said he; and he even let me hire some of his horses. Had I been a little more suspicious and cautious, I would have taken alarm at this unusual obligingness. First of all, it was risky to enter a country where Europeans were forbidden to travel, and where, in case they were admitted, they could only travel by certain routes and if provided with proper passports. Secondly, I would really be leaving Tibet upon entering Nepal, and the Tibetans might quite properly have stopped me at the frontier when I returned.

Notwithstanding this, I departed on June twentieth, and spent the night at Likse-gompa, a monastery on the south bank of the Tsangpo. Of the sights in that small monastery I will only mention the holy dog, who lived on the monks' excrement and ate their bodies when they died; and the drinking-vessels of the priests, which were human skulls that shone like ivory.

Two days later, we rode up to the 15,290-foot pass of Kore-la, in the Himalayas, the water-parting between the Brahmaputra (Tsangpo) and the Ganges, the two sacred rivers. The incline from the Brahmaputra to the pass was almost unnoticeable, the difference in altitude amounting to only 315 feet. It would thus be possible to dig a canal and force the upper Brahmaputra to become a tributary of the Ganges. As it is, these two rivers do not meet until they come to the delta of the Hugli.

The panorama from the pass was wonderful. In the south, the ridges and valleys of Nepal gleamed in the sunshine. In the north lay the Transhimalaya, bathed in sunlight. But the snowy peaks of the Himalayas were concealed by clouds; and of the Dhaulagiri (26,830 feet) nothing was to be seen.

We wandered down into Nepal. Down we clambered, to the valley of the Kali Gandak, a tributary of the holy Ganges, doing it afoot rather than topple over the horses' heads. The air grew warmer, respiration became easier, and we saw more and more plants that could not stand the Tibetan climate. When 2,800 feet below the pass, we made our camp for the night, near the village of Nama-shu, in the garden of Lo Gapu, the "King of the Land South," a prince of a state on the border, under the suzerainty of the Maharajah in Katmandu. Temperate winds fanned the luxuriant tree-tops: it was like being in Paradise. Two of Lo Gapu's men came to invite us to visit their master, in his residence, farther down the valley. But I declined. He might have made us his prisoners. By the next morning, we were mounted and on our way back to the Kore-la. But rumours of my Nepal visit reached even to the ears of the Maharajah. More than a year afterwards, when my family and friends feared greatly for my life, the Swedish Crown Prince met the Maharajah of Nepal in London. On that occasion, the Maharajah told of my visit to his state, and intimated that my apprehension at the time was groundless. But by that time I had long since been back in Tibet.

The *gova* of Tradum having got his horses back, together with the promised reward, we joined Guffaru and the caravan, and proceeded toward the west and northwest, along the southern bank of the Tsangpo, through unfamiliar country. At the monastery of Namla-gompa, we crossed the Tsangpo, which was 2,900 feet wide there, and resembled a lake. A few days later, we reached Tuksum, a village, and then assisted a lama across the river. The Tsangpo carried 3,240 cubic feet of water per second at this point. Five girls from Kham, in the extreme east of Tibet, paid us a visit at one of our camps. They had made a pilgrimage to the holy mountain of Kang Rinpoche, carrying their packs on their backs, and assisted only by staffs in their hands. They subsisted by begging their way from tent to tent.

I now approached one of the important geographical problems I wanted to solve. I had hoped to be the first white man to penetrate to the source of the Brahmaputra, and to determine its place on the map! In 1865, Nain Sing, the accomplished Indian pundit, had journeyed past, on the great caravan-road from Ladak to Lhasa. He was aware that the river came from glaciers in the southwest, but he had never gone there. In 1904, Ryder and his expedition went the same way; and his route ran thirty miles north of the source of the river. In order to solve the problem, I had first of all to measure the volume of water in the rivers forming the Tsangpo-Brahmaputra. This had to be done on a clear day, and, as nearly as possible, at the same time. I discovered that the Kubi-tsangpo, one of these rivers, was three and a half times as large as all the others combined. The point was, therefore, to follow the Kubi-tsangpo, the source of which must also be that of the Brahmaputra.

But I first sent Guffaru, with the caravan, along the main road, to the tent-village of Tokchen, not far from the northeastern shore of the Holy Lake. Only Robert, three Ladakis, and three Tibetans accompanied me. The latter were familiar with the region. They were black, dressed in sheepskin coats, and carried large muskets on their shoulders. In my diary I call them the Three Musketeers.

We followed the Kubi-tsangpo toward the southwest. South and southwest, a world of gigantic peaks towered, black, but covered with perpetual snow, pointed like wolves' teeth, mighty glacier-tongues lying between them. Higher and higher we went. Here and there we found thin bark, from birches or other trees in Nepal, which had been carried by the wind across the Himalayas. The Three Musketeers became nervous, when they observed me looking through the theodolite. They asked if it was I who kept the rain away; but I assured them that I longed as eagerly as they for rain, for the sake of the grass and the animals.

The higher we got, the mightier the nine wild, snowy peaks of the Kubi-gangri rose above us. Late one evening, intensely blue-white flashes of lightning flamed in the south; and the mountain-tops stood out pitch-black against the light background, as though cut from black paper. Holy mountains, where the Brahmaputra, the "Son of Brahma," is born! The river runs through the greater part of southern Tibet, breaks through the Himalayas, irrigates the fields of the peasants in Assam, and mingles its tremendous volume with the waters of the Ganges in the Hugli delta.

On July thirteenth, we rode up to the highest point of an enormous old moraine. From there we had an astounding view over the gigantic mountains, with their wild, black rocks, domes, and passes, their *névé* basins of perpetual snow, their huge glaciers, with dark, ribbon-like moraines on the surface and blue-green fairy-grottoes in the ice. Be-

THE GIGANTIC KUBI-GANGRI MOUNTAINS, ETERNALLY COVERED WITH SNOW
AND LARGE GLACIERS

low us was the lower part of the glacier that fed the largest of all the source-brooks of the Kubi-tsangpo, the one from the Langa-chen mountain-masses. Here was the source of the Brahmaputra, and here the altitude was 15,950 feet.

Their task fulfilled, I dismissed the Three Musketeers and gave them their wages. The whole excursion had cost thirty-five dollars! Who would not, at so low a price, have the glory of discovering the source of one of the most famous rivers on earth! The three guides thought I was mad to give them so much silver, after a ride of only a few days. And as to the glory, I am proud to share it with Nain Sing and Ryder, who travelled in these regions, even if they did not reach the source itself.

During the following days, we continued westwards; crossed, in the Tamlung-la pass, the watershed between the Brahmaputra and the Holy Lake; saw to our left the mountains, the Ganglung-gangri (where the real source of the Satlej is situated) and the high, arched peak of Gurla-mandata; followed the river of Tage-tsangpo, or Langchen-kamba, the "elephant river" (which is the upper part of the Satlej and the largest of all running waters that empty into the Holy Lake); stopped for a short while on its shore, at the miracle-working spring which, like that of Lourdes, heals the sick and protects against all kinds of evils, including famine, drought, and attacks of robbers; sighted, to the northwest, the Kang Rinpoche, the Kailas of the Hindus, with the paradise of Siva at its top, the holiest mountain of the Tibetans; and, finally, got a glimpse, at its foot, of a corner of the holy lake of Tso-mavang, the Manasarovar of the Hindus.

In Tokchen we were all assembled again. I made an important change in the caravan there. Thirteen men, under Guffaru's command, were sent straight home to Ladak, with all my superfluous luggage and three hundred pages of letters to various friends of mine. The most important of these letters was to Colonel Sir James Dunlop-Smith. I asked him to send me my post, six thousand rupees, revolvers, provisions, etc., to Gartok, where I expected to arrive in a month and a half. The remaining twelve men were to go with me. Tsering became their leader. On July twenty-sixth, our ways parted. Guffaru, with his thirteen yaks and his little troop, went homeward. Many tears were shed at parting. The division of the caravan led the Tibetans to think that we would reunite in a few days, as on the former occasion.

I went southwestward with the others, and encamped on the shore of the Manasarovar, near the convent of Serolung-gompa, the first of the eight convents which are planted along the road of the pilgrims, and set like precious stones in a holy bracelet.

CHAPTER LVII

Manasarovar, the Holy Lake

HOLY, holy, holy, is the Tibetans' Tso-mavang, or Tso-rinpoche, the Manasarovar of the Hindus, Brahma's soul. A garland of mountains rises on its banks; and golden eagles, from their nests below the permanent snow-fields on Kailas in the north and the Gurla-mandata in the south, contemplate its turquoise-blue surface, upon which the faithful from India see Siva, descended from his paradise, circling about in the form of a white swan. This lake has been celebrated for thousands of years in ancient religious hymns. In that part of the "Skandha Purana" entitled "Manasa-khanda" it says:

"When the earth of Mana-sarovara touches anyone's body, or when anyone bathes therein, he shall go to the paradise of Brahma; and he who drinks its waters shall go to the heaven of Siva, and shall be released from the sins of a hundred births; and even the beast who bears the name of Mana-sarovara shall go to the paradise of Brahma. Its waters are like pearls. There is no mountain like Himachala (Himalaya), for in it are Kailas and Mana-sarovara; as the dew is dried up by the morning sun, so are the sins of mankind dried up at the sight of Himachala."

Not without a sense of reverence did I encamp on its shores. I wanted to examine this lake; investigate its hydrographic relations to the Satlej (that being an old, moot question); measure its depth, which had not hitherto been done; and thus, by deeds, celebrate its blue-green waves. On its waters, we were 15,200 feet above sea-level. The lake is oval-shaped, its northern part swollen out. Its diameter is about fifteen miles.

And now we were to venture on the Holy Lake. We waited over July twenty-sixth and twenty-seventh, but the wind was too strong. Our Tibetans cautioned us. We would be sucked into its depths and perish. On the evening of the twenty-seventh, the wind subsided, and I decided to row across the lake during the night. I took a compass-

461

MY LIFE AS AN EXPLORER

bearing on the opposite (western) shore, and directed my course toward
S 59° W. Shukur Ali and Rehim Ali were at the oars. We took
along a lead-line, speedometer, lantern, and food for two days. The
smoke from the camp-fire rose perpendicularly toward the stars, as
we pushed off. "They will *never* reach the other shore of the lake,
the lake-god will pull them down," said our Tibetans. And Tsering
shared their fears. It was nine o'clock. The dying swell sounded
melodiously against the shore. After only twenty minutes of steady
rowing, the light from the camp-fire vanished; but the swell on the
shore was still faintly audible, far away. Otherwise, only the splashing of the oars and the singing of the oarsmen disturbed the silence.

Midnight was approaching. The whole sky flamed up blue-white,
from sheet-lightning behind the mountains in the south. For a fraction
of a second it was as bright as at high noon. The reflection of the moon
swung silver-white on the sheeny water. The depth was already two
hundred and ten feet. My oarsmen were awe-struck. They sang no
more.

In the light of the lantern, I read off the soundings and the instruments, and made my notes. A fairylike atmosphere surrounded us.
In the middle of the night, in the middle of a lake as sacred to hundreds of millions of Asiatics as the Sea of Gennesaret to the Christians! Though the holiness of the Manasarovar is thousands of years
older than the veneration accorded to the lake of Tiberias, Capernaum,
and the Saviour.

The hours of the night passed slowly. Dawn showed faintly in the
east. The heralds of the new day peeped out above the mountains.
Feather-light clouds took on rose-tints; and their counterparts in the
lake seemed to be gliding over rose-gardens. The sun-rays struck the
peak of the Gurla-mandata, and it shimmered in purple and gold.
Like a cloak of light, the reflection clothed the eastern mountain-
slope. A girdle of clouds, half-way up the Gurla, cast its shadow on
the slope.

The sun rose, sparkling like a diamond; and life and colour were
imparted to the entire incomparable landscape. Millions of pilgrims
had seen the morning proceed victoriously over the Holy Lake; but
no mortal before us had witnessed this spectacle from the centre of
Manasarovar.

Geese, sea-gulls, and sea-swallows flew shrieking across the water.

The oarsmen were sleepy; sometimes they fell asleep on their oars. The morning-hours passed, and still we continued to be the centre of the landscape. I, too, felt sleepy. I closed my eyes, imagining the sound of harps in the air, and seeing whole herds of red wild asses, chasing one another across the lake.

"No, this won't do!"

To energize my men, I gave them a shower with my hand. At the next sounding-place, where we found the greatest depth of the lake, two hundred and sixty-eight feet, we had our breakfast of goose-eggs, bread, and milk. The lake-water was as sweet as that of a well. It was noon. Now it was evident that we were approaching the western shore, for its details became visible. After eighteen hours' rowing, we finally landed.

We gathered fuel, made tea, fried mutton, smoked our pipes, chatted, changed the boat and sail into a tent, and turned in as early as seven o'clock. The next day, we sailed north, not far from the shore, passing the monastery of Gosul-gompa, on its high terrace, and spent a new night on the western shore. Long before sunrise, the west wind set in with noise and bluster. At half-past four we pushed off. We had not gone many cable-lengths from the shore, when the wave-crests rose to an appreciable height; and with the wind right from behind, we flew across the lake, back to the camp, where our people received us on the shore, happy and amazed, having waited ever since they saw our sail, like a white spot, in the distance.

On August the first, we moved the camp southward, the caravan walking on the eastern shore, while I rowed. In the south rose the Gang-lung mountains, at the foot of which, as I had proved, was the source of the Satlej. At Yango-gompa, we paid a short visit to its one nun and ten monks; and at Tugu-gompa, where we pitched our tents outside the walls, thirteen monks received us with great friendliness. They were amazed to see a boat on the Holy Lake, and could find no other explanation of my fortunate journey than my friendship with the Tashi Lama. In the dark temple-hall of the lake-deity, Hlabsen Dorje Barvas, there was a picture of the god rising from the waves, the dome of Kang Rinpoche, the holy mountain of Kailas, towering above his head.

August 7, 1907, belongs to the days distinguished by three stars in the record of my life. At sunrise, a lama stood blowing his shellhorn on the temple-roof of Tugu-gompa. A group of Hindu pilgrims were bathing at the shore, pouring water over their heads, like the Brahmins when they worship the holy Ganges on the quays of Benares. The Kang Rinpoche was obscured by clouds.

With Shukur Ali and Tundup Sonam, I entered the boat. We had with us furs, food, sail, and spare oars. But this time the lake was absolutely calm, and we had not stepped the mast. Our direction was N 27° W. After several hours of rowing, the Gosul-gompa appeared, like a speck, in the distance, on the port side. It was one o'clock. Yellow clouds of dust whirled round on the shore in the northwest, and the wind blew from that direction. Dark fringes of rain hung

THE LAMAS MAKING THEIR ACCOUNTS WITH THE INDIAN MERCHANTS

along the mountain-slopes. A heavy rain poured down upon us. It turned into hail. I had never seen the like of it! The stones were as big as hazel-nuts; they beat the water like projectiles, in billions; the water splashed and squirted as they fell; it boiled and seethed, and the spray whirled along the lake. Only the waves close by were visible. Great darkness surrounded us, but the interior of the boat was white with hail. The hail changed into pelting rain, which descended madly. I had pulled the fur over my knees, but pools formed in the folds.

It was quiet for an instant; but the very next moment a new storm set in, this time from the northeast. We heard it roar in the distance like heavy artillery. For a little while longer, we attempted to steer our course northwestward, to the point set by the compass; but the waves grow larger, and their foamy crests dashed in over the starboard rail. The water in the boat rose, clucking and gurgling with our rolling. We had to steer southwestward, in the direction of the wind. A dangerous manœuvre! But it was successful. And now a journey began that I shall never forget!

Gale! We were three men in a nutshell, in the midst of waves as high as on a stormy sea of my home-country. I did not notice how I froze as the water washed over me and in under my leather waistcoat. We sank in troughs of malachite-green water, seeing, through wave-crests as clear as glass, the sun shining in the distant south. We were lifted, amid foam, on raging crests of waves, where the boat trembled for a second, before plunging again into a dark grave of water, that seethed menacingly. Slowly the boat filled. Could we stay afloat until we reached land? If only we could have got the sail up, it would have been easier to keep our craft steady in the wind. Now it wanted to go up in the wind, and lie with starboard rail to windward. I leaned on the tiller with all my strength, and Tundup exerted all the pressure he could bring to bear on his oar.

"Pull away, pull away!" I called out.

He *did* pull away, and his oar broke with a loud report. Lost, I thought. Now we were *bound* to capsize. But Tundup was a capable fellow. Without thinking, he went for the spare oar, pulled it out of its loops, fitted it in the rowlock, and pulled away before the boat had had time to turn. The more water we shipped, the deeper we lay, and the easier it was for the waves to enter.

"Ya, Allah!" Shukur Ali called out, in a dull, grave voice.

We had been struggling for our lives for an hour and a quarter, when it cleared; and we perceived the Gosul-gompa far away, straight ahead of us. It grew rapidly in size, and the monks stood looking at us from the balconies of the monastery. We were hurled into the surf at the shore, and the boat was drawn out again by suction. Tundup Sonam jumped overboard. Had the fellow gone mad? The water was higher than his breast, but he grasped the boat firmly and pulled us in. We followed his example in shallow water, and dragged our nutshell ashore.

We were all in, after our hard struggle; and we threw ourselves headlong on the sand, without saying a word. After a while, some monks and youthful novices came down to us.

"Do you need any help? It looked nasty when you were tossed about on the lake, which is angry to-day. Come up to us, we have warm rooms."

"No, thank you! We will stay here. But give us some fuel and food."

They soon returned with sweet and sour milk and *tsamba*. Of all our food, only the tea could be used. They made a welcome fire of

THREE LAMA BOYS

twigs and dung; and we undressed by it and dried our clothes, as we had so often done after shipwrecks on the Tibetan lakes.

In the morning, Robsang rode up with fresh supplies, though everybody believed we had perished. The Tugu-gompa monks had burnt incense before the image of the lake-god, and had asked him to spare us. That was considerate of them! God bless them for that!

I stayed in the Gosul-gompa twelve hours. Now I sat, sketching, between the eight pillars in the chamber of the gods; now I observed the image of the mysterious son of Sakia, on which the monks sprinkle holy water, with peacock-feathers, from a silver bowl, all the while mumbling, *"Om a hum."* Here, too, the lake-deity, in his own hall, reigned in mysterious twilight.

I walked out on the terraced roof. The Holy Lake, which yesterday had done everything to drown us, was now smooth as a mirror. The air was slightly hazy. One could not see whether the eastern shore was mountains or sky. The lake and sky had the same values. Objects swam before my eyes. After the rough lake of the previous day, the whole temple swayed under me, and I felt as if hurled into infinite space. But beneath lay the Holy Lake, along the shores of which innumerable pilgrims had walked themselves weary, to secure peace for their souls. The Manasarovar, the hub of the wheel which is a symbol of life! I could have stayed there for years, watching the

THE MONASTERY OF GOSUL ON THE ROCKY SHORE OF THE HOLY LAKE

ice extend its roof across the depths, the winter storms driving whirling snow across land and water, the approaching spring breaking up the cover, in its turn being succeeded by the temperate summer winds, heralded by the dependable flocks of geese. I should have liked to sit there, seeing new days swept forth on the wings of the morning, and becoming one with the changing and ever equally fascinating prospects over the Holy Lake which unfold before the eyes of mortal man every day and night of the year.

But presently the day faded away and the evening glow went out. I stood in a group of lamas, went up to the railing, and called out:
"Om a hum!"

CHAPTER LVIII

Rakas-Tal, the Devil's Lake

IT was good weather when we rowed back to the Tugu-gompa. The monks welcomed us with touching friendliness. They told of the sacred tree that is rooted in the gold sand at the bottom of the lake, and that rises toward the surface of the water. A thousand monks' cells are suspended from each of its thousand branches, and the lake-god's castle is at its foot. Four rivers flow from the Holy Lake: the Karnali, the Brahmaputra, the Indus, and the Satlej.

After a ride up along the slopes of the Gurla, we rode past the Gosul-gompa once more, to the Chiu-gompa, at the northwest corner of the lake. A lone monk lived there, the sympathetic and melancholy Tsering Tundup Lama, who, having tired of his loneliness, asked permission to accompany me to the mountains. But when we were about to depart, his courage failed him and he proved unequal to abandoning his retreat. I crossed the lake a couple of times more, and made a horseback-trip up to the monastery of Pundi-gompa, near which Robsang and I barely escaped a gang of twelve robbers. They preferred to pillage a Tibetan caravan of animals and goods. In the Langbo-nan-gompa, I had tea with the twelve-year-old abbot, an attractive and wide-awake boy, who became greatly interested in my sketch-book. When we rode away, he was standing in his window, waving his hand in farewell. The Charyip-gompa was the eighth and last monastery on the lake. A solitary lama lived there, with no one to hear when he rang his large prayer-bell. But the holy syllables of *om mani padme hum* had been cast in the metal; and when the bell tolled, the sound-waves wafted out over the water-waves of the Holy Lake.

We found ourselves again at the Chiu-gompa, the point where the Manasarovar at times overflows, by way of a river-bed, into the nearby lake, to the west, the Langak-tso of the Tibetans, the Rakas-tal of the Hindus. The bed was usually dry; and the easterly lake had to rise more than six feet in order to overflow. This had happened in 1846, when Henry Strachey was there, and also in 1909, as I learned in a letter from Gulam Razul. But now the bed was dry, and a thorough investigation of the problem was one of the great tasks of my journey. That is a subject that demands a book of its own.[1]

The Tibetans were furious at all the liberties I took. The *gova* of Parka, the nearest authority, pursued me from camp to camp; but every time his men came galloping up to our tents, they were met with "He is out on the lake, catch him if you can." And before they could reach the other shore, I would be on my way back, in the opposite direction. They grew quite bewildered, and probably concluded that I was a myth. At any rate, they did not once succeed in even seeing me.

THE TWELVE-YEAR-OLD ABBOT OF LANGBO-NAN-GOMPA IN HIS CELL

But presently the *gova* sent an ultimatum to Chiu-gompa. If I did not voluntarily present myself at Parka, his men would seize all my possessions and take them on yaks to that place. "Good," I replied. "As you wish!" A small troop actually arrived, with fifteen yaks, and we gladly helped them with the loading. Thereupon they marched off, accompanied by half of my men. With the other half, I went to the Langak-tso, the Rakas-tal of the Hindus, which, accord-

[1] That book is already written, namely, Volume I and Volume II of my *Southern Tibet.*

ing to the Tibetans, in contradistinction to the Holy Lake, is peopled by demons. In the previous winter, five Tibetans had made a short-cut across the ice, which broke, and all five were drowned. The lake is shaped like an hour-glass, but the southern half is much more bulbous than the northern. We encamped on the eastern shore of the narrow neck between the two. The following morning, we were to begin sounding. In spite of a strong wind, I got across without mishap. But the wind developed into a gale, and we were marooned on the western shore the entire day and night. The next morning, we returned to the camp in a tearing wind. And after that everything seemed to conspire against us. Wind and storm prevailed day and night. We therefore had to pack up the boat, and send it on, by the last mule, from Poonch, while we rode around the rocky, savage, and beautiful shores of the lake.

One evening we pitched camp at the point of a steep promontory on the southern shore. On a line with it, a rocky island, called the Lache-to, rose out of the waves. The wild geese breed, in May, in sand and gravel, on its smooth plateau. The Lhasa Government pays three men to protect the wild geese against foxes and wolves. These men walk out over the ice, and remain on the island as long as they can safely do so. But, on one occasion, they did not have time to leave the island before a spring storm broke up the ice completely. They had to stay on the Lache-to for eight months, subsisting on goose-eggs and grass.

I, too, wanted to go out to the Goose Island. With Robert and Ishe at the oars, I pushed off from the shore. It was early in the afternoon. We were to return by evening, when a wild goose would be fried, ready for my evening meal. Our camp was sheltered by high mountain-walls; and we did not notice the wind, until we were at some distance from the shore. But then we went out to the islet at a sweeping pace, and landed with difficulty in a cove. We could not think of rowing back in such weather. We pulled the boat ashore and examined the islet. It was small enough to be walked around in twenty-five minutes.

The breeding-place of the wild geese was empty and abandoned; but as thousands of eggs remained buried in the sand, we had food enough to last until the wind should subside and we could row back to camp. We cracked some eggs, and found them rotten. We tried a great many of them, and eventually found eight which, having been preserved under sand, proved edible. Ishe had a bag of *tsamba* with him. In the lee of a stone wall, built by the gooseherds, we made a fire, baked the eggs, and supped. As at the Chargut-tso, several years before, I now again thought of the danger of our situation, if the boat were to be swept away by the wind.

We slept in the sand, and returned the next morning, before dawn lighted the east. My wild goose was dried up by that time; yet I ate it with relish. A *gova* from Parka arrived the same morning, with a new, strict ultimatum. We served him up a princely meal. I joked with him, saying, "Calm yourself, *gova*, I'll go with you"; and, pursued by storms that shrouded the whole country in flying dust, we completed our ride around the lake, crossed the old bed through which the Satlej had formerly flowed from the Langak-tso, and reached Parka late one evening.

The chieftains of the district were content, now that they had finally caught me in their net. Presently the last journey back to Ladak would begin, along the main road, by way of Khaleb, a region south of the Kang Rinpoche, the Holy Mountain, the Kailas of the Hindus. I answered the chief that I would go to Ladak, as they wished, provided they would let me stay three days in Khaleb. They did not object to this.

Accompanied by a lama of rank, his escort of red monks, and his equipment-caravan, we departed, on September second, and pitched our tents on the plain of Khaleb, in sight of the most sacred of all mountains on earth.

CHAPTER LIX

From the Holy Mountain to the Source of the Indus

BY the next morning we were ready to play a trick on the stiff-necked Tibetans. I had managed to spend a month at the two lakes, to make deep soundings on the Manasarovar, and to visit all of its eight monasteries. I now wanted, at any price, to complete the circuit of the Holy Mountain, the aspiration of all pilgrims, a tour never made by a white man.

Early in the morning, on September third, I sent Tsering, Namgyal, and Ishe, with provisions for three days, to the valley leading from the Kang Rinpoche. When they disappeared, I mounted a horse, and followed on their trail, with Robsang. My tent was left standing at Khaleb. The *gova* consequently believed that I would return in the evening.

We entered the beautiful, deep-hollowed valley between high, perpendicular walls of green and violet sandstone and conglomerate, passing several groups of pilgrims. They were all on foot. They did not talk; they only mumbled their eternal *om mani padme hum*. We took a few hours' rest at the monastery of Nyandi-gompa. At the altar in its Hall of Gods were two elephant-tusks, "which had come flying through the air from India." The Holy Mountain, as seen from the roof of the monastery, was magnificent. Its shape was that of a tetrahedron, on a pedestal with perpendicular sides. Its peak was covered with changeless snow and ice. From the edge of this ice-cap, the melted water hurtled down in foaming bridal-veils.

Higher up in the valley there was granite on both sides. It was like passing between gigantic fortifications, walls, and towers. On the right, in the opening of the valley, the peak of the Kang Rinpoche came into view now and then. No matter from which direction we saw it, it was equally fascinating, baffling in its mighty majesty.

We spent our first night among other pilgrims on the roof of the Diripu-gompa monastery. We learned from them that the source of the Indus was only three days distant! Should we continue thither? No! We must first carry out the program already made. But afterwards!

We, accordingly, continued the pilgrims' circuitous walk around the mountain. In the south it looked like an enormous rock-crystal. The trail ran through a whole forest of votive cairns erected by pious pilgrims. The body of an old man lay among the stones; he had finished his pilgrimage for good. We mounted toward a pass. The ascent was very steep. On a hill there was a colossal granite rock; and underneath it a narrow tunnel-passage led through the loose layers of earth. The Tibetans believe that a man free of sin can crawl through the passage, while one burdened with sins gets stuck. Ishe was brave enough to submit himself to the ordeal. He crawled into the

THE GIGANTIC GRANITE BLOCK BESIDE THE DIRIPU-GOMPA

dark orifice, and scrambled, on his elbows and feet, into the interior of the earth. He braced himself on the ground, straining with the tips of his toes, so that the dust whirled around them. But he made no headway. He stuck. We held our sides with laughter. Robsang roared, Namgyal had to sit down, Tsering wept with laughter. We heard the half-choked calls for help coming from the unmasked sinner underground; but we let him lie in the hole for a while, for the good of his soul. At last we pulled him out by the hindlegs. He looked like a withered clay figure, and was more disgruntled than ever.

Pilgrims from all parts of Tibet flocked to Kang Rinpoche, the "holy ice-mountain," or the "ice-jewel." That mountain is the navel of the earth. On its summit is the paradise of Siva. He who walks around the mountain, reduces the pains of transmigration and gets nearer to Nirvana. His herds prosper, his goods increase. We met an aged man who had already made nine circuits around the mountain, and had four more to do. By trudging from morning to evening, he could complete the tour in two days. Some of the pilgrims are not content to walk. They lie down prone, mark the path with their hand, rise, proceed to the mark, and prostrate themselves again. They repeat this all the way around. It takes twenty days to encircle the mountain in that fashion.

We finally reached the pass of Dolma-la, 18,600 feet high. It was marked by a giant block of stone, as well as by poles, with streamers and strings. There the faithful sacrifice tufts of their own hair, and teeth from their own jaws, which they insert in the cracks of the stone. They tear strips off their clothing, and tie them to the strings. And they prostrate themselves on the ground around the rock, in homage to the spirits of Kang Rinpoche.

From the Dolma-la our road ran steeply to the pool of Tso-kavala, which is always frozen over. Accompanied by my four Lamaist retainers on foot—for none but heathens may ride on the road of the Holy Ones—I rode from the monastery of Tsumtul-pu-gompa to the Tarchen-labrang, the third monastery in the ring. We had then completed a circle which was like a prayer-mill, where at every step one heard the eternal truth, *om mani padme hum* (Oh, the jewel is in the lotus flower, amen), that mysterious, bottomless "om" and "hum," the beginning and the end. Edwin Arnold says:

> *"The Dew is on the Lotus!   Rise, Great Sun!*
> *And lift my leaf and mix me with the wave.*
> *Om mani padme hum the Sunrise comes!   The*
> *Dewdrop slips into the shining sea!"*

Upon my return to Khaleb, I called our agreeable *gova* and told him straight out that I intended to go to the source of the Indus. After long negotiation, he agreed to it, on condition that half the caravan went direct to Gartok, there to await my arrival.

"You will have to make your excursion at your own risk," he said. "You will be stopped by our authorities, and also attacked and plundered by robbers."

I took with me five men, six beasts of burden, two dogs, two rifles, one revolver, and food for several days. We knew the first part of the route, which was as far as to the Diripu-gompa. There we left the pilgrim-road and went into the lifeless valleys of the Transhimalaya. The second night, we heard whistling and signals, and we kept strict watch over the animals. Over the pass of Tseti-lachen-la (17,900 feet) we crossed the main bridge of the Transhimalaya. It was the fourth time. We encamped on its northern slope, on the shore of the Indus, with some shepherds bound for Gertse with five hundred sheep laden with barley.

One of them, an old man, was willing to accompany us to the source of the Indus, Singi-kabab, or the "lion-mouth," as the Tibetans call this remarkable place. But he wanted seven rupees a day for his trouble. We also hired eight of his sheep and bought their store of barley, enough for our horses for one week. That man, Pema Tense, was worth his weight in gold. He was with us for five days; and, upon parting from him, we gave him his earnings, $42, an enormous sum to him. As for me I had achieved the discovery of the source of the Indus at a low price.

We advanced with Pema Tense up the gently rising valley. The famous river shrank gradually, as we left its tributaries behind us. We stayed for a while at an expansion, and caught thirty-seven fish, a welcome change in my monotonous diet. Further on, we passed a steep rock, which a herd of wild sheep were climbing. The agile animals were so engrossed by the caravan, that they did not notice Tundup Sonam stealing upon them at the foot of the rock. A shot rang out, and one of the fine-looking animals dropped down into the valley.

On the evening of September tenth, my tent was pitched at the Singi-kabab! A spring flowed from under a flat shelf of rock, in four streams, which united into a single stream. Three high cairns and a square *mani* chest, ornamented with beautiful symbolic carvings, gave evidence that the spot was sacred. It was 16,940 feet above sea-level.

About forty years earlier, an Indian pundit had visited the upper Indus. He crossed the river thirty miles from its source, without advancing to this important spot. On maps published one year before my journey, the source of the Indus was still indicated as being on the northern slope of the Kang Rinpoche (Kailas), i. e., on the southern side of the Transhimalaya, when, as a matter of fact, it lay on the northern side of that mighty mountain-system.

Arrian, writing of Alexander the Great, in his work "Indica" (Book VI, Chapter I), relates the following amusing episode:

"At first, he [Alexander] thought he had discovered the origin of the Nile, when he saw crocodiles in the river Indus, which he had seen in no other river except the Nile. He thought the Nile rises somewhere or other in India, and after flowing through an extensive tract of desert country, loses the name of Indus there; but afterwards, when it begins to flow again through the inhabited land, it is called Nile by the Ethiopians of that district, and by the Egyptians, and finally empties itself into the Inner Sea (the Mediterranean). Accordingly, when he wrote to Olympias about the country of India, after mentioning other things, he said that he thought he had discovered the sources of the Nile. However, when he had made a more careful inquiry into the facts relating to the river Indus, he learned the following details from the natives—that the Hydaspes unites its waters with the Acesines, as the latter does with the Indus, and that they both yield up their names to the Indus; that the last-named river has two mouths, through which it discharges itself into the Great Sea, but that it has no connection with the Egyptian country. He then removed from the letter to his mother the part he had written about the Nile."

At the sight of the volume of water of the huge river, rushing forth from its valley in the Himalayas, Alexander thought that he was at the very source. That he could harbour so fantastic an idea as that of discovering the source of the *Nile,* was due to his ignorance of the Indian Ocean. He believed that India was connected with the African continent, and that the large river he saw burst forth from the Himalayas curved toward the south, then northward, emptying into the Mediterranean. But he soon realized that the two continents were separated by an ocean, and that the waters of the Indus emptied into it. Hence, before dispatching his letter to Olympias, the king had an opportunity of correcting his mistake. He had not found the source of the Nile, but that of the Indus. But that, too, was an error; for Alexander had no knowledge of the upper course of the river, several hundred miles long. And more than twenty-two hundred years were to elapse before, on September 10, 1907, the real source of the Indus was discovered.

Thus I had the joy of being the first white man to penetrate to the sources of the Brahmaptura and the Indus, the two rivers, famous from time immemorial, which, like a crab's claws, encircle the Himalayas, the highest mountain-system on earth.

Being beyond reach of the authorities, we pushed on through the western part of the white spot, to the region of Yumba-matsen. Thence we took a westerly course to Gartok, crossing, on our way, the pass of Jukti-la, which attains the enormous height of 19,100 feet. We had then crossed the Transhimalaya five times. But the Jukti-la was not among my discoveries. Nain Sing had crossed it in 1867, and Calvert, the Englishman, in 1906. But no white man or pundit had ever crossed that part of the great unknown country which extended between my two passes of Angden-la and Tseti-lachen-la, a distance of three hundred miles and an area of forty-five thousand square miles. All that was known of it were the few high peaks of the Lunpo-gangri, which the Ryder expedition had triangulated. Owing to the harshness of the Tibetans and the Chinese, I was compelled to leave behind me all this territory, which had been the principal object of my journey.

I simply *had* to go there. It was unthinkable that I should return home without carrying out my plans, or reaching my goal. First of all, I would have to wait in Gartok and Gar-gunsa for the money and other things which Colonel Dunlop-Smith was to send me from India. The governors in western Tibet, the two *garpun,* were inexorable when I attempted to induce them to let me go direct to the unknown country. That meant many more dead horses and mules, six months instead of one, and a murderous winter in Chang-tang.

As a result of all the obstinate resistance I met with, my plan developed and crystallized. Gar-gunsa was now an important trading-place, where great numbers of merchants from Lhasa and Ladak set up their tents, with goods. Here I spread the rumour that I had had enough of Tibet, and intended to travel, by way of Ladak, to Khotan, in East Turkestan, and thence to Peking. My Chinese passport confirmed that route. None of my friends in India was to have the slightest suspicion of my real intentions. I even wrote Reuter's correspondent in India, my friend Mr. Buck, that I was about to go to Khotan. Only Gulam Razul, a merchant from Leh, was let into my secret. He was entrusted with arranging an entire new caravan. I purchased the twenty mules he had in Gar-gunsa; and, in addition thereto, he got me fifteen splendid horses. I, myself, still had five veterans left. Then he wrote to Leh, and on my behalf employed eleven new servitors, who were to join me in Drugub. Lastly, he procured provisions, furs, clothes, tents—in a word, the entire heavy equipment—and lent me five thousand rupees in silver. For the services he rendered me, he received a gold medal from King Gustav of Sweden, and was honoured by the Indian Government with the title of Khan Bahadur.

On November sixth, the goods from India, as well as six thousand rupees, and the post, arrived at last. It was then that I received information of the treaty between England and Russia, concluded that same year (1907), in which the following paragraph concerned me very closely:

"Great Britain and Russia bind themselves mutually not to allow, without previous agreement, for the next three years, any scientific expedition whatsoever to enter Tibet, and to summon China to do likewise."

Hitherto, I had had England, India, Tibet, and China against me. Now Russia was added. I laughed heartily at those amiable diplomats, who wrote laws for me at their green table. The problem was to slip past Ladak. From there I was to take the main caravan-route toward the Kara-korum pass, and, as in the year before, turn eastward into Tibet; and, upon reaching inhabited regions, I would travel in disguise.

As soon as everything was ready, we marched to Tanksi and Drugub. I dismissed all my old followers, Robert included; for, if any of them were to be found with me, when I reached tracts in Tibet where I had been before, my whole project was bound to fail. The parting was bitter and upsetting, as usual. But it had to be. They all wept, but they were consoled by their liberal rewards. So I stood again, absolutely alone, in interior Asia, against five governments that were united to upset my plans.

But my isolation ended when the eleven men employed by Gulam

Razul arrived in Drugub. Eight were Mohammedans, three were Lamaists. The name of the caravan-leader was Abdul Kerim. The others were named Kutus, Gulam, Suän, Abdul Rasak, Sadik, Lobsang, Kunchuk, Gaffar, Abdullah and Sonam Kunchuk. They were all Ladakis with the exception of Lobsang, a Tibetan. He was the best of them all, but they were all first-rate. I welcomed them in a speech, and hoped that they would do well on the way to—Khotan! None of them, not even Abdul Kerim, had an inkling of my real plan. He was therefore, partly excusable for taking along insufficient barley for the animals. I told him to take barley for two and a half months. But Khotan being only one month's journey distant, he took only enough barley for that length of time.

We had three tents. Mine was so small that it could hold only my cot on the ground and two boxes. Our caravan numbered twenty-one mules and nineteen horses. I rode my little white Ladaki, who had been with me during the entire previous campaign. The silver and the tinned food made four loads, the kitchen two, the tents, furs, and the belongings of the men burdened several beasts. Only I and Abdul Kerim were mounted. All the other animals carried rice, flour, and tsamba for us, and barley for the beasts. We had only two dogs, Brown Puppy and a newcomer, called Yellow Dog. In addition to this, we bought twenty-five sheep.

Thus everything was new. Brown Puppy, the white mule from Poonch, and my little mount were the only veterans. I realized that the campaign about to begin would be harder than the last. At that time we had started in August; now it was December. We would walk straight into the arms of a paralyzing winter-cold and an annihilating wind. We had already had −10°, and the temperature was sure to fall gradually to the freezing-point of mercury itself.

CHAPTER LX

Desperate Winter Days in Northern Tibet

OUR first day, on December fourth, down to the village of Shayok, was one of the most difficult of the entire journey. The road ran through a narrow glen. Most of the bottom was taken up by a river, partly frozen, partly eddying wildly. Men carried the baggage. The animals bore nothing but the pack-saddles. My porters, about a hundred men, disappeared singing down the valley. A little later, I and a companion departed on horseback. The distance was only six miles, but it took us eight hours to cover it. We had to cross the river over and over again. Some spots along the shore were marked by strong belts of ice, that ended abruptly. The horses leapt from the edge into the eddying river. The water was four feet deep. We had to press hard with our knees, so as not to be thrown into the river, over the horses' heads. We were able to avoid fording several times by sliding barefooted by the rocky base on the right shore. But the horses had to wade across. Suän tried to ford one place on horseback. It was too deep. The horse lost his footing, and Suän had to swim to the edge of the ice, where he scrambled to his feet. At the last ford, the luggage was carried by naked men, who balanced themselves across the rocky bottom, carrying staffs in their hands, and supporting one another. I rode across on a tall horse, and got a foot-bath. Why the men who went to and fro between the shores did not freeze to death, is a puzzle to me. One of them got stopped immovable in the middle of the river, and had to be rescued by his comrades. We made a fire on the shore, so that they might warm themselves.

In the village of Shayok, where all the pack-saddles were dried at fires, we were at an altitude of 12,400 feet. It was to be long before we again reached so low a level.

We celebrated the last evening with a farewell-party. The village girls danced around a big fire, and musicians played.

On December sixth, a new death-march, one of the most trying I ever experienced in Tibet, was begun. We took Tubges, a Shayok

480

shepherd, with us for a few days, to tend the sheep. He soon proved to be so good a marksman, that we kept him. Thus we were thirteen.

Slowly and laboriously we proceeded up the Shayok Valley. We met caravans from Yarkand and Khotan. A man from one of them came up to me and offered me two handfuls of dried peaches.

"Do you recognize me, Sahib?" he asked.

"Certainly, Mollah Shah."

He had not been home since leaving me in the spring of 1902! Now he begged to go with us again; but we had no place for him. Some bales of silk lay scattered about, discarded by caravans after

THE GIRLS OF SHAYOK DANCING ROUND THE FIRE

their animals died. We went northwards. The valley of Shayok was nasty. It was full of rocks, ice, and eddying water. Already the temperature was down to $-13°$. Yellow Dog lay yelping with anger at the cold. Otherwise, silence reigned, and we felt the winter-cold stealing forth from all directions. All at once I heard a strangely whining sound from the tent where Gulam, my new chef, ruled. It was Brown Puppy. She had given us four black puppies again, just as in Shigatse. Two of them were bitches, and were drowned. We took affectionate care of the other two; and during the march, Kunchuk carried them inside his fur, next to his body. This trade-route between East Turkestan and Kashmir and India is no doubt the most difficult one on earth. At any rate, it is the highest one. At the camp of Bulak, where we encountered a Yarkand caravan, twenty horses lay dead; and, on the road, we counted sixty-three cadavers during a two-hour journey.

There was no pasturage at Camp No. 283. I examined our supply of barley and found that it would serve for ten days!

"Did I not tell you to take barley for two and a half months?" I asked the old man.

"You did," he answered sobbingly; "but within two weeks we'll be able to buy barley from Shahidullah, on the way to Khotan."

I spoke very sharply to him. Anyhow, it was my own fault that I had not investigated the provisions before our departure. It was unthinkable to return to Ladak; for in that case my real plan would have been revealed. I sat up half the night, in a temperature of −31°, consulting my maps. It was ninety-six miles to Camp No. 8 of last fall, where the pasturage was good. From there it was four hundred miles to the Tong-tso, which I wanted to touch, in order to get right through the white spot south of that lake. But long before reaching the Tong-tso we would meet nomads and be able to purchase fresh animals. I *had* to carry out the plan. Forward, no matter for how many desperate days; but not one step backward!

The sooner we left the Kara-korum route (which went northwards) and turned east and southeast toward interior Tibet, the better. On December twentieth, a large lateral valley tempted us to look for a short-cut toward the east. After struggling the whole day in that direction, we found that the valley shrank into a gorge, and finally into a mere crack, through which a cat would hardly have been able to squeeze. We made camp. Not a blade of grass for grazing. The horses chewed one another's tails and ropes. The temperature sank to −31°. The next morning, we turned back on our own tracks. I rode last. Kutus went on foot in front of me. We passed Mohammed Isa's white horse, from Shigatse, which lay frozen hard as stone in the valley.

We were again on the road of the dead caravan-horses. A spooky atmosphere pervaded the valley. Cadavers were constantly seen. Several of them were half covered with snow. The dogs barked at them. A strong wind blew from the south, and red dust settled like streaks of blood on the snow-fields. Kisil-unkur (the Red Cave), had been fittingly named.

We camped there, so as to mount a thousand feet to the Dapsang heights the next morning, the day before Christmas. If we should be attacked there by a blizzard, there was every likelihood in the world that it would prove fatal. Therefore my men were in a serious mood. Only after darkness had set in, did the two men who tended the sheep turn up, with twelve of them left, the others having been frozen to death. We had no fuel. The men were sitting around some glowing sticks, singing a melancholy hymn to Allah. As a rule, they sang gay songs. But whenever I heard the deep, serious tones, I understood that they thought our situation was desperate.

The day before Christmas came with brilliant sunshine. When we had risen to the heights of Dapsang, I rode on ahead. I turned east, and left the caravan-road that led to Khotan. The men did not understand me. They had been longing for the grapes and abundant flesh-pots of Khotan, instead of which I was riding straight into this dreadful desert of cold and snow.

In places, the crust of the snow bore the weight of the horses. But it broke often enough, and the animals sank into snow-filled hollows, five and six feet deep. They plunged like dolphins through the fine, powdery snow. Everything was dead-white. The caravan stood out black against the whiteness. In our Christmas-camp, the thermometer registered $-17°$, as early as nine o'clock, and a minimum of $-38°$ during the night. The moon shone clear and brilliant over this abode of deathlike quiet. I read the Biblical passages of the day, while the cold crackled about my tent. For all I cared, a snowstorm might drive across the mountains and wipe out the tell-tale snow-prints that showed our route. One horse lay dead in the morning.

We followed an antelope-path, running east. No pasturage! Only two bags of barley remained. When they should be finished, the animals would get rice and tsamba. We had huge supplies of that. Everyone had a headache. I heard again the weird hymn to Allah. Abdul Kerim offered prayers nightly, interceding for the others. Perhaps they were right. Perhaps I had set my mark too high! We simply had to proceed, even if we should have to go begging afoot among the nomads.

We followed a valley. There was less snow. Something yellow gleamed on the slope on our left. It was grass! We settled down, and the animals ran thither with their burdens. Suän, filled with delight, began a droll dance, which raised all our spirits. One mule died on the pasture. Wild yaks had been in the neighbourhood; and so we had fuel again. Twenty-two wild sheep were climbing on a rocky slope.

I called Abdul Kerim, Gulam, and Kutus to my tent, and revealed my plan to them. I told of the large, unknown country to the southeast that I wanted to cross, of how the Tibetans kept their eyes on me, and how it was necessary that I should disguise myself as soon as ever we met the first nomads. Then Abdul Kerim would become the head of our party, and I would be the humblest among his servants. They looked at one another in amazement, but said yes and amen to everything; though they probably wondered if they had not let themselves in with a madman.

We arrived at the valley of the Kara-kash-daria, one of the two source-rivers of the Khotan-daria. I had in mind the desert-trip thirteen years before, when the Khotan-daria saved my life. Here, too, we tried to make a short-cut toward the interior of Tibet, but had to turn again, after straining our animals and ourselves unnecessarily for two heavy days. Thus badly did 1908, the new year, begin.

We had still to continue eastwards, and we crossed two high passes. A wild yak came running toward us; but becoming aware of his mistake, he turned, pursued by the dogs. The snow ended beyond the second pass. We took with us two bags full of snow from the last drift. We encamped in an open valley, where there was fuel. All the animals were taken to a grazing-ground, where a frozen spring provided them with water. During the night, the animals ran off in search of better pasturage. They wandered far, and it took all next day to round them up. Meanwhile I sat alone in my tent, with Brown Puppy and Baby Puppy for company. The other puppy had died. A weird sense of desolation possessed me. Things were tolerable as long as the sun was up, for then the strange formations and colours of the mountains and clouds were visible. But after sundown, the long winter evening and the biting cold set in.

On January eighth, a horse and a mule died. The next day, we walked only a few miles, to a copious spring. From that camp (No. 300), we saw, to the east, the region of Chang-tang, where I had been the year before. One day more, and we stopped at the good pasturage which had been our Camp No. 8. The cairn of Mohammed Isa stood like a beacon on the hill high above. On January fourteenth, the temperature sank to −39.8°! It was impossible to keep warm. Every evening I had Gulam rub my feet, which were all but frostbitten. Tubges shot a wild sheep and an antelope near Camp No. 306. Our last two sheep were therefore granted a respite.

Turning southeast, we lost ourselves in a world of mountains, and were battered by constant storms. One-fourth of the caravan had died, and presently the last mule from Poonch fell too. We were rarely able to make more than six miles a day. The barley was gone, and so the animals got rice and rice-balls. The time was one of devastation. Not a day passed without the loss of a horse or a mule.

The Arport-tso, the lake visited by Deasy and Rawling, stretched right across our route. Lobsang acted as pilot. The middle of the lake was very narrow. Lobsang walked on, across the ice, which was clear as crystal, and dark-green. In the cracks, loose snow had accumulated, offering a footing to the animals. Otherwise the raging wind would have swept away the entire caravan. On the farther shore, springs gushed forth, compelling us to get up on the hills. At an inlet there was good pasturage. Two horses and one mule were left behind there. Would we survive until we encountered nomads?

We forced our way through a storm to a pass 18,300 feet high. Two horses died on the way. Now Abdul Kerim, too, had to go on foot. We needed his riding-horse. The snow lay a foot deep. Kutus and I walked far behind the others. We found Sonam Kuchuk and Suän in a drift. They had heart- and head-pains, and could not go on. I told them to rest, and then to follow in our track. In the evening they dragged themselves up to the camp. Abdul Kerim came to my tent, downcast, saying that we would be lost, if no help came from the nomads within ten days. "Yes, I know," I replied. "Help the others to keep up their spirits, and take good care of the animals; and things will be all right."

January thirtieth proved to be a difficult day. Snow lay everywhere two feet deep, and often three. Two guides, staff in hand, led our dying train up a pass. Deep snow on a rising terrain, at this tremendous altitude, takes the life out of even the very best caravan-animals. It was snowing, and the strong wind cut through our skin like knives. We all walked in single file through the furrow trodden down by the pilots. Time and again, a horse or a mule fell, and had to be helped to its feet again. A brown horse would drop, and in a few minutes it was dead. The whirling snow covered it with a fine white shroud, while the carcase was still warm. Our progress was hopelessly slow. We doubted whether we would have strength to reach the top of this murderous pass. I sat in the saddle, to which the snow held me fast, my hands and feet being quite numb. And yet I dared not neglect my map, compass, and watch. I held the pencil as though it were a

OUR HALF-DEAD ANIMALS CLIMBING THE PASS IN DEEP SNOW

hammer-handle. This pass was as high as the previous one. We descended slowly. Soon we were stalled in snow a yard deep. The storm pressed on in all its wild rage, sweeping the fine, dry, driving snow around us, as we shovelled into the drifts and laboriously pitched the tents. And then the darkness of night set in. Even if there had been pasturage, we could not have found it, because of the snow. We kept the animals tethered. The storm howled around us; but from the men's tent I heard faintly the grave hymn to Allah. In the morning one mule was dead.

On the last day of January we were able to cover only three miles. Four old yaks were walking on a slope just above the camp, plunging in the drifts. I sifted all the luggage here. Everything not absolutely essential was piled up and burnt. We smashed all the boxes, for use later on as fuel. Their contents were packed in bags, as being lighter and more suited to the animals.

A vast amount of snow fell all night long. The last passes were sure to be blocked by snow. Had we been caught in one, we would have been bottled up. We were at least spared the fear of being pursued from the north. What awaited us in the southeast we could only conjecture. We continued down a large, open valley. The snow di-

FOUR OLD YAKS IN THE DEEP SNOW

minished. The weather cleared. We saw the lake of Shemen-tso, and made camp near its western shore, where the pasturage was good. There we stayed three days, exhausted. It had stormed incessantly for two weeks. I sat like a prisoner in my tent. Brown Puppy and I were pining for the spring. Alas, it was still four months away! Baby Puppy, born in the middle of winter, did not yet know the feel of temperate spring winds.

On February fourth, the sun returned for a peep. A horse and a mule died; and, with the last seventeen animals, we walked along the northern shore of the Shemen-tso. The landscape was beautiful, with the mountains a flame-yellow. The amphitheatrical lines of the shore indicated the drying-up state of the lake.

We saw traces of nomads or hunters daily. Two more of our exhausted animals died. I was still riding my little, white Ladaki; but now he, too, had tired. He stumbled right on the level ground, and fell; and the Tibetan soil received me roughly. After that the horse was freed from further service.

We camped in an open glen. Abdul Kerim appeared at my tent, and reported in a serious voice that three men could be seen in the north. I went out with my field-glasses. The distance was very great. The mirage made them look very tall. We watched them for a long while. At last they approached. But, alas, there were only three wild yaks grazing.

I was torn between two emotions, just like the year before. On the one hand, I longed for nomads, from whom to buy yaks and sheep. On the other, the absence of people rendered our position safer; for as soon as ever we came in contact with nomads, the rumour of our caravan would spread from tent to tent, and the risk of opposition would grow day by day. Yet it was imperative that we should find natives before the last of our caravan-animals fell.

CHAPTER LXI

I Become a Shepherd

ON February eighth, we had another remarkable day. While crossing a large, open valley, we saw a *Pantholops* antelope, one hundred feet ahead of us. It did not run away, and we noticed at once that one of his hind feet had got caught in a trap. The poor animal struggled and tore to free itself. The dogs rushed at it, but two of our men chased them away. We slaughtered the animal and encamped in the neighbourhood. The trap consisted of a funnel, made of the elastic ribs of an antelope, fastened to a firm ring of plant-fibre. This in turn was anchored at the bottom of a hole, in which the funnel was concealed. The Tibetan huntsmen knew, from time immemorial, that antelopes could be stopped in their progress by a row of small cairns, several hundred yards long. The antelopes followed the row quite closely to the end. Soon a path was beaten along the cairns, and there the traps were placed.

It was evident now that we were not far from black tents. We saw the quite fresh footprints of two men. Possibly we ourselves had been observed, and perhaps it was already too late for me to assume my disguise. I called the men to my tent and acquainted them with the parts they were to play. We were to pretend to be thirteen Ladakis, in the service of Gulam Razul, a wealthy merchant. Abdul Kerim was our caravan-leader. I was one of his twelve servants, and my name was Haji Baba.

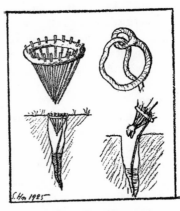

HOW THE ANTELOPE TRAPS ARE CONSTRUCTED.

Gulam Razul had commissioned us to traverse these regions, to investigate if it was worth while to send a large caravan to western Tibet next summer to purchase sheep's wool. While we were still talking, Lobsang appeared and reported seeing two tents in the distance.

I sent Abdul Kerim and two others to the place. They returned, after three hours, with a sheep and milk. Nine persons, adults and children, dwelt in the two tents. They owned a hundred and fifty sheep. But they lived mostly on antelope-meat, which they hunted with traps. Abdul Kerim paid them also for the trapped antelope which we had taken. The place was called Riochung. It was sixty-four days since we had seen another human being besides ourselves.

As we now had to be prepared to meet more nomads at any time, I put on my Ladak disguise, and thereafter appeared in the same kind of costume as my servants. Only, it was too neat and clean. But it was not long before the soot of the camp-fires and the sheep-fat of our meals soiled it.

At Camp No. 329, my little mount proved to be quite worn out. While the other animals grazed in the meagre grass, he remained standing at my tent, icicles hanging from below his eyes and nostrils. I relieved him of the icicles, and fed him with rice-balls.

On February fifteenth, our train advanced slowly up a new pass. I rode in the van. On the top of the pass (18,550 feet), I stopped and waited. The view behind, toward the northwest, was glorious. An agitated sea was as if arrested, and crowned with dazzling snow-fields. Slate, porphyry, and granite were there, in all shades. I waited till nine beasts of burden had come up. The other four were overcome with weariness, and the men had to carry part of their load up to the crest of the pass. From there we descended into a stony valley, where the snow again lay fairly deep. We were able to water the animals by melting snow over the fire. After dark, the men who had remained behind arrived with a mule. The other three animals—one of them my little white Ladaki—had died. It was one and a half years, to a day, since we had set out together from Leh. The horse had chosen a distinctive spot for his end, the very crest of the pass, where his bones would whiten under the snow of the winter storms and in the summer sunshine. His going left a great void, and we were desolate. One more such pass would have annihilated the caravan.

The burdens were now too heavy for our ten beasts. All my European clothes, except some underwear, were accordingly burnt. I discarded felt mats, unnecessary kitchen-utensils, and all my toilet-articles, including razors. I kept only a piece of soap. The whole apothecary-

stock, except a box of quinine, went. All the books that I could spare
paid tribute to the flames. We were like a balloon which throws out
ballast to keep afloat.

On the way to the Lemchung-tso, a small lake, antelopes and whole
armies of gazelles enlivened the large plain we were crossing. This
was on the border of a large spot of unknown territory. We presently
left the routes of Deasy and Rawling behind us. The lake was covered
with thick ice. We cut a hole in it, and sank some metal articles,
including some costly reserve-instruments, in it.

The next day's journey took us to fairly large gold-deposits, in

WILD ASSES RUNNING IN SINGLE FILE

shallow mines, in the bed of a brook, with stone sluices. We sighted
two nomad-tents in the distance, but ignored them. Tubges shot five
hares, which were put to good use, as our meat-supply was exhausted.
In a beautiful, wide-spreading valley, we saw at least a thousand wild
asses, in scattered herds, and, further down, five more herds. One of
them numbered a hundred and thirty-three head. It is impossible to
describe their elegant movements, as they circled round our dying
caravan, as if in mockery. One might have believed they were ridden
by invisible Cossacks, and were responding to shouts of command.
For they ran in perfect formation, their hoofs clattering, as they went
through their paces in unison.

Near Camp No. 341, we found some nomads, who sold us two sheep, milk, and butter. From there we marched toward two small lakes, in a hollow. Not far from the shore, two shepherds were tending sheep, and a man was driving six yaks. We encamped there. The altitude was only 15,200 feet. Lobsang and Tubges went to a tent near by, and an old man came out and asked:

"What do you want? Where are you going?"

"To Saka-dsong," they replied.

"You lie. You are in the service of a European. Tell the truth!"

My men were downcast when they returned. Abdul Kerim had better luck. He bought one more sheep and some milk.

We had intended to continue on the following day. But the storm that had been raging for thirty days grew into a hurricane. To break camp was absolutely out of the question. The air was so saturated with flying dust, that we could not see where the valley opened or where mountains rose in our path. So we stayed where we were. Our neighbours called on us. The cocky old man's heart softened, when he learned that we would pay thirty-eight rupees for twelve sheep. The transaction was concluded. I remained hidden in my tent. The wind roared and howled. It was cold; and I felt a strong tendency to become inert and paralyzed.

Then we went on. We now had three horses, six mules, and twelve sheep. Even the sheep bore burdens; for five sheep could carry as much as one mule. At a spot where a hill jutted out, two dogs rushed at us. We had not yet noticed two tents that stood there. The occupants sold us some sheep. Our herd now numbered seventeen head, and we hoped soon to be no longer dependent upon our weary pack-animals.

The gale constantly pursued us. It was torture to ride in such weather. The wind tore the ground into furrows. There was a roar like that made when high-pressure streams are turned on a burning house, a roar like that of rolling railway-cars, or like artillery-wagons on cobbled streets. On March sixth, we had the greatest difficulty in getting the tents pitched on the bank of a salt-lake. When my tent was finally raised and exposed to the vigorous bombardment of sand and gravel, it nearly burst with the pressure of the wind. The Ladakis had not enough strength left to pitch their own tent. I let some of them crawl into mine, while the others lay waiting in its lee. A journey through High Tibet is indeed no pleasure-trip!

The next day I rode ahead, Kutus and Gulam accompanying me. A frozen waterway, with an ice-surface as clear as glass, interrupted us. We lit a fire in a small cleft on its further side, and waited for the others. When they were crossing the ice-belt, one of our best mules slipped and sprained a hind leg, so that the animal could no longer stand up. We did everything to help her, but all efforts were in vain. She could not walk; and we had to kill her. When we proceeded southwards, the next morning, Brown Puppy and Yellow Dog stayed with the mule, and got a good meal of warm meat.

I again set out in advance, with Gulam and Kutus. Gulam walked ahead, to warn us if tents appeared out of the dense haze. The storm was raging, as usual. Suddenly he signalled us to stop. Through the haze, a stone house, two huts, and a wall were dimly visible on the right of a glen, a few hundred paces away. It was too late to turn, otherwise we would have done so; for we might now, perhaps, walk right into the arms of a chieftain, who would, of course, bar our further progress southwards. We walked past the houses, seeing neither people nor dogs, and stole into a cleft at the base of a projecting cliff, on the top of which were two *chorten* and a *mani* chest.

For a moment, as the dust-cloud lifted, we perceived a huge black tent, quite close by, on the other side of the valley. Our men arrived at last. They had lost one horse. Of the forty caravan-animals, only two horses and five mules were now left. Abdul Kerim and Kunchuk went up to the large tent. A lone medicine-lama lived there. The interior was arranged like a small temple-chamber, and the lama was the spiritual guide for the nomads of the vicinity. The district was named Nagrong. Gertse Pun, its chief, was expected home at any moment. We were lucky not to find him at home! My men were soon on good terms with his brother-in-law, who sold them five sheep, two goats, two loads of rice, two loads of barley, and some tobacco.

At sunrise, on March tenth, two other Tibetans appeared and offered sheep for sale. We were glad to buy them. I completed my disguise, stained my face brown, and walked ahead with Tubges and two of the others, driving our thirty-one sheep, all with loads, before us. The Tibetans stood and watched us. They could hardly have failed to notice that I possessed no talent for driving sheep. Never before in my life had I worked as a sheep-tender. I moved my staff as my men did, whistled like them, and uttered the same strange sounds as they. But the sheep had no respect for me; they walked where they pleased, and I ran myself out of breath. When we were well out of sight of the tents, I lay down in a cleft, to wait for the caravan, and was glad to be able to mount a horse again.

We rode through a belt of drift-sand. We were headed southwest, and the storm blew right in our faces. The constant friction of the sand-particles against my fur caused it to become charged with electricity. I needed but to touch the horse's mane to make sparks fly with a crack. We made camp at a sheepfold.

KEEPING THE SHEEP IN ORDER

Brown Puppy and Yellow Dog never arrived at Nagrong. No one had seen them since they had stayed with the fallen mule. I hoped that they would find us, as they had done so many times before. But the gale had probably obliterated our tracks and baffled their scent. We never saw them again. How often did it not seem to me, as I lay awake at night, that the tent-cloth would be raised, and that my old travelling-companion crawled in and lay down in her corner? But always it was the wind that deceived me. I imagined I could see the unhappy dog, running in despair, night and day, in valleys we had passed through, always looking for our track in vain. I saw her, with wounded paws, sitting and baying at the moon. She had spent her whole life in my caravans; and now she had lost us. The thought of Brown Puppy haunted me for long. I imagined that the ghost of a dog was present wherever I was—a poor, lone, and abandoned dog, who begged for help. But the mystery of Brown Puppy's fate—whether she and Yellow Dog stuck together and stayed with the nomads, or, exhausted, fell victims to wolves—was never solved.

OUR FAVOURITE DOG, LEFT ALONE IN THE COLD AND LONELY TIBETAN WILDERNESS

On March fifteenth, we pitched camp on the western shore of the Tong-tso, a small lake, which Nain Sing discovered in 1873. The altitude there was only 14,800 feet. We now stood on the northern edge of the unknown country. If we succeeded in going straight south, as far as to the Tsangpo-Brahmaputra, we would cross the centre of the large white spot. Now it was important that we play our cards skillfully.

Abdul Kerim looked in at two tents, and held the following conversation with two men:

"How many are you?" they asked.

"We are thirteen."

"How many rifles have you got?"

"Five."

"When you came, another man was riding ahead. You walked. He who rode was a European."

"Europeans never travel in the winter. We are wool-buyers from Ladak."

"The Ladak people never travel by this way, leastways not in winter-time."

"What is your name?" Abdul Kerim inquired.

"Nakchu Tundup and Nakchu Hlundup."

"Have you got yaks and sheep to sell?"

"What do you pay?"

"What do you want? Bring the animals."

The upshot of it all was that we bought two yaks and six sheep the next morning. We were on the northern border of the province of Bongba. The name of the district was Bongba Changma, and it was six days' journey to the tent-camp of Karma Puntso, the Governor.

We passed tents several times a day. Every time they came within sight, and every time that shepherds were encountered with their herds, I had to go and drive our sheep. I began to acquire some proficiency in the art. On one occasion, Tubges shot seven partridges. A Tibetan who noticed it remarked that only Europeans ate partridges. But Tubges assured him that Abdul Kerim, too, had that curious taste.

We were on a beaten path; and on March eighteenth, we encamped at the foot of a pass. The next morning, as we were preparing to

TAKKAR HAD TO BE HELD BY TWO MEN

break camp, three Tibetans called. I hurried out, under cover of the tents, in order to drive the sheep up the pass, with Lobsang and Tubges. We met a Tibetan, on a white horse, followed by a big, ragged watchdog, black, with two white spots. Abdul Kerim, who came after us with the caravan, bought the horse for eighty-six rupees, and the dog for two. The dog was of the "Takkar" race; so we called him Takkar. He was absolutely savage, and as ferocious as a wolf. The Tibetan helped us to tie a rope around his neck, leaving two long ends, by which Kunchuk and Sadik led him between them, to prevent him from biting.

On the other side of the pass, we descended into a glen, where there were several tents, herds, and horsemen enough to suggest another mobilization of troops. We made camp there. Takkar probably felt like Uncle Tom: he, too, had been sold into captivity. But the sight of the white horse seemed to make him happy. We needed a watch-dog, after losing Brown Puppy and Yellow Dog. To prevent Takkar from giving us the slip, we thought of tying a pole to his neck, in such a way that he could not gnaw it to pieces. But as soon as one of the men approached him, he rushed up, with bared fangs and bloodshot

TAKKAR ANCHORED

eyes, determined to get at the throat of his tormentor. The men therefore threw a thick *vojlok* blanket over the dog, and four men sat on him, while the others fastened the pole to his neck with a thick rope. Then they anchored the pole in the ground, and Takkar was moored. The operation over, he tried to hurl himself at the men, who made off in all directions. "He will be nice to have around the house," I thought.

We now came upon nomads daily. I rode when no tents were visible; but as soon as man or tent hove in sight, I dismounted, and went to driving sheep. The number of sheep was increased gradually, and the burdens of our last horses and mules grew lighter and lighter. But the sheep also served us as food. After a very difficult crossing

of the partly-frozen Kangsham-tsangpo River, which flows from the
mountain of Shakangsham, we learned from nomads that in seven
days we would arrive at the tent-camp of Tsongpun Tashi, a Lhasa
merchant, from whom the people of the vicinity were wont to buy brick-
tea in the winter.

We crossed two hard passes during the following days. Now we
went past tents and herds; now we saw wild sheep in the mountains,
and goa gazelles on the plains. We failed to get two attenuated
mules across one steep pass, and left them, alive, hoping that passing
nomads would care for them. Everywhere people talked about Tsongpun Tashi, who lived in the interior of this large unknown country. I
was in a state of extraordinary expectation. Would I succeed? Every
morning I stained my face and hands brown, and I never washed. I
wore a soiled fur, a sheepskin cap, and boots, all similar to those that
my men wore. But it was irksome to have to be on my guard all the
time, and to feel like a thief. When Gulam, who preceded us, stretched
out his arm, it meant that I had to dismount and go to the sheep.
Abdul Kerim then rode my horse. When I was in my tent, I was
virtually a prisoner; and Takkar was always kept tied in front of the
entrance.

The new dog was irreconcilable. No one could go near him. If
one of us even came out of a tent, he would bark himself hoarse.
But he was most furious at Kunchuk, who had bought him. Baby
Puppy was the only one who could approach him; he tried to make
Takkar play, but Takkar was not in the mood for it.

One mountain-range after another rose in our path, and we had
to get over them all. At the southern foot of one, a spring gushed
forth copiously and formed a crystal-clear, slow-flowing brook between
grassy banks. We caught a hundred and sixty delicious fish there.
In one deep pond, the water hardly moved; and we could see the
bottom as clearly as if the bed had been dry. Baby Puppy, who had
never in his life seen aught but crystal-clear ice, thought that the surface would carry him now, too; and so he jumped. Great was his
amazement, disappointment, and annoyance at his sudden, deep im-
mersion.

A shepherd came along. He informed us that it was but a short
day's journey to Tsongpun Tashi's tents. "Now we are in for it
again," thought I. It would be a sheer miracle, should we get past him.

CHAPTER LXII

A Tibetan Captive Again

MARCH TWENTY-EIGHTH, was a critical day of prime importance. Whistling, I drove the sheep along, while Abdul Kerim and two others went to the large tent which had been pointed out as Tsongpun Tashi's. We considered it wiser to take the bull by the horns than to steal about like thieves in the night. We passed several tent-camps. Some men came out to inquire what manner of people we were. At one camp, Abdullah exchanged a dying black horse of ours, for two sheep and a goat. One large tent was said to belong to the *gova* of that region. In another dwelt the abbot of Mendong-gompa, a monastery of which neither I nor anybody else on earth, except the Tibetans, had ever heard. Karma Puntso, the governor, was also somewhere in the vicinity. Thus we were surrounded on all sides by men of high authority. We might be stopped at any step, and made prisoners. It was really important now to be on the lookout. That we looked like beggars was decidedly in our favor. We were, in fact, a handful of tatterdemalions, with four horses, three mules, two yaks, and a score of sheep. Certainly nobody could believe that a European would be travelling with such a poor and wretched escort.

We encamped between the tents of Tsongpun Tashi and the abbot, but at a considerable distance from both. Abdul Kerim soon returned. He had purchased rice, barley, butter, and *tsamba*. We loaded it all on a horse, which he had also bought. Tsongpun Tashi had proved to be a kind old man, who believed the story which Abdul Kerim told him, and, besides, warned us of robber-bands that were quartered in the region to the south. Abdul Kerim also promised to let Tsongpun Tashi buy one of our horses cheaply—the same horse which Abdullah had already sold. Then my caravan-leader, who was doing splendidly, went to the *gova's* tent. There he was met with the information that, because of some dereliction, the *gova* had been excommunicated by the abbot of Mendong, and was not allowed to leave his tent for a certain time. "Good," thought we, "that eliminates *that* bird."

The next morning Tsongpun Tashi himself walked straight up to our tents. I hastily stained myself and stowed all suspicious articles at the bottom of a rice-bag. This time the Lhasa merchant was in quite a different humour. He was furious.

"Where is that horse I was to get? You lie; you are rascals! Now I shall examine your tents and belongings. Tie your dogs!"

We tied the dogs, and the old man entered Abdul Kerim's tent, which, as usual, was pitched alongside of mine. When he came to examine the tent in which I sat hidden, he was as angry as a bee. But Gulam had meantime released Takkar; and when the old man appeared at the opening, the dog rushed at him. He retired hastily.

"Kutus," roared Abdul Kerim, "take Haji Baba with you, and go and find the lost horse."

Kutus hurried to me, and together we ran toward the nearest mountain.

"Who is that?" asked Tsongpun Tashi.

"Haji Baba, one of my servants," Abdul Kerim replied, without winking.

"I'll stay here till Haji Baba has found the runaway horse," said Tsongpun Tashi.

However, Abdul Kerim handled the uninvited guest with diplomatic skill. From our hiding-place, on a ridge, we saw him slouch off to the abbot's tent after Takkar had once more been tied. The abbot's tent was so situated that Kutus and I could not avoid passing it. We walked rapidly, staring at the ground, as though seeking the horse's tracks; and we were certainly happy to leave the tent far behind us without further adventures. The caravan arrived soon afterwards and I took my place with the sheep; for we had to pass twenty tents, from which, as always, inquisitive people came out to look at us. When we had at last manœuvred ourselves out of this wasps'-nest, we made camp on a plain in the valley.

I heaved a sigh of relief. We had no neighbours. Takkar was, as usual, tied before my tent. I seated myself, entered the day's events in my diary, and sketched the panorama. It was a clear evening. Spring-like winds were blowing across the plain. Takkar played condescendingly with Baby Puppy. All of a sudden, the big dog came up to me, and

looked at me steadily. "Well, what do you want?" I asked. He leaned
his head to one side and started to scratch my arm with his fore-paws.
I took his ragged head in my hands and patted him. We understood each
other. He began to howl and whine with delight, leaped at me, and
seemingly implied: "Ah, come and play with me, instead of sitting there
alone and sulky." I unfastened the ropes and knots around his neck, and
freed him from the nasty pole that had weighed him down since the day
he became our captive. He stood motionless. Finally, I wiped away
the dust-clots in the corners of his eyes. Now his joy was boundless.
He shook himself so that the dust flew, and nearly upset me with his
playful leaps. He cavorted and danced, howled and barked, and seemed
both proud and happy at the confidence I had shown in restoring his
freedom. Then he darted off over the plain like an arrow. "Now he
will run back to his former master," thought I. But no; he came back at
top speed, within a minute, and gave Baby Puppy a push, the impact of
which caused the little dog to make several revolutions along the ground.
And this manœuvre was repeated over and over again, until Baby Puppy
became quite dizzy. My men were astonished that Takkar had been
tamed so quickly, and that I could play with him as safely as with the
puppy.

I played with my new friend—Brown Puppy's successor—every evening during my voluntary imprisonment; and day and night Takkar was
our best protector. He developed a violent hatred of all that was
Tibetan. He would not suffer a Tibetan to approach the tents. His
attacks were dart-like. I had to pay a number of silver rupees to peace-
able nomads for the torn clothes and bloody wounds which he caused.
He also helped me to maintain my incognito; for he would not let a soul
approach my tent. And when we feared curious neighbours, we had but
to tie Takkar before the flap, to assure me perfect peace.

I was also greatly indebted to Takkar for the successful outcome of
the sixth crossing of the Transhimalaya; and consequently I bear his
memory in warm regard.

A few peaceful days followed unexpectedly. We entered the *serpun-
lam* (the road which gold-inspectors took to western Tibet), bought a
horse and some more sheep, and discovered a lake, Chunit-tso. We
encountered salt-caravans and yak-caravans. From the easy pass of
Nima-lung-la, we admired one of the most important Transhimalayan
ranges in the south. In a bare, narrow valley, a mountain horned owl

perched above our tents, calling "clevitt!" Lobsang informed us that this bird warned travellers against thieves and robbers.

It was now the beginning of April. We were following the hitherto-unknown river, Buptsang-tsangpo, southwards. Some of the many nomads who camped on its banks told us that the river emptied into Tarok-tso, a lake several days' journey to the northwest. In the south-southeast there were two glorious, snow-covered peaks, belonging to the Lunpo-gangri. Then we reached the beautiful arena-shaped valley, in a semicircle of snow- and glacier-mountains, which contained several sources of supply of the Buptsang-tsangpo.

We traded our two weary yaks for nine sheep belonging to some kind nomads. On April fourteenth, we passed a salt-caravan consisting of eight men and three hundred and fifty yaks. These men displayed great interest in us, and asked many unwelcome questions.

The next day, we made the pass of Samye-la (18,130 feet), crossing, for the sixth time, the main ridge of the Transhimalaya, the continental watershed between that part of Tibet which has no outlet to the sea, and the Indian Ocean. Between the Angden-la in the east and the Tseti-lachen-la in the west, I had thus succeeded in establishing a new route through the white spot. And right here it came to me vividly that the vast system of mountain-ranges running north of and parallel with the Himalayas, ought in future to be called the Transhimalaya.

While I was seated on the pass, sketching, and rejoicing at this new, important conquest for geographical knowledge, Kutus whispered:

"Yaks are coming."

Down in the valley appeared the large yak-caravan, winding toward the pass like a black snake; and we heard the whistling and shrill cries of the drivers. Then we descended into the valley, on the south side; and once more I felt gratified at the thought that the brook which rippled over the gravel would sometime meet its Nirvana in India's sea.

We did not pass a single tent that whole day. The tract was too high. We met only two horsemen. Abdul Kerim stayed them long enough to buy one of their mounts. Again we passed sheep-caravans, with salt for Pasaguk. On the way to the Chaktak-tsangpo, a river known to us from the year before, we came upon nomads, who cautioned us against a band of eighteen robbers, all armed with guns. We avoided Pasaguk and Saka-dsong, and took a back way, through the mountains, to Raga-tasam. This very route was notorious for its nests of robbers.

In the evenings the Mohammedans would sing their weird hymn to Allah.

On April twenty-first, the nomad-tents again became so numerous that I had to take my appointed place with the sheep. We were soon to arrive at a large tent, that of Kamba Tsenam, who owned a thousand yaks and five thousand sheep. On April twenty-second, one of my men looked in on some nomads, in passing, to ask if they would sell us any horses. Snow fell so thickly, that I could ride for stretches without being distinguishable. Two of our men went to Kamba Tsenam's tent and bought provisions. The wealthy nomad himself was not at home, but two of his men rode to our camp in the evening and sold us a handsome white horse, for a hundred and twenty-seven rupees.

On April twenty-third, we continued eastward up to the pass of Gäbuk-la. Fortunately we found an old man, tending some horses, who went with us as a guide. He was quite voluble, and told us, among other things, of a European who had been in those parts the year before, with a big and strong caravan-leader, who died suddenly, and was put in the earth at Saka-dsong.

Camp No. 390 lay in the opening to the valley leading to the pass of Kinchen-la. It snowed wildly all through the evening and night, and once more we were in the thick of winter.

Our anxiety increased every day. Every step took us closer to the danger-line; for two days' travel would bring us to the main caravan-route (*tasam*), with its vigilant authorities. What was to happen, and how we were to elude the difficulties, was a puzzle. I had several plans. Circumstances would have to determine which of them was to be adopted. Even if we should once more be made captive by the Tibetans, I would have the satisfaction of having crossed the province of Bongba, which corresponds with the middle Transhimalaya, and which was until then unexplored.

How would *this* day end? That was my thought, on April twenty-fourth, as we started out, in brilliant sunshine, to travel through snow-clad land. We admired the massive bulk of the Chomo-uchong. As usual, I stopped to make a panoramic sketch of the pass, the Kinchen-la (17,850 feet). From there, a mighty, snowy range was to be seen in the northeast, the Lunpo-gangri in the west, and the white ridge of the Himalayas in the east-southeast. Nobody disturbed us. When I had finished my sketch, I followed the trail of the caravan. It had made Camp No. 391, in a fairly narrow glen, which afforded pasturage, fuel, and water.

We all felt that something decisive was impending. Some radical precautionary measures were accordingly adopted. My European blankets, leather instrument-cases, and all other things likely to arouse suspicion, were buried or burnt. Abdul Kerim was to take my tent; and

THE TRANSHIMALAYA AS SEEN FROM OUR CAMP

from then on I was to occupy a secret compartment, quite a tiny, enclosed crib, in his large tent. Our two tents were always placed back to back. This enabled me to creep from one to the other without being seen from the outside. Under the new arrangement, the Tibetans might search both tents without finding me, hidden as I was in the separated compartment.

I sat writing, when Abdul Kerim looked in, and, in a serious voice, and with grave mien, said:

"A group of men are coming down from the pass!"

In the tent-cloth, on each long side, there was a peep-hole. I looked through the one in the direction of the pass. Quite right! Eight men were approaching. They led nine horses, two of which bore burdens.

They were not ordinary nomads, for they wore red and dark-blue skin coats, and red headgear, and they were armed with rifles and swords.

I put everything that might arouse suspicion into the rice-bag, my usual cache. I ordered Gulam to tie Takkar before the entrance to my tent. I freshened my brown complexion and donned my soiled Ladak turban. Three of the strangers brought their horses to a spot hardly thirty paces from Takkar, who barked furiously. There they unloaded and unsaddled the horses, collected fuel, made a fire, fetched water in a pan, and made themselves at home for the night.

The other five, among whom were two evidently prominent officials, entered Abdul Kerim's tent, without ceremony, and started a lively but low-voiced conversation. I heard them mention my name; and Abdul Kerim swore as he hoped to be saved, that there was no European in our caravan. Then they went out and sat down in a circle, round their fire, for tea.

Unseen from the outside, I crawled into Abdul Kerim's tent. All my men were seated there, looking as though they had just heard their death-sentence pronounced. The leader of the group had said: "Newly-arrived salt-caravans from the north have reported you to the governor of Saka-dsong. He suspects that Hedin Sahib is concealed among you. I am commissioned to make a thorough investigation. I shall therefore go through all your luggage, turn every bag inside out, and finally examine you yourselves to the very skin. If it turns out that you have no European in your train, as you say, you will then be allowed to travel wherever you wish."

My men regarded our situation as desperate. Kutus suggested that he and I should flee to the mountains, as soon as it was dark, and hide there until the examination was over. "That is useless," Gulam whispered. "They *know* that we are thirteen."

"No," I added; "it would be in vain, now. We *are* caught. I shall go out to the Tibetans and give myself up."

Abdul Kerim and the others began to weep, thinking our last moment had come.

I rose and went out. The Tibetans stopped talking and looked at me. I stopped for a while by Takkar, to pat the dog. He whined affectionately. Thereupon I walked slowly up to the Tibetans, my thumbs in my girdle. They all rose. I made a haughtily condescending gesture, and bade them sit down. I seated myself between the two most prominent. A little to the right of me sat Pemba Tsering. I remembered him at once, from the year before.

"Do you recognize me, Pemba Tsering?" I asked.

He did not answer, but jerked his head in my direction and looked meaningly at his comrades. They were all bashful and silent.

"Yes," I went on, "I am Hedin Sahib. What are you going to do with me?"

While they sat whispering, I sent Kutus to get a box of Egyptian cigarettes. I handed them around, and they all smoked. Presently the leader regained his courage. He produced a letter, received by the Governor from the Devashung, to the effect that I was not to take another step toward the east.

I DELIVERED MYSELF INTO THEIR HANDS

"To-morrow you will go with us to Saka-dsong."

"Never!" I replied, "We have left a grave there. I shall *never* go back to that place. Last year I wanted to go up into the mountain-land north of Saka-dsong. Then you prevented me. Now I have come here, after passing through that forbidden country. So you see that you *cannot* interfere, and that I am more powerful in your own country than you yourselves. I shall now go to India; but I myself will decide by which route."

"The governor of Saka-dsong will decide that point. Will you come with us to Semoku, on the Tsangpo, to meet him there?"

"With pleasure."

A courier was immediately dispatched to the Governor.

Now the conversation became freer. The leader began:

"Last year we compelled you to go to Ladak. Now you are among us again. Why have you come back?"

"Because I like being in Tibet, and I like its people."

"It would suit us better if you liked living in your own country as well."

Thus we sat chatting and smoking till the sun went down. We became the best of friends. My servants were as happy as they were surprised at the agreeable outcome of the adventure. The Tibetans laughed heartily at Abdul Kerim's merry tale about our being wool-buyers. But they believed that I possessed secret powers, which enabled me to get through Chang-tang and escape the snares of the robber-bands. The chief, Rinche Dorche, called Rindor, took down all I said, to report it to the Governor.

A new chapter of our wandering existence really began now. I had a comfortable feeling of freedom, and no longer did I have to hide in my tent. And yet now I was really a captive. We made my tent as attractive as possible, moving out rice-bags and the like, and I was certainly glad that we had not had time to burn more of our valuable and useful articles than we had disposed of. To begin with, I underwent a thorough scouring in warm water, which was renewed four times. Then I cut my beard. I missed my razors and other toilet-accessories. But having water and a piece of soap, I could dispense with other creature-comforts.

On April twenty-fifth, we rode to Semoku, two days' journey distant. Our procession looked like a gang of prisoners. Six Tibetans went on either side of me. We found the Governor already at the meeting-place. There were present also Dorche Tsuän, his colleague Ngavang, and his son Oang Gyä. The first-named was a tall man of forty-three, garbed in Chinese silk, with skull-cap and queue, wearing earrings, finger-rings, and velvet boots. He entered my tent, polite and smiling:

"I hope that you have had a pleasant journey."

"Yes, thank you; but it was cold."

"You were ordered out of the country last year. Why, then, have you come back here?"

"Because there are parts of your country that I *did* want to see."

"Last year you went down into Nepal, to Kubi-gangri, on the lakes, to all the monasteries, around the Holy Mountain, to the source of the Indus. I know exactly where you have been. Such a thing is impossible this year. The Devashung has issued new orders, and I have informed the Government that you are here again. Now you must go back to the north by the same road that you came."

Large areas of the white spot, rich in geographical enigmas, still remained both east and west of my latest route across the Samye-la. An irresistible longing arose in me to conquer these, too, to complete the pioneer-work and block out the entire uncharted country, leaving only the work of detail to future explorers. But I was aware that nothing but the refinements of diplomacy would open the doors of these regions to me. I therefore began by saying that I wished to start back to India by way of Gyangtse.

"Impossible! You will never get permission to go by that route."

"I also want to write to Lien Darin, and send letters to my family."

"We do not forward any letters."

Being thus prevented from informing Lien Darin and my friends in India that I was still alive, my parents had no news of me until September. Hence they feared the worst. In many quarters I was already given up for dead.

Dorche Tsuän, for his part, insisted that I go back towards the north. I replied:

"You may be able to kill me, but you can *never* force me to cross the Samye-la."

"Well, then, I may allow you to return by the same road to Ladak that you took last year."

"No, thank you! I never walk in my own footprints. That is against my religion."

"You must have a strange religion! Which way will you take, then?"

"Across a pass east of the Samye-la, and then to the Teri-nam-tso and further west."

"Unthinkable! But are you willing to go with us to Kamba Tse-nam's tent for further negotiations?"

"Certainly."

Before we left, I wrote out a list of what we needed in the way of clothes and provisions; and Dorche Tsuän sent a courier to a wealthy merchant in Tsongka, near the southern border of Tibet, two days' journey from Semoku. Dorche Tsuän had fallen in love with a Swedish army-revolver I had, and asked to buy it; but I told him that it was not for sale. However, I offered it to him as a present, provided they allowed me to choose my own route.

"It is strange," he said. "You are dressed more poorly than all your servants, and yet you have so much money!"

A brown horse, for which we had paid a hundred rupees, was attacked by wolves and devoured. The Tibetans took this mishap calmly. But they were frantic when Tubges shot a wild goose; and young Oang Gyä came to my tent, on the verge of tears and lamented:

"It is murder! Do you not understand that the other goose will die of sorrow, now that you have destroyed its mate? Kill any animals you want, but leave the wild geese in peace."

Then we departed on our journey across four passes. As we were making camp in the valley of Namchen, the merchants arrived with the required articles. My men got new clothes; and Abdul Kerim fashioned a genuine Tibetan robe of heavy red cloth for me, like those worn by the gentry of the land. I bought a fur-lined Chinese cap, elegant boots, a rosary to wear around the neck, and a sword in a silver scabbard, adorned with turquoises and corals, to be worn in the girdle. We purchased rice, barley, flour, *tsamba*, tea, sugar, paraffin-candles and cigarettes, sufficient for two or three months and also several horses and mules. The Tibetans' eyes grew big at the sight of the silver coins piled up on my tent-rug.

Thus far everything went well. Only the question as to the route remained.

THE AUTHOR IN TIBETAN DRESS

We held a council for several hours in Dorche Tsuän's tent.

"There is no other pass but that of Samye-la," they said.

"Yes, there is," I answered, "the Sangmo-bertik-la."

"That road is so poor that we do not hire out yaks for a journey there," one nomad put in.

"Then I will buy the yaks."

"We do not sell them."

"Large bands of robbers run riot in that region," the Governor added.

"Then it is your duty to give me an escort."

"The soldiers I have belong to the Saka-dsong garrison."

"Let us divide in two parties. Abdul Kerim will go with the bulk of the caravan across the Samye-la; and I, with a small caravan, will take the eastern road. Afterwards we'll meet at the lower Buptsang-tsangpo. You will give me ten men as escort. Each one of them will get two rupees a day. You will then be able to supervise my movements, besides being assured that I will not make any long roundabout excursions, seeing that I have to pay so much."

Dorche Tsüän did some thinking, and went out to hold a private council with his trusted men. When he returned, I had my way; and he only asked that I sign a paper, assuming entire responsibility for the consequences.

The captain of the bodyguard was immediately introduced to me.

NIMA TASHI, THE CHIEF OF OUR ESCORT

His name was Nima Tashi. He looked like a good fellow, and wore a large, bulging fur coat. Panchor, elder brother of Kamba Tsenam, a fifty-five-year-old yak-hunter, was to be our guide. He was a wrinkled old man and an arrant rascal.

On May fourth, we all went to Kamba Tsenam's camp, where quite a tent-town had grown up in the valley. Having passed there on April twenty-second, we had thus described a loop around the Chomo-uchong mountain-masses. In the evening, Kamba Tsenam stole into my tent. He confided to me that Panchor would take me and the escort anywhere we wished. He told me of his own accord that he was on friendly terms with all the robbers in the entire region. "I am the father of all robbers," he said.

May fifth was our last day together. In the evening, we had a farewell-party for Dorche Tsuän and all his men. I sat with the chieftains at the entrance to my tent and had tea. Outside, in front of us, there was a big fire, around which my men performed Ladak dances and enjoyed themselves heartily. Two men, covered with a blanket, with two sticks for horns, simulated a wild beast, which stole up to the fire, and was brought to earth by a lurking hunter. The comical Suän executed a love-dance toward a woman who was represented by the staff which he bore in his hand. The audience clapped their hands rhythmically, the Ladakis sang, and the Tibetans, in a solid circle around the arena, howled with delight. Dorche Tsuän assured me that never in their lives had they had so good a time. Meanwhile, the snow fell! thickly; and the smoke from the fire and the whirling snow joined in the dance. It was a picturesque and successful evening. It was midnight before the guests departed and the fire went out.

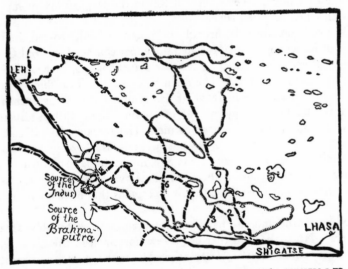

LARGE SPOTS IN TIBET INDICATE UNEXPLORED REGIONS UNTIL 1906. NUMBERS I TO 8 SHOW MY CROSSING OF THE TRANSHIMALAYA RANGE

CHAPTER LXIII

New Travels Through the Unknown Land

ON the morning of May sixth, our roads separated. Gulam,
Lobsang, Kutus, Tubges, and Kunchuk went with me. All
were mounted. Nima Tashi and his nine soldiers likewise
rode horses. We had yaks for the luggage; and on the way
we bought sheep. Abdul Kerim and the other six men went by way of
the Samye-la, with instructions to wait for me near the Tarok-tso. As
my little troop had to be as lightly-equipped as possible, I made the
mistake of handing over to Abdul Kerim the larger part of my funds,
or twenty-five hundred rupees.

We rode northwards through the unknown land, crossed the mighty
range of Kanchung-gangri, reached the upper course of our old Chaktak-
tsangpo River, and encamped at Lake Lapchung-tso, surrounded on all
sides by high mountains. The main ridge of the Transhimalaya, with
huge snow-peaks, rose in front of us. Our road took us even higher;
and this complicated labyrinth of mountain-ranges, valleys, rivers, and
lakes became increasingly clear to me. The terrain was difficult. We
walked over mossy rocks, along paths rarely used except by wild yaks.
But finally we stood on top of the Sangmo-bertik-la, 19,100 feet above
the sea. There I crossed the Transhimalayan system for the seventh
time, whereupon we descended again to regions that have no outlet to the
sea.

Nima Tashi and his handful of warriors were terribly afraid of
robbers. No sooner did they see a few horsemen in the distance, than
they expected an attack. They began to make trouble, and wanted to
turn back. But after I suggested that they receive their twenty rupees
every evening, they stayed. Panchor entertained us with stories of
robberies, and he also told us that there were spooks at night at the
grave of Mohammed Isa.

The country was rich in game, goa gazelles, *Pantholops* antelopes,
wild sheep, wild yaks, and wild asses. We passed tent-camps here and

there; and once, when we made camp, sixty inquisitive Tibetans crowded around us.

Across the river of Soma-tsangpo, we got to the little Teta-la pass. Its threshold afforded an indescribably beautiful view of the salt-lake of Teri-nam-tso, intensely turquoise-blue, and surrounded by naked mountains, in violet, yellow, red, pink, and brown shades. In the northwest rose the Shakangsham, in the southeast the Targo-gangri, in the south and southwest the Transhimalaya—all of them with dazzling snow-fields. I sat for hours entranced by all this grandiose beauty, and sketched a panorama of the lake, in colours. The pundit Nain Sing had

A GROUP OF TIBETANS

heard of the Teri-nam-tso, in 1873, but had never seen the lake; hence I had the satisfaction of being the first to see it and confirm its existence. It was situated 15,360 feet above sea-level.

From the Teta-la, I could see, sharply and distinctly, through field-glasses, all the Targo-gangri peaks, snow-fields, and glaciers; and my old longing for the Dangra-yum-tso, the Holy Lake, lying at its foot, returned. It was only a few days' journey distant. I negotiated with Nima Tashi and Panchor, in our camp on the shore of the Teri-nam-tso, promising them big rewards. But they dared not accede; and fearing that in one way or another I would make my way to the Dangra-yum-tso against their wishes, they called the chieftain Tagla Tsering, who the previous year had taken part in stopping me near the southern bank of the Holy Lake. He arrived, with twenty horsemen, in a warlike outfit, with lances, swords, and rifles, and wearing tall white hats. He himself was dressed in a panther-skin and red cloak, with a ribbon bearing six silver idol-cases on his shoulder. He was jovial and witty; and we had a nice time together during the four days I spent at the lake. Nevertheless, he was adamant, and I could not demoralize him. Not one step to the

TAGLA TSERING AND A FEW OF HIS MEN

east, was his ultimatum. Nor was I allowed to visit the Mendong-gompa, a monastery which was situated west of the Teri-nam-tso, and of which we had heard before. The only road open to me was that to the Tarok-tso, where I was to meet Abdul Kerim. Consequently I had to give up the Dangra-yum-tso trip for the third time. Several years later, this lake was visited by the distinguished English geologist, Sir Henry Hubert Hayden, who recently perished in a mountain-ascent in the Alps. He is, as far as I know, the only European who penetrated the unknown land north of Tsangpo subsequent to my journey; but owing to his untimely death, his observations have not been published.

On May twenty-fourth, we bade farewell to good Tagla Tsering and his soldiers, and rode westward along the southern shore of Teri-nam-tso (the Heavenly Lake of the Throne-Mountains). We encamped at the

Mendong-gompa, in spite of the prohibition. It was a small white-and-red convent. The monks and nuns lived in tents. West of the "Gazelle Pass" (Goa-la) we discovered the peculiar Karong-tso, surrounded by a tangle of ridges and promontories. And a few days later, we again entered the province of Bongba, and made camp on the bank of the Buptsang-tsangpo. On June fifth, we took leave of the escort, who said they had performed their task. They returned with Panchor to Saka-dsong. Thus, being alone, and having procured two unassuming nomads as guides, we were at absolute liberty to go where we would. But the most important task now was to find Abdul Kerim and his detachment. No one had seen any signs of them. We therefore went on, along the river, toward the Tarok-tso.

Although it was the beginning of June, the most violent, whirling snow-storm fell upon us here, and the whole country became white as chalk. Thunder clashed in the Transhimalaya, one of the mightiest ridges of which rose southwest of the Buptsang-tsangpo valley. Baby Puppy, who had never before heard the roar of thunder, became so frightened that he ran into my tent, his tail between his legs, and lay there snarling and barking at the peals. The experienced Takkar met the noise with the utmost calm.

Our camping-grounds on the Buptsang-tsangpo were so beautiful, that I would have liked to stay there a longer time, if for no other reason than to observe the wild geese and the trig yellow goslings that swam on the river. We finally pitched our tents near the southern shore of the Tarok-tso. Nowhere did we see a trace of Abdul Kerim and his troop. Instead, two district chiefs and a score of horsemen called on us. They had heard nothing of Abdul Kerim, but promised to find him. They declared that the only route open to me led across the pass of Lunkar-la, to the Selipuk-gompa monastery, the very way I wanted to take; for it ran right through the largest tract of the unknown land that still remained "unexplored."

And so we proceeded, on June ninth, to the little monastery of Lunkar-gompa, temporarily closed, and up to the Lunkar-la pass (18,300 feet), from the top of which we had a splendid view of the Tarok-tso and the Tabie-tsaka, a salt-lake, famous for its very rich yield.

All the nomads and chiefs whom we met in this region were friendly and helpful. At Poru-tso, a newly-revealed lake, *gova* Pundar, of Rigi-hloma, paid his respects to us, and procured the supplies we needed.

Here the enormous outlying ranges of the Transhimalaya system ran from north to south. We crossed one of them by the pass of Sur-la, 19,100 feet high, surrounded by a world of magnificent, snowy cupolas, peaks, and shimmering blue glaciers. Then we descended into the valley of Pedang-tsangpo, where the river flowed north. The Sur-la range then lay on our right, its valley-front capped by snow-covered tops. The consciousness of being the first white man to traverse this region, gave me an indescribable feeling of satisfaction. I felt like a powerful sovereign in his own country. There are bound to be future expeditions into this country, which is one of the most notable on earth, from the point of view of orography and geology. In centuries to come, it will be as well known as the Alps. But the discovery is mine. That fact will never be forgotten.

But where was Abdul Kerim? He had vanished without leaving a trace. Had he been attacked by robbers? I consoled myself with the knowledge that all the results of the last stage, from Drugub on, were in my possession: collections, diaries, and maps. But of money I had only eighty rupees ($27) left.

The Pedang-tsangpo River took us to the lake of Shovo-tso, another new discovery. Its basin, too, was surrounded by mighty mountains. The "gold route" ran across the Ka-la pass, in the northeast. The Nganglaring-tso, a large, sparkling, turquoise-blue salt-lake, ringed with brick-red and violet mountains—an extremely fantastic landscape, wonderfully permeated with colour—met our gaze from the Tayep-parva-la pass, on June twenty-third. Not a tree, not a bush; only occasional meagre pasturage, in a glen. Barren and gaunt it was like everything else in High Tibet. One of Captain Montgomerie's pundits, having heard of this lake, some forty years before, called it Ghalaring-tso. But neither he nor anyone else had been there.

We settled down on its shore, and afterwards on the banks of the Sumdang-tsangpo, a river which emptied into it. There were plenty of wolves in the vicinity, and we had to keep careful watch over our animals. Once a pack of wolves came quite close to us in broad daylight. Lobsang caught a little ferocious wolf-cub at the Sumdang-tsangpo, and we kept him in a leash at the camp. Takkar and Baby Puppy treated him with a certain respect, and kept at arm's length. In an unguarded moment, the wolf-cub managed to free himself from the rope, and fled to the river, intending to swim across to the other bank. But Takkar thought this was going too far. He emitted a howl, threw himself into the river, overtook the young wolf, held him under the water until he was drowned, swam back to our bank with the wolf in his teeth, and ate him up, skin, bones, and all.

We came to the Selipuk-gompa monastery on June twenty-seventh. The prior, Jamtse Singe, received us very cordially. To allay our fears about Abdul Kerim, he consulted his sacred books, and ascertained that our men were still alive, that they were in the south, and that we would meet them within twenty days. My cash was down to twenty rupees, and I was quite ready to sell rifles, revolvers, and watches. Then we would certainly be able to reach Tokchen and the Manasarovar, and from there send a courier to our old friends in Gartok.

Previously, at Shovo-tso, we had seen a large yak-caravan, which now also encamped at Selipuk. It belonged to the governor of Chokchu, on the Dangra-yum-tso, who was on a pilgrimage to Kang Rinpoche, the Holy Mountain, with a hundred persons, four hundred

THE ABBOT OF SELIPUK-GOMPA

yaks, sixty horses, and four hundred sheep. I became friends with him and his two brothers. They visited me in my tent, and I had dinner with them. The name of the governor was Sonam Ngurbu. He was of a striking type, copper-brown face, broad, clumsy nose, a lion's-mane of black hair (undoubtedly richly stocked!), and a cherry-red cloak. He and his two brothers had two wives in common—or two-thirds of a wife each—which, in view of the ladies' looks, seemed to be an ample sufficiency. The women were old, ugly, and dirty.

I tried to sell a fine Swedish gun; but when Sonam Ngurbu offered ten rupees, I said the gun would be his when he produced three hundred silver rupees. A gold watch, worth two hundred rupees, astonished him exceedingly. He thought it strange that human beings could make such small fine things. But as twelve and six o'clock were all the same to him, when he had the sun in the sky gratis, he refrained from bidding. He offered me sixty rupees for our last Swedish army-revolver.

"No, indeed," I replied. "I am not a beggar; and sixty rupees mean nothing to me." I lied, of course; for I *was* a beggar, and in as deep a hole as in Kermanshah, twenty-two years before. However, Sonam Ngurbu presented us with rice, *tsamba,* and sugar, so that we were able to make our way to Tokchen; and, by way of return, I gave him a watch.

The *gova* of Selipuk was amusing. He came to my tent, with a band of loafers, to inquire, by virtue of his office, what kind of bird I was. He had heard of a European's arrival, and was extremely amazed to find a stranger, in Tibetan attire, surrounded by five veritable vagrants. The problem was too much for his intellect, and I made no attempt to solve it for him. He went away with something to think about.

We departed on June thirtieth, and made camp on the plain of Rartse, whence the saw-toothed, snowy ridge of the Transhimalaya offered a magnificent sight. Toward sunset, Lobsang appeared, and announced the approach of four men and four mules. Out came the field-glasses. Aha! It was Abdul Kerim, two of our men, and a guide. The others arrived a few days later. I was brimming over with abuse for my caravan-leader; but he got off lightly, partly because the silver was intact, partly because he had really been attacked by robbers, who got away with a horse and a mule, and finally because of his encounter with hostile district-chiefs, who forced him to take rough roads north of the Tarok-tso.

Only the final crossing of the unknown country remained to be accomplished. It led to many important discoveries, for which there is no room in this book. We went over the Ding-la, a pass 19,300 feet high, the loftiest one we had negotiated during this entire journey in Tibet, and across Surnge-la, 17,300 feet high, situated on the continental water-parting. On July fourteenth we reached Tokchen.

I had then crossed the Transhimalaya eight times, by eight different passes, of which only one, the Jukti-la, had theretofore been known. Between the Jukti-la in the west and the Khalamba-la in the east, there was a region five hundred and seventy miles in length, which no European had ever before visited, and which, on the latest English map, was marked with nothing more than the word "Unexplored." Although the existence of a mighty mountain-system in the east and the west was well known before, it became my happy lot to describe the enormous intervening gap. The exploit was accomplished when I finally reached Tokchen.

All the highest mountain-ranges in the world are situated on the gigantic elevation of the earth's crust of which Tibet occupies the greatest part. They are the Himalayas, the Transhimalaya (which merges with the Kara-korum in the west), and the Kun-lun, which includes the Arka-tagh. As for that part of the Transhimalaya which I had explored, it might be said that in general its passes are five hundred metres higher than those of the Himalayas, but its peaks are fifteen hundred metres lower. All the rain-water that falls on the Himalayas flows to the Indian Ocean; but the Transhimalaya is the water-parting between the ocean and the table-land which has no outlet. Only the Indus has its source on the northern slope of the Transhimalaya, breaking through that system as well as through the Himalayas.[1]

After my return home, the name which I had given to the mountain-system north of the Tsangpo was objected to by British geographers in certain quarters. The reason was that Sir Alexander Cunningham had already used the name, in the 1850's, to denote one of the ranges of the northwestern Himalayas. Back in India it had been proposed that the system be named for me, an honor which I declined. In this connection I may be pardoned for quoting the opinion of the late Lord Curzon of Kedleston, one of the most distinguished connoisseurs of the geography of Asia. After alluding to my discoveries in Bongba, he says:

"Alongside of this great discovery I would place the tracing for hundreds of miles, and the assurance of a definite orographical existence to the mighty mountain-palisade, or series of palisades, to which he has, in my opinion very appropriately, given the title of Transhimalaya. This range has been surmised to exist in its entire length for many years; it has been crossed at its extremities by Littledale and by native surveyors. But it was reserved for Dr. Hedin to trace it on the spot, and to place it upon the map in its long, unbroken, and massive significance. . . . It is no mean addition to human knowledge that we should realize the assured existence of one of the greatest mountain-masses in the world. As regards the name which Dr. Hedin has given to it, I will only say that the desiderata for the title of a new and momentous geographical discovery appear to be these: (1) that the name should, if possible, be

---

[1] A detailed account of the Transhimalaya, and an account of all that was known about this mountain-system prior to my expedition, may be found in Volume III and Volume VII of my work, *Southern Tibet* (Stockholm, 1917 and 1922).

given by the principal discoverer; (2) that it should not be unpronounceable, unwritable, over-recondite, or obscure; (3) that it should, if possible, possess some descriptive value; and (4) that it should not violate any acknowledged canons of geographical nomenclature. The name Transhimalaya combines all these advantages, and it has a direct Central Asian analogy in the Transalai, which is a range of mountains standing in the same relation to the Alai that Transhimalaya will do to Himalaya. I am not in the least impressed by the fact that the name was once given to another range, where its unsuitability secured its early extinction. Any attempts to substitute another title on the present occasion will, in my opinion, be foredoomed to failure."—*Geographical Journal,* April, 1909.

CHAPTER LXIV

To India

WE were delayed in Tokchen for nine days, owing to the implacability of the heads of the district. On the whole, they were friendly and courteous. But they had got into trouble, the preceding year, when I went about at will, without permission; and so they were reluctant to get into another scrape on my account. I had no passport. Consequently they could not let me travel by any other road than that by which I had come. The authorities along that route had to be responsible for my passage. The Tokchen officials could not permit me to hire yaks, or to buy provisions. But in case I wished to return northwards, to Selipuk, they would render me all the assistance possible.

The Tibetans are an odd folk! The year before, I had had recourse to all sorts of tricks and stratagems to get into the unknown land north of the Tsangpo, and yet I had failed. In the end, I had been compelled to sacrifice about a year's time, a whole caravan of forty animals, and thousands of rupees, to attain my object. And now, after many crossings and recrossings of the unknown land, and when I longed for nothing else than to get down to India, they wanted to *force* me back north of the Tsangpo!

At last my patience gave out, and I departed, with my twelve men and ten horses, without assistance. We followed the northern shore of the Manasarovar, and I called on our friends, the young prior in Langbonan and the lonely Tundup Lama in Chiu-gompa. At the monastery of Tirtapuri, I divided the caravan. Only Lobsang, Kutus, Gulam, Suän, Tubges, and Kunchuk were to accompany me to India; the others, under Abdul Kerim, were to go direct to Ladak.

My journey along the Satlej and across its deep-lying tributaries was one of the most interesting I ever undertook in Asia, because we crossed the Himalayas crosswise. Words fail to describe the landscapes of overwhelming grandeur which our eyes encountered everywhere. To see them once, is to possess a lifelong memory of the high mountain-peaks, with their dazzling snow-fields, and the steep, rocky walls which enclose the valley of Satlej; and one even imagines hearing the mighty roar of the foaming river.

The journey from Tirtapuri to Simla took a month and a half. Here I will recount only two memories of this king's highway, that intersects the highest mountain-range on earth.

At the monastery of Kyunglung, the Satlej was spanned by a sagging wooden bridge, constructed of two beams, with cross-pieces. It was four feet wide and forty-two feet long, and without a rail. A few feet

THE FRIGHTENED HORSE JUMPED FROM THE SHAKY BRIDGE INTO THE
FOAMING RIVER

beneath the bridge, the Satlej, pinched between cliffs, rushed by at a dizzying speed, seething, boiling, foaming; and, a few hundred paces farther down, it widened out, with a hollow and awesome roar. The river ran very deep in its chiselled, rocky bed. One dared not be dizzy, crossing the bridge. The men carried the luggage. Two of the horses gave us considerable trouble. My white horse, the one I had bought of Kamba Tsenam, and which I had ridden four hundred and eighty miles, was the last to cross. I dismounted, and we removed his saddle. The animal was frightened by the angry water; and he had never in his life seen a bridge. He trembled all over. We tied a rope around his nose; and two men pulled him out onto the bridge, while the others urged him on with whips. Everything seemed to be going well. Trembling in every limb, the horse advanced to the middle of the bridge. But there he saw the heaving foam of the whole river below him, and became panic-stricken. He stopped and turned crosswise on the bridge, his head pointing up-river. He pricked up his ears, his eyes flamed, he distended his nostrils, snorted, and made a death-jump right into the river.

"He is lost, he will be ground to pulp against the rocks," was my first thought. And my second was: "Lucky that I did not ride him across the bridge!" But the strangest thing of all was that the horse rose to the surface, in the expansion below the bridge, and swam briskly ashore to the left bank. With one leap he was up, and began to graze, just as though nothing had happened!

We had to cross all the tributaries of the Satlej. They were deeply grooved, like the Canyon of the Colorado, though of course on a much smaller scale. Yet some of them were entitled to no little respect. At the edge of the Ngari-tsangpo gorge, the gigantic river-valley was right below. We descended on foot, by hundreds of precipitous zigzags, 2,720 feet down to the river; then mounted again as high, and at the same grade, on the other side. The greater part of a day was needed to cover a few miles.

Near the Shipki-la, we crossed the border-line of Tibet and India. Here, for the last time, we were at an altitude of 16,300 feet. I remained long, gazing toward Tibet, the land of my victories and my sorrows, the inhospitable land, where both man and nature create obstacles for the traveller, and from whose dizzying heights the traveller returns with a whole world of unforgettable, precious memories, in spite of the difficulties.

Within a stretch of a few miles, we had mounted 5,620 feet, from the river to the pass. Presently we descended from the upper cold and wind, down to the river, where we enjoyed temperate summer winds, blowing through the apricot-trees. We were on the left bank. Poo, the first village on the Indian side, lay high up in the hills on the right side, embedded in luxuriant vegetation. Here there was a Moravian mission, established many years ago, and still conducted by German missionaries.

But how were we to cross the immense river, which at this point was squeezed into a narrow passage, between perpendicular rocks, and roared in foaming eddies through its bed? Not a living creature was to be seen on the shore, and Poo was obscured. Only a steel cable, as thick as my thumb, stretched across the abyss, which yawned about a hundred feet below. The bridge that once was there had broken down. The only remains were the stone abutments at both ends, and the adjoining beams which used to be the bridge-heads.

TIBETAN BOY FROM THE WEST

Ngurup, our last guide, knew what to do. He wound a rope around the cable a few times, secured himself in the loop, grasped the cable, and hauled himself across. Then he ran to Poo, and soon returned with two missionaries and some natives. They brought a wooden yoke, grooved to fit the cable, and wound around with ropes. Other ropes served to haul it back and forth along the cable. And now we began the transit. Mules, horses, dogs, boxes, and men were hauled across. I put my legs through loops in the ropes, grasped the yoke with my hands, got another rope looped around my waist, and was thus hauled across the abyss. It was a hazardous trip. With legs dangling I swayed between heaven and earth. It was a hundred and fifteen feet to the middle, but the distance seemed endless. With a sense of relief, I finally glided in over the bridge-head on the right bank, and felt safe.

It was August 28, 1908; and, until Mr. Marx and his companion met me, I had not seen a European since August 14, 1906. I stayed with them a few days. On the Sunday, I attended their impressive high mass, celebrated for the native children.

From Poo, we descended to ever lower levels. It grew warmer, day by day. Takkar suffered agonies with his thick black coat of hair. With tongue hanging out, and dripping, he ran from shade to shade; and he lay down, outstretched, in every brook, to cool himself. Half a year ago, he had come to us, while Tibetan winter storms hurled the drift-snow round our tents. As far as the Shipki-la he had breathed the fresh, cold air of his home-country, and had seen the last yaks. We had now brought him to a land of infernal heat. He pondered and cogitated. He was conscious of loosening bonds. We had taken him from the nomad-herds by force; and now, again treacherously, we were luring him down to a country, the heat of which he could not endure. He felt more and more like a stranger among us. He was frequently out of sight the whole day; but in the cool of the evening he would come to our camping-place. He felt lonely and for-saken, and noticed that we left him heartlessly. One evening he failed to turn up. We never saw him again. He had doubt-less gone back to Tibet, to the poor nomads and the biting snow-storms.

On September ninth, I got the post in Gaura; and on the four-teenth, I encamped in Fagu. I had left my entire caravan sev-eral days earlier, and now trav-elled alone. On September fif-teenth, I entered Simla and wrote "Camp No. 500" in my diary.

The very next day, I attended one of those brilliant state balls at Lord Minto's court—I who had loafed like a beggar, and tended sheep, a short while ago! I could see the Himalayas from my windows in the Viceregal

CROSSING THE BOUNDARY BETWEEN TIBET AND INDIA

Lodge. Behind its snowy crest, my beloved Tibet lay dreaming. The doors to the forbidden country had been closed again.

From Simla I went to Japan. And then began a series of splendid receptions by Academies, Geographical Societies, Kings and Emperors. The many years that followed I spent working out my scientific discov-eries and undertaking journeys to Asia and America. But that is quite another story. So here I close "My Life As An Explorer." What my remaining years may bring forth, rests in the hands of God.

EPILOGUE

Peter Hopkirk

Some eighteen years were to pass before Hedin set out on another major expedition to Asia. Much of this time was spent touring the world and lecturing, not to mention writing books and being fêted. But it also saw his first foray into Swedish, and then European, politics. Throughout his life Hedin feared that his country, and eventually much of Europe, would be swallowed up by Russia, whose advance eastwards had been halted by the Japanese. He believed that Britain, being concerned only with its own empire, could not be relied upon as an ally for Sweden against an expansionist Russia. Only one other country, he was convinced, was powerful enough to serve as a bulwark, and that was Germany, a country he had come to admire greatly during his student days there.

At the outbreak of World War I, therefore, he offered his services as a neutral observer and war correspondent to Kaiser Wilhelm II of Germany. He also advised the German High Command that Muslims throughout the East—including those of British India and Russian Central Asia—were ready to join a German-sponsored Holy War against the Allies. As a result of his allying himself with the enemy, a number of countries withdrew the honours they had bestowed upon him. Meanwhile, during 1914 and 1915, he toured the German frontlines in Europe, and the following year the Turkish and German lines in the Near East, providing both governments with valuable propaganda, particularly for use in the United States and other neutral countries. He maintained his belief that Germany would win the war, almost to the end.

After the war he was still highly regarded in Germany although beyond the pale as far as Britain and France were concerned. In 1926 he was asked to mount an expedition to China with the aim of planning an air route that would link Peking to Berlin via Central Asia, which involved finding locations for refuelling and weather stations. The dramas and difficulties he encountered on this and other

527

between-the-wars expeditions to China are beyond the scope of this epilogue. They are, however, vividly described in several popular narratives he wrote around them, including *Big Horse's Flight* (1936) and *The Silk Road* (1938).

In 1939 the world was once more plunged into war, and again Hedin offered his services to Germany, convinced that this time it would emerge triumphant. In Berlin a square and a street had been named after him in gratitude. But by 1945, it was clear that he had now backed the losing side twice, leaving his reputation in tatters and robbing him of any remaining friends he might have had outside Germany. In 1952, surrounded by mementos of a long and most remarkable life, the great Swedish explorer died in Stockholm, a lonely and forgotten man. Perhaps now, nearly half a century later, Hedin's political misjudgements should be forgiven, and his immense scientific achievements allowed to speak for themselves. The publication of *My Life as an Explorer* is at least a beginning.

London
January 1996

INDEX

A

THE END

KODANSHA GLOBE

International in scope, this series offers distinguished books that explore the lives, customs, and mindsets of peoples and cultures around the world.

ON FAMILIAR TERMS
To Japan and Back,
A Lifetime Across
Cultures
Donald Keene
1-56836-129-7

KNOTTED TONGUES
Stuttering in History
and the Quest for a
Cure
Benson Bobrick
1-56836-121-1

LIVING IN, LIVING OUT
African American
Domestics and the
Great Migration
Elizabeth Clark-Lewis
1-56836-124-6

ECHOES OF DISTANT
THUNDER
Life in the United
States, 1914–1918
Edward Robb Ellis
New Preface by the Author
1-56836-149-1

GRINGA LATINA
A Woman of Two Worlds
Gabriella De Ferrari
1-56836-145-9

LOOKING FOR THE LOST
Journeys Through a
Vanishing Japan
Alan Booth
1-56836-148-3

IN GOOD HANDS
The Keeping of a
Family Farm
Charles Fish
1-56836-147-5

YANOAMA
The Narrative of a
Young Girl
Kidnapped by
Amazonian Indians
Ettore Biocca
Translated by Dennis
Rhodes
New Introduction by
Jacques Lizot
1-56836-108-4

JOURNEY TO KHIVA
A Writer's Search for
Central Asia
Philip Glazebrook
1-56836-074-6

A BORROWED PLACE
The History of Hong
Kong
Frank Welsh
1-56836-134-3

SINGER AND THE SEWING
MACHINE
A Capitalist Romance
Ruth Brandon
1-56836-146-7

MY LIFE AS AN EXPLORER
The Great Adventurer's
Classic Memoir
Sven Hedin
Translated by Alfild
Huebsch
New Introduction by
Peter Hopkirk
Illustrated by the Author
1-56836-142-4

To order, contact your local bookseller or call 1-800-788-6262 (mention code G1). For a complete listing of titles, please contact the Kodansha Editorial Department at Kodansha America, Inc., 114 Fifth Avenue, New York, NY 10011.